Rodney Hilton's Middle Ages:

An Exploration of Historical Themes

OXFORD JOURNALS
OXFORD UNIVERSITY PRESS

OXFORD
UNIVERSITY PRESS

1 Great Clarendon Street, Oxford OX2 6DP

Oxford University Press is a department of the University of Oxford.
It furthers the University's objective of excellence in research, scholarship,
and education by publishing worldwide in

Oxford New York

Athens Auckland Bangkok Bogotá Buenos Aires Cape Town
Chennai Dar es Salaam Delhi Florence Hong Kong Istanbul Karachi
Kolkata Kuala Lumpur Madrid Melbourne Mexico City Mumbai Nairobi
Paris São Paulo Shanghai Singapore Taipei Tokyo Toronto Warsaw

with associated companies in Berlin Ibadan

Oxford is a registered trade mark of Oxford University Press
in the UK and in certain other countries

Published in the United Kingdom
by Oxford University Press Inc., New York

ISBN 0-19-954210-4
ISBN 978-0-19-954210-9

Subscription information for Past & Present is available
from:jnls.cust.serv@oxfordjournals.org

Typeset by Cepha Imaging Pvt Ltd, Bangalore, India
Printed by Bell and Bain Ltd, Glasgow, UK

Past and Present Supplements

Supplement 2, 2007

Rodney Hilton's Middle Ages:
An Exploration of Historical Themes
*Edited by Christopher Dyer, Peter Coss,
and Chris Wickham*

Rodney Hilton's Middle Ages:
An Exploration of Historical Themes

CONTENTS

The Transition from Feudalism to Capitalism

Conclusions 304

Appendix

Index 329

List of Figures

List of Tables

Contributions and Communications (two copies), editorial correspondence, etc., should be addressed to The Editors, *Past and Present*, 175 Banbury Road, Oxford OX2 7AW, UK. Tel: +44 (0)1865 512318; Fax: +44 (0)1865 310080; E-mail: editors@pastandpresent. demon.co.uk. Intending contributors should write for a copy of 'Notes for Contributors'.

The Past and Present Society is a company limited by a guarantee registered in England under company number 2414260 and a registered charity under number 802281. Its registered office is at 9400 Garsington Road, Oxford.

Typeset by Cepha, Bangalore, India, and printed by Bell and Bain Ltd, Glasgow, UK

Preface

The origins of this book are described in the Introduction. Briefly, Rodney Hilton's friends, colleagues and admirers, in the year after his death in 2002, participated in a conference not just to celebrate his work, but to indicate new directions in the historical themes to which he gave special prominence. The venture was encouraged and assisted by Jean Birrell, Rodney's widow, who also translated the paper by Monique Bourin. The essays in this book were presented as papers at the conference.

The conference attracted eighty participants, who demonstrated Rodney Hilton's international reputation by travelling from twelve different countries. The event was organized impeccably by Heather Swanson, and facilities were provided by the University of Birmingham. Barrie Dobson, Janos Bak and Paul Slack chaired sessions. Other contributors included Halil Berktay who responded to the session on the 'Transition from feudalism to capitalism'. Six contributors from overseas were funded by the British Academy, for whose support we are extremely grateful. The conference was held in a convivial and positive atmosphere, and the papers provoked questions and comments from the participants which helped to improve them as published essays.

We received consistent support and encouragement in the planning and financing of the conference, and in the preparation of this book, from the Past and Present Society, and particularly from the chairman of the Board, Paul Slack, and from the co-editor, Lyndal Roper. Three anonymous referees provided constructive criticism and propelled us forward through the last stages of revision and editing.

We thank everyone who has been involved in this book, but above all we express our profound gratitude to Rodney Hilton, whose acuteness of mind, commitment to ideas, enthusiasm, energy and boisterous good humour not only enabled him to produce so much excellent scholarly work, but also inspired so many others to follow his example.

Christopher Dyer, Peter Coss, Chris Wickham
July 2006

Introduction. Rodney Hilton, Medieval Historian

Christopher Dyer

This book has an unusual background, and the purpose of this introduction is to explain how it came into existence. It is of course commonplace for a senior and distinguished historian such as Rodney Hilton to be presented with a volume of essays in his honour, and indeed such a book was given to him and published in 1983, at the time of his retirement.[1] When he died in 2002, there was a strong and widely held feeling that some gathering in his memory was needed, at which his many friends and admirers from different parts of the world could express their admiration for him. We immediately thought how inappropriate it would be to mark his passing with lengthy expressions of praise and affection, partly because one knew how he would have reacted to anything that smacked of piety, and which contained excessive reference to personality: 'What a lot of nonsense' would have been the comment, or stronger words to that effect. The only way to honour him was to make reference to his own achievements, but above all to celebrate the subjects that he studied by looking forward to new developments in medieval social history. As he would have wished, this would be an event involving not only established scholars but also young people, and it would be held in a convivial atmosphere. The best memorial, in other words, was to carry forward his project, and as much as possible in his style.

The conference was held in September 2003. The historians who were invited to contribute were chosen from three categories: Hilton's own research students; colleagues, friends and admirers from this country and abroad; and younger researchers who had worked on subjects that he had pioneered. They were expected to cover the themes chosen by the organizers. One ought to add that there were many more who would have responded had they been asked, and it was a difficult and invidious task to select those who gave papers. The conference was well attended, including visitors from twelve different countries, and the papers were received with enthusiasm. There was

---

[1] T. H. Aston, P. R. Coss, C. Dyer, and J. Thirsk (eds), *Social Relations and Ideas. Essays in Honour of R. H. Hilton* (Cambridge, 1983).

no doubt that the contributions deserved publication, and the essays in this book represent the bulk of the papers given on that occasion.

Why did this historian attract so much attention, affection and admiration? Why did such a variety of scholars accept the invitation to contribute to the conference and this volume? Why did they all go to the trouble of writing essays appropriate for the man and occasion? To some extent his own character and personality explain these responses. But the contributors were also celebrating the school of thought and approach that he represented, and they were expressing their interest in his fields of inquiry which were selected for discussion at the conference.

Rodney Hilton's life can be briefly summarized.[2] He was born into an upper working class family in 1916. He benefited from the educational system which provided scholarships for bright pupils at an excellent school (Manchester Grammar), at Balliol College, Oxford (1935–8), and then at Merton College as a postgraduate student. After five years in the army (1940–6), he took up a lectureship at the University of Birmingham, and remained there, becoming first a reader and then a professor, until his retirement in 1982. In his academic career he published a dozen books and pamphlets, edited almost as many texts and collections of essays, and wrote sixty articles and essays.[3]

He was paradoxical in his ideas and attitudes. He was brought up in a strong scholarly tradition based on hard work, the acquisition of technical skills, accuracy, honesty, and integrity, and which put a particular premium on the critical interpretation of evidence, leading to discussion, debate and innovation. He remained throughout his life true to that approach, though he regarded the University of Oxford, where he was educated in these methods and principles, in a critical spirit because of its conservatism and stuffiness. He was for twenty years an active and loyal member of the Communist Party, the other great institution which played a big part in his life, but left after the crises of 1956, disillusioned with its rigidity and disgusted by Stalin's crimes. He remained loyal to the ideals of communism, and indeed rejoined a much changed Party in the 1980s. He was consistently committed to Marxist ideas, though it is difficult to depict him simply as a Marxist, as he was very open to new developments in scholarship, and was influenced by such non-Marxist thinkers as Weber.

---

[2] Biographical details can be found in C. Dyer, 'Rodney Howard Hilton, 1916–2002', *Proceedings of the British Academy*, 130 (2005), 52–77.

[3] See below, 317–24.

He always saw himself as pitted in battle against the Establishment, whether represented by right-wing governments in Britain or abroad, or high-ranking academics such as Deans, Vice-Chancellors and other 'big-wigs' (his phrase).

At the same time he was rather successful as a university administrator (Chairman of the School of History at Birmingham in the 1960s), was elected a Fellow of the British Academy, and founded, nurtured and administered *Past and Present*, once regarded as subversive, but later the leading historical journal in the English-speaking world.

He researched primary sources with care and thoroughness, and took on the exacting scholarly task of editing texts. Hilton's writings were quite formally structured, and argued in a rigorous fashion. Those who knew his publications were often surprised to find when they met him that he was very informal in manner. His conversation was often bantering and light hearted, and he was fond of good food and drink. He encouraged seminars which were accompanied by wine—the 'feudal booze-up' was his name for the evening series of meetings at Birmingham in the 1960s known officially as the 'Research Society'. In conversation and to some extent in seminar papers he spoke directly and used a colloquial style. His company was both stimulating and enjoyable, and memories of this historian who took pleasure in his subject, and made it pleasurable for others, helped to ensure a positive response to the proposal for a conference in 2003.

Hilton belonged to a particular school of thought, and worked during a high point in the practice of history. He was of course part of the group known collectively as the 'British Marxist Historians', who were students before, during and just after World War II. He was linked with such figures as Hill, Hobsbawm, the Thompsons and Kiernan, and encountered them and others at the meetings of the Communist Party's Historians' Group.[4] He was the only member who specialized in the study of the middle ages. After the crisis which ended the Group's meetings in 1956, he continued in the Marxist tradition of historical interpretation for the rest of his life. Beginning with his doctoral thesis on monastic estates in Leicestershire, published in 1947, he had worked on such themes as the dynamics of the feudal economy, class consciousness and class struggles, the crisis of the feudal order and the transition to capitalism.[5] As he pursued these ideas in

[4] E. Hobsbawm, 'The Historians' Group of the Communist Party', in M. Cornforth (ed.), *Rebels and their Causes* (London, 1978), 21–48; H. J. Kaye, *The British Marxist Historians. An Introductory Analysis* (Cambridge, 1986).

[5] R. H. Hilton, *The Economic Development of some Leicestershire Estates in the 14th and 15th Centuries* (Oxford, 1947).

the 1960s, 1970s and 1980s he adapted them and took note of the new developments in thinking among historians and the social scientists.

He showed a great openness to new approaches to history. From an early stage Hilton was concerned with the history of localities, as only in particular places could social and economic trends be observed. Confrontations between lords and peasants were to be found in the records of such villages as Stoughton and Kibworth Harcourt, and the lessons applied to feudal society in general.[6] He admired the French explorations of the total history of regions, and was stimulated by such works as Fourquin's study of the Paris basin to write his book on the west midlands, *A Medieval Society*.[7] He practised social history when it was still a minority interest, and embraced the new wave of urban history. One of the earliest explorations of medieval women's history was included in his Ford Lectures.[8] In his last book, on English and French towns, when he was in his late seventies, he was engaging with cultural history in a chapter on how towns were imagined.[9] As he adopted these innovations in historical writing himself, he was able also to encourage their development more generally through the journal *Past and Present*. In the 1960s and 1970s as higher education expanded and historians felt the liberating effects of the new age, history was enjoying its greatest flourishing since the end of the nineteenth century. Hilton's part in this was recognized overseas. His writings had a universal appeal because although his empirical work related to English history, his theoretical perspectives and concerns for general themes could be applied to other countries and societies. He had always had close links with French historians such as Georges Duby, and now he was celebrated in India, Japan, the United States, and throughout Europe. He was held in especially high regard in Spain, where the arrival of academic freedom in 1975 coincided with the heyday of the historical renaissance.

[6] R. H. Hilton, 'A Thirteenth-Century Poem on Disputed Labour Services', *English Historical Review*, 56 (1941), 90–7; id., 'Kibworth Harcourt: a Merton College Manor in the Thirteenth and Fourteenth Centuries', in W. G. Hoskins (ed.), *Studies in Leicestershire Agrarian History* (Leicester, 1949), 17–40, reprinted in R. H. Hilton, *Class Conflict and the Crisis of Feudalism. Essays in Medieval Social History* (London, 1985), 18–35.

[7] R. H. Hilton, *A Medieval Society: The West Midlands at the End of theTthirteenth Century* (London 1966; 2nd edn, Cambridge, 1983).

[8] R. H. Hilton, *The English Peasantry in the Later Middle Ages: The Ford Lectures for 1973 and Related Studies* (Oxford, 1975), 95–110.

[9] R. H. Hilton, *English and French Towns in Feudal Society. A Comparative Study* (Cambridge, 1992), 105–26.

When the organizers of the 2003 conference came to select the themes that would be covered, they sought to reflect Hilton's range of concerns, and particularly those which were still current and developing in the new century.

The first section of the conference (as in this book) was devoted to 'lordship and society', which for Hilton meant the problems of defining the feudal ruling class, showing how lords and lordship changed over time, and particularly exploring the relations between lords and peasants. For him the failure of lords' own productive role to develop after about 1300, and the challenges from the peasantry, precipitated the crisis of the whole feudal order. He had first presented these ideas as a general scheme in an article in *Annales* in 1951, and was still investigating such issues as lords' investment in their estates and the impact of serfdom in the 1960s.[10] The first paper in this section by Davies deals with the origin of the feudal order and lordship around the year 1000, which was not a period on which Hilton wrote much, but he was very interested in Bloch's idea of a new feudal age about that time, and the concept's subsequent development by Duby and his successors as the 'feudal transformation' or '*mutation féodale*'.[11] The stratification of the aristocracy was also a concern of Hilton's, which is explored here in Coss's paper. Hilton gave seminar papers in the 1960s on the crisis of the knights in the thirteenth century, many of whom were reduced to debt, and Coss as his research student developed the idea. Hilton explained the feudal crisis by arguing that feudal rent damaged the peasant economy; the peasants, however, did not accept this oppression, but actively opposed it and eventually made it more difficult to enforce. Schofield and Dyer explore the way in which lordship affected peasant society, putting special emphasis on their social consciousness and resentment of the idea of serfdom.[12]

The second section of the book takes the analysis of the lower ranks of society further by exploring the 'peasant centred' themes which Hilton helped

---

[10] R. H. Hilton, 'Y eût-il une crise général de la féodalité ?', *Annales, Économies, Sociétés, Civilisations*, 6 (1951), 23–30, reprinted in English translation in *Class Conflict*, 239–45; R. H. Hilton, 'Rent and Capital Formation in Feudal Society', in *Second International Conference of Economic History: Aix-en-Provence* (Paris, 1965), vol. 2, 38–68, reprinted in *English Peasantry*, 174–214; R. H. Hilton, 'Freedom and Villeinage in England', *Past and Present*, 31 (1965), 3–19, reprinted in R. H. Hilton (ed.), *Peasants, Knights and Heretics: Studies in Medieval English Social History* (Cambridge, 1976), 174–91.

[11] M. Bloch, *Feudal Society*, 2nd edn of the English translation (London, 1962); the historiography of the 'feudal revolution' debate is discussed and itemized in articles in *Past and Present*, 142 (1994); 152 (1996), and 155 (1997).

[12] R. H. Hilton, 'A Crisis of Feudalism', *Past and Present*, 80 (1978), 3–19, reprinted in T. H. Aston and C. H. E. Philpin (eds), *The Brenner Debate. Agrarian Class Structure and Economic Development in Pre-industrial Europe* (Cambridge, 1985), 119–37.

to define. These concern the autonomy and self-government of peasant communities, and the knotty problem of stratification in peasant society. Did the peasantry form a single class? Or did the wealthier peasants exploit their poorer neighbours? He always emphasized the inequalities among the peasantry, but in *The English Peasantry in the Later Middle Ages* he argued that even around 1400, after the fall in population gave the upper ranks of peasants access to larger holdings of land, the common interests of all villagers were still more important than the factors which separated them.[13] Alfonso, Bourin, and Müller re-examine these arguments. Müller reasserts Hilton's view, and Bourin sees peasant solidarity in the thirteenth century, which was threatened by the rise of an elite in the fourteenth. Bourin also highlights quarrels between villages. Alfonso explores the underclass of servants and labourers within villages.

The third group of papers turns to Rodney Hilton's main concern in the later stages of his academic career, medieval towns. His main contention was that towns were an integral part of feudal society, and that urbanization did not represent the rise of a precocious precursor of capitalism which threatened to undermine the traditional hierarchy of lords and peasants.[14] This provides Holt with his theme for his analysis of Norwegian towns, which were underdeveloped just as lords were weak and not able to dispose of a large surplus. Goddard looks at feudal lords' investment in urban property, and Roberts takes Hilton's comparison between French and English towns into the sixteenth century, when feudalism was changing, but the towns were still not rampantly capitalist.

Hilton gave popular rebellions, our fourth theme, a central place in his interpretation of change within medieval society, beginning with his early essays on peasant movements and his book on the English rising of 1381. He reviewed the whole European history of peasant revolts, with a focus on 1381, in 1973.[15] Others such as Postan believed that the medieval economy expanded and contracted because of the impersonal fluctuations in levels of population, with growth and over-exploitation of resources up to 1300, and consequent decline and stagnation.[16] Hilton agreed with the chronology of

[13] *English Peasantry*, 1–19.

[14] R. H. Hilton, 'Towns in English Feudal Society', *Review (Journal of the Fernand Braudel Institute for the Study of Economies, Historical Systems and Civilizations)* 3 (1979), 3–20, reprinted in *Class Conflict*, 175–86.

[15] R. H. Hilton, *Bond Men Made Free: Medieval Peasant Movements and the English Rising of 1381* (London, 1973).

[16] M. M. Postan, 'Medieval Agrarian Society in its Prime: England', in M. Postan (ed.), *Cambridge Economic History of Europe*, vol. 1, 2nd edn (Cambridge, 1966), 548–632.

expansion followed by the fourteenth-century crisis, but argued that the clash of class interests, and the growth of subversive ideologies, lay behind the faltering of economic growth and the failure of the lords to reassert their power after the Black Death of 1348–9. This view is supported here by Razi's analysis of serfdom as a form of class oppression. Cohn demonstrates the number and variety of rebellions, with a change in their character after the Black Death. Hilton always emphasized the ideas that lay behind rebellion, though reconstructing the thinking of illiterates is always difficult. He advocated the value of literature for this purpose, and revived the study of the Robin Hood ballads.[17] Justice here pursues this problem, exploring the religious ideas among the peasants in 1381. Sanchez and Whittle examine the social background of rebels and the ideas behind revolts at the end of the middle ages.

Finally, for Hilton the problem of the transition from feudalism to capitalism always formed the backdrop of all of the subjects which he explored. He published a vitally important essay about the definition of capitalism in 1952,[18] and much of his writing about rural society, the feudal crisis and towns had emergent capitalist relations as their underlying concern. In 1976 he edited a collection of essays written twenty years earlier, and brought the subject up to date in a lengthy introduction.[19] He also contributed to the 'Brenner debate', but did not write at full length on the transition. This remains one of the most intractable of historical problems. Here van Bavel advances our understanding of wage labour, both in the Netherlands and more generally. Dimmock looks at small towns and in particular their innovative role in the market and industrial economy, taking forward the subject of small towns and marketing which Hilton pioneered in the 1980s.[20] Epstein took a broader theoretical view, which pointed out that previous authors on the subject, including Hilton, paid insufficient attention to the role of the state.

This book cannot reflect all of Hilton's contributions to our understanding of the middle ages. A glance at the bibliography will show that, for example, he encouraged the use of archaeological and architectural evidence, and

---

[17] R. H. Hilton, 'The Origins of Robin Hood', *Past and Present*, 14 (1958), 30–44, reprinted in *Peasants, Knights and Heretics*, 221–35.

[18] R. H. Hilton, 'Capitalism—What's in a Name?', *Past and Present*, 1 (1952), 32–43, reprinted in *Class Conflict*, 268–77.

[19] R. H. Hilton (ed.), *The Transition from Feudalism to Capitalism* (London, 1976).

[20] E.g. R. H. Hilton, 'Small Town Society in England before the Black Death', *Past and Present*, 105 (1984), 53–78; id., 'Medieval Market Towns and Simple Commodity Production', *Past and Present*, 109 (1985), 3–23.

made contributions to the history of technology. He wrote about sources, the management of aristocratic estates, and on agricultural history in general. But we hope that these essays reflect some of his most significant contributions to medieval history. The authors of the papers in this book accord him and his memory great respect, above all because he had the ability to identify the really important problems, but they often depart from his views. The subject moves on, and looks forward to new interpretations, exactly as Rodney Hilton would have expected.

Lordship and Community: Northern Spain on the Eve of the Year 1000

Wendy Davies

Rodney was my colleague when I came to Birmingham in 1970 to my first teaching job. Working with him—designing courses, co-teaching, graduate seminars—was a revelation and has had a profound impact on the work I have tried to do ever since. What follows picks up some of the themes which always interested him, but does so in the context of northern Spain in the tenth century—northern Spain because the extension of lordship is a key issue in historical writing about social change in the central middle ages; the tenth century because there is a large mass of available text, following an era of very little surviving written material, and this allows us to look into the nature of peasant society both before and during the changes of that period. The documentation includes large numbers of charters, that is, records of property transactions and disputes which are rich in personal, topographic and narrative detail.[1]

---

[1] The main editions used here are: A. Ubieto Arteta (ed.), *Cartulario de Albelda* (Valencia, 1960)—charters are hereafter referred to by number, as A1, A2, etc.; L. Serrano (ed.), *Cartulario de San Pedro de Arlanza* (Madrid, 1925)—hereafter Ar1, Ar2, etc.; G. Martínez Díez (ed.), *Colección documental del monasterio de San Pedro de Cardeña* (Cardeña/ Burgos, 1998) (older edition: L. Serrano (ed.), *Becerro Gótico de Cardeña*, Silos/ Valladolid, 1910)—charters from the 1998 edition hereafter C1, C2, etc.; J. M. Andrade (ed.), *O Tombo de Celanova*, 2 vols. (Santiago, 1995)—hereafter Cel1, Cel2, etc.; E. Sáez and C. Sáez (eds), *Colección documental del archivo de la catedral de León 775–1230*, vol. I (775–952), vol. II (953–85), J. M. Ruiz Asencio (ed.), vol. III (986–1031) (León, 1987, 1990, 1987)—hereafter L1, L2, etc.; L. Sánchez Belda (ed.), *Cartulario de Santo Toribio de Liébana* (Madrid, 1948)—hereafter T1, T2, etc.; P. Floriano Llorente (ed.), *Colección diplomática del monasterio de San Vicente de Oviedo (años 781–1200)* (Oviedo, 1968)—hereafter Ov1, Ov2, etc.; J. M. Mínguez Fernández (ed.), *Colección diplomática del monasterio de Sahagún*, vol. I (León, 1976)—hereafter S1, S2, etc.; A. Ubieto Arteta (ed.), *Cartulario de San Juan de la Peña*, vol. I (Valencia, 1962)— hereafter JP1, JP2, etc.; A.Ubieto Arteta (ed.), *Cartulario de San Millán de la Cogolla* (Valencia, 1976)—hereafter SM1, SM2, etc.; M. Desamparados Perez Soler (ed.), *Cartulario de Valpuesta* (Valencia, 1970)—hereafter V1, V2, etc.

Past and Present (2007), Supplement 2

Context

It is an understatement to say that Rodney Hilton was invariably interested in the domination of the peasantry by landlords and in the mechanisms by which this was extended. Writing about England and France, he stressed the importance of the extension of private jurisdictions, and of the significance of adding 'seigneurial' to 'domanial' jurisdiction over peasants (that is, adding ruler-like coercive powers over 'subjects' to the power a landlord has over tenants) in order more fully to expropriate the peasant surplus:

> It was in this institution [the *seigneurie*] that the two great classes met face to face—the landowners great and small and the peasants rich and poor, the first to receive, the second to give their labour or the fruits of their labour, in cash or in kind. It was the principal theatre of that act of coercion . . . by which the infinitely scattered surpluses of the peasant economy were concentrated into the hands of the politically and socially dominant class.[2]

Recent discussion of the process of increasing exploitation in western Europe has largely been pursued within the construct of 'feudal revolution', also the subject of much of Jean Birrell's translation work.[3] Interest centres on the change to what is described as a feudal mode of production, characterized not only by the domination of private lords over the persons, labour and surplus of a largely servile peasant population, but also by the disappearance of slavery and by the fragmentation of the public power of the state and its dispersal among the greater private lords. This access to public power was manifest in the lord's capacity to raise private military followings, to levy taxation of many kinds and to hold judicial courts. Hence the emergence of the *seigneurie*, the sphere in which these private powers were exercised, and the process of 'seigneurialization', the establishment of such spheres.

---

[2] R. H. Hilton, 'Feudalism or *féodalité* and *seigneurie* in France and England', reprinted in id., *Class Conflict and the Crisis of Feudalism* (London, 1985), 227–38, at 230 (first published 1979).

[3] See the debate in *Past and Present*: T. N. Bisson, 'The "feudal revolution"', *Past and Present*, 142 (1994), 6–42; 'Debate: The "feudal revolution"', *Past and Present*, 152 (1996), contributions by D. Barthélemy and S. D. White, 196–223; and by T. Reuter, C. Wickham, and T. N. Bisson in *Past and Present*, 155 (1997), 177–225. For earlier statements: G. Duby, *La société aux XIe et XIIe siècles dans la région mâconnaise* (Paris, 1953), and below, n. 4; for recent comment, D. Barthélemy, 'La mutation féodale a-t-elle eu lieu?', *Annales, économies, sociétés, civilisations*, 47 (1992), 767–77, and 'Qu'est-ce que le servage, en France, au XIᵉ siècle?', *Revue historique*, 287 (1992), 233–84; E. Bournazel and J.-P. Poly (eds), *Les féodalités* (Paris, 1998).

In the last ten to fifteen years the debate has especially focused on the speed of the change (gradual mutation or sudden rupture), on the persistence or otherwise of ancient slavery till a date well into the central middle ages, and on the role of aristocratic violence. The most extreme approaches focus on the year 1000, or on a short period in the eleventh century, as a moment of— rather rapid—change.[4]

Iberia has a different early medieval background, but a central medieval development that has many points of contact with that of France and England. Most of the peninsula had experienced rapid Arab conquest in the eighth century, and the tenth, eleventh and early twelfth centuries saw the to-and-fro of 'Christian' kings campaigning from the north and 'Muslim' leaders campaigning from the south.[5] The kingdom of Asturias, in and beyond the mountains in the north and north-west, and that of Pamplona (Navarre) in the north, meanwhile sustained the Christian rulerships that appear to have controlled those areas since the early eighth century in the former case and the early ninth in the latter. It remains the standard view that much of the long river basin of the Duero was 'recovered' for the Christian kingdom of Asturias-León by 900, while the southernmost part of the basin and the upper waters of the river were recovered in the late eleventh century, leaving the Ebro valley to the east within Arab hands until the mid-twelfth (Fig. 1). It is part of the dominant historiographical tradition that the Duero basin was depopulated as a consequence of the Arab conquest, and that repopulation by 'free' settlers followed in the wake of the sustained Christian reconquest of the later ninth, tenth and subsequent centuries.[6] It is these 'free settlers' who were long seen to give rise to the peasant communities of the central middle ages. The reality of depopulation,

---

[4] P. Bonnassie, *From Slavery to Feudalism in South-western Europe*, trans. J. Birrell (Cambridge, 1991) (first published 1968–90); G. Bois, *The Transformation of the Year One Thousand. The Village of Lournand from Antiquity to Feudalism*, trans. J. Birrell (Manchester, 1992) (first published 1989).

[5] For broad general surveys in English, see for example, T. F. Glick, *Islamic and Christian Spain in the Early Middle Ages* (Princeton, 1979); H. Kennedy, *Muslim Spain and Portugal: A Political History of al-Andalus* (London, 1996); B. F. Reilly, *The Contest of Christian and Muslim Spain 1031–1157* (Oxford, 1992).

[6] See for example, C. Sánchez Albornoz, *Despoblación y repoblación del valle del Duero* (Buenos Aires, 1966); id., 'Repoblación del Reino Asturleonés', in his *Viejos y nuevos estudios sobre las instituciones medievales españolas*, 3 vols. (Madrid, 1976–80), vol. II, 581–790 (first published 1971); Reilly, *Contest*, 28–9; R. Collins, 'The Spanish Kingdoms', in T. Reuter (ed.), *The New Cambridge Medieval History*, vol. III, *c.900–c.1024* (Cambridge, 1999), 670–91, at 673.

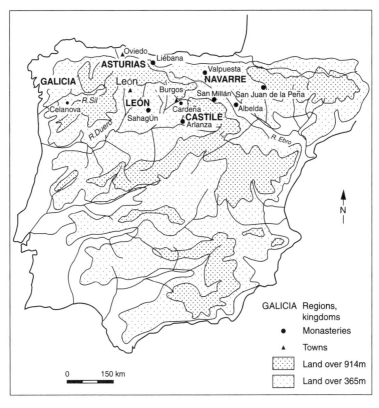

Fig. 1. Northern Spain *c.*1000

however, is very questionable, and has been strongly challenged in recent years.[7] The significance of free settlers in determining the nature of peasant

[7] See J. Escalona Monge, *Sociedad y territorio en la alta edad media castellana. La formación del alfoz de Lara* (BAR International Series no. 1079, 2002), esp. 7–14; M. C. Rodríguez González and M. Durany Castrillo, 'Ocupación y organización del espacio en el Bierzo entre los siglos V al X', and J. M. Mínguez, 'Continuidad y ruptura en los orígenes de la sociedad asturleonesa. De la *villa* a la comunidad campesina', both in *Studia Historica* 16 (1998), 45–87, 89–127; J. L. Quiroga and M. R. Lovelle, 'Ciudades atlánticas en transición: la "ciudad" tardo-antigua y alto-medieval en el noroeste de la Península Ibérica (s.v–xi)', *Archeologia Medievale*, 26 (1999), 257–68; I. Martín Viso, *Fragmentos del Leviatán. La articulación política del espacio zamorano en la alta edad media* (Zamora, 2002), esp. 43–55; S. Castellanos and I. Martín Viso, 'The Local Articulation of Central Power in the North of the Iberian Peninsula, 500–1000', *Early Medieval Europe*, 13 (2005). Cf. J. Escalona Monge, 'De "señores y campesinos" a "poderes feudales y

society has therefore also been challenged, although the disappearance of free peasant communities in the tenth and eleventh centuries remains a prominent theme in the debate.

There is a very large and important literature on 'feudal revolution' and related issues in Spain, the debate running in one form or another for most of the past century.[8] This both engages with the French framing and has distinctive preoccupations of its own. These are conditioned by a transition from late antiquity which was interrupted by Arab invasion and consequent political domination of much of Iberia; and influenced by the existence of a long military frontier east-west across the peninsula and active military engagement with Arabs and their clients during the central middle ages.

Assessment of societal change in the tenth and eleventh centuries in Spain is complicated by the extreme paucity of pre-tenth-century texts. This is not so different from the situation in other centuries and other regions of western Europe in the early middle ages, but in Spain the contrast is more extreme than elsewhere. Nonetheless, despite this difficulty, by the late 1990s, very broadly, and allowing for regional differentiation and individual nuance, some consensus is apparent on several aspects of change. Firstly, ancient slavery was weakening across the third to eighth centuries AD, so that there was scarcely any slave population left by 1000. Secondly, seigneurialization began in the last quarter of the tenth century but was mainly a feature of

---

comunidades". Elementos para definir la articulación entre territorio y clases sociales en la alta edad media castellana', in I. Álvarez Borge (ed.), *Comunidades locales y poderes feudales en la edad media* (Logroño, 2001), 115–55, at 122–9.

[8] For an indication of the range: C. Sánchez Albornoz, 'Las behetrías. La encomendación en Asturias, León y Castilla', *Anuario de Historia del Derecho Español*, 1 (1924), 158–336, esp. 196–240; H. Grassotti, *Las instituciones feudo-vasalláticas en León y Castilla* (Spoleto, 1969) and *eadem*, ' "Senior" y "seniorium" en la terminología jurídica de Castilla y León (siglos X–XIII)', *Cuadernos de Historia de España*, 65–6 (1981), 31–58; P. Bonnassie, 'From the Rhône to Galicia: Origins and Modalities of the Feudal Order', in Bonnassie, *Slavery to Feudalism*, 104–31 (first published 1980); C. Estepa Díez, 'Formación y consolidación del feudalismo en Castilla y León', in *En torno al feudalismo hispánico. I congreso de estudios medievales* (León, 1989), 157–256; J. A. García de Cortázar and E. Peña Bocos, 'Poder condal ¿y "mutación feudal"? en la Castilla del año mil', in M. I. Loring García (ed.), *Historia social, pensamiento historiográfico y edad media* (Madrid, 1997), 273–98; J. J. Larrea, *La Navarre du IVe au XIIe siècle* (Paris, 1998), 301–37; J. M. Salrach, 'Les féodalités méridionales: des Alpes à la Galice', in Bournazel and Poly (eds), *Féodalités*, 313–88, at 320–38; A. Isla Frez, *La alta edad media. Siglos VIII–XI* (Madrid, 2002), 279–92.

the eleventh century, through the imposition of new lordly constraints and demands and the erosion of the liberty of most of the peasantry. Thirdly, this was in part effected by the enormous expansion of monastic lordship in the tenth and eleventh centuries, both through the acquisition of small-scale free peasant properties and through the creation of immunities, although there is much stress in the literature on a new emerging lay aristocracy. And fourthly, the exercise of public power by the king and his agents continued through the tenth century; for some historians (and some regions) the real weakening of royal power came in the mid-eleventh century, while for others royal power also continued through much of the eleventh century, with the real change coming in the early twelfth.[9] In other words, very few would see a sudden rupture; most would see 150 or more years of gradual change; most would see seigneurialization as central to the change; and most would put this later than the passage of comparable changes in the Frankish world. Most people nowadays would also see the ensuing social formations as essentially similar to those of the Frankish world, although there are some very clear northern Spanish variations.

The extension of lordship: some problems

What follows is designed to raise some questions about recent interpretations. Before that, there are three warnings, all obvious, but essential to keep in mind. Firstly, although we have several thousand tenth-century texts from northern Spain, we often cannot quantify in any meaningful way because the records do not have a standardized format—and that is consistently problematic. Secondly, as everywhere, our perceptions are heavily influenced by the language of the person writing the record; both the Latin terminology and the conceptual apparatus of the scribes are often very localized. So, when comparing one place with another, language can make similar things look different, and vice versa. This is especially true of charter collections for the monasteries of Cardeña and Arlanza, which are (differently) variant from

---

[9] J. A. García de Cortázar y Ruiz de Aguirre, *La sociedad rural en la España medieval* (Madrid, 1988), 6–7, 48–9; R. Pastor, 'Sur la genèse du féodalisme en Castille et dans le León, X^e–XIIe siècles. Point de départ pour une histoire comparative', in H. Atsma, A. Burguière (eds), *Marc Bloch aujourd'hui. Histoire comparée et sciences sociales* (Paris, 1990), 259–70, at 266–8; Bonnassie, 'From the Rhône to Galicia', 117, 122; Larrea, *Navarre*, 235–79, 341–73; Salrach, 'Les féodalités', 366; I. Álvarez Borge, 'Estructuras de poder en Castilla en la alta edad media: señores, siervos, vasallos', in *Señores, siervos, vasallos en la alta edad media. XXVIII Semana de estudios medievales, Estella, 16 a 20 de julio de 2001* (Pamplona, 2002), 269–308, at 278–81; C. Estepa Díez, *Las behetrías castellanas*, 2 vols. (Valladolid, 2003), vol. II, 388–90.

many of the others: Cardeña has a greater emphasis on donation and reciprocities, and Arlanza, in which the tenth-century material is a small group anyway, is heavily comital and clerical in interest. However, despite their distinctive qualities, they condition the way many people think about Castile. Since texts from Castile have often been focal to the assessment of change in northern Spain (partly because of the increasing prominence of the count of Castile), we need to be wary of their unusual nature. More than that, amongst the thousands that survive we see a handful of the same texts used over and over again by historians to make or break arguments (the supposed immunities of Barrio, Berbea and San Zadornil in 955, of Los Ausines in 972, of the Covarrubias foundation document of 978, of Nave de Albura in 1012, as also the *caballeros* [knights] and their *seigneur* of the Castrojeriz *fuero* of 974, and the *infanciones* [minor nobility] of Espeja c.1017). While they are obviously important, we need to remember that their character is unrepresentative; and, on top of that, most have suspect elements—additions and emendations of later times.[10] Thirdly, there are in any case plenty of forged texts in Spanish charter collections; many of these claim a tenth-century context for specific royal or comital powers, claims which are often obviously anachronistic. There has been much recent high-quality editing, which has drawn attention to the suspect character of some of the not so obviously anachronistic charters as well. This is extremely important work, but there is a danger of circularity here: more charters become suspect as more people come to doubt the practical realities of royal and comital power in the tenth century.

Public power

It is obviously impossible to measure the quantity and quality of power that a Spanish king could or did hold. Despite this, one might say that a sense of royal authority, and of public power as conveyed through royal authority, pervades many tenth-century texts; hence we find dating by reference to regnal years, royal authorizations and confirmations, royal initiatives, royal confiscations, royal handling of cases of dispute, and so on. This is a much stronger sense of the public than one finds in many parts of France or in western Britain or Ireland at that time. However, while the image of ruling

---

[10] SM67; C153; G. Martínez Díez (ed.), *Fueros locales en el territorio de la provincia de Burgos* (Burgos, 1982), no. 1, 119–22; L. Serrano (ed.), *Cartulario del infantado de Covarrubias* (Madrid-Valladolid, 1907), no. VII; SM144; JP54. See Álvarez Borge, 'Estructuras de poder', 281 n. 22 and 298; and id., 'Sobre la formación de la gran propiedad y las relaciones de dependencia en Hampshire (Wessex) y Castilla en la alta edad media', in id. (ed.), *Comunidades locales*, 21–63, at 27 n. 9.

kings is strong, the practical implications of royal power are not much evident in uncorrupted tenth-century texts: holding a law court is clear enough, but tax-taking and the control of public obligations are much more questionable at that time (early eleventh-century evidence is much firmer).[11] There is, then, a strong sense of the public without much evidence of any institutionalization of practical powers associated with ruling. Royal rights were also clearly alienated from the early tenth century onwards, through grants of land and populations to laymen or bishops or monasteries, although unambiguous grants of specified immunities are extremely hard to find in unchallengeable tenth-century text.[12] It is therefore evident that fragmentation of such royal power as existed was under way from at least the early tenth century. However, public power does not appear to have been very precisely defined and may well not have been very great.

Seigneurial power in the tenth century
From surviving grants of land and populations it is abundantly clear that all kinds of landlord, lay and ecclesiastical, had 'authority' over dependent cultivators on large estates from the late ninth century onwards.[13] This is the case from Galicia to Castile, although it is notable that references markedly increase from the 970s—a significant numerical difference given the relative decrease in available text in those three last decades of the tenth century. We don't always know what kind of authority this was, since texts that mention cultivators when property changes hands do not usually specify the nature of the subjection, but it sometimes involves payment of dues and occasionally performance of specific duties, both often simply called 'service' (*servitium*). This kind of authority is most easily interpreted as straightforward landlordly, domanial, power over persons, following Carlos Estepa's classic paper reminding us to distinguish domanial from seigneurial elements in the tenth century.[14] It is also perfectly clear that some powerful lords, lay

---

[11] See Larrea, *Navarre*, 251–5, on fiscality. Texts like the Fuero of León (1017) indicate quite a range of royal powers: see A. García Gallo, 'El fuero de León. Su historia, textos y redacciones', *Anuario de Historia del Derecho Español*, 39 (1969), 5–171, at 152–65.

[12] Many grants appear to be of royal property (i.e. landlordly power) rather than of any royal power to command, although the latter do occur. Estepa, 'Formación y consolidación del feudalismo', 169–79, is critical here: unless the grants were made *ad imperandum*, he argues, they cannot be taken to confer anything more than domanial power.

[13] For example: S19 (of 920), C82 (of 952), L333 (of 960) and L461 (of 978), the latter two being originals.

[14] Estepa, 'Formación y consolidación del feudalismo'; at 161–3 he expresses the distinction as between three, rather than two, forms of lordly power, *propiedad dominical, dominio señorial, señorío jurisdiccional* (roughly 'landlord power, seigneurial lordship, the full

and ecclesiastical, had powers of control over territories and populations, in their own right, howsoever they originated, such that residents had to *obey their orders* as well as pay dues to them in the tenth century, both early and late. This looks like more than landlordly power: although undeveloped, it has a touch of the seigneurial.[15] However, what we do not find at this time are disputes centring on peasant objections to new impositions, such as those that crop up in eighth- and ninth-century Carolingian contexts.[16] By contrast, there is well-documented 'resistance' in the eleventh century and later.[17] It therefore looks as if the beginnings of seigneurialization were indeed under way by the early tenth century, if not before, but there is little to suggest any increase in burden or change in its character in the tenth century itself. These are extremely low levels of seigneurialization by European standards, despite much stronger comment in the literature, where Estepa's reminder has not always been heeded, and where the term 'seigneurialization' has often been used to describe changes which were essentially an increase in landlordship and a decrease in small proprietorship.

Commendation

It is a major theme of the Spanish historiography that an increase in commendation (becoming committed to a lord), especially in the latter half of the tenth century, was one of several factors contributing to the seigneurialization process. There is a very large literature on some aspects of this, but direct and unambiguous evidence of acts of commendation is in fact difficult to find in the tenth century. There are certainly a number of charters recording gifts to laymen, laywomen and clerics to secure patronage, by defending the donor's

---

seigneurie', where the latter is the 'concrete expression' and development of seigneurial lordship).

[15] For example: S6 (of 904), Cel207 (of 929), L549 (an original of 991).

[16] Cf. J. L. Nelson, 'Dispute Settlement in Carolingian West Francia', in W. Davies and P. Fouracre (eds), *The Settlement of Disputes in Early Medieval Europe* (Cambridge, 1986), 45–64, at 51–2, and, for references to other cases, 52, n. 27.

[17] R. Pastor de Togneri, *Resistencias y luchas campesinas en la época del crecimiento y consolidación de la formación feudal. Castilla y León, siglos X–XIII* (Madrid, 1980), 99 ff.; Bonnassie, 'From the Rhône to Galicia', 123–4; Salrach, 'Les féodalités', 364–6. Reyna Pastor argues for resistance from the 920s (75–86) by pointing to repeated conflicts over ownership (for example, as implied by groups of villagers agreeing to pay dues on land they had colonized, sometimes following a court case, L290 (of 955), Cel446 (of 959), Ar18 (of 965)); this obviously occurred, but it is not the same kind or degree of resistance as an open challenge to new, and new kinds of, imposition.

property, giving the donor support in court, and so on.[18] Several of these texts use the formula *bonum mihi facere* ('I give you this so that you may do good to me, defend my farms, etc.'), a phrasing that is much discussed, especially in the context of the development of the *behetría* (a particular kind of lay lordship characteristic of Castile in the later middle ages).[19] Although one early Liébana text (of 875) does directly associate this kind of gift with commendation,[20] the formula does not have to imply full personal commendation in the sense that we normally understand it in the early middle ages: it may mean gaining a protector but it does not have to imply personal, much less exclusive, commitment.[21]

In fact, a number of these 'doing good' texts are associated with practical support. The same language is used but the social level varies: 'I give you this [not so that you may defend my farms but] so that you can feed and clothe me, or take me into your house, or look after me when I am old and sick'; here 'doing good' is about getting care in old age, in a number of different ways. Indeed, far from recording personal commendation, some of the 'personal care' texts are clearly business transactions: in effect long-term care is purchased (and at least two texts, one from Oviedo of 937 and one from León of 978, frame the transaction in terms of sale not gift).[22]

The *bonum mihi facere* formula has several meanings and is no guide to the amount of commendation in the tenth century. While commendation, including collective commendation, certainly happens in the eleventh century, there does not appear to be much of it in the tenth; it must be very doubtful that it is a significant determinant of change.

Villages

The role of free village communities is a prominent theme in the Spanish historiography. The older view of Sánchez Albornoz, that the Spanish peasantry prior to 1000 had exceptional and unusual freedom (by contrast with peasantries elsewhere in western Europe), arising from the circumstance of fresh colonization of a depopulated landscape, has largely been set aside.

---

[18] For example, L222, S332, T64. I deal fully with these cases in *Acts of Giving. Individual, Community and Church in Tenth-Century Christian Spain* (Oxford, 2007).

[19] On which see now the publication of Estepa Díez, *Las behetrías castellanas*.

[20] T13.

[21] Cf. Estepa and Jular, 'Prólogo', in C. Estepa Díez and C. Jular Pérez-Alfaro (eds), *Los señoríos de behetría* (Madrid, 2001), 9–18, at 10, who make this point very strongly (*pace* Sánchez Albornoz, 'Behetrías', 205–25); Estepa Díez, *Behetrías*, vol. I, 42–3.

[22] Ov8 (an original), L462.

However, many still argue that it is the existence of free village communities that both delayed the development of local aristocratic power until the eleventh century and determined the character of some of the *seigneuries* of the later middle ages.[23] Others, arguing on a different basis, maintain that it is not the individual village but a supra-local entity (in effect, a group of villages) that determines some later forms of lordship.[24]

There are some very questionable assumptions suffusing these arguments. On the issue of free village communities: that there were free peasants in the tenth century makes sense and accords with a mass of evidence.[25] The relevant evidence includes: anecdotes of behaviour, especially family conflict, in the context of small-scale property owners and their disputes; a pattern of transactions in relation to very small properties—there is an enormous volume of sale, for price, especially in Galicia and León—which is difficult to see as anything other than the activity of peasant proprietors;[26] and the use of guarantors (*fidiatores, fideiussores*) to guarantee small-scale transactions as well as agreements.[27] The latter are found across northern Spain, from west to

---

[23] See above, pp. 20–2 and n. 7. C. Sánchez Albornoz, 'Pequeños propietarios libres en el reino Asturleonés. Su realidad histórica', *Settimane di studio del centro italiano di studi sull'alto medioevo*, 13 (1966), 183–222; id., 'El régimen de la tierra en el reino asturleonés hace mil años', in id., *Viejos y nuevos estudios*, vol. III, 1313–521, esp. 1447–514. Bonnassie, 'From the Rhône to Galicia', 116; Pastor, 'Sur la genèse du féodalisme', 264–5; Larrea, *Navarre*, 312–22; cf. Salrach, 'Les féodalités', 364–8, and Escalona Monge, 'De "señores y campesinos" a "poderes feudales y comunidades"', 118.

[24] García de Cortázar, *Sociedad rural*, 14; Larrea, *Navarre*, 262–3; J. Escalona Monge, 'Unidades territoriales supralocales: una propuesta sobre los orígenes del señorío de behetría', in Estepa and Jular (eds), *Señoríos de behetría*, 21–46.

[25] By a peasant of free status in this context I refer to the person who had a capacity to alienate property rights and to move where he wished, who was not subject to arbitrary demands, and who could go to court and participate in local decisions. Cf. Escalona's sensible comment on the nature of freedom, 'De "señores y campesinos" a "poderes feudales y comunidades"', 151.

[26] The small proprietor as social determinant was a favourite argument of Sánchez Albornoz (see 'Pequeños propietarios libres' and also 'Behetrías', 201–3). One does not have to accept his approach to accept the fact of petty proprietorship (*pace* Pastor, *Resistencias*, 51 and n. 55); cf. Larrea, *Navarre*, 318 and Álvarez Borge, 'Estructuras de poder', 291.

[27] T66 gives us an excellent example of precisely what a *fideiussor* did: he took the principal to court to confirm an agreement and was to make good the transaction himself if the latter defaulted. For comparative material, see D. B. Walters, 'The General Features of Archaic European Suretyship', and R. Stacey (trans.), '*Berrad airechta*: an Old Irish Tract on Suretyship', both in T. M. Charles-Edwards, M. E. Owen and D. B. Walters (eds), *Lawyers and Laymen* (Cardiff, 1986), 92–116, 210–33; cf. for Breton examples, W. Davies, 'Suretyship in the *cartulaire de Redon*', ibid., 72–91, at 79–80.

east, and there are many examples from the charters of Celanova, León, Sahagún, Liébana, Cardeña, Valpuesta and San Millán. As private mechanisms for guaranteeing contract, they are an important pointer to community mechanisms, mechanisms which essentially depend upon the force of local reputation in a society where everyone knows everyone and community support can make or break an individual.

So, the argument for the existence of free peasants and free peasant communities in the tenth century is entirely reasonable. However, some peasant groups were undoubtedly dependent (and there were still some slaves too, especially in the north-west): the populations of whole villages changed hands and had obligations to the landowner summarized as 'service'. They may have been legally free but they were economically and socially dependent. This happened from Galicia to Castile, early and late, both for large tracts of land and individual villages. The presence of free peasant groups must have been punctuated by dependent groups and individuals already in the early tenth century. The landscape of 'freedom' must have been more uneven in the tenth century than is commonly portrayed.

Secondly, quite apart from the distinction between dependent and free, the 'peasantry' was not a homogeneous mass, as one or two current writers point out; there were tenants as well as proprietors, and richer and poorer peasants.[28] (One would in fact expect, as in ninth-century Breton villages, that some rich peasants would have been slave-owners.) Now, social differentiation and 'hierarchization' has long been a theme of the literature on this period. However, the burden of these analyses has been to focus on the separation of the minor nobility from the peasant mass—that is, a top (rich) layer of peasants who became minor nobles, *milites* being increasingly distinguished from *rustici* and *infanzones* from *villanos*.[29] Without questioning the obvious importance of such differentiation, there really ought to be more to peasant social analysis than this. Those who remained peasants are unlikely to have been an undifferentiated mass; and one would expect leading peasants to have played a role in community organization just as they did in even better documented periods.

---

[28] I. Álvarez Borge, *Poder y relaciones sociales en Castilla en la edad media. Los territorios entre el Arlanzón y el Duero en los siglos X al XIV* (Valladolid, 1996), 27–34; id., 'Estructuras de poder', 290–2; Salrach, 'Les féodalités', 364–5.

[29] Pastor, 'Sur la genèse du féodalisme', 265; García de Cortázar, *Sociedad rural*, 27–36; Estepa, 'Formación y consolidación del feudalismo', 191; Larrea, *Navarre*, 327; García de Cortázar and Peña Bocos, 'Poder condal', 293; Álvarez Borge, 'Estructuras de poder', 289, 293.

Authority, chiefs and communities

Discussion of emerging aristocratic power makes much of issues of authority in the villages and the supra-localities. Some writers favour a model which has villages and/or supra-localities with 'chiefs', and some favour the chiefless 'community of the village'—hence the alternative models of the 'hierarchical' rural community with its chief, or the 'communitarian' community without chief; many see the models having different regional application, and some would have a hybrid of leading lineages dominating the village beneath the supra-local chief.[30]

There are many issues here. Let me focus on two. Firstly, there are texts that refer to people called *seniores* [elders] in and around the villages. There is a prevailing tendency to view these *seniores* as the forerunners of later *seigneurs* as, obviously, at a linguistic level, they clearly are; and the famous, and much-cited, Castrojeriz text of 974 does make the point implicitly.[31] In fact, most tenth-century examples of *seniores* come from Castile and Navarre texts and in Castile texts, especially, *seniores* look more like aristocrats or public functionaries than peasants; documents may, for example, mention exemption from service due to king or *senior*. It is however worth raising the issue of what a *senior* was in contemporary tenth-century understanding? Was he a local big-man, the chief who gave orders, whether in his own right or as the agent of public power? Or was he ever a respected local man, elevated by the community and answerable to it, its representative and its voice? The word is used collectively in some Navarre texts,[32] and I can think of comparative material that is suggestive. There is Welsh material of the eighth century, where *seniores* (the term is the same, though *meliores* is also used) were an independent regional petty aristocracy, who attended meetings and witnessed transactions.[33] There is also Breton material of the ninth century, where the term is again the same, but the people related to villages rather than regions and were demonstrably peasants. They were explicitly those called

---

[30] Pastor, 'Sur la genèse du féodalisme', 264–5; García de Cortázar, *Sociedad rural*, 12–15, 22–7; Escalona Monge, 'De "señores y campesinos" a "poderes feudales y comunidades"', 147–8.

[31] Martínez Díez (ed.), *Fueros locales*, no. 1, 119. See García de Cortázar, *Sociedad rural*, 49; Álvarez Borge, *Poder*, 35–6; García de Cortázar and Peña Bocos, 'Poder condal', 283; Larrea, *Navarre*, 332–3; Estepa Díez, *Behetrías*, vol. I, 45. Note Estepa's reservation (45, n. 28) about the date of all elements of this text.

[32] Larrea makes the sensible point that the terminology is unstable in *Navarre*, 228–9. For the relatively late appearance of the word *senior* in León texts, see Grassotti, ' "Senior" y "seniorium" en la terminología jurídica', 34–5.

[33] W. Davies, *An Early Welsh Microcosm* (London, 1978), 108–20.

upon to give evidence of local situations in cases of dispute, about a fifth of those who went to village meetings, and not necessarily the richest; most never appeared outside their own village territory, although a few went to meetings in neighbouring villages. They seem literally to have been 'elders', experienced, respected and trusted local freemen.[34] Although there are differences of scale here, what is common is that these are people who went to meetings, leading freemen whose judgment was respected. Could some of the *seniores* of Spanish texts have been the respected, and not necessarily the most wealthy?

The second issue is that of village councils—*concilia*—which appear characteristically in a number of tenth-century texts. Was the *concilium* the meeting of chiefs/big-men, for example of a supra-locality? Was it the meeting of dominant lineages of a village? Or was it an expression of all the free families of a region?[35] A simple reading of the texts shows *concilia* in León and Castile from the 930s. From the contexts the word (*collacio* is sometimes used as a variant) clearly refers to a collectivity—that of the village, or of a monastery, or very occasionally of a town or a group of villages (though the texts are suspect in the latter case). Some texts go out of their way to emphasize that the collectivity is the whole group, male and female, old and young, greater and lesser (though again the most detailed of these are suspect); other texts are clear in indicating that leading persons might represent the collectivity, with numbers varying from 9 to 42. Equally interesting is the fact that action by a collectivity in some villages does not merit the label.[36] Given the numbers, it is very difficult to see a village *concilium* as other than an assembly of a wide range of different households, and it is difficult to deny that a larger or smaller group might take responsibility in speaking for the collectivity. Given the names of those named, such groups cannot be associated with either chiefs or dominating lineages. Why should they not have been like 'elders',

---

[34] W. Davies, *Small Worlds. The Village Community in Early Medieval Brittany* (London, 1988), 146–52.

[35] García de Cortázar, *Sociedad rural,* 14–15; Escalona Monge, 'De "señores y campesinos" a "poderes feudales y comunidades" ', 148–9. Pastor, *Resistencias,* pp. 28–9, has *concilium/colegium* as the group with the power of making decisions, such as a family group.

[36] C89, with 17 named and 'all the council' unnamed; 'de minimo usque ad maximo', A27; C70, C192, C151 (Burgos), C153 (suspect); SM67 (suspect); L466, with 13 named and others not; S268, S298, with 17 named and others not, S338. *Collatio* as synonym for *concilium,* S44, with 9 named, S335; V43; T45; cf. the list in Estepa, 'Formación y consolidación del feudalismo', 191 n. 136. M. del C. Carlé, *Del concejo medieval castellano-leonés* (Buenos Aires, 1968), 21–2, notes the range of early meanings.

whether or not they were so termed—experienced, respected and trusted local freemen—rather than necessarily the richest or most powerful?

Extending the analysis

There is certainly a sense of public power in northern Spanish texts of the tenth century, but the quality and quantity of it looks very fragile and the full-blown immunity is rarely evidenced. As Rodney Hilton showed in the case of England, seigneurialization could happen *without* public power fragmenting.[37] Here too, the issue is not so much one of the fragmentation of public power but of building new, multiple and divided, powers of control over the free. And as lords acquired powers, so did kings: the very fact that alienated regalian rights are specified much more precisely in eleventh-century texts than earlier shows that royal powers were in fact developing too. A simple model of transfer of public power from king to lords is not appropriate here.

Even if we allow for fewer free village communities and some element of seigneurialization at the start, increasing seigneurialization in the tenth century is probably too much emphasized in the literature (as are also the fact and amount of commendation and the presence of village chiefs in the tenth century): there does not seem to have been much development of domanial power into something else in this period. Extension of lordship, as such, there certainly was: the extension of episcopal and monastic lordship—which is a very clear feature of the tenth century, increasing in the last decades—is often under-emphasized.

Attention to social differentiation within peasant communities, by contrast, has been so focused on the emergence of new noble strata that differentiation *within* the peasant mass may be suggested but goes uninvestigated; it is potentially significant in respect of authority *within* the village and in understanding the process of social change in more ways than is customary. As Rodney Hilton pointed out many times, leading peasants consistently played a role in community organization in the later middle ages.[38] One would expect the same to have happened in these Spanish villages: the alternatives are not simply *either* chiefs *or* whole communities; and they are not simply *either* lords infiltrating the village from outside *or* rich peasants acquiring horses and starting to dominate. The actions of some village *concilia* may point towards the emergence of peasant elites and not to the emergence of strata which became noble.

[37] Hilton, 'Feudalism or *féodalité*', 231–4; id., ' "*Seigneurie française et manoir anglais*" Fifty Years Later', in Atsma and Burguière, *Marc Bloch aujourd'hui*, 173–82, at 177–8.

[38] For example, Hilton, *Class Conflict and the Crisis of Feudalism*, 141–2; cf. id., ' "*Seigneurie française et manoir anglais*" ', 178.

The tenth century is unquestionably a time of extending lordship because it is unquestionably a time of extending landlordship. The acquisition strategies of many of the larger monasteries are strikingly evident—and new—in the tenth century (although for San Millán, which plays such a large part in the historiography, this is an eleventh- as much as a tenth-century phenomenon).[39] Extending the *powers* of lordship may happen a little (there are fragile hints of some ecclesiastical justice in the tenth century[40]), but it is not the most striking characteristic of that time. The main development, as the consensus has it, comes later, but probably later than is usually allowed.

It is important to pursue social differentiation at village level in northern Spain. This could be taken forward by systematic analysis of the mass of documentation, with much less of a focus on texts that may ultimately have a tenth-century origin but have been massaged in later centuries. It *is* possible to do the analysis, because the texts are so rich in detail of people and places. Once done, we stand a better chance of understanding changing power structures within the rural community and of understanding the bases upon which lordship itself developed in the eleventh century.[41]

---

[39] See J. A. García de Cortázar, *El dominio del monasterio de San Millán de la Cogolla (siglos X a XIII). Introducción a la historia rural de Castilla altomedieval* (Salamanca, 1969), and J. M. Mínguez Fernández, *El dominio del monasterio de Sahagún en el siglo X* (Salamanca, 1980) for classic studies; see also W. Davies, 'Buying with Masses: "Donation" *pro remedio animae* in Tenth-Century Galicia and Castile-León', in F. Bougard, C. La Rocca, and R. Le Jan (eds), *Sauver son âme et se perpétuer* (Rome, 2005), 401–16.

[40] C55, L479, SM26, Ov23, for example.

[41] I am most grateful to Chris Dyer, Chris Wickham, and Isabel Alfonso for their comments on a draft of this paper.

Hilton, Lordship and the Culture of the Gentry

Peter Coss

The history of the gentry was not one of Rodney Hilton's central concerns. In much of what he wrote—on the structure of society, on the constitution of estates, on lord–peasant relations, on towns in feudal society—the gentry tended to be subsumed within the broader, secular landowning class. This was so, partly because lesser families have left comparatively little in terms of private records compared to great landowners, both secular and ecclesiastical, but also because the structure and role of the gentry per se were not his prime interests. He was very much aware, however, of problems surrounding status: of the changing nature of knighthood, for example, of the issue of gentility, and of the question of social gradation, and he had things to say on the blurring of distinctions in the decades after the Black Death and on the specific problem of the franklin. On one occasion he spoke of 'an old problem in English social history—the identification of the "gentry"'.[1]

Although he was very much aware of the directions in which the study of the gentry might go, these issues were less important to him than the ones he chose to follow centrally in his own research. Gentility was seen primarily as part of the system of oppression under which the medieval majority lived. He highlighted not only famous statements like 'When Adam delved and Eve span, who was then the Gentleman?', but also figures like the leading character among the shepherds in the Towneley Plays who is in reality a landholding husbandman and who complains of being harassed by 'gentlery men'.[2]

Hilton noted that 'the members of the landowning class with whom the peasants came most into contact were the gentry', not least in their capacity as agents of the state.[3] At the same time, however, he was well aware that social relations between gentry and peasants were not necessarily antagonistic.

---

[1] R. H. Hilton, 'Ideology and Social Order in Late Medieval England', in his *Class Conflict and the Crisis of Feudalism: Essays in Medieval Social History* (London, 1985), 246. This essay was first published in French in 1978.

[2] R. H. Hilton, *The English Peasantry in the Later Middle Ages* (Oxford, 1975), 23.

[3] Ibid. 223–4.

Past and Present (2007), Supplement 2

They could be involved together in rebellion and disturbances of one sort and another, as his discussion of Cade's Rebellion in the Ford Lectures shows. Moreover, as he points out 'there was nothing new [in the fifteenth century] about the presence of husbandmen in the retinues of the country gentry'.[4]

Although the gentry was not a specific focus of Hilton's work his programme was such that it helped to inspire the study of the medieval gentry which took off in the 1970s and which has been a feature of medieval studies in England ever since. Of course he supervised theses on the gentry, as did others, but that is not primarily what I mean. He played a major part in determining the agenda. For one thing he brought contemporary French scholarship—pre-eminently that of Georges Duby—into the British arena. The study of knighthood from this perspective gave rise to Sally Harvey's famous essay on the knight and the knight's fee,[5] while the debate on the crisis of the knightly class, jointly inspired, as was often the case, by Hilton and Michael Postan, developed—for good or ill—not long after.[6] Hilton was agnostic at best, I think, when it came to E.A. Kosminsky's view that the small manors—predominantly those of lesser lords—were by their nature proto-capitalist, at least as regards the period before the Black Death.[7] However, Richard Britnell, drawing inspiration from Hilton's famous essay on rent and capital formation and from a parallel essay by Postan, used the rare survival of lesser landowners' manorial accounts from Essex to show that Kosminsky was wrong and to illuminate the actual workings of gentry estates.[8] Christopher Dyer, pre-eminently, has looked at gentry estates in the later fourteenth and fifteenth centuries.[9] In a recent study he has identified some fifteenth-century landlords as among the proto-capitalists of the era, a development determined not so much by the specifics of estate structure

---

[4] Ibid. 69.

[5] S. Harvey, 'The Knight and the Knight's Fee in England', *Past and Present*, 49 (1970), 3–43; repr. in R. H. Hilton (ed.), *Peasants, Knights and Heretics* (Cambridge, 1981), 133–73.

[6] For the contributions to this debate see P. Coss, *The Origins of the English Gentry* (Cambridge, 2003), 69–108.

[7] See his introduction to T. H. Aston (ed.), *Landlords, Peasants and Politics in Medieval England* (Cambridge, 1987), 3–4.

[8] R. H. Britnell, 'Minor Landlords in England and Medieval Agrarian Capitalism', *Past and Present*, 89 (1980), 3–22; repr. in Aston (ed.), *Landlords, Peasants and Politics*, 227–46.

[9] See for example, C. Dyer, *Warwickshire Farming 1349–c.1520: Preparations for Agricultural Revolution*, Dugdale Society Occasional Paper, 27 (1981).

as by the radically changed nature of the fifteenth-century economy.[10] In my own recent work I have endeavoured to bring some of the conceptual rigour I thought was lacking into the study of the gentry by offering a six-point definition and arguing that the gentry was formed from the lesser nobility in 'an accelerating process' between the mid-thirteenth century and the mid-fourteenth.[11] In *The Origins of the English Gentry* I have refined the thesis and in doing so placed the accent more firmly upon the 1290s to the middle of the fourteenth century in terms of the full realization of the gentry.[12] These are all works by scholars whose approach to medieval society was not greatly dissimilar from Hilton's own. But his work has also inspired studies of aspects of gentry life by scholars who are not remotely connected either to his affinity or to Postan's. One thinks of the debate on the audience and dissemination of the ballads of Robin Hood, for example, and of his discussion of 'honest felons and well-born bandits', which has become one of the benchmarks in the study of gentry violence: its genesis, purpose and its true incidence.

Of course, there have been many other influences upon modern gentry studies and it is to some of these that I now wish to turn. One of them is constitutional history. Now constitutional history as such may be largely dead, at least in its true sense, but its ghost ever walks among us. From the perspective of the gentry there are two dimensions to its influence, one active, the other reactive: that is to say participation in justice and local government on the one hand, and political action in the defence of liberty on the other. The former tends to be seen as the product of self-government at the king's command, while the latter is often seen from the perspective of the evolution of parliament. In practice, these two dimensions have tended to run together. In an influential essay R. F. Treharne wrote of the period of baronial reform and rebellion in the mid-thirteenth century as marking a critical phase in the rise of the knightly class, a new class that 'had proved its worth, and had arrived, in national politics, at a position which gave it the opportunity of asserting itself in proportion to its economic and social standing, and to its experience in the practical work of daily government'. Moreover,

> In knowledge, competence and awareness of their responsibilities and powers, the knights of mid-thirteenth-century England matched in the field of local government the public spirit and

[10] C. Dyer, 'Were there any Capitalists in Fifteenth-Century England?', in J. Kermode (ed.), *Enterprise and Individuals in Fifteenth-Century England* (Stroud, 1991), 1–24.

[11] P. R. Coss, 'The Formation of the English Gentry', *Past and Present*, 147 (1995), 38–64.

[12] Coss, *Origins of the English Gentry*, esp. 239–51.

sense of responsibility shown by the magnates in the "state of the realm" in 1258 . . . . The development of government in England between 1216 and 1258 provides several instances to show that a new principle was achieving recognition, by both the Crown and its officials on the one hand, and the knights on the other—the principle that government is for the sake of the governed, and not solely for the good of the rulers, with the corollary that good government must carry with it the goodwill of those who operate the system.[13]

Treharne was writing some time ago and few would tend to write quite in that vein today. But shorn of Whiggery and the grandiloquent language of scholars like Treharne, this interactive approach has continued to the present day to shed considerable light on local society and its relationship with central government. The evolution of parliament is central to it, and parliament is undeniably of great significance within gentry history. John Maddicott, in particular, has used this approach to great effect.[14] But it does have its dangers. Whiggery is one; another is the suggestion of an innate English exceptionalism. Some recent work on the late Anglo-Saxon state, for example, seems to be predicated upon a sense of English difference, and some of those who argue that the gentry already existed before the Norman Conquest seem to have this sort of exceptionalism in mind.[15] A third danger is the over-ready ascription of public spirit. The motives of those landowners who participated in the exercise of public justice, for example, are more often assumed than analysed, in a way reminiscent of F. W. Maitland's business-loving gentlemen. For Maitland the county court was an assembly 'formed out of miscellaneous elements . . . great men and small men . . . . Many of them were knights, the predecessors of the country gentlemen who for centuries to come will do justice and manage the county business *because they like the work* [my italics]'.[16]

---

[13] R. F. Treharne, 'The Knights in the Period of Reform and Rebellion, 1258–67: A Critical Phase in the Rise of a New Social Class', *Bulletin of the Institute of Historical Research*, 21 (1946–8), 9–10.

[14] See, to take just one example, J. Maddicott, 'The County Community in the Making of Public Opinion in Fourteenth-century England', *Transactions of the Royal Historical Society*, 5th ser., 28 (1978), 27–43.

[15] For a critique of this position see P. Coss, 'Was there a Gentry in Late Anglo-Saxon England?', in R. Evans (ed.), *Lordship and Learning: Studies in Memory of Trevor Aston* (Woodbridge, 2004), 95–107.

[16] F. Pollock and F. W. Maitland, *The History of English Law before the time of Edward I*, 2nd edn, 2 vols (Cambridge, 1968), vol. I, 543.

Mention of Maitland reminds us of the role of legal history in gentry studies. In the past much of its influence was allied to constitutional history. In recent years, however, that influence has become stronger, and again from two angles. The first is through a deepening understanding of the complex relationship between law and social change, rather than seeing legal developments as the product of genius, of Henry II for example, and social and institutional changes as the by-product of a largely autonomous legal sphere. This latter approach was once satirized by Rodney Hilton when he wrote that, according to this view, the English ruling class invented villeinage in a fit of absent-mindedness.[17] The Angevin legal reforms are now seen as part of a more complex process of change rather than as its prime initiator, as *deus ex machina*.[18] The second angle is the study of lawyers and allied professionals— the prosopography of the law, if I might call it that—which has now begun to open new perspectives.[19]

Another strong influence upon medieval gentry studies as they developed during the 1970s and 1980s came from the early modern period, most especially from the concept of county community which underlay many gentry regional studies. From the late 1960s the county rapidly became *the* focus of gentry studies within Tudor and Stuart historiography, stimulating young medievalists to follow suit.[20] Given that the shire community already figured in constitutional and legal history and that the county was an important administrative unit in the middle ages this was, in any case, a wholly natural development. The first book-length study, of fourteenth-century Gloucestershire, came in 1981, and others soon followed.[21] As the 1980s progressed,

---

[17] R. H. Hilton, *The Decline of Serfdom in Medieval England* (London, 1967), 9.

[18] See, in particular, J. Hudson, *Land, Law and Lordship in Anglo-Norman England* (Oxford, 1994), esp. 250–81.

[19] See, especially, P. A. Brand, *The Origins of the English Legal Profession* (Oxford, 1992) and A. Musson, *Medieval Law in Context: The Growth of Legal Consciousness from Magna Carta to the Peasants' Revolt* (Manchester, 2001), 36–83.

[20] For the influence of early modern scholars upon the study of the medieval gentry see especially C. Carpenter, 'Gentry and Community in Medieval England', *Journal of British Studies*, 33 (1994), 340–80.

[21] N. Saul, *Knights and Esquires: the Gloucestershire Gentry in the Fourteenth Century* (Oxford, 1981). However, both Michael Bennett and John Maddicott had already submitted important essays on the medieval county community: M. J. Bennett, 'A County Community: Social Cohesion amongst the Cheshire Gentry, 1400–1425', *Northern History*, 8 (1973), 24–44; Maddicott, 'The County Community and the Making of Public Opinion'. Bennett's full study soon followed Saul's: *Community, Class and Careerism: Cheshire and Lancashire in the Age of Sir Gawain and the Green Knight* (Cambridge, 1983).

however, doubts began to creep in over the viability of the concept.[22] Moreover, the role of the county court in the formation of gentry opinion came to be questioned.[23] These growing doubts among medievalists once again matched concerns within early modern historiography. Most scholars began to take a cautious and nuanced, perhaps one might say ambivalent, approach towards the county community.[24] Some were more forthright. At the extreme end of the spectrum lies Christine Carpenter, who has suggested that the county community is a weak and redundant analytical tool and should be removed from the historian's vocabulary.[25]

The questioning of the county community has had positive benefits in encouraging historians to look more broadly at the whole issue of gentry identity, highlighting the dimensions that were sub-county—Nigel Saul's 'county of communities'[26]—as well as those that were regional or national, and to examine the whole phenomenon of gentry networks of association.[27] The issue of elites within the gentry, especially in a county context, has also come under scrutiny. Arguably, the greatest lesson gentry historians have

---

[22] See, for example, S. M. Wright, *The Derbyshire Gentry in the Fifteenth Century* (Chesterfield, 1983), 58, 146; N. Saul, *Scenes from Provincial Life: Knightly Families in Sussex, 1280–1400* (Oxford, 1986), 57.

[23] See, for example, S. J. Payling, *Political Society in Lancastrian England: The Greater Gentry of Nottinghamshire* (Oxford, 1991), 160. See also, more recently, J. R. Lander, 'The Significance of the County in English Government ', in P. Fleming, A. Gross, and J. R. Lander (eds), *Regionalism and Revision: The Crown and its Provinces in England 1200–1650* (London, 1998), 15–27. For early doubts about the role of the county court in the thirteenth century see my 'Knighthood and the Early Thirteenth-Century County Court', in P. R. Coss and S. D. Lloyd (eds), *Thirteenth Century England II* (Woodbridge, 1988), 54–5; and my *Lordship, Knighthood and Locality: A Study in English Society c.1180–c.1280* (Cambridge, 1991), 4–5.

[24] See, for example, E. Acheson, *A Gentry Community: Leicestershire in the Fifteenth Century, c.1422–c.1485* (Cambridge, 1992), 77–9, 106.

[25] Carpenter, 'Gentry and Community in Medieval England', 340–80. See also Lander, 'The Significance of the County', and C. E. Moreton, *The Townshends and their World: Gentry, Law and Land in Norfolk, c.1450–1551* (Oxford, 1992), 80–1, 195–6.

[26] Saul, *Scenes from Provincial Life*, 60. For a discussion of forms of territorial identity in the thirteenth and early fourteenth century see my 'Identity and the Gentry c.1200–c.1340', in M. Prestwich, R. H. Britnell and Robin Frame (eds), *Thirteenth Century England VI* (Woodbridge, 1997), 49–60, repr. in *The Origins of the English Gentry*, 202–15. For a regional study see A. J. Pollard, *North-eastern England during the Wars of the Roses: Lay Society, War, and Politics, 1450–1500* (Oxford, 1990).

[27] Christine Carpenter has become the particular champion of this mode of analysis. See 'Gentry and Community', 364–80, and her *Locality and Polity: A Study of Warwickshire Landed Society, 1401–1499* (Cambridge, 1992), esp. 281–346.

learned from the county approach and its offshoots, however, is a stronger appreciation of the varieties of gentry experience, across time and space.

Perhaps the strongest influence upon medieval gentry studies as a whole, however, has been the work of K. B. McFarlane.[28] McFarlane believed that the study of England's ruling class was the most urgent task facing its historians, and he embarked upon a thorough examination of its history across the later medieval period, from the reign of Edward I to the Reformation. Explicit in his programme was the dethroning of the narrowly conceived and rather stultifying constitutional history bequeathed by Stubbs and his school which had become so dominant in British universities. His aim was to replace it with a political history of a much broader kind, modelled to a degree upon the prosopographical approach of Sir Lewis Namier which, with its emphasis upon the workings of patronage, was currently illuminating eighteenth-century politics. It was, as Maurice Keen puts it, 'an encyclopaedic approach'.[29] The central entry in that encyclopaedia was bastard feudalism, for beyond a doubt it is through this concept and its implications for how we see later medieval society that McFarlane's impact upon gentry studies has been most keenly felt. The institutions of bastard feudalism have been closely studied, pre-eminently the retinue itself, and important work has been done on assessing the impact of the magnate affinity.[30] The content of indentures of retainer has been minutely scrutinized, and the broader impact of the magnates upon the workings of local society and local government has been brought into view.[31] Arbitration by great lords, for example, has become a particular focus of attention and is now generally felt to be complementary rather than antagonistic to the workings of the common law.[32] In consequence, vertical relations between the gentry and the higher nobility have become part of the stock-in-trade of students of the medieval gentry

---

[28] What follows has been adapted from a broader discussion of McFarlane and his influence in my essay 'From Feudalism to Bastard Feudalism', in N. Fryde, P. Monet and O. G. Oexle (eds), *Die Gegenwart des Feudalismus* (Göttingen, 2002), 79–107.

[29] M. Keen, 'English Political History of the Late Middle Ages 1272–c.1520', in A. Deyermond (ed.), *A Century of British Medieval Studies* (Oxford, 2007), 51–69.

[30] See, especially, M. Cherry, 'The Courtenay Earls of Devon: The Formation and Disintegration of a Late Medieval Aristocratic Affinity', *Southern History*, I (1979), 71–97, and C. Carpenter, 'The Beauchamp Affinity: A Study of Bastard Feudalism at Work', *English Historical Review*, 95 (1980), 514–32.

[31] See now M. Jones and S. Walker (eds), *Private Indentures for Life Service in Peace and War 1278–1476* (Camden Society Miscellany 32, 5th ser., 3, Royal Historical Society, 1974).

[32] See, for example, E. Powell, 'Arbitration and the Law in the Late Middle Ages', *Transactions of the Royal Historical Society*, 5th ser., 33 (1983), 49–67.

alongside office-holding under the crown and the accumulation and protection of estates.

Some of McFarlane's pupils, pre-eminently Gerald Harriss—'Elisha to McFarlane's Elijah', as Maurice Keen so aptly calls him[33]—have developed his approach into a strongly consensual model of the operation of later medieval politics.[34] Harriss's own pupil, Christine Carpenter, has extended the reach of the McFarlane enterprise into the study of the gentry's own network of alliances and produced a compelling model of a remarkably cohesive aristocratic world based on 'the mutually reinforcing interplay of gentry networks with lords' affinities'.[35] A notable recent product of this school of thought has been Helen Castor's re-examination of the workings of the gentry world insecurely inhabited by the upwardly mobile Pastons in East Anglia.[36]

This is not to suggest, however, that studies of the workings of gentry society in the fourteenth and fifteenth centuries have been entirely monolithic. Some have questioned the all-embracing focus upon the magnate affinity. As early as 1981 Nigel Saul had argued that despite all the influences pressing men to retain and be retained there were, nonetheless, 'numerous unattached gentry' in fourteenth-century England.[37] In 1990 the idea that later medieval magnates were successful monopolists in the exercise of power came under strong attack from Simon Walker in his study of the great affinity of John of Gaunt.[38] Even he, one of the most powerful of all magnates in fourteenth-century England, found his power circumscribed by the social realities of his day. The independent-mindedness of the gentry was a phenomenon which McFarlane himself stressed and he and later scholars have been able to show times when they opposed the excesses of magnate power in parliament. Despite the general coincidence of interests, there were nevertheless times when magnate and gentry views were inclined to collide. The essential brake upon the exercise of magnate power appears to have been the relationship

---

[33] Keen, 'English Political History of the Late Middle Ages'.

[34] See his 'Political Society and the Growth of Government in Late Medieval England', *Past and Present*, 138 (1993), 28–57.

[35] See, especially, her *Locality and Polity*, 281–398. The quotation comes from C. Carpenter (ed.), *The Armburgh Papers* (Woodbridge, 1998), 42.

[36] H. Castor, *The King, the Crown, and the Duchy of Lancaster: Public Authority and Private Power 1399–1461* (Oxford, 2000).

[37] Saul, *Knights and Esquires.* The quotation comes from p. 102. See also the same author's *Scenes from Provincial Life*, 56, and Wright, *The Derbyshire Gentry in the Fifteenth Century*, 65–6.

[38] S. K. Walker, *The Lancastrian Affinity, 1361–1399* (Oxford, 1990), esp. 235–61.

between resources and numbers. According to this view the active gentry within the counties were too numerous and magnate resources too limited for the latter easily to dominate local society. Invoking Namier, Walker suggested that the most the magnates could achieve was to 'follow, not to force, the bent of the county'.[39] Simon Payling, focusing on the independence of the 'greater gentry' in particular, comes to similar conclusions, broadly on the same basis, while Colin Richmond, in a characteristic intervention adds: 'Drs Walker and Payling tackle that old, senile adversary, Bastard Feudalism. It is dealt a knock-out blow; it may hereafter be resurrected only as an Aunt Sally . . . we are left in no doubt: Bastard Feudalism is dead: I don't think I ever believed it was alive'.[40]

Whether bastard feudalism remains a viable concept, in traditional or modified form, is a matter of some debate. Its questioning is part of a continuing re-evaluation of McFarlane's legacy.[41] This began during the 1980s when several scholars working within his framework began self-consciously to redirect that legacy. In 1983, in the context of a wide-ranging review of works on fifteenth-century England, Richmond expressed some regret that McFarlane's disciples were not more like the master himself, 'prone to oppose *idées reçues* and to establish his own insights by way of antithesis'. In particular, he lamented 'the mechanistic tendency' which he felt resulted from too much attention to the affinity and to patronage.[42] Richmond, meanwhile, was developing his own, fundamentally empathetic, approach to the gentry. This was already present, in embryo, in his study of John Hopton, published

---

[39] L. B. Namier, *The Structure of Politics at the Accession of George III* (London, 1929), 91; Walker, *The Lancastrian Affinity*, 252.

[40] Payling, *Political Society in Lancastrian England*, 87–108; C. Richmond, 'An English Mafia?', *Nottingham Medieval Studies*, 36 (1992), 240.

[41] The breakdown in McFarlane's chronology—which saw the reign of Edward I as the point at which a contract, indenture-based army replaced forces based on the fief—has helped to fuel a debate among historians of the twelfth and thirteenth centuries over the role of the honour and the way in which aristocratic society was articulated: P. R. Coss, 'Bastard feudalism Revised', *Past and Present*, 125 (1989), 27–64; D. Crouch, D. Carpenter, and P. R. Coss, 'Debate: Bastard Feudalism Revised', *Past and Present*, 131 (1991), 165–203; D. Crouch, 'From Stenton to McFarlane: Models of Societies of the Twelfth and Thirteenth Centuries', *Transactions of the Royal Historical Society*, 6th ser., 5 (1995), 179–200; D. A. Carpenter, 'The Second Century of English Feudalism', *Past and Present*, 168 (2000), 30–71. M. Hicks, *Bastard Feudalism* (London, 1995) is essentially a restatement of McFarlane's position but without his precise chronology.

[42] C. Richmond, 'After McFarlane', *History*, 68 (1983), 46–60.

in 1981.[43] Of course, studies of individuals and of individual families have long been a feature of gentry studies. Richmond's programme, however, has been rather different. Through him we see (perhaps one should say we 'feel') from the vantage point of one individual, then another, as they connect, interact, clash. What he is searching for is a sort of history from the inside, taking us far beyond the description of interest and the assessment of motive. This project reached fruition in his extraordinary three-volume study of the Pastons and their associates, whose letters provide the most fertile ground for such an enterprise within the entire corpus of medieval gentry sources.[44] Richmond, however, is no mere bystander, observing the fair field full of (gentle) folk. He actively mediates between them and us, but not in any neutral way. Thus, for example, '[William Worcester] is the character which binds the centrifugal story of the affair of Fastolf's will together. Were it not for John Paston II's ever-sanguine, ever-admirable, ever-lovable personality, William's would be the one which makes its telling bearable, such an account of everyday covetousness is it'.[45] Reading Richmond one is obliged to engage palpably not only with Sir John Fastolf, Sir John Paston, Margaret Paston and the rest of the characters, but also with their historian. We are reminded constantly that they shared a humanity which binds us all. However one judges this—epic, romantic or whatever—it is a long way from mainstream approaches to the subject, and a very long way from the essentially self-effacing analytical approach of Rodney Hilton.

On McFarlane's legacy, similar points to Richmond's were made by Edward Powell in 1989, but with a different emphasis, when he advocated 'a more complete constitutional history' which would integrate 'the new learning with the old'; a constitutional history 'in which analysis of the economic position of the landowning classes and the workings of power politics can be related to institutional and administrative changes, and to those developments in political theory which influenced relations between the king and his subjects'.[46] Christine Carpenter, too, had been thinking along these lines.

---

[43] C. Richmond, *John Hopton: A Fifteenth-Century Gentleman* (Cambridge, 1981). In a footnote Richmond quotes with approval: 'Attempts to write biographies without empathy for the subject of the work . . . are schoolboys' jokes or exercises in sleights of hand'. J. Namier, *Lewis Namier* (1971), 306.

[44] C. Richmond: *The Paston Family in the Fifteenth-Century: The First Phase* (Cambridge, 1990); *The Paston Family in the Fifteenth-Century: Fastolf's Will* (Cambridge, 1996); *The Paston Family in the Fifteenth-Century: Endings* (Manchester, 2000).

[45] Richmond, *Endings*, 10.

[46] E. Powell, *Kingship, Law and Society: Criminal Justice in the Reign of Henry V* (Oxford, 1989), 4.

The aim of her study of the landed society of fifteenth-century Warwickshire, published in 1992, was 'to investigate the political morality and ideologies of landowners as a group in the later middle ages'.[47] In her contribution to the 1993 conference on *The McFarlane Legacy*, she offered a new definition of constitutional history, namely to study 'political and governmental structures and the beliefs of those who participate in them about how those structures should operate'.[48] The effect of concentrating over much on patronage and the affinity has led, she maintained, to 'bastard McFarlanism'.[49] She ended with a rallying cry:

> We need to regenerate a subject that can too easily come to seem an intellectual backwater. To do so, we must place our studies of politics firmly within the parameters of constitutional history; not the history McFarlane inherited from the Whigs and rejected, but, following McFarlane, something far more difficult and challenging, a constitutional history conceived in terms of the world that our late medieval protagonists knew and grappled with.[50]

To call this constitutional history might be considered bizarre and it is certainly problematic. It would be better on the whole, it seems to me, if one thought more in terms of the 'political culture' of the later middle ages. Whatever one calls it, however, this initiative looks set to complement the advances in understanding which have followed from the Namier-inspired structural approach pursued by McFarlane. In a recent contribution, for example, John Watts has very profitably analysed the conceptual framework within which the politics of the reign of Henry VI were played out.[51]

Ideas, political or otherwise, do not subsist in a social vacuum. The study of political culture necessarily opens up the issues of how political ideas and assumptions are generated, how they are sustained, how some are chosen for emphasis within a broader stock of ideas, how they are de-emphasized, re-emphasized, and so on. One needs to understand the relationship between ideas and material concerns. In *Locality and Polity: A Study of Warwickshire Landed Society, 1401–1499*, Christine Carpenter stresses the preservation of estates as the strongest motivating force behind the attitudes and actions

---

[47] Carpenter, *Locality and Polity*, 1.

[48] C. Carpenter, 'Political and Constitutional History: Before and After McFarlane', in R. H. Britnell and A. J. Pollard (eds), *The McFarlane Legacy: Studies in Late Medieval Politics and Society* (Stroud, 1995), 176.

[49] Ibid. 191.

[50] Ibid. 198.

[51] J. Watts, *Henry VI and the Politics of Kingship* (Cambridge, 1996).

of medieval landowners.[52] At the McFarlane conference she came under attack for this position from Anthony Gross, who argued that we should look to their libraries for their thought-processes rather than to their accounts.[53] The latter is of course an approach which has a considerable pedigree behind it, including the whole weight of manuscript study. It is also an important point at which the interests of the historian and the literary scholar intersect. Considerable advances have been made in recent years in discerning the social context of specific manuscripts and groups of manuscripts and in understanding the processes involved in their production and circulation. As far as the pre-Black Death period is concerned particular attention has been paid recently to the trilingual manuscripts Digby 86 and Harley 2253, the one of definite gentry, the other of at least distinctly local, provenance.[54] As far as the later fourteenth and fifteenth centuries are concerned, a concerted effort has been made to comprehend the parameters of literary culture, and to understand how the many varieties of text, including what one might call normative ones, intersect.[55] Recent work on Thomas Malory might be taken as an example. Raluca Radulescu has examined what she calls 'the political literature consumed in the gentry household' alongside the attitudes expressed in their letters, as means of comprehending the gentry values contained in the *Morte Darthur*; principally values surrounding honour, loyalty and lordship and attitudes towards matters such as counsel and governance. In this way, she argues, the reception and impact of Malory's work can be better understood.[56]

When all of this has been said, however, and great profit drawn from it, the implied antithesis between material interests and library-induced values is a false one; and Carpenter is surely correct in putting a strong emphasis upon the protection of estates in understanding the political ideas and general attitudes of the medieval landowners. But the protection of estates is not just a matter of forming alliances and of adopting new legal processes to protect one's interests, one's family and one's heirs. Beneath these levels of operation lies the economy of the estates themselves and hence the social

[52] Carpenter, *Locality and Polity*, 244–62, 621.

[53] A. J. Gross, 'K. B. McFarlane and the Determinists: The Fallibilities of the English Kings, c.1399–c.1520', in Britnell and Pollard (eds), *The McFarlane Legacy*, 49–50.

[54] See J. Hines, *Voices in the Past: English Literature and Archaeology* (Woodbridge, 2004), 71–104, which brings together, and extends, recent work on these two manuscripts.

[55] See, for example, the various essays in J. Griffiths and D. Pearsall (eds), *Book Production and Publishing in Britain 1375–1475* (Cambridge, 1989).

[56] R. L. Radulescu, *The Gentry Context for Malory's Morte Darthur* (Woodbridge, 2003); the quotation is from p. 4.

relationships that underpinned them. Consequently, more basic considerations must also have underlain landlords' beliefs and prompted their actions.
As Radulescu's extended discussion indicates, honour or 'worship' was
multifaceted.[57] Centred upon social esteem or reputation, worship could
be augmented or lost in a whole variety of ways. More was involved, however,
than reputation for correct behaviour and right dealing among one's peers.
Worship involved respect for one's 'lifelode', the estates that provided
the sustenance and sustainability of one's family and lineage. A careless or
dissolute attitude to these would provoke rebuke. So, too, would a failure to
protect one's tenants. As Margaret Paston wrote to her eldest son, 'if thei haue
hasty help it shall be the grettest wurchep that euer ye had, and if thei be not
holpen it shall be to you a gret diswurchep, and loke neuer to haue favour of
your neybores and frendes but if this spede wele'.[58] A similar point is made,
but more broadly, by Philippa Maddern in her extended study of honour
in the Paston Letters: 'the forum of honour for these people lay in their
quotidian relationships with tenants, servants, clients and fellow magistrates;
and their means of attaining honour were likely to be legal, peaceful and
mundane'.[59]

Concepts like worship (or honour) and 'the protection of tenants' were,
and are, ideologically charged. They open up major issues within feudal social
relations and, at least by implication, within capitalist ones too. What was
really at stake for the Pastons here was the strength and hence the viability of
their lordship. Vital though peer-group alliances were, they were operable
only insofar as one could sustain lordship in the first place. The political
attitudes, assumptions and, indeed, behaviour of the gentry are likely to
have reflected this. Let me illustrate the point from my own research on the
period of gentry formation.[60]

From the 1290s onwards there was an explosion in the number of royal
commissions, judicial and otherwise, and of the percentage of knights
involved in them. This resulted in what can best be described as a partnership
between the crown and the gentry, a partnership manifested in the emergence
of the justice of the peace as the mainstay in the exercise of royal authority

---

[57] Ibid. 17–24.

[58] N. Davies (ed.), *Paston Letters and Papers of the Fifteenth Century*, 2 vols (Oxford, 1971 and 1976), vol. I, 340–1.

[59] P. Maddern, 'Honour among the Pastons: Gender and Identity in English Provincial Society', *Journal of Medieval History*, 14 (1988), 357–71. The quotation is from the précis on p. 357.

[60] What follows is a précis of what is said in *Origins of the English Gentry*, 159–61 where the details will be found.

over the populace in the counties and in the legislation in favour of the manorial economy which followed the Black Death. The explosion in commissions was triggered in large measure by the needs of the crown in prosecuting its wars but it could not have happened without the willing participation of the lesser landowners. Even before the 1290s, however, a proportion of knights had involved themselves in gaol delivery and such like. It is necessary to ask why it was that they were keen to be involved in the exercise of royal justice. Direct rewards were not great. They did not receive salaries, although they were accustomed to hospitality. There was certainly the prospect of indirect rewards through the exercise of royal patronage, ranging from wine and timber, through grants of free warren and the exercise of minor franchises, to the possibility of a wardship or marriage of an heiress at the top end of the scale. In addition, no doubt, they tended to gain some prestige within lesser landowning ranks and perhaps access to networks of power. But there was also a more mundane reason propelling them into the exercise of royal justice.

Courts, as Hilton showed clearly, lay at the very heart of seigneurial life, given that control over their tenantry was the real guarantor of seigneurial income. In his book on the west midlands at the end of the thirteenth century he examined the jurisdictional situation in some detail:

> It was considered at this time to be the natural right of any lord to hold a court for his tenants. It was not simply that the tenant–lord relationship had much wider implications than in modern times, but that many lords had, in addition to jurisdictional rights over their tenants with respect to the holdings and the services due from them, a number of other rights and privileges. These other rights and privileges were often of doubtful origin, or, from the point of view of the crown, legality. But they buttressed the lord's powers considerably, and jurisdictional rights and claims of different character tended to come together in a body of customary practices in the manor court.[61]

Now, it has been justly said that the royal courts 'cast a longer and longer shadow over private and local jurisdictions' as people increasingly invoked them.[62] There were various ways in which lords responded to this. It has been argued persuasively that manor court rolls first appeared in the

---

[61] R. H. Hilton, *The West Midlands at the End of the Thirteenth Century* (London, 1966), 227–30.

[62] J. S. Beckerman, 'Procedural Innovation and Institutional Change in Medieval English Manorial Courts', *Law and History Review*, 10 (1992), 197.

mid-thirteenth century precisely because landlords needed to adopt the superior procedures of the royal courts if they were going to keep their free tenants coming.[63] Another response, for those landlords who did not already possess it, was to acquire view of frankpledge, that is to say the inspection of tithings—the, normally, ten-man security system—and receipt of their presentments properly held by the sheriff in the hundred court. In this way private courts could receive presentments of breaches of the peace and other offences. There were further minor franchises which added to a lord's jurisdiction over the peasantry: the right to take the assizes of bread and ale, for example, the right to a pillory and tumbril, and even the right to hang thieves from private gallows. The grant of a weekly market, and often an annual fair, included the right to hold a court to handle trading matters while the grant of free warren, conveying minor hunting rights over such small animals as rabbits, hares and foxes, involved jurisdiction over poaching.[64] Such things could be lucrative and considerably strengthened lordship. Moreover, a lord exercising franchises was in effect the equivalent of a commissioned royal justice.[65]

In other words, an increasing response to the exercise of royal justice in the thirteenth century, by means of royal grant or usurpation, was to harness it. A further means of harnessing royal authority emerged. It cannot have escaped the landowner's notice that seigneurial and royal justice were becoming complementary. Moreover, in a world of increasing geographical mobility and the perception of a growing crime wave and threat to authority, it became more and more apparent that a further dimension of social control was required. The need to harness royal authority goes a long way towards explaining why many lords were willing to involve themselves in commissions of gaol delivery and the like. What the gentry wanted, and what in large measure they achieved through the advent of the justice of the peace, was the devolution of royal justice.[66]

---

[63] Z. Razi and R. M. Smith, 'The Origins of the English Manorial Court Rolls as a Written Record: A Puzzle', in Razi and Smith (eds.), *Medieval Society and the Manor Court* (Oxford, 1996), 36–68.

[64] There is a recent reminder of the gentry's concern to control access to their warrens and to fine those who infringed them in R. Lock (ed.), *The Court Rolls of Walsham Le Willows*, 2 vols (Suffolk Record Society, 1998 and 2002). See, for example, vol. I, 47, 77, 158, 212, 224, 250, 267, and vol. II, 56, 74, 85, 145.

[65] See D. W. Sutherland, *Quo Warranto Proceedings in the Reign of Edward I, 1278–1294* (Oxford, 1963), 13.

[66] The rise of the justice of the peace has been the subject of much revisionism in recent years, especially by A. Musson and M. Ormrod. In an extended treatment of the issue I have taken their revisions into account: *Origins of the English Gentry*, 180–5.

After the Black Death, however, and more especially after the failure of the seigneurial reaction which followed the Black Death, the world changed profoundly. The fifteenth century saw an increasingly mobile tenantry, the blurring of tenures, the withering of serfdom and the decline of the manor court. It saw an increase in the ranks of the justices of the peace and a steady extension of their role. The quarter sessions waxed as the manor court waned.[67] The fifteenth century saw major shifts in the demand structure of the economy and higher standards of consumption, as well as increased opportunities for upward social mobility. There was a broadening of interest in gentility and civility, as witnessed by the production and circulation of courtesy books teaching good manners.[68] There were shifts also, and potential shifts, in the balance of rural power. In this world the protection of one's tenants took on a new meaning. The retention of tenants was now a vital concern. Thus the maintenance of the 'lifelode' was not only a matter of access to a well-functioning legal system, to patronage and to arbitration, of participating in a network of alliances, and of effective central and local governance. Relationships on the ground, as it were, were equally important, and it would be a mistake to study political culture in isolation from them. In other words, lordship needs to be studied in the round. The ways in which material concerns impacted upon the world of ideas should be at the heart of the gentry historian's programme.

By this point the reader will have realised that what I wish to advocate is not a new constitutional history but a new cultural history of the gentry, of which political culture, understood in the broadest sense, is one component. In advocating a cultural history I am not, of course, saying anything remarkable or new. Over the years there have been many studies of aspects of gentry culture, or of noble and gentry culture combined. Moreover, in terms of the cutting edge of history the baton has been passing from the social to the cultural historian in sphere after sphere for quite some time and historians of the gentry are following suit. A fine compendium of essays on later medieval gentry culture has recently appeared, for example, which covers a variety of dimensions, from politics to music. Centring on the fifteenth century, it establishes numerous benchmarks and will undoubtedly stimulate further

---

[67] M. Bailey, *The English Manor c.1200–c.1530* (Manchester, 2002) gives a good summary of fifteenth-century developments.

[68] There is a good account of courtesy books in K. Mertes, 'Aristocracy', in R. Horrox (ed), *Fifteenth-Century Attitudes: Perceptions of Society in Late Medieval England* (Cambridge, 1994), 42–60.

study.[69] What I am advocating is the study of gentry culture in its totality: a re-focusing that will allow us to move beyond the mere juxtaposition of aspects of gentry culture. In my view, a cultural history if it is to be viable has to be embedded in social practice. Hence the historian needs to examine the wide range of social relations into which its members entered, the impact of those relationships upon its culture, and ultimately the cultural significance and consequences of those relationships. They include relationships entered into as a result of the running of households and estates, as well as through the legal protection of those estates. These are as important as the vertical relationships with the higher nobility and the horizontal relationships between themselves as equals or near equals which have often been a mainstay of gentry studies. There are also broader associations of various kinds to consider, including a variety of professional contacts in the public as well as the private spheres of life. One thinks here, in the first instance, of the several varieties of lawyer, so essential in this highly litigious age bedevilled as it was by an overly complex land law, as well as administrators, civil servants, and of course the many levels of churchman, from village parson and chantry priest to bishop and abbot. And then there is the still under- researched issue of the interactions between an essentially rural gentry on the one hand and members of the mercantile/urban elites on the other. Nor should we omit the military side of gentry life and the contacts that engendered.[70] An exploration of the full range and interlocking of these social contacts should in my view underpin the study of gentry culture.

There is not the space here to review all the various manifestations of gentry culture that would need to be encompassed in a full study. Suffice it to say that it should include not only literary tastes, political culture, and attitudes to law, lordship and gentility, but also visual culture, seen especially from the vantage point of social display.[71] One thinks, inter alia, of the constant refinement of, and adornment to, seigneurial dwellings—of Stokesay Castle, Longthorpe Tower and so on—and of the accumulation of high-value possessions, of remarkable and sumptuous books like the Luttrell Psalter, of silver, furnish-ings and chests, of clothes and other personal artefacts. This approach could also inform the study of religious beliefs and sensibilities—the growing

---

[69] R. Radulescu and A. Truelove (eds), *Gentry Culture in Late Medieval England* (Manchester, 2005).

[70] See, for example, P. Morgan, *War and Society in Medieval Cheshire, 1277–1403* (Chetham Society, 1987), esp. 149–84, and A. Ayton, 'Sir Thomas Ughtred and the Edwardian military revolution', in J. S. Bothwell (ed.), *The Age of Edward III* (York, 2001), 107–32.

[71] For the parameters see the essays in P. Coss and M. Keen (eds), *Heraldry, Pageantry and Social Display in Medieval England* (Woodbridge, 2002).

preoccupation with purgatory, for example, and the attachment to the Virgin and to particular saints—not just in their own right, but as they interlocked with various forms of social projection in the adornment of the medieval church.[72] Art historians are revealing increasingly just how colourful parish churches became through the thirteenth century and beyond, a phenomenon in which the gentry must have played no little part, just as they contributed to the dissemination of architectural styles.[73] The sheer variety of sepulchral monuments is being appreciated more and more, as comparatively neglected forms like incised slabs are rejoining stone effigies and monumental brasses as subjects of antiquaries' expert scrutiny.[74] And then there is heraldry, a powerful and pervasive expression of elite identity whose study is providing sharper and sharper insights into how gentle society was articulated. It reminds us that the civilian and military aspects of the lives of the gentry and indeed of other combatants have tended to be studied in isolation from one another, a situation which is slowly being rectified.[75] This, too, should come firmly within the cultural historian's purview.

The gentry was pivotal in later medieval English society. Its social contacts, as we have seen, looked in all directions. It offers, therefore, a peculiar vantage point for analysing patterns of consumption and dissemination as well as such matters as social anxiety and social aspiration.[76] The impacts of fashion, and especially perhaps of court-sponsored styles, upon the localities remain under-studied. The sheer splendour of some of the stained glass constructed under secular stimulus, for example, and the grandeur of building schemes undertaken by men associated with the court, is likely to have aroused both admiration and resentment, the latter heightened perhaps during unpopular reigns like those of Edward II and Richard II. As a hypothesis this is at least worthy of examination. The ways in which ladies participated, often enthusiastically, within what was in many ways a male-orientated gentry culture

---

[72] An example of this sort of study is N. Saul, *Death, Art and Memory in Medieval England: The Cobham Family and their Monuments 1300–1500* (Oxford, 2001).

[73] See, especially, R. Marks, *Image and Devotion in Late Medieval England* (Stroud, 2004).

[74] See, S. Badham and M. Norris, *Early Incised Slabs and Brasses from the London Marblers* (London, 1999), and S. Badham, ' "A new feire peynted stone": Medieval English Incised Slabs?', *Church Monuments*, 19 (2004), 20–52.

[75] The issue has been put on a new footing by M. Keen, *Origins of the English Gentleman: Heraldry, Chivalry and Gentility in Medieval England c.1300–c.1500* (Stroud, 2002).

[76] For an attempt to understand the cultural role of the gentry see P. R. Coss, 'Aspects of Cultural Diffusion in Medieval England: The Early Romances, Local Society and Robin Hood', *Past and Present*, 108 (1985), 35–79.

also deserves more emphasis and consideration.[77] In short, sensitively han-
dled gentry culture offers us the opportunity of seeing human society once
again as a whole, in the way that the neo-Marxists and Annalistes famously
attempted to do.

Finally, more attention needs to be paid to change within gentry culture.
Marooned in our chosen centuries or other restrictive blocks of time we have
tended to lack the broader perspectives from which to gauge and appreciate
the degree and the pace of change. Perhaps, echoing Colin Richmond, this is
one of the reasons why, sitting on the shoulders of giants like Hilton and
McFarlane, we still don't see quite so far as we should.[78]

---

[77] I have made some suggestions along these lines in P. Coss, *The Lady in Medieval England,
1000–1500* (Stroud, 1998).
[78] Richmond, 'After McFarlane', 47.

Lordship and the Peasant Economy, c.1250–c.1400: Robert Kyng and the Abbot of Bury St Edmunds

Phillipp R. Schofield

The nature of production under feudalism was, according to Maurice Dobb, 'petty'. The basic social relation, again to follow Dobb—as numerous other Marxist commentators and historians—rested upon the extraction of the surplus production of these petty producers, an extraction achieved by extra-economic compulsion. That extra-economic compulsion varied according to the type of feudal rent levied.[1]

Rodney Hilton, a key player in that first generation of British Marxists which included Dobb, tested these fundamental relations of production throughout his work as a historian and recognized, as a Marxist, that, since 'variations in the incomes of the landed ruling class and its state . . . were crucial', it was the nature of that income and the principal factor(s) in its fluctuation which determined that nature of production, that is the mode of production. Identification of the nature of the relationship of lord and tenant, 'a crucial element in determining the level of rent', was of signal importance in discussing the transition from a feudal to a capitalist mode of production.[2] To quote Dobb once more, who cited Hilton's work in making the assertion: 'it is upon . . . revolt among the petty producers that we must fix our attention in seeking to explain the dissolution and decline of feudal exploitation. This rather than vague concepts like "the widening of the market" or "rise of money economy" '.[3]

The transition from feudalism to capitalism, as an historical and observable phenomenon, dominated Hilton's early contributions to medieval

---

[1] M. Dobb, 'From Feudalism to Capitalism', in R. H. Hilton (ed.), *The Transition from Feudalism to Capitalism* (London, 1976), 165–6.

[2] R. H. Hilton, 'Introduction', in T. H. Aston and C. H. E. Philpin (eds), *The Brenner Debate. Agrarian Class Structure and Economic Development in Pre-industrial Europe* (Cambridge, 1985), 5. For discussion of the intellectual engagement of Hilton and Dobb, see, for instance, H. J. Kaye, *The British Marxist Historians* (Basingstoke, 1995), 48–9.

[3] Dobb, 'From Feudalism to Capitalism', 166–7.

history, as it did the work of all Marxist historians operating in the 1940s and 1950s. While the transition debate, a debate that involved only Marxists and was characterized by a deliberate and inevitable combination of close theoretical reading and empirical research, lost ground to other Marxist (socialist-humanist approaches epitomized by 'history from below') and non-Marxist (new social history, cultural history, etc.) approaches to the past from the 1960s, it had encouraged a close engagement with issues of long-term change and their explanation which have not been forsaken by economic historians, and perhaps especially medievalists.

Hilton was both too good a historian and too good a Marxist to employ either a cavalier approach to his sources or a vulgarity to his theory. While Hilton was keen to stress, throughout his long publishing career, that it was the relationship of lord and tenant that was paramount, he was very much aware of the additional factors that played upon the peasant economy and, in some measure, stood as challenges to the characterization of the feudal mode of production. There is, in Hilton's work, the not infrequent warning to the unwary lest they be deceived into treating certain types of relation as of greater significance than they actually were, and certainly as of greater significance than that of the lord–tenant relationship, a political relationship founded on non-economic compulsion.[4] This insistence upon the primacy of a particular political relationship and the reduction of others to a secondary level of importance reflects, as previously, Hilton's grounding in the historiography and theory of transition. What interested Hilton there, as he had articulated in 'Capitalism—What's in a Name?', later published as 'further material' to the 'transition debate', was the extent to which the historian could identify the *predominant* methods and relations of production in any period.[5] While we should attempt to identify process and progress, Hilton argues that the 'history of trade alone will not tell us how and when the characteristic relations of feudalism gave place to those of capitalism, how peasant agriculture and artisan industry gave place to large concentrations of capital and of wage labourers . . . . Political conditions need closer attention'.[6] Hilton quotes Marx in distinguishing between modes of production and noting that the capitalist mode of production could not establish itself

---

[4] See, for instance, R. H. Hilton, *The English Peasantry in the Later Middle Ages* (Oxford, 1975), 52–3; id., *Bond Men Made Free. Medieval Peasant Movements and the English Rising of 1381* (London, 1977), 35.

[5] R. H. Hilton, 'Capitalism—What's in a Name?', in *Transition from Feudalism to Capitalism*, 153.

[6] Ibid., 153–4.

while the 'solidity and internal articulation' of feudalism remained sufficient to prevent it. Thus, to follow Hilton further, again in paraphrasing Marx:

> since men make their own history, *the historian must know what part the political and social consciousness of the various classes played in advancing or retarding the tempo of capitalist development* [my italics]. Since that consciousness is by no means a direct reflection of the economic activity of these classes, the historian cannot but concern himself with law, politics, art and religion . . . . Society and its movements must be examined in their totality, for otherwise the significance of uneven developments, and of contradictions, between the economic foundation of society, and its ideas and institutions, cannot be appreciated.[7]

In Hilton's call for what was essentially a total history, and one that encapsulated mentality and the intellectual culture of the period in ways that illustrate perfectly his close engagement with the Annalistes and considerably pre-date some of the apparent shifts of new social history, he encourages a nuanced investigation of peasant mentality and the extent to which lords featured in the calculations of their tenants. This, then, takes us beyond simple calculation: it is not enough to say, for instance, that, in a modelled budget, 'tenant x' owes 'lord y' only 1 per cent of his or her surplus as rent and therefore 'lord y' is of no great significance to 'tenant x'. It is both in the extent to which 'lord y' does or does not dominate other production economies, both of 'tenant x' and his or her peers, and the degree to which 'tenant x' cares about the role of 'lord y' in his or her world, that the character of the mode of production is established.

As Hilton noted, that relationship was not solely an economic one and so challenges simple attributions of temporal or spatial distinction. In fact, he wrote of the disparities and apparently inconsistent chronologies of the agrarian economy in the middle ages. Whilst his principal focus was on the west midlands, he wrote also of other parts of England and recognized distinct developments within these regions. For Hilton, as for other Marxist commentators, such as Dobb, the extent of this disparity was evidence for the long-drawn-out transition between feudalism and capitalism which 'laid the basis for some accumulation of capital . . . , and hence for the start of a process of class differentiation within that economy of small producers . . . . This social polarisation in the village . . . prepared the way for production by wage-labour and hence for bourgeois relations of production'.[8] Citing

---

[7] Ibid., 157–8.
[8] Dobb, 'From Feudalism to Capitalism', 167.

Marx—*Capital*, volume III—Dobb notes that the rise of capitalists from the ranks of producers was 'the really revolutionary way' of transition (in comparison to a top-down process which was likely to stall at some mid-point).[9]

Hilton seems to have felt that, in terms of scale and potential, the rise of capitalists in medieval England in the manner envisaged by Marx was not achieved until after the mid-fourteenth century. The relationship, at that point, between the producers' surplus and the extent of non-economic exploitation on the part of landlords can be shown to have altered for this post-plague period and is a feature that Hilton detected in his early studies of Leicester estates in the fourteenth and fifteenth centuries.[10] It is one that has since been discussed by a number of commentators and is chiefly characterized as a redistribution of incomes in the fifteenth century.[11] But it was in earlier periods also, in certain parts of the country, that we can see similar developments to those described more typically for the fifteenth century.[12] This would not have surprised Hilton, of course, and for the reasons already elaborated but it behoves us to reflect, albeit briefly, upon the nature of the relationship between lord and tenant in the more obviously and precociously market-focused parts of the country. In exploring the relationship between producers and lords, a relationship mediated through the non-economic exploitation of surplus, we can revisit some of the questions which Hilton saw as vital if we are to make sense of change in the medieval and early modern economy and find room to explain that change.

The political nature of feudal rent

On a simple level, as already suggested, it is possible to glean some sense of the economic relationship between lord and tenant from an examination of rent in the context of estimated or, occasionally, calculated surplus. E. A. Kosminsky was generally dismissive of earlier attempts to model the peasant budget, seeing them as far too optimistic and inclined to reduce

---

[9] Ibid., p. 168.

[10] R. H. Hilton, *The Economic Development of some Leicestershire Estates in the Fourteenth and Fifteenth Centuries* (Oxford, 1947), 129–30.

[11] C. Dyer, 'A Redistribution of Incomes in Fifteenth-Century England', *Past and Present*, 39 (1968), 11–33; R. H. Britnell, *The Commercialisation of English Society, 1100–1500* (Cambridge, 1993), 217–23.

[12] See, for instance, studies of the land market in eastern England in the thirteenth century: R. M. Smith, 'Families and their Land in an Area of Partible Inheritance: Redgrave, Suffolk 1260–1320', in R. M. Smith (ed.), *Land, Kinship and Life-cycle* (Cambridge, 1984), 135–95; P. R. Schofield, 'Dearth, Debt and the Local Land Market in a Late Thirteenth-Century Suffolk Community', *Agricultural History Review*, 45 (1997), 1–17.

the exploitative nature of rent: 'the main body of the English peasantry, the villeins occupying virgates and half-virgates, were not rich, solid peasants, but a middle peasantry crushed by feudal exploitation'.[13] Few historians would now subscribe to such a wholly bleak characterization of the peasant economy in relation to lordship; as more recent exercises in peasant budget modelling have illustrated, the extraction of rent could still, for the more substantial peasants, leave a meaningful surplus.[14] For some peasants, clearly, the evidence is of extensive capital accumulation that belies any sombre, strict Marxist-Leninist characterization of the kind employed by Kosminsky. Where we can compare evidence of capital accumulation, through rare examples of peasant inventories, detailed taxation assessments or occasional evidence of particular outlays, with rental and account information we can again make some meaningful comparison between peasant rent obligations and usable surplus. On occasion, the disparity, even in the thirteenth century, between economic activity, managed in capital outlay and surplus, and feudal rent appears considerable. Christopher Dyer has already described, for eastern England, some of these discrepancies. He notes, in his discussion of ancient demesne pleas in the thirteenth and fourteenth centuries, that the rents which litigant peasants paid were relatively low and certainly diminutive in comparison to the outlay made to cover the fees of lawyers.[15] Taxation assessments also illustrate the huge surpluses which peasants could enjoy; set against contemporary or near-contemporary rentals, the extent of the rental element within such peasant budgets must have been fairly small.[16]

However, even where the immediate economic consequences of rent for the peasant tenantry were reasonably light, peasants were still keen to escape them. For Dyer, as also for Hilton, it was the uncertainty of obligation rather than the fixity of it that explains this peasant resistance. We see that resistance manifested in a number of ways; Hilton described many of these manifestations, including violent resistance, rent strikes and plaints, in one of his most important articles, discussing peasant movements in England prior to 1381,

---

[13] E. A. Kosminsky, *Studies in the Agrarian History of the Thirteenth Century* (Oxford, 1956), 230–42; quote, p. 240.

[14] C. Dyer, *Standards of Living in the Later Middle Ages. Social Change in England, c.1200–1520* (Cambridge, 1989) 110–18; H. Kitsikopoulos, 'Standards of Living and Capital Formation in Pre-plague England: A Peasant Budget Model', *Economic History Review*, 53 (2000), 237–61.

[15] C. C. Dyer, 'Memories of Freedom: Attitudes towards Serfdom in England, 1200–1350', in M. Bush (ed.), *Serfdom and Slavery. Studies in Legal Bondage* (Harlow, 1996), 289–90.

[16] Note, for instance, J. Masschaele, *Peasants, Merchants and Markets. Inland Trade in Medieval England, 1150–1350* (Basingstoke, 1997), 36–54.

and it is a theme that he and his students have revisited on a number of occasions.[17]

This 'political' nature of feudal rent is not however always manifest. It is sometimes hard to conceive that the wealthy villein tenant in parts of eastern England, owing relatively low rents, most of which were commuted into fixed payments, and with interests in land that were akin to freehold, should have had any cause, other than a misguided sense of paranoia, to see his lord as the principal obstacle to his prosperity and that of his family. Ultimately, the potential of lordship to threaten the schemes and expectations of the tenantry may have resided not so much in rent per se as in the *consuetudines non taxatas* (unfixed customs) and the subtle shifts of seigneurial policy. Thus, for instance, seigneurial resistance to outsider dealing, be it education, marriage, out-migration, the use of common law or ecclesiastical jurisdiction, could well present the prosperous kulak with the sorts of impediments that he—and more likely he than she—had the advantage and opportunity to recognize and thereby to resent. Other restrictions within the manor, including seigneurial expectations regarding the nature of the land market or the employment of legal instruments, were also likely to be causes of tenant discontent and we can see them as such from the thirteenth century in eastern England, and probably elsewhere.

In the section that follows we can explore an example of lord–tenant relations in the later fourteenth century which draws upon incidence of villeinage from a century earlier. The case, from the estates of the Abbot of Bury St Edmunds, and more particularly from the Abbey's manors at Wattisfeld and Hinderclay, is predicated upon the range of demands of lordship and the concomitant tokens of villeinage discussed above; it can be used to suggest the ways in which the demands of villeinage could ultimately count for a great deal, notably in the imposition of bonds and impedimenta that, irrespective of their economic worth, weighed upon tenants and their families and for much longer than individual lifetimes.

---

[17] R. H. Hilton, 'Peasant Movements in Medieval England', *Economic History Review*, 2nd ser., 2 (1949), repr. in E. M. Carus-Wilson, ed., *Essays in Economic History*, ii (London, 1962), 73–91 (from where subsequent references are taken). See also Dyer, 'Memories of Freedom'; Z. Razi, 'The Struggles between the Abbots of Halesowen and their Tenants in the Thirteenth and Fourteenth Centuries', in T. H. Aston, P. R. Coss, C. Dyer and J. Thirsk (eds), *Social Relations and Ideas. Essays in Honour of R. H.Hilton* (Cambridge, 1983), 151–67; P. Franklin, 'Politics in Manorial Court Rolls: the Tactics, Social Composition, and Aims of a pre-1381 Peasant Movement', in Z. Razi and R. M. Smith (eds), *Medieval Society and the Manor Court* (Oxford, 1996), 162–98.

Robert Kyng and the Abbot of Bury St Edmunds

On Monday 3 March 1393, the abbot of Bury St Edmunds and brother
William Bray, by force and arms, with swords, bows, and sticks, seized
Robert Kyng at Hinderclay (Suffolk) and imprisoned him there. They later
took him from his prison at Hinderclay to the prison at Bury St Edmunds
where he remained for two weeks. Kyng was only released when three pledges,
Almaric Grym, John Goodewyn and Simon Clerk, stood surety through a
written obligatory of £20. In May 1393, Robert brought a writ of replevin
against the abbot, claiming wrongful imprisonment according to the grounds
of the writ, namely that he had not been imprisoned as a result of special
order of the king nor on account of a homicide nor on account of forest law
nor for other reason of common law that would render him irreplevisable
(that is, in a condition which rendered him incapable of generating a claim
of wrongful imprisonment).[18] Following the writ, pleas were entered in
Trinity term 1393. Robert claimed that the action of the Abbot and his
men had been contrary to the King's peace and claimed damages of £100.
The Abbot's defence was that Robert was his villein from his manor at
Wattisfeld, a manor which he held by right, and that he enjoyed all 'advantages' against Robert and his *sequele* as a villein. The Abbot also explained that
on the day of the alleged trespass (i.e. the wrongful imprisonment), Robert
had, in the lord's court at Hinderclay and in the presence of brother William
Bray and Edmund Lakynghethe, the steward, denied his villeinage and caused
a great affray in open court, *menciendo prefatum Seneschallem sedentem
in eadem curia et faciendo affraiamentum in eadem curia contra ballivos et
servientes eiusdem abbatis* (threatening the abovesaid Seneschall seated in the
same court and causing an affray in the same court against the bailiffs and
servants of the same Abbot). It was on account of this affray that Robert was
arrested and placed in gaol.[19]

The case was soon brought to arbitration and overseen by the earl of
Arundel and Surrey (Richard Fitzalan III); in January 1394 the abbot undertook to produce for the earl all evidence pertaining to Robert, *quel Robert nous
clamons pour notre neiff de sank* (which Robert we claim for our neif by
blood). The evidence included that *tochant le claim du dit Robert Kyng et
de sa sequele et stoke et le lignage du dit Robert ovesque les autres incidences
cestes matires touchantes* (concerning the claim of the said Robert Kyng and of

---

[18] B.L. Add. 31970, f. 31b. On replevin and the writ *de homine replegiando*, see J. H. Baker,
An Introduction to English Legal History, 3rd edn. (London, 1990), 536, 538; Sir F. Pollock
and F. W. Maitland, *The History of English Law before the time of Edward I*, 2nd edn.
(2 vols., Cambridge, 1968), vol. 2, 584–6.

[19] B.L., Add. 31970, f. 31b-32.

his brood and stock and kin of the said Robert along with those other incidents concerning these matters).[20] The case book of the Abbot of Bury St Edmunds, compiled in the early fifteenth century records this evidence, in much the same way as, presumably, it had been gathered for arbitration. Over three folios, eighty separate court entries are produced to illustrate the neifty, that is the hereditable condition of villeinage, of the Kyng family. These eighty entries are drawn from seventy-three courts held between the mid-thirteenth century and the late-fourteenth century.[21] They detail a considerable range of activity, including a substantial proportion of what we might identify as core economic dealing. Thus, unsurprisingly given the importance of merchet payment as proof of villeinage at common law, the payment of, or failure to pay, marriage fines is the largest category recorded as evidence in the list (19 entries; 23.7 per cent); importantly, the buying and selling of unfree land feature almost as prominently in this recording of evidence (18; 22.5 per cent). Also noteworthy is the attention given to minor trespasses against the lord and his property (10; 12.5 per cent) and to absence without licence from the lord's domain (9; 11.25 per cent of entries). Further entries are also potentially revealing, including the record of the lease of the sub-manor of Wattisfeld to a Thomas Kyng in March 1341 and earlier, in April 1309, the record of a surrender of all lands and tenements 'which he previously held in villeinage' by Adam Kyng to Peter Clopton, the Abbey chamberlain to hold in demesne in pereptuity. Adam was paid 100s. 'for this demise and concession'.[22]

Some of this evidence had, in fact, already been gathered prior to the events of 1393/4. Twenty years earlier, in a court held on 26 November 1373, Robert Kyng was claimed as the lord's neif by blood, *calumpniatus fuit per dominum fore nativus de sanguine*. In order to make good his claim, the lord discovered amongst his muniments evidence arising, as it was described, from the general process, namely an entry from a late thirteenth-century court roll describing the merchet obligations of one Berard Kyng.[23] Robert, present in

---

[20] B.L., Add. 31970, f. 33.

[21] B.L., Add. 31970, ff. 27-30. The earliest courts recorded here also coincide with the earliest manor court rolls surviving for Hinderclay; these are probably therefore not just the earliest surviving manorial court rolls but the earliest courts recorded on the manor; for the appearance of the manor court roll in the mid-thirteenth century, see Z. Razi and R. M. Smith, 'The Origins of the English Manorial Court Rolls as a Written Record: A Puzzle', in Razi and Smith (eds), *Medieval Society and the Manor Court*, 38–42.

[22] B.L., Add. 31970, ff. 28, 29.

[23] *dominus invenit inter munimentia sua in processu videlicet in curia generali tenta apud hildercle die jovis post festum Epiphanie anno regno regis Edwardi xxio in hec verba.*

court, requested a stay until the next court before responding and produced pledges that he would neither remove himself nor his goods or chattels in the meantime. By the next court the lord had amassed a wealth of entries as further evidence of Robert's neifty, including late thirteenth- and fourteenth-century instances of merchet payment, of receipt of land in villeinage, of office-holding by neifs, childwyte (a fine paid by villeins for conceiving a child out of wedlock), all by members of the Kyng family. Again, Robert sought a delay in order to gather his response. At a later court, held on 31 May 1375, not Robert but Thomas Kyng, the son of Oliver Kyng, came into court and made fealty to the lord through his body and chattels, acknowledging his neifty on account of the evidence of the rolls of court and the oath of the homage. In the same court it was recorded that, inter alia, a William Kyng was illegally absent from the lord's domain, at Feltwell.[24] Robert Kyng, it seems reasonable to suppose, refused to accept the force of the same evidence, his resistance ultimately leading to the dispute in 1393.

As above, the litigation of 1393 and its subsequent removal to arbitration appear to have generated a further spate of trawling through the Abbey muniments. In proof of Robert Kyng's villeinage the Abbot sought to produce further evidence and this time by examining the activity of previous generations of the Kyng family. Neifty by blood was, of course, an inherited condition; it was unavoidable and to deny one's neifty was also therefore to deny one's lineage. Hence the abbot searched manorial courts to the earliest surviving (1257/8) and presented genealogies and evidence, over a number of generations, of activity carried out by the Kyng family consistent with villeinage and, in particular, neifty by blood. The establishment of genealogies appears, at least, to have been based almost exclusively upon the written records of the manor court. At no point, save in the instance of Thomas Kyng in 1375, as noted above, does a jury or inquest explicitly pronounce upon lineage. While it seems reasonable to suppose that local knowledge was exploited in compiling the Kyng 'family tree', listings were chiefly compiled from court roll entries and genealogical associations largely deduced therefrom. It seems clear that the starting point was the extraction of relevant material consistent with neifty, from which material, once gathered, suitable

---

De Berardo Kyng quia maritavit se sine licencia et pro licencia se maritus, B.L. Add. 31970, f.29b. The original entry survives, Joseph Regenstein Library, University of Chicago, Bacon MS [hereafter Bacon] 117, m. 8, court of 8 January 1293.

[24] B.L., Add. 31970, f. 30.

associations to Robert Kyng would need to be constructed. Certainly, the genealogical links are far from compelling.[25]

Quite how the dispute ended is not clear from this record. The final entry of the relevant materials includes the opening clause of an indenture made between the parties to the dispute but which then ends abruptly with the note that the details of the indenture cannot be continued at this point of the collection. Court roll entries for the manor of Hinderclay suggest that the dispute rumbled on in some form into the early fifteenth century.[26]

Importantly, at Wattisfeld and at Hinderclay it was not the villeinage of the Kyng family alone that was subject to scrutiny in this period. While the case of Robert Kyng and his relatives features most prominently in the record and has the feel of a local contemporary *cause célèbre*, perhaps in ways not wholly

---

[25] To quote the summary result of this genealogical research:

> And let it be known that Thomas Kyng who was in court held on Wednesday before Christmas 43 Henry III [18 December 1258] was the father of Thomas Kyng. And this Thomas and Oliver were the first sons of Thomas Kyng.
> Also Walter Kyng the son of John Kyng was the father of Berard Kyng, Thomas Kyng and Adam Kyng.
> Also John Kyng was the son of Berard Kyng and Robert Kyng was the son of the said John Kyng the brother of John Kyng the father of Robert Clerk. And Thomas Kyng living in Walsham is the son of Robert Kyng the brother of John Kyng the father of Robert Clerk. And John Kyng living in Hawle is the son of John Kyng and the brother of Robert Clerk.
> Also John Kyng was the son of Adam Kyng of Wattisfeld. (B.L., Add. 31970, f. 31).

'Robert Clerk' appears to have been a pseudonym for Robert Kyng, a point that the compilers of the genealogy were keen to make, for instance, B.L., Add. 31970, f. 30 and f. 31.

[26] *Cest indenture fait par entre le abbe de seint Edmundbury et William Bray seneschal compigne dun part et Robert Kyng de Watlesfeld dautre part tesmoigne que les parties avauntdit touchaunt certeins debates entre il* [sic]. *Vide postea in in litterra v in verbo Watlesfeld qui hic non potest continueri* [*folio 3A in Gallic'*—added], (B.L., Add. 31970, f. 33). For reference to the dispute in later manorial courts, see court of 15 June 1402, *Fidelitas servilis. Robertus Clerk de Hyldercle alias dictus Robertus Kyng', Thomas Kyng' filius Oliveri Kyng', Johannes Kyng' et Johannes Kyng' filii Robert Kyng' nativi domini de sanguine de manerio de Wattlesfeld venerunt in plena curia et fecerunt fidelitatem servilem ut nativi de sanguine deberent facere in presencia Johannis Wade parsoni de Thelnetham, Edmundi Caterton amigeri et aliis.*

. . .

Finis vis. viiid. Item quod predicti Robertus Kyng', Thomas Kyng', Johannes Kyng' et Johannes Kyng' nativi domini de fine pro rebellione et contradictionibus suis. (Bacon 129, m. 7)

dissimilar to that of the Ketels in the late thirteenth and early fourteenth centuries at Halesowen,[27] it is quite clear, and to be entirely expected, that the shadow of seigneurialism fell more widely. The folios immediately preceding the evidences against the Kyng family contain a larger listing of instances of neifty and villeinage as indicated by activity recorded in the manor court. Headed *Evidencie extracte per venerabilem patrem dominum Willelmum Gratfeld dudum abbatem et nuper camerarium ex diversis rotulis curie contra disclamantes esse nativi manerii de Hildercle* (Evidences extracted by the Venerable Father lord William Gratfeld, whilst abbot and once chamberlain, from diverse rolls of court against those claiming not to be neifs of the manor of Hinderclay), the listing offers a series of transcripts from the earliest surviving courts, October 1258, until June 1300. In all there are transcripts of 274 entries from this period, detailing the recorded activities of eighty-four families (identified as such by surname only) which marked them out as neifs. Individual family names, often through the recording of a number of their members, appeared more than once, a fact identified by the compiler of the transcripts who attempted to maintain a running tally, in Arabic numerals, against family names in the marginalia.[28] The range of cases is consistent with the expectations of a common law of villeinage and, while it lacks some of the closer focus of the Kyng 'portfolio' described above as well as the sense of simmering tensions, it covers broadly similar ground. Thus the majority of entries relate to merchet payments, either performed or avoided. A significant proportion of entries also deal with childwyte and chevage (essentially a fine for non-residence) payments. Finally, as well as a small number of single entries in relation to a range of misdemeanours contrary to seigneurial expectations of villeinage, including the issuing of contracts through chirograph, there are a group of entries which deal with alienation of land or chattels.

It is perhaps revealing that much activity recorded as distinctively 'villein', both in the case of the Kyng family and in that of other tenants at Hinderclay, was also consistent with the sort of enterprise that underscored the local economy. The payment of merchet, the principal badge of villeinage by the close of the thirteenth century, may also be seen as a licence to alienate or

---

[27] Razi, 'Struggles', 161–3.

[28] The heading of these evidences includes the explanatory note, *Et nota quot pro quolibet nomine per algorisium* (And it is noted how much by each name by algorism). Thus, for instance, the entry transcribed from the court held on the Friday after the feast of St John ante portam latinam 25 Edward I (10 May 1297)—*de Waltero le Kyng pro se et Isabella Bonseriant pro licencia simul nubendo iis*—is supported by the marginal note *Kyng 12 Bonseriant*. (B.L., Add. 31970, f. 25)

transfer real and movable property.[29] The same is also clearly true of other activity associated with villein status and accordingly cited here. Thus, the *inter-vivos* transfer of customary land was a mainstay of the local economy in parts of eastern England by the close of the thirteenth century, attracting speculative accumulation and providing lords with a significant tranche of their income.[30] Similarly, the alienation of chattels or peasant mobility, activities which both required seigneurial sanction, can be seen as indices of peasant economic activity in a context that extended far beyond the lord's domain.[31] The lord's commitment to villeinage also censured those villagers caught making use of common law, including written proof of contract or specialty and recourse to courts other than his own. Intriguing also is the extent to which the manor court, both in its initial use by tenants and in the subsequent exploitation of its record by lords, served as a basis of proof for genealogies and for activity consistent with neifty. Since, as has been argued, the manor court should be perceived as a vehicle of peasant advancement in the thirteenth century as much as an instrument of seigneurial exaction, the extent to which activity recorded in the court roll could redound to the ultimate disadvantage of the tenantry cannot but impress.[32]

It was then in everyday activity, including such central elements of proto-capitalism as the buying and selling of customary land, that the Kyngs and their neighbours in the decades either side of 1300 were laying down unfortunate precedent for later generations of their own families. The case of Robert Kyng and the additional transcripts in relation to a host of villagers

---

[29] See, for instance, E. Searle, 'Seigneurial Control of Women's Marriage: The Antecedents and Function of Merchet in England', *Past and Present*, 82 (1979), 1–43, where she also makes explicit the connection between wealthier villagers and the payment of merchet, ibid., 24; and for responses that are far from dismissive of the association between property transfer and merchet payment, P. A. Brand and P. R. Hyams, 'Seigneurial Control of Women's Marriage', *Past and Present*, 99 (1983), 123–33; R. Faith, 'Seigneurial Control of Women's Marriage', *Past and Present* 99 (1983), 133–48. On merchet as proof of villeinage, see especially P. R. Hyams, *King, Lords, and Peasants in Medieval England. The Common Law of Villeinage in the Twelfth and Thirteenth Centuries* (Oxford, 1980), 187–91.

[30] On seigneurial income from *inter-vivos* transfers in customary land, see R. M. Smith, 'Some Thoughts on "Hereditary" and "Proprietary" Rights in Land under Customary Law in Thirteenth and Early Fourteenth Century England', *Law and History Review*, 1 (1983), 116–17. See also studies cited above, n. 12.

[31] Masschaele, *Peasants, Merchants and Markets*, 47–54.

[32] Razi and Smith, 'Origins of the English Manorial Court Rolls', 67–8; see also J. S. Beckerman, 'Procedural Innovation and Institutional Change in Medieval English Manorial Courts', *Law and History Review*, 10 (1992), 197–252.

from the thirteenth century illustrate usefully the ways in which the institution of lordship could and did respond—or fail to respond—to economic developments in both centuries. This response was sometimes perverse and contrary to rational expectation, including the expectation of some of the main players. And the main players here were not just lords but included petty though cumulatively significant producers such as Robert Kyng, his immediate family and his progenitors, as well as a host of other villein families from Wattisfeld and Hinderclay.[33] Like a number of their neighbours, the Kyngs of the late thirteenth and early fourteenth century were moderately successful peasant producers. They do not appear to have been the most significant economic players within their communities but they were not amongst their poorest members either. From Wattisfeld there are three Kyngs—Thomas, Hugo, and Almer—recorded in the 1283 lay subsidy assessment for Blackbourne Hundred; Thomas's movable wealth, assessed at £2 12s. 7d., with a sizeable proportion of that wealth in wheat (more than three quarters, that is, the fifth largest quantity of the forty-six individuals assessed for the vill) suggests in particular that he was a reasonably prosperous villager.[34] The *inter-vivos* transfers of the Kyng family, used as evidence of their neifty by the second half of the fourteenth century, are also testimony to their relative prosperity. Between 1289 and 1307, individuals with the surname Kyng were involved in eleven transfers of land recorded in the manor court, buying land on three occasions and selling in eight instances. We have also seen that members of the Kyng family surrendered land to the abbey in lucrative agreements and were able to enter into large-scale leasing arrangements with their lord. Finally, of the 170 entries recorded in the manor court at Hinderclay between 1289 and 1307 involving members of the Kyng family, sixty-one involved inter-personal litigation, another useful index of reasonably high-level economic activity.

Robert Kyng, in the later fourteenth century, appears to have been a villein of significant means. Either as Robert Kyng or as Robert Clerk,[35] he appears with some frequency in the court and account rolls as bailiff, and as a buyer, lessee and lessor of land, including substantial units. In a single court held at Pentecost 1384, a Robert Clerk was identified in separate entries as holding four acres, and one half rod of land in neifty and one half rod freely, nine acres, three rods and a further thirty-two acres in diverse parcels at farm (a rod was

---

[33] Masschaele, *Peasants, Merchants and Markets*, 45–6.

[34] E. Powell (ed.), *A Suffolk Hundred in the year 1283. The assessment of the hundred of Blackbourne for a tax of one thirtieth, and a return showing the land tenure there* (Cambridge, 1910), assessment sheet n. 35.

[35] See above, nn. 25 and 26.

¼ acre). Interestingly, in the light of his disputes with his lord, Kyng or Clerk had failed, in more than one instance, to pay rent or farms on part of this extensive portfolio of landholding.[36]

With families such as the Kyngs, and their neighbours at Wattisfeld and Hinderclay, we are in the presence of those who, as Hilton and Dyer have both described, were reasonably well-placed but who, as their struggles within and outside of the law illustrate, sought greater freedoms for themselves and their successors.[37] By the late fourteenth century, when we encounter Robert Kyng in his struggle with the Abbot of Bury St Edmunds, the force of lordship was challenged by a radically altered demographic landscape. The response of many of the greater landlords to recurrent plague, and a greatly changed economic environment characterized by rising wages and falling prices, was to dig in their heels and to tighten their demands on their tenants.[38] The tenants' response was, of course, to seek greater opportunities, bargaining for lower rents, accumulating holdings and, where need or chance required, fleeing their manors. The advantage, as has been described on numerous occasions, rested increasingly with the tenantry in this period. The case of Robert Kyng can stand therefore as one example of a potentially advantaged tenantry whose opportunity was challenged by an increasingly desperate seigneurial sector. It was also a sector that was in the process of handing over its control of so much of this everyday activity to a burgeoning state system in

---

[36] Bacon 127, m. 16 (face and dorse), court of 31 May 1384. In the early 1380s, a Robert Kyng and a Robert Clerk, almost certainly the same person, are also noted as serving as manorial bailiff, an office consistent, inter alia, with substantial landholding, Bacon 127 m. 9 (dorse), court of 4 March 1381 (Robert Clerk); also, in the manorial accounts, for example, Bacon 489, account of Michaelmas 1377 to Michaelmas 1378 (Robert Kyng); Bacon 490, account of Michaelmas 1378 to Michaelmas 1379 (Robert Clerk). On the increasingly important role of bailiffs at Hinderclay in the later fourteenth century, see D. Stone, *Decision-making in Medieval Agriculture* (Oxford, 2005), 219–21. Investment in the skills of the bailiff, as outlined by Stone, is one further index of the variety of response by lords to changing agrarian demands and, in this instance, may conceivably help to explain some of the particular tensions.

[37] Hilton, 'Peasant Movements', 85–90; Dyer, 'Memories of Freedom', 277–95. For instances of other well-placed villein families at Hinderclay, see Schofield, 'Dearth, Debt and the Local Land Market', 11–17.

[38] See, for instance, on post-plague incidence of merchet payments, C. Dyer, 'The Social and Economic Background to the Rural Revolt of 1381', in R. H. Hilton and T. H. Aston (eds), *The English Rising of 1381* (Cambridge, 1984), 23; L. R. Poos, *A Rural Society after the Black Death. Essex 1350–1525* (Cambridge, 1991), 246.

which oversight of, inter alia, inter-personal activity, the regulation of marriage, of morality and of mobility would increasingly come to reside.[39]

However, while it is undoubtedly true that Robert Kyng and his like were the victims of a too-late reaction intended to save an already moribund system, this is not to say that, in a different climate a century earlier, the political culture of villeinage and neifty somehow counted for less. In fact, we should almost certainly include the thirteenth century within that same era of transition, where economic opportunity and a developing money economy effected significant changes in social structure and in lord–tenant relations, and especially perhaps in parts of eastern England, including the environs of Bury St Edmunds.[40] The economic opportunities presented to wealthier tenants in the thirteenth century and to their descendants in the second half of the fourteenth, were contained by lordship, and tenants reacted against this in a variety of ways, including violence, flight, and use of the law courts. Whilst circumstance may have contrived to heighten tension between lord and tenant in the later fourteenth century, this was a fairly extreme manifestation of a persistent condition. It was in fact the very persistence of that condition, rather than any resurrection of it, that informed the later fourteenth-century articulation of seigneurialism and the impositions upon villagers such as Robert Kyng.

Conclusion

The level of importance which the Kyngs and their peers attached to lordship remains one of those key questions which has been posed for us by Rodney Hilton and which offers no easy answers: namely how important was the role which the *political and social consciousness of the various classes played in advancing or retarding the tempo of capitalist development?* While it may seem a little too nebulous to identify the feudal mode of production as a persistent state of mind as much as or more than an economic reality, doing so, as Hilton recognized, allows us to accommodate the variety of experiences

---

[39] See, for instance, M. K. McIntosh, *Controlling Misbehavior in England, 1370–1600* (Cambridge, 1998), 23–45; C. Given-Wilson, 'The Problem of Labour in the Context of English Government, c.1350–1450', in J. Bothwell, P. J. P. Goldberg and W. M. Ormrod (eds), *The Problem of Labour in Fourteenth-Century England* (York, 2000), 85–100; R. C. Palmer, *English Law in the Age of the Black Death, 1348–1381* (Chapel Hill, 1993), 139–44 and following chapters.

[40] See, for instance, E. Miller, *The Abbey and Bishopric of Ely. The Social History of an Ecclesiastical Estate from the Tenth Century to the Early Fourteenth Century* (Cambridge, 1951), 145–53; also D. C. Douglas, *Social Structure of Medieval East Anglia* (Oxford, 1927), 113–30.

and expectations which the lord–tenant relationship embodied in the high and late middle ages. We do not have to wait until the late fourteenth century to discover that, in some parts of the country, engagement with the market and expansion of holdings, use of law and the sophisticated extension of credit by wealthy peasants were central facets of the peasant economy. At the same time, however, it would be incorrect to suggest that, for peasants such as these, lordship was of little or no consequence. Living as they did, in a period of transition, peasant tenants were sometimes scorched by the failing flame of seigneurialism which, in its dying could still occasionally burn fiercely, if only briefly. Perhaps, in their new proto-capitalist dealings, peasants sometimes lost sight of that; but sometimes it is clear that they also received unwelcome reminders.

The Ineffectiveness of Lordship in England, 1200–1400

Christopher Dyer

This essay is concerned with the English aristocracy, meaning lay and clerical lords, from the gentry to dukes and archbishops, mainly in the thirteenth and fourteenth centuries. It examines critically the reputation that the lords have gained in modern times for playing a very decisive and forceful role in the economy.[1]

The aristocracy, especially the magnates, are often depicted as attaining a pinnacle of economic success in the thirteenth century. They had been faced with grave problems around 1200, as inflation threatened to reduce the value of their fixed incomes, and a predatory Angevin monarchy increased its financial demands on them. By the end of the thirteenth century, they had increased their landed revenues; embraced direct management of agriculture on their estates; honed an effective system of private administration; completed the imposition of a new form of serfdom; developed written records as an aid to exercising profitable private justice; squeezed large sums from the peasantry; founded a network of new markets and towns; invested in property in the larger urban centres; embraced technological innovations such as windmills; and changed the landscape by clearing land from wood and marsh, and by creating impressive buildings and parks.[2]

---

[1] I am grateful for the comments made at the conference in September 2003, including the hostile ones, which have helped me to focus my ideas more precisely. I was also influenced by hearing a paper by Bruce Campbell on a similar theme at the Economic History Conference at Glasgow in 2001, though in some respects he drew different conclusions. The paper has subsequently been published: B. M. S. Campbell, 'The Agrarian Problem in the Early Fourteenth Century,' *Past and Present*, 188 (2005), 3–70.

[2] There is a vast literature on these themes, and these are some of the works which reflect the current state of knowledge: R. A. L. Smith, *Canterbury Cathedral Priory. A Study in Monastic Administration* (Cambridge, 1943); E. Miller, *The Abbey and Bishopric of Ely* (Cambridge, 1951); B. M. S. Campbell, *English Seigniorial Agriculture, 1250–1450* (Cambridge, 2000), esp. 3–6; N. Denholm-Young, *Seignorial Administration in England* (London, 1937); P. D. A. Harvey, *Manorial Records* (British Records Association, Archives and the User, no. 5, 1999); M. Bailey, *The English Manor c.1200–c.1500*

Past and Present (2007), Supplement 2

All of these things happened, but when the significance of these changes is questioned closely, the level of achievement must be qualified. It will be argued here that in some respects we must regard the thirteenth century as marking a phase in the failure of lordship.

Rodney Hilton emphasized the coercive powers of lords, which allowed them to extract the peasants' surplus, so he would not have welcomed this line of argument. He was, however, opposed to mechanical, economistic conceptions, and distrusted dogmatic ideological positions which were not informed by empirical observation. If our evidence undermines a generalization, then that position must be revised or restated. The observations presented here to some extent draw on his ideas about peasant self-reliance and activism. He pointed out that the peasant economy was autonomous, and that peasants could live without lords; they derived strength from that potential independence.[3] Far from all-powerful lords oppressing cringing demoralized peasants, Rodney Hilton showed that although lords put pressure on their subordinates, the peasants could resist because they had their own resources in terms both of their material goods and their ideas. In his broad theory of the crisis of feudalism he argued that the feudal regime around 1300 failed to sustain its earlier growth, and this paper attempts to explore the inherent weaknesses in the power of lords which contributed to the crisis.[4] Hilton would have welcomed a critical appraisal of the aristocracy, whether medieval or modern, but he would have said that the jurisdictional power and the selfish ruthlessness of lords should not be underestimated.

(Manchester, 2002); R. H. Hilton, 'Freedom and Villeinage in England', *Past and Present*, 31(1965), 3–19; Z Razi and R. M. Smith (eds), *Medieval Society and the Manor Court* (Oxford, 1996), 36–68; B. F. Harvey, *Westminster Abbey and its Estates in the Middle Ages* (Oxford, 1977), 216–43; R. H. Britnell, *The Commercialisation of English Society, 1000–1500* (Cambridge, 1993), 79–90; D. Keene, 'Landlords, the Property Market and Urban Development in Medieval England', in F.-E. Eliassen and G. A. Ersland (eds), *Power, Profit and Urban Land. Landownership in Medieval and Early Modern Northern European Towns* (Aldershot, 1996), 93–119; J. Langdon, *Mills in the Medieval Economy. England 1300–1540* (Oxford, 2004), 21–64; O. H. Creighton, *Castles and Landscapes* (London, 2002), 65–84.

[3] R. H. Hilton, *Bond Men Made Free: Medieval Peasant Movements and the English Rising of 1381* (London, 1973), 41.

[4] R. H. Hilton, 'Was there a General Crisis of Feudalism?', in R. H. Hilton, *Class Conflict and the Crisis of Feudalism. Essays in Medieval Social History* (London, 1985), 240–1. He made the point again in 'A Crisis of Feudalism', *Past and Present*, 80 (1978), 8–10.

Weaknesses of the seigneurial regime

First of all, the evidence itself must be considered, because the abundant documentation of estate management by its very existence represents a major achievement of private administration. If we move from being impressed by the sheer bulk of manorial rolls, registers and cartularies to examining their contents, the rising rents and manorial profits in the thirteenth century can readily be observed. Admirers of lords point to the skill with which central estate administrators, like those of Norwich Cathedral Priory, calculated the annual profits of each manor.[5] The local knowledge and quick decision-making of the reeves who managed individual manors could raise profits by adjusting the balance of crops from year to year. Their annual accounts reflected the quality of their performance, a judgement which could be made by the estate administrators as well as by modern historians.[6]

The usefulness of the profit calculations, however, is not always apparent, and modern observers wonder how much practical use could have been made of them. Lords like Merton College, Oxford, seem to have been reluctant to lease out their demesnes around 1300, even when their own accounts suggested that this move would have yielded a larger income.[7] The documents tell a story of lords' defensiveness in the face of real threats to their property and incomes. Surveys and extents of manors, for example, with their detailed records of lords' revenues and entitlements, were designed to conserve and protect lords' rights. They looked back to old customs and traditional payments and obligations, which were often described in archaic language. The surveys were not the starting point for some new venture to increase demands, but they were concerned with settling any areas of uncertainty or debate, and ensuring that rents and services were performed by reluctant tenants; they were designed to maintain the existing structure of tenant holdings. Extents, which valued demesne assets and tenant obligations, provided authoritative information for use by those auditing annual accounts, and those documents, for all of their potential for assessing profits, had a major function of protecting the lords' revenues from the dishonesty and inefficiency of officials. The rolls of the manorial courts reflect a new and

---

[5] E. L. G. Stone, 'Profit-and-loss Accountancy at Norwich Cathedral Priory', *Transactions of the Royal Historical Society*, 5th series, 12 (1962), 25–48.

[6] D. Stone, 'Medieval Farm Management and Technological Mentalities: Hinderclay before the Black Death', *Economic History Review*, 54 (2001), 612–38; id., *Decision-Making in Medieval Agriculture* (Oxford, 2005).

[7] T. H. Aston, 'The External Administration and Resources of Merton College to circa 1348', in J. I. Catto (ed.), *The History of the University of Oxford*, vol. 1 (Oxford, 1984), 321–3.

more systematic approach to the management of private jurisdiction, but again they were conceived as a means of recording precedents and past decisions with a view to maintaining the lords' authority. One of their advantages for the lord was their continuous record of the names of tenants (and especially those of servile status), and the terms on which they held the land. Written court records to some extent succeeded in their aims, but tenants, as well as resenting the documents which perpetuated memory of their disadvantages, also saw the benefits of obtaining evidence of title from copies of the court roll. They could also appeal to the authority of precedent for asking for a search of the rolls which they hoped would be helpful to them, for example in pursuing a claim to the inheritance of land.[8]

We can suspect that some of the most successful lords in the thirteenth century were not the magnates with their growing piles of documents, but the gentry who kept very few records, but were able to behave in a much more innovative, even buccaneering style. For example, individuals were building up new manors by buying land, sometimes by exploiting the indebtedness of their neighbours, and carving out new cultivated fields and enclosed pasture from wastes at the expense of the common grazing rights of their neighbours. Such enterprising and acquisitive gentry have been revealed as operating in the countryside around Coventry in Warwickshire, where the development of a thinly populated woodland landscape gave them opportunities, especially in the vicinity of an expanding city.[9]

The image that the aristocracy projected of themselves provided a basis for their claims to wealth and power. Long before the thirteenth century the secular lords had been represented as having a legitimate military role as the protectors of the rest of society, and the clergy prayed on everyone's behalf. These simple functions became ever more elaborate, with the development of heraldry, seals and tournaments, and the growth of courtly behaviour.[10]

Castles, which had begun as useful watch towers and strong points, were being designed to make a statement to visitors about the power of their builders and owners. They had always been centres for administration, and residences appropriate for a large household, but this aspect received ever more emphasis, with styles of building which provided a backdrop for ceremonies, entertainment and leisure. The castles of the secular lords, and the residences of the bishops and abbots, which in some cases were also

---

[8] L. R. Poos and L. Bonfield (eds), *Select Cases in Manorial Courts, 1250–1550* (Seldon Society, 114, 1997), lvi–lxxii.

[9] P. Coss, *Lordship, Knighthood and Locality. A Study in English Society c.1180–c.1280* (Cambridge, 1991), 93–119.

[10] D. Crouch, *The Image of Aristocracy in Britain, 1000–1300* (London, 1992).

fortified, gave the impression of being part of a planned and controlled land-scape. Members of the household could enjoy walks in a large garden attached to the castle, from which they could view the high towers or broad moats. Beyond lay a much larger area of parkland, stocked with deer and provided with fish ponds.[11] The park was an extensive enclosed private space, in which the lord and his companions could enjoy the pleasure of the chase, and obtain supplies of venison, which (like fish from the pond) was a scarce and presti-gious foodstuff. At the castle gate the visitor would be impressed by a built environment called into existence by the powerful lord. There would be at least a large parish church, perhaps with a college of clergy, or in the case of magnates, a monastic establishment. A planned town with a wide market place would complete the picture by demonstrating that the lord commanded the local economy.

This public face of lordship was in some measure mere window dressing. The de Montforts of Beaudesert in Warwickshire impressed visitors with a hill-top castle, an architecturally pretentious parish church, park, ponds and town, but the family can be categorized as either superior knights, or in the very lowest rank of barons. The Mohuns of Dunster in Somerset were undoubtedly barons, and mounted an even grander show, with an impressive castle, a priory, and a prosperous town, but their income was not very high, and the family experienced some financial difficulties. In the fourteenth cen-tury they included in their cartulary a poem which gave advice on keeping up appearances on modest expenditure.[12]

A familiar aspect of medieval aristocrats is the occasionally extravagant language in which lords or their officials expressed their claims over their subordinates. When serfs brought cases to the royal courts disputing their status, one of the tests that could be invoked was their liability to pay tallage 'high and low, at the will of the lord', which implied that the sum was variable, and that the charge could be made at any time that the lord wished.[13] In an extreme situation in 1280 when his servile tenants had successfully used

---

[11] M. Johnson, *Behind the Castle Gate: From Medieval to Renaissance* (London, 2002).

[12] R. H. Hilton, *A Medieval Society. The West Midlands at the End of the Thirteenth Century* (Cambridge, 1983), 47, 174–5; H. Riley and R. Wilson-North, *The Field Archaeology of Exmoor* (Swindon, 2001), 119–20; S. Painter, *Studies in the History of the English Feu-dal Barony* (Baltimore, 1943), 171, 174–5; J. Beauroy, 'Sur la culture seigneuriale en Angleterre: un poème anglo-normand dans le cartulaire des barons de Mohun', in C. Duhamel-Amado and G. Lobrichon (eds), *Georges Duby. L'écriture de l'histoire* (Brussels, 1996), 341–64.

[13] P. R. Hyams, *King, Lords and Peasants in Medieval England. The Common Law of Villeinage in the Twelfth and Thirteenth Centuries* (Oxford, 1980), 191.

common law procedures against him, the abbot of Burton could say that their animals, which he had seized, were his property and the serfs have 'nothing except what they have in their bellies'.[14] Other lords, like Worcester Cathedral Priory, implied the same when they announced in their manorial courts that they had seized their serfs' chattels into their own hands.[15]

Lords applied these bold claims as much as they could in their estate administration. In many manorial surveys and extents, tallage, marriage fines and other dues which derived from the lord's control of the persons of his serfs were not mentioned, or at least were not given a fixed value, justifying the 'high and low' claim.[16] The recognition fine owed when a new lord took over an estate is a good example of an unpredictable payment, the timing of which depended on the accident of death and succession. Again, this does not appear in surveys, but could be recorded in manorial court rolls and reeves' annual accounts.

In practice, however, these payments were not as variable and arbitrary as lords and the lawyers wished to believe. Tallage was often a well-established amount of money shared among the customary tenants. A sum in the region of £5 or £10 on a manor with between thirty and sixty tenants would be collected annually, which had the effect of adding a few shillings to the rent charged on each holding.[17] The recognition payment was similarly fixed in size, though uncertain in its timing. Marriage fines were collected from individuals, usually either the women themselves or their fathers, and commonly the amount was levied at 2s. or 3s.4d. or 4s., though the lord reserved the right to charge more if the family seemed rich enough. These sums were a burden, and peasants had to adjust their budgets to afford them, and in bad years they would cause real hardship, but they were not as punishing or unpredictable as the phrase 'high and low, at will' might imply. Similarly, whatever the legal position over peasant property, in practice their possessions were respected by lords, who normally expected to ratify the hereditary succession of holdings, and registered the transfer of land by gift or sale, as

---

[14] D. Crook, 'Freedom, Villeinage and Legal Process: The Dispute between the Abbot of Burton and his Tenants of Mickleover, 1280', *Nottingham Medieval Studies* 44 (2000), 123–40.

[15] R. H. Hilton, *The English Peasantry in the Later Middle Ages. The Ford Lectures for 1973 and Related Studies* (Oxford, 1975), 61.

[16] W. H. Hart (ed.), *Historia et Cartularium Monasterii Sancti Petri Gloucestriae* (Rolls Series, 1863–7), vol. 3, 191, contains a survey of Eastleach in 1267 which notes the existence of tallage, merchet and entry fines, but without giving them any values.

[17] Harvey, *Westminster Abbey*, 224.

long as the court was notified.[18] Servile peasants, many of whom worked holdings of above average size, could accumulate considerable quantities of goods, both livestock and equipment for the farm, and household goods, furniture and clothing.[19] Lords only interfered with peasant goods in extreme situations, such as the rebellion of the peasants of Mickleover (Derbyshire) which provoked the abbot of Burton's intemperate remark. There was an element of bluster and bravado in the routine claims by lawyers that lords could dispose of their serfs' property as they pleased. They were aware of the looming presence of the state, which inhibited lords' powers of justice through enquiries into franchises, and offered the peasants at least a hope of protection, for example if they could show that they lived on manors which had previously formed part of the royal demesne. Perhaps lords and their advisers needed such pretences because they felt at least a little insecure in their position.[20]

If we turn from image making to a more objective test of the success of lords in the thirteenth century, their incomes undoubtedly grew. The thirteenth-century expansion in the market, and consequent increase in the prices of grain, wool and livestock gave the demesnes every opportunity to make profits. The rising surplus of more substantial tenants should have been reflected in the rents that they paid. The recorded rise in lords' incomes reflects the market opportunities. For example, the bishops of Worcester expanded their annual revenues from £345 in 1211–12 to £1,162 in 1311–12, which was an impressive increase of just over 200 per cent.[21] In the same century the price of grain doubled, and wool and livestock prices went up two and a half times, so the estate managers added value, though part of that came from acquiring new assets rather than from the increased profits of existing land and holdings.[22] Lords' real incomes increased a little more than their cash revenues, as they employed much labour and wage rates tended to stagnate or rise by only a small degree. In the late thirteenth century

---

[18] R. M. Smith, 'Some Thoughts on "Hereditary" and "Proprietary" Rights in Land under Customary Law in Thirteen and Early Fourteenth Century England', *Law and History Review*,1 (1983), 95–128.

[19] A striking example is William Lene of Walsham le Willows, Suffolk, who died in 1329 owning goods worth £26 9s. 11d.: R. Lock (ed.), *The Court Rolls of Walsham le Willows, 1303–50* (Suffolk Records Society, 41, 1998), 133–5.

[20] C. Dyer, 'Memories of Freedom: Attitudes towards Serfdom in England, 1200–1350', in M. L. Bush (ed.), *Serfdom and Slavery. Studies in Legal Bondage* (London, 1996), 283–6.

[21] C. Dyer, *Lords and Peasants in a Changing Society. The Estates of the Bishopric of Worcester, 680–1540* (Cambridge, 1980), 52–5.

[22] D. L. Farmer, 'Prices and Wages', in H. E. Hallam (ed.), *The Agrarian History of England and Wales*, vol. 2, 1042–1350 (Cambridge, 1988), 788, 790, 801, 805, 807, 809.

they were better off than their predecessors had been in *c*.1200, as can be seen in the elaboration of the architecture of their buildings, but they had benefited from favourable circumstances rather than great enterprise. Some lords were only able to double their incomes in the thirteenth century, and a substantial number of lords, wealthy monasteries as well as vulnerable gentry, mismanaged their affairs and fell into debt.[23] The whole class found that the rise in incomes of the thirteenth century could not be sustained for long after 1300.

A major weakness of demesne production was identified by both Hilton and Postan as a lack of investment. More recently students of lords' agriculture have found examples of higher levels of expenditure on capital improvements, and have seen efficiency and rationality in demesne management which historians had previously not recognized.[24] Nonetheless the administration of the great estates seems to have been ponderous and slow to respond to new ideas, for example in the adoption of windmills after 1200.[25] Many smaller estates were unable to profit greatly from the market, because if they had a demesne of no more than 200 acres of arable land, which was often the case, the grain crop was only enough to feed the animals and servants on the manor, provide seed for the following year, and to supply the lord's household. Larger peasant holdings, which could regularly sell a third of their crops after setting aside seed corn, could be more orientated to the market than were the small self-sufficient aristocratic estates.[26]

The lord–tenant relationship was closely integrated into the demesne economy. The labour for demesne cultivation was provided partly by the services of the peasants. Rodney Hilton always presumed that such forced labour, grudgingly provided, achieved only low levels of productivity. Now the poor performance of servile labour has been demonstrated with careful calculations, by comparison between the output of wage labour and tenant

---

[23] Harvey, *Westminster Abbey*, 63; E. Jamroziak, 'Rievaulx Abbey as a Wool Producer in the Late Thirteenth Century: Cistercians, Sheep and Debts', *Northern History*, 40 (2003), 197–218.

[24] R. H. Hilton, 'Rent and Capital Formation in Feudal Society', in id., *English Peasantry*, 174–214; M. M. Postan, 'Investment in Medieval Agriculture', *Journal of Economic History*, 27 (1967), 576–87; I. Kershaw, *Bolton Priory. The Economy of a Northern Monastery 1286–1325* (Oxford, 1973), 117–31; R. H. Britnell, 'Minor Landlords in England and Medieval Agrarian Capitalism', in T. H. Aston (ed.), *Landlords, Peasants and Politics in Medieval England* (Cambridge, 1987), 227–46, esp.238–42.

[25] R. Holt, *The Mills of Medieval England* (Oxford,1988), 22–30.

[26] C. Dyer, *Standards of Living in the Later Middle Ages. Social Change in England c.1200–1520*, revised edn (Cambridge, 1998), 112–15; Britnell, *Commercialisation of English Society*, 120–2.

services in mid-fourteenth century Wisbech.[27] Lords recognized this, and labour service even in the late thirteenth century, accounted for a fraction of the work performed on demesnes.[28] Manorial demesnes, and the running of the manor courts, depended on the services of peasant administrators, recruited from among the tenants. The astuteness of some reeves as agricultural managers has already been noted, but not all of them possessed either talent or motivation. On some manors new reeves were elected frequently, which not only deprived the manor of continuity in administration, but also ensured that at intervals it must have been put into the hands of a foolish or ill-disposed official. Reeves were at least under constant supervision, and their accounts were audited, so that the lord was protected from excessive corruption and incompetence. A reeve who overreached himself by taking too many liberties with the lord's property would be amerced in the manor court.

The courts also depended on the cooperation of peasant officials who carried out the roles of jurors, chief pledges, tithingmen and others, who, for example, were responsible for reporting cases to the court. These men were content to gain some influence for themselves for the unpaid work that they did, and the lord, in exchange for their cooperation, had to accept that the courts would not serve exclusively as tribunals enforcing his rule. Occasionally we find a presentment in a court that chief pledge or a jury 'concealed' an offence, showing that the lord could intervene and prevent the court being manipulated too blatantly by the peasants. At other times a court might catch up with a concealed offender years after the event.[29] Such cases arouse our suspicions that the court was not fully aware of all that went on in a manor.

Many lords could not extract a great deal from their peasants because limited tenant obligations had evidently been built into the manorial structure of some regions and types of estate. Rodney Hilton's first investigation of a medieval rural society, in Leicestershire, uncovered some very light obligations, in which few peasants owed work every week, and where cash rents predominated.[30] When he turned to Warwickshire he found contrasts between the lightly burdened peasants of the woodland district, the Arden, and the more oppressive regime in the Feldon, where a high proportion of the

---

[27] D. Stone, 'The Productivity of Hired and Customary Labour: Evidence from Wisbech Barton in the Fourteenth Century', *Economic History Review*, 50 (1997), 640–56.

[28] Campbell, *Seigniorial Agriculture*, 3.

[29] P. R. Schofield, *Peasant and Community in Medieval England, 1200–1500* (Basingstoke, 2003), 42–4.

[30] R. H. Hilton, 'Medieval Agrarian History', in *Victoria County History of Leicestershire*, vol. 2 (1954), 173, 179.

inhabitants were servile tenants. But even here week work was demanded in only a minority of villages, eight from a total of forty-eight, and in eighteen the peasants performed only light services or none at all.[31]

Hilton was much influenced by the work of Kosminsky, who analysed all of the printed Hundred Rolls of 1279–80, and compared them with manorial extents. Kosminsky showed that a very high proportion of tenant obligations were paid in cash, and that regions such as the north lacked a conventional manorial system. Even in the midlands and the south the majority of lords, being laymen, gentry, or small church institutions with limited powers of jurisdiction could not require their tenants to do heavy labour services. The burdens conventionally linked with peasant servitude were owed mainly on the manors of large church estates, which had attracted historical attention because of the survival of lords' surveys. Periodically this important insight into medieval society is rediscovered; although Kosminsky emphasized the disadvantages of the customary tenant's payment of feudal rent, his statistics showed some strong variations, from the high rents in Huntingdonshire to modest payments in Oxfordshire, and these figures have now been recalculated and confirmed. In Huntingdonshire annual customary rents averaged 8d. per acre, compared with 5d. in Oxfordshire.[32]

Some historians now explain the relatively low rents and services that are found through much of rural medieval England as the result of custom. Just as the free tenants were protected from increases in rents by the royal courts' common law, so the lords' courts operated a customary law which regulated the conditions of unfree tenure. Custom in the manor courts was not an inanimate force of nature, but was under the influence of the common law, and was constantly moulded by the actions of lords and peasants.[33] The competing forces in rural society had been at work in a long process going back before the Norman Conquest. Factors in the relatively strong bargaining position of peasants in eastern and northern England would have been the relatively late breakdown of the early medieval 'great estates', and the upheavals in land holding after the Scandinavian conquest of the ninth century and

[31] R. H. Hilton, 'Social Structure of Rural Warwickshire in the Middle Ages', in id., *English Peasantry*, 113–38, esp.125–9.

[32] E. A. Kosminsky, *Studies in the Agrarian History of England in the Thirteenth Century* (Oxford, 1956), 243–6; J. Kanzaka, 'Villein Rents in Thirteenth-Century England: An Analysis of the Hundred Rolls of 1279–80', *Economic History Review*, 51 (2002), 593–618.

[33] Razi and Smith (eds), *Medieval Society and the Manor Court*, 96–116.

the assertion of English rule in the tenth.[34] But such political and institutional changes cannot be invoked to explain the relatively low level of rents found on many manors in all regions. We can only imagine the silent tussle that must often have taken place, with lords attempting coercion, only to encounter peasant resistance. Peasants sought to minimize their obligations, and lords had to be vigilant to prevent a service being reduced, or an occasional rent being forgotten. Occasionally we glimpse these early frictions, in the problem of peasant migration which troubled officials on the Hatfield (Hertfordshire) estate in the early eleventh century, or the peasant rising on the estate of Much Wenlock Priory in Shropshire in c.1163 when labour services were refused in a public display of defiance.[35] We become aware of the ability of eleventh-century peasants to take collective action when village communities became the lessees of manors.[36] Much of the hidden struggle between lords and tenants involved not violent confrontations, but latent coercion and grumbling resistance, which are scarcely discernible in early written sources.

Lords in the thirteenth and fourteenth centuries often appear to have treated their tenants gingerly. Peasant administrators were valued not just because of their cheapness and local knowledge, but also because their status and connections within their own communities helped to make seigneurial rule more acceptable. The persistence of an untidy and confusing plethora of small rents and dues suggests the sensitivity of lords and officials to the perceptions of peasants. Surely no lord would have maintained in c.1300 archaic payments, often worth a few pence, with their strange names—fishfee, grasearth, fustale, stuck, and woodhen—unless it was thought that many small payments seemed less onerous than one larger sum? And the names reflected their origin and justified the payment by indicating the benefit to the tenant— woodhen allowed the peasant to collect fuel, and a grasearth gave access to grazing.[37]

Lords clung to the fiction that they were participating in a reciprocal relationship with their tenants. It did not matter that the tenants were often

[34] D. Hadley, *The Northern Danelaw. Its Social Structure, c.800–1100* (London, 2000), 165–215.

[35] D. Pelteret, 'Two Old English Lists of Serfs', *Mediaeval Studies*, 48 (1986), 470–513; R. Graham, 'The History of the Alien Priory of Wenlock', *Journal of the British Archaeological Association*, 3rd ser., 4 (1939), 124–5.

[36] R. Hoyt, 'Farm of the Manor and Community of the Vill in Domesday Book', *Speculum*, 30 (1955), 147–69.

[37] C. Dyer, 'The Language of Oppression. The Vocabulary of Rents and Services in England, 1000–1300', in M. Bourin (ed.), *Pour une anthropologie du prélèvement seigneurial dans les campagnes de l'occident médiévale: les mots, les temps, les lieux* (Paris, 2006), 71–85.

obliged to pay their lords money and labour which they could ill afford, while lords' grants to them were confined to an occasional meal at major harvest and ploughing boons. Lords could still portray themselves as patrons, who were entitled to receive rents and services in exchange for privileges for the peasants: holdings of land, access to pastures and woods, and the famous 'protection'. Concrete examples of the last service provided by lords prove elusive in our sources. New peasant tenants, just like knights and aristocratic vassals, took an oath of fealty on a public occasion, in the manor court, supposedly establishing a bond of loyalty and personal commitment to the lord.

Some of the lords' rights were valued highly by them because they were not limited by custom. In the case of tallage, perhaps they hoped by insisting on its variability that they would one day in the future be able to raise the sum above the level that had become customary. The implementation of the Provisions of Oxford and Westminster in 1258–60 gave peasants the opportunity to make complaints about ill-treatment by their lords, and these included a claim from Surrey that the steward of Geoffrey de Lusignan on three manors had increased tallage from 40s. to 100s. This shows that lords did sometimes push up their demands, but of course it also demonstrates that such increases were regarded as unjust, and in these cases were overturned.[38]

The profits of justice were changeable. The level of individual amercements were supposedly restrained by the affeerors, that is two leading peasants who were consulted by the steward about the amount to be levied, and who were presumably responsible for the occasional statement that an amercement had been condoned because of poverty. The number of offenders, however, might increase with the growth of the population, or the vigour with which the offences were uncovered. Occasionally a court roll records swingeing fines exacted from an especially difficult individual tenant, or we read that a large collective fine, such as £20, was imposed on a whole community.[39]

The largest sums that were paid into most manorial courts came from the entry fines for holdings that had changed hands through inheritance or purchase. Lords' officials could often bargain with the incoming tenant for a sum that reflected the value of the land, which varied with the quality and profitability of the soil, and with the level of demand. A recent survey of entry fines in the period 1270 to 1348, when demand for land was relatively high, suggests that in much of England, including the areas of strong lordship and

---

[38] D. Carpenter, 'English Peasants in Politics 1258–67', *Past and Present*, 136 (1992), 21.

[39] R. K. Field (ed.), *Court Rolls of Elmley Castle, Worcestershire, 1347–1564* (Worcestershire Historical Society, 20, 2004), 13. (in 1356 a jury was amerced £20 for finding that a serf was free).

potentially high land values in the midlands and the south, incoming tenants commonly paid around 12d. per acre. In counties such as Suffolk or Somerset where pressure on land was especially high, or the land was particularly fertile, the level of fine rose to about 24d. per acre, or £3 for a standard virgate or yardland holding. As is well known, on occasion a powerful lord at the right moment could demand from a tenant in Somerset much higher sums, even above 240d. per acre or £30 per yardland, but the normal figures are equivalent to the rent of between one and three years. Such sums would be inconvenient for the new tenants, and would have sent them to money lenders as they would not usually have such a large sum in ready money. The fine must sometimes have discouraged them from buying a piece of land. A perspective on the outlay involved in paying an entry fine, however, is provided by the occasional survival of evidence of the price of land paid by the incoming tenant to his or her predecessor, which was usually far above the fine, even ten times the sum. For example at Alrewas in Staffordshire in 1260 the fine was 3 ½d. per acre, and the purchase price 3s.2d. (38d.) per acre. Seen in this light, the lord could be seen as taking the opportunity to exact a share of the large sums of money changing hands among the peasantry, though of course the fine was also taken from an heir taking over a holding after the death of the tenant, when (apart from the heriot and mortuary) the lord's fine was the sole payment for the land.[40]

Lords were not always very effective in enforcing the rules and regulations which they claimed over their tenants. Before the Black Death there was no great build-up of the arrears of local officials, so the sums of money demanded were generally collected. Tenants were still able to evade the notice of the authorities, and anyone counting marriage fines in a run of court records notices flurries of payment and suspiciously long gaps, suggesting that marriages were taking place without being taxed, until the authorities caught up with the evaders.[41] A fine such as leirwite, levied on women who were involved in sexual activity outside marriage, was to some extent dependent on village gossip, and therefore makes a very intermittent appearance in the court records. In the case of the migrations of servile young men, which supposedly required permission from the lord and the payment of chevage, the rules were enforced very inconsistently. After all, before the plague caused

---

[40] C. Dyer, 'Seigniorial Profits on the Landmarket in Late Medieval England', in L. Feller and C. Wickham (eds), *Le marché de la terre au moyen âge* (Rome, 2005), 219–36.

[41] E. Searle, 'Merchet in Medieval England', *Past and Present*, 82 (1979), 26–9; M. Müller, 'The Function and Evasion of Marriage Fines on a Fourteenth-Century English Manor', *Continuity and Change*, 14 (1999), 169–90.

a scarcity of tenants and labour, lords were not harmed by the movement of surplus people out of the manor.

Compelling tenants or inhabitants to pay for the use of the lord's mill encountered considerable problems. Suit of mill was an issue in disputes such as that at Darnhall and Over in Cheshire, and any series of court rolls will contain occasional amercements of tenants who avoided their obligation of suit of mill, either by grinding their corn at home on a hand mill, or by taking it to a mill belonging to another lord. Langdon has argued that lords might use coercion, but were more often involved in competition with their neighbours in securing customers at their mill, by providing a good service.[42] A resolution of a dispute at Walsall in Staffordshire in 1395–6 supports this argument. The miller of this small town complained to the officials of the lord, the earl of Warwick, that the mill lacked business and was unprofitable, and accused the townspeople of going to other mills. The officials responded by urging him to attract customers by providing a better service and charging lower tolls: he should 'serve truly my lord's tenants, and in such manner treat them, that he might have their good will'. They recognized the futility of compelling attendance at the mill.[43]

Suit of court, that is compulsory attendance at the manor court, was one of the obligations of tenants, and the whole notion of private justice suggests a world of coercion. However, innovations in court procedures and conveyancing in manor courts in the thirteenth and fourteenth centuries, based on changes in the royal courts, suggest that the private courts were competing with the royal courts for business.[44] Analysis of the private litigation brought before manor courts has shown such great variations in the number of cases, that the most plausible explanation is that a lord such as Crowland Abbey was providing in its courts a convenient and effective service for litigants. Those with claims for the repayment of debts or compensation for trespass felt that some courts offered a better chance of success, or speedier actions, than others. Their custom was attracted, and their presence added to the profits of the lord.[45]

Lords are sometimes given credit for initiatives which promoted economic growth, such as the foundation of markets, fairs, towns, and industrial facilities such as fulling mills. There were plenty of successes to celebrate. The fair at St Ives brought profits not just to Ramsey Abbey but also to the merchants

[42] Langdon, *Mills*, 257–87.
[43] S. Shaw, *The History and Antiquities of Staffordshire* (London, 1801), vol II, 71–2.
[44] Razi and Smith (eds), *Medieval Society and the Manor Court*, 67–8.
[45] C. Briggs, 'Rural Credit, Debt Litigation and Manor Courts in England, *c.*1290–*c.*1380', unpublished PhD thesis, University of Cambridge, 2002.

and economy of eastern England. New towns flourished, such as Salisbury, founded by its bishop. The failures should not be forgotten, however, including the many markets for which charters were granted in the thirteenth century but which showed little evidence that they ever functioned. Some urban ventures were planned, but failed to attract a large or permanent population.[46]

Lords were often most anxious to encourage commercial and industrial development on their least valuable, most thinly populated, and very remote estates. They were seeking ways to increase profits when the conventional methods, such as expanding the cultivated area or the number of tenants, were not so easy. There were more seigneurial boroughs in Shropshire than in Norfolk, for example, and a very high density of markets in Devon. Towns and markets sprouted in Norfolk without needing a great deal of institutional support. Ventures in the bleak economic climate of uplands or woodlands were more likely to come to nothing. Lords had little power to give help to new markets, towns, or fulling mills in their early stages of growth. They might hope to compel their rural tenants to sell their produce in their lord's own market place, but they lacked the machinery to do this. Much depended on the siting of the market or town in relation to road and river routes, the planning of the town in a manner which would be convenient and attractive to the potential tenants, and the provision of the right tenurial and institutional framework by fixing rents and giving privileges, such as burgage tenure. Decisive lordship could be used in order to acquire land for the new streets and house plots, and to divert roads outside the town to bring traffic through the main streets, and this was often done.[47] Existing tenants would have been cajoled or pushed into losing land and common rights. Townspeoples' surnames sometimes show that they had migrated from other manors on the lord's estate. For example at Stratford-upon-Avon, a new town of the bishop of Worcester, founded in 1196, the Kempsey family had come soon after the foundation from another episcopal manor, 22 miles away, beyond the main catchment area for migrants.[48] This may have resulted from a policy of recruitment by the lord's officials, but more likely through informing people of the opportunities in the new town than by compulsory

---

[46] J. Masschaele, 'The Multiplicity of Medieval Markets Reconsidered', *Journal of Historical Geography*, 20 (1994), 255–71; M. W. Beresford, *New Towns of the Middle Ages. Town Plantations in England, Wales and Gascony* (London, 1967), 290–307.

[47] Beresford, *New Towns*, 55–225.

[48] E. M. Carus-Wilson, 'The First Half-Century of the Borough of Stratford-upon-Avon', in R. Holt and G. Rosser (eds), *The Medieval Town. A Reader in Urban History, 1200–1540* (London, 1990), 58–60.

relocation. Lords could also ensure, by invoking the lawyers' rules to avoid one market encroaching on another, that rival markets were not established too near. Lords initially used some power to help the new commercial centres, but in the long run entrepreneurial skills in the choice of site, and the response of traders and artisans, determined the success or failure of a town.

Competitiveness weakened the authority of individual lords. They showed class solidarity in the adverse circumstances after the Black Death in 1348–9, but when the economic climate had encouraged expansion before 1300 lords were very ready to welcome migrants from other estates to take burgage plots in towns or to cultivate cleared land in zones of colonization. Even before the great exodus of serfs in the fifteenth century, a *neif* who moved to another lord's manor would be regarded in his or her new home as free. Nor were lords averse to exploiting the misfortunes of others. The history of landed estates in the thirteenth century is full of lords, both monastic and lay, buying land from indebted unfortunates 'in urgent need', and even taking over a whole inheritance encumbered with debt, and arranging for the last lord and lady to end their days in a retirement home.[49] Families competed with one another for the advantages of marriage into a rich inheritance. And periodically disputes over marriage, inheritance or even patronage of a parish church led to violent confrontation. There were well-founded resentments by laymen against church lords, which helped to bring about the mortmain legislation in 1279, and there were tensions also between lesser landowners and lay magnates.[50]

Conclusion

The undoubted influence that lords enjoyed over medieval society came only partly from their direct wielding of coercive powers. Their jurisdiction was exercised through courts run largely by their own tenants. Their military capacity, away from their castles, came as an ultimate and distant threat rather than as a constant presence of armed men. They had no monopoly over weapons. Their tenants carried arms too, and representatives of the peasantry were recruited into armies. Lords used their position to manipulate, channel and pressurize their inferiors into acting in the seigneurial interest. Large numbers of people in medieval society were caught up in a network, not just of paying money and performing service, but also collecting rents,

---

[49] P. R. Coss, 'Sir Geoffrey de Langley and the Crisis of the Knightly Class in Thirteenth-Century England', in Aston (ed.), *Landlords, Peasants and Politics*, 168–77.

[50] S. Raban, *Mortmain Legislation and the English Church, 1279–1500* (Cambridge, 1982), 3–9; E. King, 'Large and Small Landowners in Thirteenth-Century England: The Case of Peterborough Abbey', in Aston (ed.), *Landlords, Peasants and Politics*, 141.

supervising work, sitting on juries, informing courts on wrongdoing, assessing tallage and other variable payments and all the other tasks that made the system work. Lords set a tone and style which was widely accepted by a society which could be deferential, but also collaborated out of self-interest.

Accepting the limitations on lords' powers, and their ineffectiveness in terms of some modern expectations of their ability to command, bully and dictate to others, leads us into drawing the conclusion that feudal society had a capacity to change within its own structure. This was becoming particularly apparent around 1300. The incompleteness of seigneurial power gave the peasantry some opportunities, and it is a commonplace that the upper peasantry could take advantage of the market by selling produce profitably and buying land.

Some readers may be tempted to take the argument further than I have attempted to do, and play down the antagonism between lords and peasants. I would warn against such a tendency. For all of the weaknesses in the lords' position, they retained powers of jurisdiction and control. In the midlands, for example, the tenurial structure of yardlands and oxgangs survived intact for centuries, and inheritance by a single son prevented fragmentation and enabled services to be levied on traditional holdings. Servile peasants on many manors suffered serious disadvantages when they were paying heavy annual rents in excess of 20s. per yardland (8d. per acre), and incurring extra payments such as entry fines on top.

Lordship cannot be regarded as benevolent. Even the common lawyers, in their reflective moments, found it difficult to justify serfdom in terms of natural law.[51] Peasants resented the power of lords, whether it was weak or strong. They acted in concert and saw a common interest which united the whole village against their lord. They objected to all labour services, so that even if they only owed a few each year, they could still be matters for contention. Indeed it was often the small demands, rather than such major payments as entry fines, which provoked peasant agitations. The marriage fine, a relatively modest sum of perhaps 2s., and much lower than the dowry provided by the bride's father to the couple under the marriage contract, was still resented as an imposition. Although we can find rebellions on old oppressive church manors, like the 1348 incident at Badbury in Wiltshire, many protests took place on manors such as Halesowen in Worcestershire where the burdens were not especially heavy.[52] Customary or servile tenants

---

[51] S. E. Thorne (ed.), *Bracton on the Laws and Customs of England* (Cambridge, MA, 1968), vol.II, 30.

[52] M. Müller, 'The Aims and Organisation of a Peasant Revolt in Early Fourteenth-Century Wiltshire', *Rural History*, 14 (2003), 1–20; Z. Razi, 'The Struggles between the Abbots of

resented the variability of tenures and payments, and any element of uncertainty; lords valued their ability to raise extra money and to be unpredictable. Their freedom of action, as we have seen, was hedged about with limitations, which leads us to regard lords as lacking effectiveness. Their inability to exercise full control over the peasantry, their competitiveness and internal subdivisions, and the tension between their interests and those of the state, all contributed to Rodney Hilton's 'crisis of feudalism', and made the landlords vulnerable to subsequent changes.

Halesowen and their Tenants in the Thirteenth and Fourteenth Centuries', in T. H. Aston, P. R. Coss, C. Dyer and J. Thirsk (eds.), *Social Relations and Ideas. Essays in Honour of R. H. Hilton* (Cambridge, 1983), 151–69, esp.156.

Exploring Difference within Rural Communities in the Northern Iberian Kingdoms, 1000–1300[1]

Isabel Alfonso

Historical studies in Spain have been dramatically revitalized since the 1970s and 1980s, not just for the medieval period but in general. This has meant the gradual integration of Spanish work into debates and developments in other countries. The myth of Spanish difference, for long so carefully fostered by official ideology in almost every sphere, was thus questioned in its medieval dimensions as well. It is not my intention here, however, to address these historiographical developments, which are well known.[2] Rather, I will examine some issues relating to peasant communities in the north of the peninsula, in particular in regard to internal forms of inequality, a theme on which Rodney Hilton wrote many illuminating pages.[3] His influence, indeed, played a pivotal role in the shift from legal and institutional history to more social approaches among Spanish medievalists.[4]

---

[1] I am most grateful to Julio Escalona for his comments on a draft of this paper, and to Simon Doubleday (Hofstra University, New York), for the English translation.

[2] One of the most recent historiographical studies in the field of medieval rural history is J. A. García de Cortázar and P. Martínez Sopena, 'Los estudios sobre historia rural de la sociedad medieval hispanocristiana', in a collective study of 'La historia rural de las sociedades medievales europeas: trayectorias y perspectivas', ed. I. Alfonso, which also includes articles on England (C. Dyer and P. Schofield), France (G. Brunel and B. Cursente), *Historia Agraria*, 31 (2003), 57–83; and on Italy (L. Provero), Poland (P. Górécki), and Germany (J. Demade), *Historia Agraria*, 33 (2004), 12–103; now in English: *The Rural History of Medieval European Societies. Trends and Perspectives* (Turnhout, 2007).

[3] R. Hilton, 'Reasons for Inequality among Medieval Peasants', in *Class Conflict and the Crisis of Feudalism*, 2nd edn (London, 1990) 66–78 [Translated into Spanish as, *Conflicto de clases y crisis del feudalismo* (Barcelona, 1988)]; id., *The English Peasantry in the Later Middle Ages* (Oxford, 1975).

[4] Two of his most influential books, *Bond Men Made Free. Medieval Peasant Movements and the English Rising of 1381* (London, 1973), and *The Transition from Feudalism to Capitalism* (London, 1976), were almost immediately translated into Spanish and the second of these two books, which introduced one of the main debates about the origins of

The changing approach by historians to rural communities in medieval Castile has unquestionably been closely related to new ideas concerning the development of feudal society in the peninsula, and has benefited greatly from new critical editions of documentary sources. These allow a better appraisal of both the information these sources contain and the contexts in which they were compiled. Sadly, with a few notable exceptions, historians have been slow to integrate into their field the great potential contribution of archaeology, which in Spain is underdeveloped and usually under-funded.[5]

Scholars agree to some extent that local society offers a variegated picture in the period between the eleventh and thirteenth centuries. Diverse forms of lordship and internally divided communities are recognized, although the formalization of such differences also varied. In many cases, there were two clearly defined groups among charter witnesses, representing the free population of a community: a group of knights, and the rest of the population. The names given to these two respective groups varied according to the context. The first group were generally known as *milites* or *caballeros*, and they enjoyed certain privileges with respect to their neighbours, from whom they were distinguished by ownership of a horse and their corresponding (at least nominal) military duties. Those belonging to the remaining population were known as *pedites* or *peones, homines, pecheros, labradores, rústicos, collazos*, to cite the most common terms. Together both groups formed the body of seigneurial dependants (sometimes called vassals[*6]), although villages rarely depended on a single lord and most communities were divided in their attachments to social superiors.

But there were other differences, too, both between the two groups and within their ranks, partly corresponding to material wealth but also dictated by networks of social relationship. There were some knights, for instance, who were recognized as nobles or *infanzones*, along with others (*caballeros villanos*) who only in part avoided the obligations that were normally

---

capitalism, appeared in three Spanish editions within a very short period of time. [Spanish translations: *Siervos liberados: los movimientos campesinos medievales y el levantamiento inglés de 1381* (Madrid, 1978); *La transición del feudalismo al capitalismo* (Barcelona, 1978, 1979, 1980).

[5] On this problem, Julio Escalona has been particularly eloquent: 'Paisaje, asentamiento y Edad Media: reflexiones sobre dos estudios recientes', *Historia Agraria*, 20 (2000), 227–44. See also M. Barceló (ed.), *Arqueología medieval. En las afueras del medievalismo* (Barcelona, 1988).

[6] 'Vassals', a word confined to socially elevated feudal tenants in England, is applied in Castile to all the tenants of a lord.

rendered by the commoners. Our understanding of the processes of social mobility which led to this type of differentiation within the most elevated ranks of peasant society has improved considerably in recent decades, as the result of attempts to identify mechanisms of seigneurial domination which influenced and/or made possible such differentiation.[7] Nevertheless, more research is still needed on a number of matters, such as the position of local knights in regard to rural communities (were they essentially outsiders, or privileged members of a cohesive social body?), or the extent to which they were involved in agricultural production and direct management of their holdings. We also need to know more about the chronology of social differentiation and its regional variations.[8]

In villages where we witness this kind of internal stratification, we can also see that the remaining peasant population was not homogeneous, either. The sources we have in Spain for the study of inequality among peasant holdings, although far sparser than those available, for example, to English historians, allow us to trace a widespread, tripartite, social structure of peasants with large, medium and small holdings: that is to say, with a varying capacity for subsistence. Taking cyclical patterns into consideration, these differences mean that some households had insufficient manpower in the nuclear household, and others enjoyed a surplus. Certainly, it is not easy to go beyond generalized descriptions, or to know the relative proportions of the different sizes of peasant holding or their precise distribution in different

---

[7] The bibliography, already abundant, can be reviewed in the articles in two important collective volumes arising from an explicitly comparative approach to similar problems in other societies of the medieval European west: I. Álvarez Borge (ed.), *Comunidades locales y poderes feudales en la Edad Media* (Logroño, 2001); and, *Señores, siervos, vasallos en la Alta Edad Media*, XXVIII *Semana de Estudios Medievales. Estella 16 a 20 de julio de 2001* (Pamplona, 2002). See also n. 4 above.

[8] For my immediate area of concern, J. M. Monsalvo, 'Transformaciones sociales y relaciones de poder en los concejos de frontera, siglos XI–XIII. Aldeanos, vecinos y caballeros ante las instituciones municipales'; I. Alfonso, 'Poder local y diferenciación interna en las comunidades rurales gallegas', both in R. Pastor (ed.), *Relaciones de poder, de producción y parentesco en la Edad media y moderna* (Madrid,1990), 107–70, 203–23; R. Pastor, I. Alfonso, A. Rodríguez and P. Sánchez, *Poder monástico y grupos domésticos en la Galicia foral (siglos XIII–XV), La casa. La comunidad* (Madrid, 1990); and R. Pastor, E. Pascua, A. Rodríguez and P. Sánchez, *Transacciones sin mercado: Instituciones, propiedad y redes sociales en la Galicia monástica. 1200–1300* (Madrid, 1999) [Translated into English as *Beyond the Market: Transactions, Property and Social Networks in Monastic Galicia, 1200–1300* (Leiden, 2003)]; C. Estepa, *Las behetrías castellanas* (Valladolid, 2004), vol. 2, 275–6.

lordships and regions, but a growing interest in family structures and community interaction has opened new avenues of scholarly inquiry.[9]

My aim here is to explore this differentiation within villages, paying special attention to the most dependent seigneurial peasants, those least visible in the sources. I believe this will allow us to identify some of the problems which underlay social antagonisms, at the same time generating less easily apparent forms of solidarity. I will concentrate on information relating to labour services exacted from the recipients of *fueros*, village franchises, in the villages of Castile and León by lay or ecclesiastical lords, in the expectation that this will throw light on stratification among the peasantry.[10] I will address three questions: 1) how these labour services affected different segments of the population, 2) who performed these services in practice, and 3) how the work was assigned within peasant households.

Seigneurial *fueros* and social differentiation among dependent peasants

Local laws (*fueros*), which varied widely in length and content, multiplied across Christian Iberia between the eleventh and thirteenth centuries, in small hamlets and villages as well as in major urban centres. The normative character that was attributed to these documents until recently has obscured the fact they are valuable sources of information for issues other than the regulation of peasant life by the lords, traditionally seen as the only social agents in the elaboration of these local statutes. Less juridical approaches have allowed us, among other things, to recognize the influence of the broader population in the design of such laws. A majority of the *fueros* were the result of resistance and struggle, the result of sustained conflicts—many of them conducted in legal terms—and prolonged negotiations.[11]

---

[9] See notes 7 and 8.

[10] I will use the following compilations of *fueros*: J. Rodríguez (ed.), *Los fueros del reino de León*, 2 vols. (León, 1981); J. Rodríguez (ed.), *Los fueros locales de la provincia de Zamora* (Salamanca, 1990); J. Rodríguez (ed.), *Palencia. Panoramica foral de la provincia* (Palencia, 1981); E. González (ed.), *El regimen foral vallisoletano* (Valladolid, 1986); G. Martínez (ed.), *Fueros locales en el territorio de la provincia de Burgos* (Burgos, 1982). Charters from these collections are hereafter referred to using the abbreviations FL, FZ, FP, FV respectively, and by the number of the document.

[11] I. Alfonso, 'Campesinado y derecho: la vía legal de su lucha (Castilla y León, siglos X–XIII)', *Noticiario de Historia Agraria*, 13 (1997), 15–31. For more details on the nature and content of these sources in a comparative context, see P. Martínez Sopena, 'Autour des fueros et des chartes de franchises dans l'Espagne médiévale', I. Alfonso, 'La contestation paysanne face aux exigences de travail seigneuriales en Castille et León. Les formes et leur signification symbolique', and C. Reglero 'Le prélèvement seigneurial

Labour services, known as *sernas* in Castile and León, or sometimes simply described by reference to the required tasks, were generally quite light, since week-work was exceptional. Most common were one or two days of labour service each month, or even three or four days per year. Nonetheless, the peasant perception of these obligations appears to have been very negative, and, as elsewhere in Europe, they performed them without the 'goodwill' that their lords demanded.[12] The differences we observe in the *fueros* regarding the labour services that were required from a community or a group of vassals under the lord's jurisdiction or holding land from him (*vassallos, homines, collazos, populatores, moradores*) seem to have corresponded to a desire to exploit the particular resources of peasant families. These differences—which also existed in relation to other forms of payment—corresponded to the size of the peasants' landholdings; the number of working animals (one or two oxen or donkeys were most common); or whether they depended only on their own labour. Although there is no evidence that peasants in the same community were required to work more days than others, each was required to perform labour services related to his resources.

But these differences also had a social, juridical and political dimension, which tended to give privileges—in a wide range of conditions and contexts—to free men over bondmen, clerics over laymen, those with a horse over *peones*, the lord's officials (*alcaldes, jueces, merinos*) over others, those with a supervisory role over their neighbours, and the recently-married and widows over the rest. These privileges meant total or partial exemption from services owed by others, and, given the limited number of days of service demanded, appear to have entailed not only an economic advantage, but also a symbolic distinction and a certain prestige within the community.

Sub-dependants as substitutes

The perception of labour services as quintessentially servile work—a picture largely drawn from the charters themselves—has obscured the fact that those

---

dans le royaume de León. Les évêchés de León, Palencia et Zamora', in M. Bourin and P. Martínez Sopena (eds), *Pour une anthropologie du prélèvement seigneurial dans les campagnes médiévales (XIe–XIVe siècles). Réalités et représentations paysannes* (Paris, 2004), 211–37, 291–320, and 411–42 respectively.

[12] For further detail, see I. Alfonso 'Las sernas en León y Castilla. Contribución al estudio de las relaciones socio-económicas en el marco del señorío medieval', *Moneda y Crédito*, 129 (1974), 153–210. I have studied the way in which peasants view their condition in 'La contestation paysanne face aux exigences de travail seigneuriales'; the classic study of resistance is R. Pastor, *Resistencias y luchas campesinas en la época del crecimiento y consolidación de la formación feudal. Castilla y León, siglos X–XIII* (Madrid, 1980).

who really performed these services were not necessarily direct seigneurial vassals. In reality, the latter could oblige, request, or pay others to fulfil the services in their place. There are frequent references to peasants who had not managed to gain exemption like their more privileged neighbours, but who sent substitutes to perform them. It is worth investigating the character of these substitutions, and the relationship between dependants and substitutes, by examining a few cases.

Mojados is a village to the south of the Duero river, 14 km from Valladolid, from which we have a number of extant documents. It is an ecclesiastical lordship between two large towns, and was linked successively to the bishops of Palencia and Segovia. The bishop of Palencia had received it in a donation by Alfonso VIII in 1175, along with all its *collazos*, a term which we might translate as 'villeins' or simply 'tenants'; they were ostensibly free but actually dependent peasants. One year later, in 1176, the bishop agreed on a *fuero* with these local inhabitants.[13] This document takes the form of a charter addressed to all the vassals, without exception, so that by 'living honestly' according to the *fuero* and good customs they might merit eternal life and happiness.[14] Of its twenty-three clauses, we are especially interested in three here. One allows tenants to possess more than one *solar* where they can accommodate their ploughmen (*yugueros*) or other workers, male or female.[15] Another establishes that all residents, male and female—except salaried workers—with

---

[13] 1176/FV, doc. XI.

[14] '*facio cartam . . . uobis hominibus meis et fidelibus vasallis de Moiados generaliter omnibus sine exceptione aliqua tam presentibus quam futuris de uestris foris et bonis consuetudines quibus in hoc seculo recte et honeste uiuatis, et hec iuste et fimiter semper tenendo ab hac temporali vita ad eternam que Christus es procul feliciter perueniatis*'.

[15] [2] '*Et placet mihi quod habeatis aliut solare tantum preter uestrum ubi si neccesarie fuerit et teneatis iugueros uestros uel quoslibet homines uel mulieres*'. The word *solar* is the common term for the peasant holding, the place where the house is constructed, the central nucleus of seigneurial exactions, to which cultivated lands (sometimes described as the *heredad*) are conjoined. The growing complexity of peasant tenancies, and the process of separation between *solar* and *heredad*, seems quite well developed by the thirteenth century, although we do not yet understand all their implications. For these questions, see C. Estepa, 'Proprietà, evoluzione delle strutture agrarie e trasformazioni sociali in Castiglia (secoli XI-XII), in G. Dilcher and C. Violante (eds), *Strutture e trasformazioni della signoria rurale nei secoli X-XII* (Bologna, 1996), 411–43; and I. Álvarez Borge, 'Sobre las relaciones de dependencia en las behetrías castellanas en el siglo XIII: hipótesis a partir del caso de Las Quintanillas', in E. Sarasa and E. Serrano (eds), *Señorío y feudalismo en la Península Ibérica, ss. XI–XIX* (Zaragoza, 1993), vol. 4, 225–40; and Luis Martínez, 'Los campesinos solariegos en las behetrías castellanas', in C. Estepa and C. Jular (eds), *Los señoríos de behetría* (Madrid, 2001), 187–225.

more than 10 *maravedíes* of money, shall pay and serve the bishop.[16] The third
clause obliges them to perform labour services (*sernas*) twice a year, once to
plough the land and once to sow the seed, besides other duties.[17] The *fuero*
does not, then, appear to be directed to the poorest members of society, even
though the term *collazos*, applied to the population in the royal donation of
the previous year, might seem to suggest this. In these clauses of the text, one
can observe that references to the local population make a number of fine
distinctions.[18] They distinguish vassals with more than one *solar*; those who
implicitly have only one; men and women who live in someone else's *solar*;
vassals with more than 10 *maravedíes*; those who implicitly have less than this,
and the salaried labourers (*soldariegos*). The latter two categories are explicitly
excluded from paying tribute or performing service to the bishop. These
distinctions, although they reveal a differentiated social fabric, should not
be taken as clearly defined social strata; indeed, what needs to be investigated
is the overlapping, fluidity and contingency which might be involved in these
situations. The term social 'stratum' therefore needs to be understood here in
a loose sense.

We know that the village of Mojados subsequently passed to the crown,
which then re-granted it to the bishop of Segovia, in whose hands it remained
until it was sold in the sixteenth century.[19] It was one of the bishops of Segovia
who issued another *fuero* in 1294,[20] and who tells of the disputes over their
duties that his predecessors had experienced in the course of the thirteenth
century. These disputes, the new *fuero* stated, had damaged the bishops and
given the peasants a poor reputation (*mala fama*) as vassals. The new *fuero*
consolidates some improvements in regard to taxation, and, although it does
not modify the frequency of labour services, it lays down some changes in
how they are to be performed and allows us to observe more clearly the
different social strata living in this peasant community. Labour services are
to be performed by all peasants who work using oxen or mules, but those with

[16] [3] '*Pretera constituo quod omnes homines uel mulieres, cuiuscumque generit [sic] sint, quicumque in uilla de Moiados commorauerint, nisi fuerint soldariegos, habentes ualiam X morabetinorum et ultra in hereditate uel in quolibet mobili, omnes pro arbitrio et mercede episcopi pectent et seruiant domino episcopo suo*'.

[17] [5] '*Mando eciam quod faciatis mihi duas sernas in anno, unam in barbechar et alteram in seminar*'.

[18] A separate clause regulates the obligations of the Jewish inhabitants. The term *vecino* is used to regulate horizontal relationships in general, and as a global term of reference the word *qui* is used.

[19] G. Martínez Díez, 'Los fueros inéditos de Mojados,' in *Estudios en homenaje a don Claudio Sánchez Albornoz en sus 90 años*. Anexos CHE (Buenos Aires, 1983), vol. 2, 450–7.

[20] FV, doc. XXX.

more than one pair of oxen are to perform the services with just one of these pairs, while those with only one ox or mule should bring it to be yoked to another. Those with only donkeys, meanwhile, no longer have an obligation to perform labour services.[21] All tenants with this obligation are to receive bread, wine and cheese twice a day. But the officials (*alcaldes*) and other 'good men' (*boni homini*) supervising the labour services are to receive meat instead of cheese[22] and do not have to perform these boon works.[23] Therefore, these arrangements do not seem to have affected the knights (*caballeros*) as they did in other communities,[24] but rather those who formed the apparatus of the local council (*alcaldes, juez* and *escribano*) and the generic 'good men'. It is likely, although not certain, that most of the latter belonged to the privileged sector of the village. However, we can see that not all the wealthier peasants were formally exempt from work services, with all their servile connotations, since these services were due also from those who had more than one pair of oxen and had other people under their protection (*su bien fazer*) and authority (*gouernio*),[25] even though, as in 1176, they did not have to pay for the place (*solar*) where these people were lodged. The evidence allows us to deduce that in practice it was often the sub-dependants—when the tenant possessed them—who performed the labour service.

We know little about this last-mentioned sector of peasant society, especially those who lived in villages and hamlets, except that they were excluded from the rights afforded to their more privileged neighbours. In some cases, their domestic character is clear: in Mojados, they appear to have formed a part of the peasant household, living in an adjoining building. It is true, nonetheless, that the ambiguous expression *morar en sus casas*, which we

---

[21] [1] '...*Estas sernas deuen fazer todos los que labraren con bueys o con bestias mulares en esta guysa: el que labrare con vna yunta que faga serna con vna yunta, el que mas oyuere non sea tenudo de dar mas de vna yunta; et el que ouyere vn buey o vna bestia mular que la de para yuntar con otra; et los que labraren con bestias asnares que non sean tenudos de fazer serna*'.

[22] [1] '...*et el dia que fizieren la serna mandamos que a los alcalles et a los otros omes buenos que lo endereçaren que les den pan et vino et carne dos vezes al dia a comer, et a los otros que labraren con los bueys que les den pan et vino et queso dos vezes al dia con el ero, et a la noche quando dexaren de la lauor denles sendos panes et sendos medios quartos de vino*'.

[23] [6] '...*et tenemos por bien que los alcalles et el iuez et el escriuano que sean escusados de nos fazer serna et de nos dar enfurçion*'.

[24] The fact that *caballeros* are not exempted does not mean that they were obliged to perform labour services, since there is no evidence that there were any in the village.

[25] [2]'...*tenemos por bien que sin la casa en que morare cada vno pueda aver otro solar sin enfurcion en que tenga sus bueys o omes que esten a su bien fazer de gouernio et en otra manera non*'. The term '*gouernio*', besides authority, implies a sense of responsibility for providing what was necessary for carrying out the tasks at hand.

find in other references to express the link between these workers and the seigneurial tenants, may signify either possession or cohabitation in these houses, so we have to assess carefully the nature of these residential arrangements.[26] Another group of references poses similar problems:

1. Fuero de Fuentesauco (1133): the men of the bishop of Zamora, in this village, obliged to perform five days of labour each year, are authorized to have as vassals only the ploughmen and gardeners 'living in their houses'.[27]
2. Fuero de Villarmildo (1129): Countess Estefanía grants similar authorization to her *collazos* in this village, among the few who are subject to week work, for having the same type of workers under their dependency.[28]
3. Fuero de Villalonso and Benefarces (*c.*1147), also a lay lordship: its men, obliged to perform only four days of *serna* each year, may have their ploughmen as vassals.[29]

In these cases, what the references reveal—at least as much as the domestic character of this population—is a subordinate level of vassalage, permitted and recognized by the lord. This is a form of dependency which, without doubt, must have encompassed a variety of situations, from servants in husbandry on yearly contracts, or labourers hired by the day, to some type of sub-tenancy, but we lack sufficient information to be precise about the nature of their accommodation. Take the case of the ploughmen (*yugueros*). These are better known from urban *fueros*, in which they are mentioned receiving lands and animals for working these lands separately with their families in exchange for one fifth of the product. However it is not clear

[26] The dimensions of the *solar* are unknown, but the well-entrenched equation between *solar*, house and family needs to be re-evaluated, given the many indications of complexity. What are we to think, for instance, of the ten *fuegos* within a single *solar*, used as a criterion for the *servicium temporale* owed by clerics and laymen to the abbot of Oña *rationi soli*? I. Oceja (ed.), *Documentación del monasterio de San Salvador de oña (1032–1350)* (Burgos, 1983–86), 4 vols. doc. 107, *c.*1209. On these questions see I. Alfonso, 'Resolución de disputas y prácticas judiciales en el Burgos medieval', in *Burgos en la Plena Edad Media. III Jornadas burgalesas de Historia* (Burgos, 1994), 211–44, at 226.

[27] 1133/FZ, doc. 7 [1] '*Ut nullus homo habeat ibi vassalum nisi suum iugarium vel suum ortolanum qui moratus fuerit in sua propia kasa*'.

[28] 1129/FV, doc. 5: [15] '*Et uos meos populatores dono uobis foro, que abetis super uos uestros ortolanos et uestros iukeros sine alio seniore super se in domos suas*'.

[29] *c.*1147/FZ, doc. 10, [2] '*Et illos homines . . . habeant suos iugueros perdonatos er pro suos vasallos, ut non faciant facienda nulla*'.

that the situation of rural ploughmen can be equated to that of their urban counterparts.[30]

These forms of dependency were the object of specific negotiation in some cases. For instance, let us observe the choice the bishop of Zamora gave to one of his vassals in 1224 as the result of a dispute. He might choose either to reside personally in the hamlet of Almaraz as a direct vassal of the bishop, performing all the corresponding labour services and owing all the relevant taxes, and to keep all the holdings (*cortes*)[31] populated with his own vassals. Or he might choose to leave, and to cede these sub-vassals to the direct lordship of the bishop.[32] We do not know what decision the bishop's vassal took; his options were, however, no different from those in many other cases. More generally, the possibility provided by some *fueros* of keeping a house legally inhabited, even if one did not live in the place implied the option of substituting another worker to do his services. Nonetheless, in this kind of situation, the lord's preference appears to have been that the substitute be his direct vassal, even if this vassal were to have other workers in his service.

Why this seigneurial preference? Why allow in the lordship this extra social stratum of dependants of his peasant vassals, these *vassalli vassallorum* which one document mentions alongside the landless (*proprios labores non habentes*)?[33] Before trying to answer these questions, it is important to stress that although the explicit legal recognition that others might take one's place in performing tenant obligations seems to be a later phenomenon, in practice this kind of substitution had been occurring for a long time. In order to show this, I will use a different kind of source—an inquest—which provides rich information on the practice of work on the demesne, and which reinforces and complements what we know from the *fueros*. The inquest was conducted by the cathedral of León in the late thirteenth century to ascertain the

[30] J. C. Martín Cea, 'Una pequeña contribución al conocimiento del campesinado castellano: el yuguero', in *Primer Congreso de Historia de Castilla y León* (Burgos, 1983), vol. I, 101–12. See also n. 37.

[31] The terminology here is rather unclear, with a dynamic rather than a fixed meaning, indicating processes that we can only partially understand at present (see n. 15, 26). This further complicates research into the nature of these sub-dependants, and the nature of their relationship with the peasants for whom they work. The problem is not unique to our sources, as has been shown in regard to the *garciones* listed in the court rolls by H. S. A. Fox, 'Exploitation of the Landless by Lords and Tenants in Early Medieval England', in Z. Razi and R. Smith (eds), *Medieval Society and the Manor Court* (Oxford, 1996), 518–68.

[32] We have various documents on this hamlet (*aldea*), which was first under lay lordship and then under episcopal lordship: 1175/FZ, doc. 20; 1194–1217/FZ, doc. 38; 1224/FZ, doc. 46.

[33] 1197/FP, doc. 29, Fuero de Pozuelos.

obligations their *fuero* vassals owed in Villavicencio, a village some way from the centre of their estates. One witness, asked whether he knew whether Domingo López or his wife, Sol García, performed labour services, answered that he did not, but that he had seen their ploughman (*yuguero*) doing so, and that this ploughman, who lived in their houses in Villavicencio, was using their oxen.[34] The context of this information makes one doubt, again, whether these ploughmen were servants in husbandry, living with the direct vassals of the cathedral in the houses they possessed in this village. Alternatively, the witness's response may equally be read to mean that the houses were inhabited by the tenants' dependent *yugueros* who went to work the demesne while the direct vassals lived in the nearby settlement of Villalpando. Another witness in the some inquest states that he is not sure whether those he has seen performing *sernas* for the bishop were doing so for money or for some other reason (*se por dineros si por otra cosa*). Again, we have evidence here of the various methods which tenants on church estates might use in order to fulfil the demands associated with tenancy and/or seigneurial dependency. Another, later source indicates the same. In 1417, on their own behalf or for another, the inhabitants of Oteruelo, vassals of the abbot of San Marcelo de León, had to perform the service of threshing; moreover, those with oxen had to perform the service of ploughing with their animals and with their own personal labour, or else provide someone else to do it (*o dar a otro por sy que hare con los dichos buees*). They had also to gather the vintage for one day, or provide workers, male or female, every year (*o dar obreros o obreras cada año*).[35]

The very terminology used to designate these workers, which seems rather imprecise to us, indicates the diversity of situations about which we have, in fact, very little information.[36] Again, the contrast is striking with the more extensive *fueros* of the cities and major towns which regulate very precisely the forms of work and payment for the segment of the population employed to cultivate the land by the (internally differentiated) group of landowners and taxpayers.[37] But in the brief *fueros* of the small seigneurial villages under

---

[34] 1291/CL, 2560, '*que la vio fazer al su jugero que tenie los sus bues e que moraua en las suas casas de Domingo Lopez e de Sol Pelaz que auien en Vilauicens e que la fazia con los sus bues de Domingo López e de Sol Pelaz*'.

[35] 1417/FL, doc. 132, Fuero de Oteruelo.

[36] See Reglero, 'Le prélèvement seigneurial dans le royaume de León'.

[37] The classic study is that of R. Gibert, who from a juridical perspective analyses source material that still remains insufficiently used: 'El contrato de servicios en la España medieval', *Cuadernos de Historia de España*, 15 (1951), 5–130. More recently, J. C. Martín Cea, 'El trabajo rural en el mundo rural bajomedieval castellano', in *El trabajo*

consideration here, one hardly catches a glimpse of the *'no heredes'*, *'soldar-iegos'*, *'mancipios'*, *'yugueros'*, and *'obreros'*, who we find—albeit not exclusively—in the employ of the most substantial tenants of the manor. All the same, in these villages there were similar groups of landless peasants, who directly fed seigneurial demands for manpower.[38] They also, as I have tried to show, met those needs of peasant tenants which were associated with the greater size of their holdings, cyclical necessities, and/or seigneurial pressure. The paucity of data make it difficult to make comparisons with the interesting interpretation of H. S. A. Fox regarding landless peasants on the manors of Glastonbury Abbey *c.*1300.[39] Suffice it to say that given the lightness of labour services in the lordships of Castile and León, it is not possible to attribute the tenants' need for their manpower to satisfy heavy seigneurial demands, or to a seigneurial desire to profit from a tax on their labour, as in the manors Fox has studied, since they were generally exempt from any payment as dependants and tenants. In Castile-Leon, the seigneurial strategy of indirectly accepting their labour perhaps should be better understood as a more effective means of controlling both tenancies and rents.

Within the peasant household

Despite the scarcity of detailed evidence, it seems clear that one sector of the recipients of the *fueros* were peasants who had at their disposal another source of manpower that could be used for fulfilling labour services on seigneurial lands. But there are also signs that children or old people might be used as substitutes for the male head of the household, presumably to reserve the effective labour of men in their prime for the cultivation of the peasant holding. This was the case, above all, in less privileged peasant households

---

en la historia (Salamanca, 1996), 91–128. Nonetheless it is the late medieval studies that bring a more complex vision of these questions: J. C. Martín Cea, *El mundo rural castellano a fines de la edad media. El ejemplo de Paredes de Nava en el siglo XV* (Valladolid, 1991) and R. Oliva, *La Tierra de Campos a fines de la Edad Media. Economía, sociedad y acción política campesina* (Valladolid, 2002) a study which shows the influence of Rodney Hilton and Chris Dyer in the analysis of standards of living in medieval communities.

[38] For instance, the dependent household (*criazon*) of 25 individuals of the monastery of San Zoilo de Carrión in the area of San Zoles in 1240, J. A. Pérez Celada (ed.), *Documentación del monasterio de San Zoilo de Carrión (1047–1300)* (Palencia, 1986), doc. 101; see also P. Martínez Sopena, 'Las solidaridades campesinas en la Tierra de Campos durante la Edad Media', in J. Barrull, J. Busqueta and E. Vicedo (eds), *Solidaritats pageses, sindicalisme i cooperativisme. Segones Jornades sobre Sistemes agraris, organització social i poder local als Països Catalans* (Lleida, 1998), 93–113.

[39] Fox, 'Exploitation of the Landless'.

which did not have dependants, or which were at that stage in the tenant's lifecycle when no sons were available for work. It is quite true that one of the issues in which knowledge needs to be extended is the internal organization of the domestic household. The difficulties of penetrating this sphere are practically insuperable, particularly when it comes to the issue of exactly who, among its members, including servants, had to perform labour services. One does not have to know who made this kind of decision within the household to guess that sending those members of the family who for physical reasons were least productive must have been one of the ways households avoided losing the labour of adult males. This decision simultaneously represented a form of resistance. Hence the seigneurial demand that children should not be sent,[40] that the replacement be as strong as the person with the obligation, and that frail and elderly villeins work separately.[41] Lords did not reject the work of women on the demesne, however. Although exemptions for widows are very generalized, in some *fueros* it is stipulated that a widow who cannot provide a male for the haymaking shall do so herself, receiving the same food in compensation as the rest of her neighbours.[42] Some other evidence further suggests that women might be obliged directly to perform these services: in a well known case of 1040 from the famous monastery of San Millán de Cogolla, a peasant woman refused to go with her neighbours to do so, considering it an *opus servile*.[43] We have seen that women are also mentioned among dependent workers of the tenants.

It is also in this context that one must address the question of those peasants' sons who were used as servants in the houses of other peasants. This question is closely related to the character of the sub-dependent workers, whom Fox not only associates with the temporary periods characterizing the so-called servant cycle but also shows were sometimes more permanent.[44] In the case of Galicia, Reyna Pastor has shown the influence of the seigneurial policy of land concessions upon strategies of family reproduction among peasant households, which diminished or grew in size—through a kind of

[40] 1234/FZ, doc. 53. Fuero de Cañizo [12]. 1208/FZ, doc. 33 Fuero de Belver [50].

[41] P. Ilarregui, S. Lapuerta (eds), *Fuero General de Navarra* (Pamplona, 1964) '*Et si algun villano quisiere imbiar en su logar ombre logado, si el seynior non quisiere non recibrá, nin mancebo soldado, si non fuere tal que saque ombre al mudado. Si oviere algunos villanos flacos ó vieios, labren apart*', L III, t. V, cp. XVII, 51

[42] 1217/FL, doc. 67, Fuero de Abelgas: [12]' . . . *Sed uidue que non dant uiros ad secandam herbam, ipsemet debent uenire ad colligendum eam tam in prato quam in domo et dominus dabis eis ad comendendum*'.

[43] This text is edited in Alfonso, 'La contestation paysanne', Annexes [2].

[44] Fox, 'Exploitation of the Landless', 554–60.

self-regulation well-known in later periods—to adjust to offers of seigneurial land. Pastor, nonetheless, unlike Fox, considers that the practice of young peasants serving for a period of time in the houses of their neighbours did not develop.[45] The dichotomy between periodic and permanent circulation perhaps responds more to the type of sources available than to historical reality, since the consideration of a population of rural servants or domestic workers is coming to be seen as a fundamental component in the re-evaluation of rural work. Studies of family structures need to be re-assessed along these lines, and we need a more systematic exploration of other documentary sources.

Underlying these brief remarks on social differentiation within the village, there have been two main objectives: firstly, to emphasize the existence, even in small rural communities, of a sector of the population dependent on other peasants, a sector which the documents reveal more in negative terms—as those that do not have lands, houses, or animals—than in terms of the work these dependants perform; secondly, to underline the character of this dependency, which appears to have excluded them from a direct seigneurial relationship, and also to have deprived them of communal rights. The study of the internal dynamic of the community, which has advanced so much in the last decade, must explore more deeply both the reasons for such inequality, and the role of labourers and servants in peasant communities, as Rodney Hilton indicated in works that continue to represent a valuable guide.

[45] R. Pastor, 'Poder monástico y grupos domésticos forero' in Pastor, Alfonso, Rodríguez, and Sánchez, *Poder monástico*, 49–234.

Peasant Elites and Village Communities in the South of France, 1200–1350

Monique Bourin

The medieval village, said Rodney Hilton, introducing a paper on 'Village Communities in Medieval England' at the 1982 Flaran Colloque, was not an organic or a harmonious community in which everyone played their part. Drawing on his own work on the west midlands, amplified by more recent studies, he described a society in conflict. The fiercest disputes were between communities and their lords, but the community was also divided within itself; it was a stratified society in which the elite both led the resistance to the lord and itself behaved violently, especially towards the lesser villagers.[1] Do we find this type of combative and overbearing elite when we look at the sources for the south of France, and in particular Languedoc? It is hard to tell, but let us look at how elites were constructed, both economically and politically, in the villages of Languedoc (See Fig. 1). We will then be able to return briefly to the English parallel.

The apparent poverty of the sources

The Languedocian documentation for the thirteenth and fourteenth centuries is disappointing when compared either with the wealth of the English manorial sources or with the detailed notarial records found for regions beyond the borders of the kingdom of France, both across the Rhône, in the direction of Provence, and over the southern frontier, in the direction of Roussillon or Catalonia. This absence of notarial registers is puzzling; all Languedocian villages had notaries from the 1220s and the ubiquity of these officials needs to be emphasized.[2] But their records have not survived, other

---

[1] R. H. Hilton, 'Les communautés villageoises en Angleterre au Moyen Age', in *Les communautés villageoises en Europe occidentale*, Flaran 4 (Auch, 1984), 118–28; R. H. Hilton, *A Medieval Society. The West Midlands at the End of the Thirteenth Century*, 2nd edn (Cambridge, 1983). I am grateful to Jean Birrell for translating this essay.

[2] F. Bréchon, 'Autour du notariat et des nouvelles pratiques de l'écrit dans les régions méridionales aux XIIe et XIIIe siècle', in P. Guichard and D. Alexandre-Bidon (eds), *Comprendre le XIIIe siècle. Etudes offertes à Marie Thérèse Lorcin* (Lyons, 1995), 161–72.

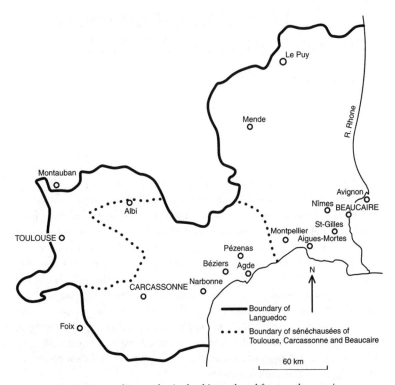

Fig. 1. Towns of Languedoc in the thirteenth and fourteenth centuries

than for a few *bourgades* (small towns), especially in the eastern part of Languedoc.[3] We have to resign ourselves, consequently, to having only a limited knowledge of the socio-economic fabric, credit networks and specific and concrete forms assumed by inheritance practices.

The seigneurial archives provide valuable information, if not on the scale of the English court rolls; the documents are not judicial and they tell us little about the manorial or seigneurial community. Accounts are few. Although the documents make plain that by the thirteenth century the lords—or at least their officials and the village elite—knew exactly what average income could be expected from a lordship, only a handful of the accounts of ecclesiastical lords survive, preserved in the papal archives (*Registres d'Avignon* and

---

[3] C. Béghin and F. Bréchon, *Les archives notariales médiévales de la sénéchaussée de Beaucaire. Répertoire numérique des registres antérieurs à 1500* (Lyons, 1998).

Introitus et Exitus); fewer than a dozen pre-date the Black Death. Among the various sources of income, these accounts mention taxes on land transfers; we are able, therefore, to gain at least some knowledge of the transfers themselves.

For the most part, the seigneurial archives consist of isolated acts recording the movement of tenures, that is, sales between tenants liable to a tax (*laudimium* or *foriscapium*) or the re-leasing of a vacant holding, that is, leases *ad novum accapitum* (at the new taking).[4] Though they are well preserved for some estates, such as those of the Templars and Hospitallers, it is difficult to build up a picture of the movement of land on the basis of these documents. However, these seigneurial archives, lay and ecclesiastical, include a large number of 'terriers', that is, the records of the seigneurial recognizances made by the tenants before a notary over a period of several weeks, then collected by him into a register. For the first half of the fourteenth century,[5] they survive in their thousands, especially for the year 1338. Given that, in each village, lordship over the land was divided between several lords, these terriers do not usually record all the land held by all the villagers. It is possible, however, to reconstitute a picture of the distribution of land between tenants, bearing in mind that the allod had virtually disappeared during the course of the twelfth century. Unlike those of other regions,[6] these documents do not record changes of tenancy, so they paint a static picture, but when they are collated with the information we have about land transfers, especially that in the accounts, we have the basis for an investigation of social differentiation within the village population.

The hierarchy of tenures

For the beginning of the fourteenth century, the terriers reveal a very fragmented pattern of land tenure, made up of tiny plots, but forming an ensemble of *terroirs* constructed in a coherent and homogeneous manner on the basis of the *castrum*, in line with one of the familiar patterns of the

---

[4] The taxes were established during the course of the twelfth century, and the leases, at the end of the century, under the influence of the revival of Roman law, were called emphyteutic. But unlike the Roman emphyteusis, or long lease, and Italian medieval contracts, these were leases in perpetuity, which gave the tenant very strong rights in his tenure.

[5] M. Bourin-Derruau, *Villages médiévaux en Bas-Languedoc: genèse d'une sociabilité* (Paris, 1987), vol. II, *La démocratie au village*, 265–82, 402–11.

[6] G. Brunel, O. Guyotjean, and J. M. Moriceau (eds), *Terriers et plans terriers du XIIIe au XVIIIe s. Actes du colloque de Paris (23–25 septembre 1998)*, (Bibliothèque d'histoire rurale, Rennes-Paris-Geneva, 2002).

Mediterranean landscape.[7] Each tenant made 'recognizance' to the lord for one or more houses and a number of plots scattered in various *terroirs*. It was the number as well as the average size of plots that determined the hierarchy of land ownership.

In Conas, a village in the valley of the Hérault, for which we can collate the information in several terriers,[8] the situation is as follows:

> 5 per cent of the population held a quarter of the land;
> a third of the population held slightly more than half of the land;
> the rest, a little less than two-thirds, held a fifth of the land.

In the absence of court records, we have no way of knowing how many persons were without land.

How does this stratification differ from the overall estimates given by Rodney Hilton in the early 1980s for the same period in England?[9] Hilton estimated the village elite, those who held between 12 and 20 hectares of land, at about 20 per cent of the population; in Languedoc the elite appears smaller. But the middling landowners seem to form a solid and substantial group; intensive farming practices, vines and gardens, probably made it possible for them to avoid subordination to the elite.

Landholding seems to have been highly volatile in the first half of the fourteenth century. There are many signs of this, in particular when we compare terriers drawn up at intervals of a few years: these reveal a very high turnover of tenants, which is not a consequence of an instability of personal names.

An analysis of land transfers shows that familial readjustments, such as sales within the family or sales by widows, following some unforeseen misfortune, constituted only a tiny proportion of all transactions, less than 10 per cent. The sellers and buyers of land were different people; it was therefore a market with winners and losers. A few sales were intended to pay off debts, such as that by a tenant who appears to have embarked on an unsuccessful project to convert his land to vines.[10] Some of the debts were owed to urban creditors. The buyers were for the most part priests, notaries or artisans.

---

[7] This model, described many times since, was especially well defined by one of the first authors to show interest in it: P. Toubert, *Les structures du Latium médiéval. Le Latium méridional et la Sabine du Xe siècle à la fin du XIIe siècle* (Rome-Paris, 1973), vol. I, 200–337.

[8] Bourin-Derruau, *Villages médiévaux en Bas-Languedoc*, vol. II, 226–31. The village concerned is some 20 km north of Béziers.

[9] Hilton, 'Communautés villageoises', 127.

[10] Archives du Vatican, Registri Avenionenses 122, fols 491–6v.

These were all men with strong links with the archiepiscopal lordship which employed them. The inhabitants of towns were not directly involved.

The land market was more active in large villages, and even more so in the *bourgades*. It was related, therefore, more to the intensity of secondary or tertiary activities than to the effects of agricultural production. Overall, it seems not to reveal either major reversals of fortune or the spectacular creation of new landed fortunes. The price of land was low, suggesting that demand was not higher than the amount of land available to sell.

The wealth of the elite: land or credit?

This situation is probably due in part to the fact that agricultural production was only one of the interests of the village elites, as the will of Bonnet de Saissac nicely demonstrates.[11] This rich man, who left his property to the monastery of Prouille, was a miller and the son of a miller. He had no arable land; his grain came from the multure. He had a few vines and some livestock, leased out *en gasaille*.[12] But above all he owned debts and his financial activities were certainly more profitable than his viticulture. He was also *bayle*[13] of the monastery of Prouille in Saissac, in line with the long-established practice by which the village elites served as intermediaries for lordship.

Landed revenues seem not to have been central to the process of enrichment and growth, even if they supported them; nor does the village elite seem to have been characterized by a rapacious acquisition of land. In any case the landed property of this elite differed more markedly from that of the nobles and lords than from that of the 'middling' villagers. At the centre of the village lands, a few very big plots, including the best soils, mark aristocratic landowning in the landscape; these plots were called *condamina*. By their size and by their status,[14] which put them beyond the regulation of custom, they formed a threshold between the nobles of old descent and other 'rich'

---

[11] Jean Guiraud (ed.), *Cartulaire de Notre-Dame de Prouille* (Paris, 1907), vol. II, 14–16.

[12] The *gasaille* or livestock lease was a contract by which animals were put out to a livestock farmer and, at the end of the contract, shared between lessor and lessee, with the natural increase, according to fixed rules.

[13] The *bayle* (*bajulus*) was the representative of the lord in all the administrative and financial aspects of seigneurial power; the exercise of justice, when not performed by the lord, was entrusted to a judge.

[14] The principle by which the nobility escaped the *alivrement*, or valuation of landed property, basis for the distribution of the *taille*, is not, however, attested in all villages in the fifteenth century, when the *livres d'estime* which recorded the declarations of the inhabitants and the valuations of their property, survive in large numbers for Languedocian villages. In some villages, for a long time and not without conflict, the property deemed

landowners; they were carefully tended by their owners. Only their peers were able, by credit, to wrest them from the original owners.

The 'new rich', merchants, butchers and also a few peasants, acquired land, but not the *condamina* of the nobles. Similarly, they bought rents, but the taxes on land transfers were retained by the lords.[15]

The village community in the Languedocian sources: the Toulousain and Mediterranean Languedoc

The sources for Languedoc may be lacking in density and depth for a discussion of the land market or the financial stability of lordships, but they still offer a means of approach to the functioning of the community; which might better be called something like 'university', since the juridical term used was *universitas*. In fact the sources for the 'community' are the most original element in the documentation for this region, even more precocious than for Provence. But they are of different types in the western and eastern (or Mediterranean) parts of Languedoc.

The west: the region of *chartes de franchise*

The west, what might be called Gascon Languedoc, was a region of *chartes de franchise* (charters of liberties). About two hundred of these have survived, dating from between 1100 and 1350. Only fifteen concern towns; the *chartes* are primarily a document of peasants and their lords. They are rich texts, often long, sometimes with a preamble, and usually including a wide variety of clauses recording a range of concessions. They have been much studied, and are currently the subject of a project at the University of Toulouse.[16] It is well known that these charters can be deceptive. They summarize, at a crucial moment when it was committed to writing, what was an often hidden or gradual evolution, a conflictual dialogue constantly being renewed between lords and villagers, which the *chartes* are at pains to conceal. They are also deceptive in that they describe a theoretical state and not its operation in reality. And they are deceptive, lastly, because the *charte* is a sort of stage-managed presentation of relations between lord and community. All the

---

noble—that is, owned by the nobles when the system of *alivrement* was instituted—was exempt from payment of the *taille*; in others, the *condamina* were subject to the *taille*.

[15] Except for the rare cases where these new rich had managed to acquire a whole lordship, lands (*condamina*), rents and taxes on land transfers.

[16] M. Mousnier, 'Seigneurs en quête d'*universitas* dans la France méridionale: de la corne d'abondance à la fontaine de miséricorde', in M. Bourin and P. Martinez Sopena (eds), *Pour une anthropologie du prélèvement seigneurial: les mots, les temps, les lieux. Actes du colloque de Jaca, 5–9 juin 2002* (Paris, 2007), 197–228.

same, they are of particular interest for the subject of my article because they show us peasants in action, and not only the complaints of the dominated. But which peasants? The *chartes* assert a unanimity on the part of the community which we should take note of, but also, of course, question.[17]

These customs were always granted to a single village community, and not a group of communities, even by a great lord or prince. They refer to an exclusive lord/community relationship. Joint ownership was very common in this region, but if many lords were associated, they dealt as one single authority with a community whose unity was affirmed.

The *chartes de franchise* were granted to communities which appear to be at different stages in their formation as legal entities. Sometimes the *charte* was granted to a community called a *universitas*, which might be represented by consuls. In other cases it was granted simply to the men of such and such a place (rarely women, because the communities were almost exclusively masculine) or to the inhabitants. The *chartes de franchise*, at least in the state in which they have come down to us, were a powerful boost to the identity of the communities concerned, but did not always mark their official birth.

In this region, the *chartes de franchise* never define the composition of the community. Was it necessary to hold land to be a member of it? Did it have to be a legal body? Did it have to participate in common taxes? Nothing in the texts of the *chartes* throws light on this.

Between a community and its lord (or lords), the *chartes* evoke the reciprocity of love and loyalty, even if seigneurial domination is left in no doubt.[18] But the grant might be made in return for services rendered by the community. Above all, it was generally bought, and bought dearly. The *charte de franchise* can be seen as an exceptional, but heavy, form of seigneurial taxation. The overt objective was often the common profit and good, especially after the middle of the thirteenth century. The general principle is a modification of seigneurial taxation for a lump sum, probably in whatever way best suited the lords and their peasant interlocutors.

---

[17] These observations are taken from B. Cursente, 'Franchises et prélèvement dans le France des XIIe et XIIIe siècles', in M. Bourin and P. Martinez Sopena (eds), *Pour une anthropologie du prélèvement seigneurial, dans le campagnes médiévales (Xie–XIVe s.). Réalités et représentations paysannes* (Paris, 2004), 115–32.

[18] The existence of these *chartes de franchises*, in their own peculiar style, together with the frequent absence of other documents, especially those revealing actual practice or judicial documents, helps to give relations between lords and peasants a much more serene, even irenic, image than that emerging from the English documents used by Rodney Hilton.

That it was the village elites who were in dialogue with their lord or lords is clear, which provokes two observations. First, how far was the new tax system, which was often the key element in the measures recorded in the *charte*, to the benefit of the community, and how far to that of this elite? Second, the *chartes* are all strongly marked by notarial influence, which is a reminder of the role of notaries within the elite; they appear as its most important element, perhaps because they are most visible in the written documentation.

The functioning of village communities in Mediterranean Languedoc

It is easier to pursue these two points on the basis of the documentation for Mediterranean Languedoc. Here the documents are of a different type. If *chartes de franchise* existed, they have virtually disappeared. A rare example, that of Laurens, survives in a late copy, the original of which has been lost, indicative in itself of the small importance attached to it.[19]

Yet the village communities are present in the archives of the late thirteenth and even more the early fourteenth centuries. As in Gascon Languedoc, they developed institutions in the form of rural consulates, which are first visible in the mid-thirteenth century. West of Carcassonne these consulates are subject to and appointed by the lords,[20] but between Carcassonne and Montpellier they enjoyed real autonomy, and were required only to swear an oath. A few of these villages have preserved fragments of their archives, which the consuls stored in a chest (*archa*), though where these were kept is not clear.[21] In this region, where writing was extensively used for public and even more for private business, we have to imagine a different and perhaps more flexible type of relationship with the lords than that characteristic of the regions of the *chartes de franchise*.

The sphere of operation of the community might differ slightly from one village to another but as a general rule the lord delegated to it everything that concerned the administration of communal life, the policing of the territory and the internal division of taxes, in particular the *tailles* (tallages). The consuls, with their council, applied custom and were in a sense the executives

---

[19] The paper copies date from 1640 and 1663: Archives Départementales de l'Hérault I E 110; the text has been published and discussed by Marcel and André Gouron, 'Un affranchissement de serfs à Laurens (1270)', in *Hommage à André Dupont. Etudes médiévales languedociennes* (Fédération Historique du Languedoc Méditerranéen et du Roussillon, Montpellier, 1974), 159–66.

[20] J. Ramière de Fortanier, *Recueil de documents relatifs à l'histoire du droit municipal en France: chartes de franchises du Lauraguais* (Paris, 1939).

[21] The communities had as yet no consular houses at this early stage in their existence.

of the community. The agreement of the inhabitants, and usually the lord, was necessary for any alteration to this custom and for any innovations, hence for all regulation of internal and external disputes.

To this end, the community had to meet; and the records of this *parlement* are instructive.[22] The meeting was summoned by a public crier and held in a church or some other customary venue. The official record noted both the quorum (three-quarters or more of the *universitas*) and the names of those present. Ecclesiastics never participated, but could be observers. Depending on the village, the knights who were not lords might take part, or constitute a separate order and elect their own representative.[23]

The order and the form of the list of names was important. A small number of lists have a very specific structure: they are juxtapositions of groups of close male relatives, with the nature of the relationship indicated. Lists of this type are characteristic of villages which had as yet acquired little autonomy, some-times even of villages that had remained servile, especially in the region of Narbonne.[24] But for the great majority of these *parlements*, the community consisted of the coming together of individually listed heads of household. The order in which those present was recorded was clearly hierarchical, at least for those who came first, the former consuls and local notables. Not all those attending carried the same weight. But the listing of the rest of the names by the notary was not strictly hierarchical and it allowed for ties of neighbourhood, friendship and family.

The village elite in the functioning of the community

The construction of the village elite was far from simple. In little *castra*, of a few dozen households, it was extremely restricted and the same names recur in every capacity. In big villages, swollen by demographic growth, the elite consisted of several strata. The nobles were a group apart, even if they parti-cipated in the *parlement* and were sometimes consuls. At the highest level came either the consul or the lord's *bayle*. This had to be a man who was solvent, capable of expressing himself with reasonable facility and in a posi-tion to devote time to community affairs, in particular to represent it in judicial matters, above all in appeals. It was probably also essential for a consul or *bayle* to come from an old local family, which is suggested by the

---

[22] The texts use the word *parlamentum*.

[23] For these points see, Bourin, *Villages médiévaux en Bas-Languedoc*, vol. II, *Démocratie au village*.

[24] M. Bourin-Derruau, 'Village Communities of the Plain and the Mountain in Languedoc ca 1300', in K. L. Reyerson and J. Drendel (eds), *Urban and Rural Communities in Medieval France: Provence and Languedoc, 1000–1500* (Brill, 1998), 131–62.

fact that the most frequently recurring village surnames were also those of the consuls, although not all consuls enjoyed significant family support. It was also necessary to want to take on these responsibilities. Not all who were qualified by their social position or membership of an old village family were so inclined.

Some fifteen or twenty advisers, former consuls or permanent councillors, supported the consul. These men clearly came from a fairly large group of *probi homines*, 'wise men' who could be counted on to give sound advice. They made up about a quarter of the population present at the *parlements*, and were probably those, as at Conas, who had the most land. They were also witnesses to transactions, assessors for the payment of *bans*,[25] appraisers of property, apportioners of the *taille*, jurors at inquests and rectors of charitable bodies. With the emergence of consuls, institutions—a consulate and its council—were added to the initial, more informal, forms of the community. In this early phase in the history of the communities, the more or less fluid group of the *probi viri* advised and directed it, even if they were unable to represent it formally.[26]

The election of consuls took various forms but always boiled down to a choice by a small group which was then ratified by the *parlement*. Nevertheless, specific crises apart, of which only a small number are known, the impression is not one of a gulf between the group consisting of consuls, former consuls and their families and the other *probi viri* and middling villagers.

It would therefore be improper to assume in principle that this elite were *potentes* exploiting to their own advantage their position as intermediaries between lord and village. In agrarian matters in particular, they were anxious to abolish ownership boundaries so that the fields could be open for common pasture. In many disputes the whole community was united against neighbouring villages. The other type of conflict, especially in the communities whose boundaries included large uncultivated areas, set the whole community against the lord if he tried to lease them to outsiders.

---

[25] The *bans* were the sums paid for infractions of the customs regulating agriculture. The offender paid the *ban* (fine) to the lord (or to the community, in the rare cases where this concession had been won from the lord) and paid the *tales* (damages) to the victim at a level decided by the village 'assessors'.

[26] During the thirteenth century the term *probi viri*, always in the plural, replaced that of *boni homines*, which was older and, more importantly, more ambiguous in its social content because also applied to members of the high aristocracy. See M. Bourin-Derruau, 'Les *boni homines* de l'an mil', in *La justice en l'an mil* (La Documentation Française, Paris, 2003), 53–66.

If we compare Languedoc to England, the first impression is that Languedocian communities had a more peaceful internal atmosphere than those of the English midlands described by Rodney Hilton. This is, in part, only a question of sources; English manorial records, particularly those which tell us about justice, give us evidence about internal conflict which notarial documentation, orientated as it is towards communal government, inevitably elides. But it seems to me that the difference is also one of periodization. The late twelfth and thirteenth centuries in Languedoc appear to be a period in which there was a dynamic of relative mutual confidence between local elites and their neighbours, perhaps because the role of interlocutor between lords and villagers gave an obviously useful social role to elites. Even their activity as money-lenders does not seem to have been seen as negatively as later, when discourses against usury (particularly by Jews) multiply. It was only from the years 1325–30 that tensions show themselves in Languedoc, above all in towns but also in some villages, and they grew from that time on. The violent demographic fall following the Black Death did not put an end to the rise in social violence, and the poverty of the countryside, which had to pay for both the armies of the Hundred Years' War and the royal treasury, exacerbated it further. Even then, however, it is hard to generalize; local circumstances, including immediate personal relationships, made potential conflicts more, or less, serious in different localities. Let us finish by looking briefly at this later period.

Disputes deriving from the fiscal policies of the fourteenth century

The unanimity of the thirteenth century in Languedoc was undermined, especially after 1325, when the majority of consulates embarked on expensive policies involving a variety of purchases, for example of franchises,[27] common lands, ovens or fairs, or the building of bridges or improvement of roads.[28] These 'investments' were probably of more benefit to some villagers than others. The purchases were also no doubt gratifying to those who aspired to lead the community, bearing the glorious title of consul, and their utility was more obvious to those who administered the community and so saw the advantage of possessing permanent legitimate institutions. The value of this expenditure was far from clear, on the other hand, to those who experienced it principally as an increase in charges.

[27] Here as elsewhere, the king now demanded payment for the concession of a consulate. The communities which had failed to get this right recognized by 1270, or even before the reign of Philip the Fair (1285–1314), were in future obliged to pay dearly for it.

[28] See Bourin, *Villages médiévaux en Bas-Languedoc*, vol. II, *Démocratie au village*.

Further, to these charges were added not only the seigneurial *tailles*, which were familiar and modest, but the first royal tax demands. Taken together over the long term, royal taxation was still low, but in the years when it was demanded the tax burden was significantly increased. The demands of an impecunious monarchy sparked collective responses, organized between neighbouring villages, for example in 1344 against the aid demanded for the king on the occasion of the knighting of his son, regarded as contrary to the customs of Languedoc.[29] But the king was also able to take advantage of local needs, and engaged in sordid but hard bargaining, for example over the issue of the maintenance or suppression of the gabelle on cloth.[30]

As a result, the problem of financial charges on the community and their internal distribution suddenly became pressing. This marked a rupture in the history of the village communities. The same problem arose in urban communities, which were only a little ahead in instituting a degree of fiscal equity by the introduction of a form of proportionality.[31] At this stage, that of the first increases in communal expenditure, many choices were possible. In the case of extraordinary expenses, direct taxation was complemented by indirect taxes, on transport or consumption. As a general rule, the communities relied on indirect taxation, and, while awaiting the arrival of the sums due, resorted to borrowing. They were in debt, but the levels were never unmanageable in the years preceding the Black Death.

For the regular *tailles*, direct taxation was the only solution. It was always the community which was responsible for its collection, this being the simplest solution both for the lords and the king. There remained the problem of the basis of the assessment. The trend was for this basis to be land, with payment according to each household's assessed landed wealth; movables were sometimes taken into account. This system gradually became general, though more rapidly in some places than others, for reasons which seem to

[29] Archives Municipales de Roujan, CC 10 no. 2; Archives Municipales de Pézenas B/3/1/12.
[30] G. Romestan, 'Les consuls de Béziers et l'abolition de la gabelle des draps', in *Béziers et le Biterrois* (Montpellier, 1972), 191–220.
[31] Many works have recently been devoted to taxation, especially urban taxation. See, in particular, *La fiscalité des villes au Moyen Age* (Toulouse, 1996). In the three-volume collection P. Contamine, J. Kerhervé and A. Rigaudière (eds), *L'impôt public au moyen âge fin XII-début XVIe, colloque tenu à Bercy les 14, 15, 16 juin 2000*, Ministère de l'Economie, des Finances et de l'Industrie. Comité pour l'histoire économique et financière de la France (Paris, 2002), see in particular A. Rigaudière, 'Les origines médiévales de l'impôt sur la fortune', vol. I, 227–88. For a specific example, see A. Castaldo, *Le consulat médiéval d'Agde* (Paris, 1974), where the author examines the city's *compoix* (or *livres d'estime*) for the years 1320–30. We should also remember the work of P. Wolff on the *livres d'estime* for Toulouse.

relate primarily to local circumstances or protagonists. However a number of issues remained unresolved. The first concerned the contribution of land-owners from outside; every village tried to make them pay and clashed with the villages to which they belonged. This was one of the most common reasons for the disputes between neighbouring villages that were a way of life for Languedocian communities in the later middle ages. But there was also, in the case of the 'indigenous' landowners, the question of whether there was to be a global assessment or a declaration by each regarding each of his properties. Whatever the case, the decision fell to the body of *talhatores*, who were chosen by the community—which did not mean that it always escaped criticism, or that it was never influenced by their personal animosities. The assessments were not kept up to date and failed to reflect changes in the price of land, fields, vines or meadows. But it has to be said that the majority of villages have left no trace of internal crises in this sphere, any more, for that matter, than in other spheres. Is the prevailing silence a sufficient basis on which to conclude that only a minority of villages were troubled by the question of equitable taxation?

In the long thirteenth century, we see the development of an elite with new features in the villages of Languedoc. It was characterized not so much by its landed wealth as by a wealth based on a multiplicity of activities, especially credit and—even less 'worthy'—artisanal skills. It was instrumental in open-ing the village to the 'new economy', serving as intermediary between the town and the villagers. It was also the intermediary with the lordship and even more with the new powers, princely and royal. This was a role that could only be played thanks to the widespread diffusion within its ranks of new forms of knowledge, which were incarnated in the notary and the frequency of writing, but which extended well beyond and permeated the sense of space, time and numbers.

It is possible that the tensions between this elite and the rest of the popula-tion were masked by the political events which shook Languedoc at this period.[32] But I am inclined to think that the thirteenth century represented

---

[32] I refer here to the conquest of Languedoc by the crusaders of the Albigensian Crusade and the annexation of Bas Languedoc by the king of France in 1228. The area was still shaken by revolts in 1240 and 1242, but there followed, from the end of the 1240s, a real paci-fication, even though this was the heroic age of the capture of the Cathar refuge of Montségur. The tensions persisted, as is shown by the revolt of Carcassonne at the time of Bernard Délicieux, but the old quarrels were essentially, if not forgotten, at least buried. See *Effacement du catharisme? (XIIIe–XIVe s.)*, (Cahiers de Fanjeaux, 20, Toulouse, 1985).

a brief moment of shared belief in new possibilities, a sort of illusion of solidarity and communality. Only after 1325 did the means offered to this elite by the new institutions and various developments draw them, at least in some villages, into an unacceptable and ruinous megalomania.

But it would probably be mistaken to think that, even if this communal existence became more conflictual in the first half of the fourteenth century, after the relative harmony of the second half of the thirteenth, the villages of Languedoc were riven by internal dissension. It was in battles against neighbouring communities that they acquired and felt their identity. A sense of community was quickly restored when a risk emerged of encroachment on the common land or an incursion, voluntary or involuntary, of flocks from outside. Led by the elite, no calmer than the majority, the village rose as one in defence of local interests and went out on the attack against its neighbours, the hereditary enemy.

A Divided Class? Peasants and Peasant Communities in Later Medieval England[1]

Miriam Müller

Few areas in the study of medieval peasants have attracted quite as much disagreement as the debate over peasant communities. Historians cannot escape their own contemporary preoccupations and experiences, and it seems to be particularly in the discussions of communal living that approaches have been influenced by longings for a better world.

One area of concern has been the changes after the Black Death of 1348–9. Some historians have argued that both familial ties and communal bonds were weakened by a rise of individualism in English villages after 1349.[2] They look back to a largely imaginary era of the medieval village, which was defined by cooperation and solidarity, before the demographic collapse, when the village community was torn asunder from the inside by social strife, and from the outside by migration and economic change.[3]

From a different angle, Macfarlane attacked the notion that peasant communities ever existed in later medieval England. He held that the village, even before 1348–9, was dominated by individualistic farmers, who in a proto- or pseudo-capitalistic way were engaged in the pursuit of profit.[4] From this perspective then, later medieval English villages were not inhabited by peasants at all, if they are defined as small agricultural producers who functioned

---

[1] I would like to thank all participants at the Rodney Hilton's Middle Ages Conference for their comments on the earlier version of this paper. I am very grateful to Chris Dyer and Chris Wickham for their helpful and encouraging comments.

[2] See for instance J. A. Raftis, *Warboys: Two Hundred Years in the Life of an English Medieval Village* (Toronto, 1974); E. Britton, *The Community of the Vill. A Study in the History of the Family and Village Life in Fourteenth Century England* (Toronto, 1977); J. A. Raftis, 'Changes in an English Village after the Black Death', *Mediaeval Studies*, 29 (1967), 158–77.

[3] Z. Razi, 'The Toronto School's Reconstruction of Medieval Peasant Society: A Critical View', *Past and Present*, 85 (1979), 141–56.

[4] A. Macfarlane, *The Origins of English Individualism* (Oxford, 1978); see also: A. Macfarlane, 'The Myth of the Peasantry; Family and Economy in a Northern Parish' in R. M. Smith, (ed.), *Land, Kinship and Life-cycle* (Cambridge, 1984), 333–49.

within communities, and were bound together by familial ties and kinship networks.[5]

According to these interpretations the village community either did not exist even before the plague, or was in terminal decline by the later fourteenth century. This latter view in particular, as has been shown by historians like W. Rösener and Christopher Dyer, can be seen as reflecting rather romanticized and idealistic views of the medieval village, which were fashionable mainly in the later nineteenth and twentieth centuries.[6] Writers were reacting to the brutality of industrialization, which drove some, both from the left and the right, to hark back to a largely imagined simpler, cleaner, and more harmonious village life. This view is not perhaps too dissimilar to J. R. R. Tolkien's visions of the simple and idealized life of Hobbiton in the Shire in his Lord of the Rings, and indeed it is a view which still persists to this day. We would therefore be justified in de-romanticizing the medieval village. However, the total denial of the village community takes, as Dyer has argued, the revisionism too far.[7]

Rodney Hilton showed that the peasantry constituted a recognizable class, in effective possession, but not ownership of their holdings. Following largely Marx's analysis in *Capital*, volume 3, Hilton argued that peasants were forced to render dues, rents and services to their lords, not through economic necessity like the modern working-class whose members are forced to sell their labour for wages, but because of the judicial powers of the ruling class.[8] As an

[5] For discussions on the definitions of peasants see for example: E. R. Wolf, *Peasants* (Englewood Cliffs, New Jersey, 1966); T. Scott 'Introduction', in T. Scott (ed.), *The Peasantries of Europe, from the Fourteenth to the Eighteenth Centuries* (London and New York, 1998), 1–19; C. Dyer, *Standards of Living in the Later Middle Ages: Social Change in England c.1200–1520* (Cambridge, 1989) 22–3.

[6] W. Rösener, *Bauern im Mittelalter* (Munich, 1991), 9–12; C. Dyer, 'The English Medieval Village Community and its Decline', *Journal of British Studies*, 33 (1994), 418; C. Dyer, 'Power and Conflict in the Medieval English Village', in C. Dyer, *Everyday Life in Medieval England* (London, 2000 edition), 1.

[7] C. Dyer, 'Power and Conflict', 1.

[8] These relationships have been explored in many papers by Hilton. Among the most recent are the perhaps less well known entries by Hilton in T. Bottomore (ed.), *A Dictionary of Marxist Thought*, 2nd edn (Oxford, 1997), 'Feudal Society', 191–6, and 'Serfdom', 494–6. See also his chapter on 'The Nature of Medieval Peasant Economy', *Bond Men Made Free. Medieval Peasant Movements and the English Rising of 1381* (London and New York, reprinted 2003), 25–62. An excellent summary can also be found in the chapter 'The Peasantry as a Class', in R. H. Hilton, *The English Peasantry in the Later Middle Ages. The Ford Lectures for 1973 and Related Studies* (Oxford, 1975), 3–19. Other examples are: 'Feudalism in Europe: Problems for Historical Materialists',

exploited class, whose surplus was extracted from them by the landlords, peasants did not however constitute a homogeneous mass. Hilton saw divisions and inequalities as part of the dynamics governing the relationships within the peasant class, which were also being influenced by factors exogenous to the peasant community. Hilton explored the nature of the peasant community in the context of relationships between peasant and lord and between different strata of people. Following Lenin's *Development of Capitalism in Russia*, for example, a growth in stratification among late medieval peasants, by the accumulation of land by a minority, was seen as the necessary precursor to the development of agrarian capitalism.[9]

Hilton explored causes for inequality and stratification among peasant communities even before developments of differentiation, which took place at a growing pace in the post-Black Death period. He highlighted factors such as unequal landholding, as well as differences in demands made on individual peasant households by the community or lords, such as the variety of obligations of the free and the unfree, or divisions due to office holding.[10]

Historians have continued to explore divisions in peasant communities, which were far from egalitarian societies. The wealth of individual peasant households could profoundly influence the number of children who survived into adulthood.[11] The village elite, recognizable in manorial records as haywards, reeves, constables and such like, tended to be drawn from the upper ranks of the village community, and such office holding tended to run in families. These local officials found themselves in the often awkward position

---

in *Class Conflict and the Crisis of Feudalism*, 2nd edn (London and New York, 1990), 1–11. See also K. Marx, *Capital Volume 3, A Critique of Political Economy* (London, 1991), esp. ch. 47: 'The genesis of capitalist ground rent', 917–50. For the necessity for extra-economic compulsion in the extraction of surplus from the peasant class see pp. 926–7.

[9] V. I. Lenin, *The Development of Capitalism in Russia*, 2nd edn (Moscow, 1977). R. H. Hilton, 'Reasons for Inequality among Medieval Peasants', in Hilton, *Class Conflict and the Crisis of Feudalism*, 66–78. These discussions are linked to the development of agrarian capitalism. See for instance the discussions published in R. H. Hilton (ed.), *The Transition from Feudalism to Capitalism* (London, 1976); or Hilton's introductory comments in T. H. Aston and C. H. E. Philpin (eds), *The Brenner Debate. Agrarian Class Structure and Economic Development in Pre-industrial Europe* (Cambridge, reprinted 1993), 1–9.

[10] See especially Hilton, *English Peasantry*, 20–36, see also: his 'Reasons for Inequality', 66–78; A detailed discussion can also be found in Hilton, *Bond Men Made Free*, esp. 32–8.

[11] Z. Razi, *Life, Marriage and Death in a Medieval Parish; Economy, Society and Demography in Halesowen 1270–1400* (Cambridge, 1980), 71–93.

of mediating between their neighbours, the lords and the state, but they could exert a profound influence on local communal affairs.[12]

Others have explored the nature of intra- and inter-familial conflicts within peasant communities, examining factors of gender and the influence of local customs, such as the rules of inheritance.[13] Some have explored borrowing and lending, activities which, as Hilton has shown, seem to combine elements both of cooperation and conflict.[14] Inequalities in wealth and status in peasant communities also meant that the poorer cottagers worked for their wealthier peasant neighbours for wages.

These inequalities between poor and rich in particular have led some to argue that internal differences were more important to peasants than any class divisions between lords and peasants.[15]

Men and women were not equal in village communities, and gender can be cited as another divisive factor. Hilton, as probably the first historian to devote a whole chapter to the role of peasant women in their communities, bemoaned the fact that it was necessary to devote separate space to discuss half the members of the class.[16] For Hilton, however any such divisions and

---

[12] Dyer, 'Power and Conflict', 1–11, esp. 7; C. Dyer, 'Taxation and Communities in Late Medieval England', in J. Hatcher and R. Britnell (eds), *Progress and Problems in Medieval England. Essays in Honour of Edward Miller* (Cambridge, 1996), 168–190. See also the contributions to the subject area of families, status, and stratification by E. Britton, *The Community of the Vill*; E. B. DeWindt, *Land and People in Holywell-cum-Needingworth, Structures of Tenure and Patterns of Social Organisation in an East Midlands Village* (Toronto, 1972) and Raftis, *Warboys*.

[13] R. M. Smith, 'Kin and Neighbors in a Thirteenth-Century Suffolk Community', *Journal of Family History*, 4 (1979), 219–56, reprinted in: G. Crow (ed.), *The Sociology of Rural Communities*, vol. 1 (Cheltenham, 1996), 244–81; B. A. Hanawalt, 'The Peasant Family and Crime in Fourteenth-Century England', *Journal of British Studies*, 13 (1974), 1–18; M. Müller, 'Conflict, Strife, and Cooperation: Aspects of the Late Medieval Family and Household', in I. Davis, M. Müller, and S. Rees Jones (eds), *Love, Marriage and Family Ties in the Later Middle Ages* (Turnhout, 2003), 311–29; B. A. Hanawalt, *Crime and Conflict in English Communities* (London, 1979); B. A. Hanawalt, *The Ties that Bound: Peasant Families in Medieval England* (Oxford, 1986).

[14] P. R. Schofield, 'Dearth, Debt and the Local Land Market in a Late Thirteenth-Century Village Community', *Agricultural History Review*, 45 (1997), 1–17; P. R. Schofield, 'Access to Credit in the Early Fourteenth-Century Countryside', in P. R. Schofield and N. J. Mayhew (eds), *Credit and Debt in Medieval England c.1180–c.1350* (Oxbow Books, 2002); Hilton, *The English Peasantry in the Later Middle Ages*, esp. 44–53.

[15] Britton, *The Community of the Vill*, esp. 168–72, and 122–3.

[16] Hilton, *English Peasantry*, 95.

inequalities should be seen and analysed in the context of wider class relationships.

The 'community' operated on different levels and in varying contexts, and can be defined in various ways.[17] One could talk about a religious community, based on the parish, local churches and fraternities, and brought together by religious rituals and festivals.[18] In the secular sphere it makes sense to talk about a village and a manorial community, one defined primarily by territory and local government, and one by lordship and jurisdiction.[19] The 'different' communal levels (village, parish, manor) overlapped significantly. In some cases they coincided to such an extent that they could be one and the same. I will concentrate here on the secular aspects of peasant society, the village and the manorial communities.

Manorial court records allow excellent insights into the daily lives of peasants albeit through the constant prism of lordship, in whose interest the documents were compiled. This paper uses these records to explore some aspects of internal divisions within village communities and ask whether it is appropriate to speak of the peasantry as a class, or whether they were hopelessly divided.

I will examine the manorial court evidence for the Suffolk manors of Walsham le Willows, in the hands of two lords in the early fourteenth century, Lady Mary Rose and the de Walsham family, and also Brandon, held by the bishop of Ely. The analysis will include three manors located in Wiltshire, namely Longbridge Deverill, Monkton Deverill and Badbury, all held by the abbot of Glastonbury. Rather than focusing on the problematic areas highlighted earlier, associated with developments in the post- Black Death period, this essay will instead raise some general themes relating to social friction, possible points for comparisons, and further research.

The nature of peasant communities

Just as peasants were not some homogeneous mass, neither were the communities in which they lived. The level of rents, extracted from peasants by lords,

---

[17] For a discussion about defining the 'community' see P. R. Schofield, *Peasant and Community in Medieval England 1200–1500* (Basingstoke and New York, 2003), 5–7.

[18] For a discussion of the parish in relation to peasant communities see Dyer, 'Medieval Village Community', esp. 413; C. Dyer, *An Age of Transition? Economy and Society in England in the Later Middle Ages* (Oxford, 2005), 56–8. P. R. Schofield, *Peasant and Community*, 186–212.

[19] See on the village and the manor Dyer 'Medieval Village Community', 408.

depended to some degree on the type of lord, the local economy and the ability of the peasant class to resist the various demands of lordship.[20] The nature of peasant resistance and the ability of peasants to more or less successfully counter seigneurial demands also has to be contextualized in individual styles of lordship. Larger ecclesiastical lords tended to have a reputation for conservatism, especially the regime of the Abbey of Glastonbury and the Bishopric of Ely, whereas smaller, and perhaps lay lords may have been more amenable. Local differences could impact on the local economy, but also influence peasant cultures, mentalities and possibly even the outlook and aims of peasants in popular revolts.

The topography of communities could also influence the nature of local hierarchies, divisions, cooperation and kinship networks.[21] Compact settlements where manor and village coincided, such as Badbury or Brandon, would experience different internal dynamics from communities which comprised a number of smaller hamlets, brought together by one manorial court and joint agricultural production.

Urban characteristics also influenced communities, and I would include here smaller market villages, such as Brandon in Suffolk, which show some signs of urbanization, while still being more firmly rooted in agricultural production.[22] In such villages there was more occupational diversity, for example in Brandon we find a taverner, shoemakers, and the occasional travelling merchant, or dealers of wool, among a range of trades and crafts.

Proximity to larger towns could influence production for the market as well as patterns of mobility, marriage and the circulation of news and gossip. The pull of London together with the commercialism prevalent in the East Anglian region, for example, has been cited as an important precipitating factor in the region's strong engagement in the rising of 1381, as economic changes and pressures clashed perhaps more clearly and strikingly here than in other areas with remaining ties of bondage.[23] Communities depending

---

[20] For the importance of resistance to rents see for instance Hilton, 'Feudalism in Europe', 4–6.

[21] Some studies indicate that local inheritance structures could influence the nature and extent of intra-familial conflicts. Smith, 'Kin and Neighbors', 219–56; B. A. Hanawalt, 'Peasant Family and Crime', 1–18.

[22] See for a stronger position on Brandon's urbanism: M. Bailey, 'Trade and Town in Medieval England: New Insights from Familiar Sources', *The Local Historian*, 29 (1999), 194–211.

[23] See especially Hilton, *Bond Men Made Free*, 166–74.

mainly on agriculture, such as Badbury, might have been more inward looking, parochial but perhaps more cohesive.[24]

Economic specialization in the region could also affect communities. The
Wyle river valley was probably one of the more commercialized areas in
Wiltshire, where fulling mills could be found in numbers along the river.[25]
This specialization is reflected in occupational surnames like 'Wybbe' and
'Touker' in the Glastonbury manors of Monkton Deverill and Longbridge
Deverill.[26]

Internal stratification was based on the varied size of tenants' holdings.
Villages contained smallholdings, middling-sized tenements and larger holdings of about thirty acres or more. The size of holdings could be an indicator
of wealth and status, but not always. Some smallholders could have alternative sources of income, which gave them a special role in the village, such as
smiths. Other smallholders were genuinely impoverished, eking out a living
from small plots of land and supplementing their incomes by unskilled wage
labour.

The divisions in wealth could be quite marked, as can be seen in tax records.
Although the poorest members of communities would have been exempt
from taxation, we can gain some insights by comparing the middling and
upper strata of the communities. Some villages, especially in the densely
settled areas like East Anglia had larger numbers of smallholders and hence
perhaps poorer peasants than some villages in more thinly settled regions,
such as Wiltshire. In the Liberty of Longbridge Deverill in Wiltshire forty-two

---

[24] One might consider here Badbury's appeal to ancient demesne status: M. Müller,
'The Aims and Organisation of a Peasant Revolt in Early Fourteenth-Century
Wiltshire', *Rural History*, 14 (2003), 1–20; see also R. Faith, ' "The Great Rumour" of
1377 and Peasant Ideology', in R. H. Hilton and T. H. Aston (eds), *The English Rising of
1381* (Cambridge, 1984) 43–73.

[25] E. M. Carus-Wilson has argued that in the south-western area of Wiltshire was an 'emerging . . . specialised clothmaking area', which is apparent from the evidence of occupational surnames in the fourteenth century. E. M. Carus-Wilson, 'The Woollen Industry
before 1550', in E. Crittall, (ed.), *Victoria County History, A History of Wiltshire, Volume
IV* (London, 1959), 122. For fulling mills along the Wyle River see 116, 119–20.

[26] Examples can be found in a roll dated 1299, Glastonbury Abbey Documents held at
Longleat House, sourced from microfilm prepared by Cedric Chivers Ltd Portway,
Bath, 1981 (hereafter cited as GADL) MS 9629, Skin 1, where a certain Stephen Fulling
is also mentioned. A certain Andrew le Touker is mentioned in Longbridge Deverill MS
9633 Skin 5, and William Toukere in the Liberty of Longbridge Deverill. D. A. Crowley
(ed.), *The Wiltshire Tax List of 1332* (Wiltshire Record Society, 45, 1989), 23.

taxpayers were recorded when the lay subsidy was collected in 1332, and of these over 16 per cent paid 4s. or more, and three paid a substantial tax of 6s. or more.[27] At the Wiltshire village of Badbury thirty-two taxpayers were recorded, of whom rather more, namely just over 21 per cent paid taxes of 4s. or more.[28]

At Brandon in Suffolk the lay subsidy return for the twentieth of 1327 lists thirty-nine taxpayers at the manor. Here five taxpayers (12.8 per cent) had a total taxable wealth of 91s. or more (paying in excess of 4s.6d.), but none of Badbury's taxpayers was this wealthy. At the same time only 37.8 per cent of Brandon's taxpayers had a taxable wealth of between 60s. and 21s., and 41 per cent of Brandon's taxpayers had a taxable wealth of 20s. or less. At Badbury 53.1 per cent of taxpayers had a taxable wealth of between 60s. and 21s., and 25 per cent had a taxable wealth of 20s. or less.[29]

It is therefore possible to conclude that in the more urbanized manor in the comparatively commercialized region of Suffolk we appear to find a wider range in the distribution of wealth among the lower to middling and upper income peasants than at the more remote and agricultural village of Badbury. Here we find fewer rich peasants, but a more sizeable middling income block, which is very thin in Brandon. Larger settlements with urban features and regular markets might also contain numerous landless or nearly landless inhabitants.

Internal stratification was linked to local inheritance customs. A manor where partible inheritance was practised would probably produce more smallholders than a manor where primogeniture was the norm. However, the effects of this should not be exaggerated, as it has been shown that peasants in communities where a single son inherited often arranged for non-inheriting offspring to acquire some land.[30] Divisions in wealth could also be masked through kinship ties, by providing loans and credit to the less well off or by providing non-inheriting children or other relatives with financial means to set up their holdings, or indeed through marriage arrangements. On the other hand non-inheriting children of substantial peasants could also sink into smallholdership. The effect these fluid structures had should not be underestimated, as peasant communities were not static. They meant that

---

[27] Crowley, *Tax List of 1332*, 23–4.

[28] Crowley, *Tax List of 1332*, 24.

[29] S. H. A. Hervey (ed.) *Suffolk in 1327; being a Subsidy Return* (Suffolk Green Books, 9, 1906), 196–7.

[30] Z. Razi, 'Family, Land and the Village Community in Later Medieval England', *Past and Present*, 93 (1981), 3–36; see also Razi, *Life, Marriage and Death in a Medieval Parish*, 50–1.

permanent divisions between different peasant strata were highly unlikely.[31]

Inheritance structures also influenced gender relationships by disadvantaging peasant women. Invariably they were only able to inherit land in the absence of sons, or in widowhood. This does not mean, however, that there were no unmarried women in peasant societies participating fully in most economic and social activities. Women could and did take up or buy land, and lease land, or sell it in their own right, and even if they were married they were rarely without rights over land in manorial customs.

In Walsham le Willows, for example, husbands were prevented from simply alienating land held jointly with their wives, and some rather extraordinary court roll entries tell us how the halimote felt it had to make sure that the woman in such cases had not agreed to the alienation after undue pressure had been placed on her by her husband. In 1366, for example, John Margery and his wife Hilary Margery surrendered 12½ acres of land in addition to 2 acres of meadow, 1 acre of woodland and a ½ messuage, which they held in bondage, for the joint use of their daughters Joan and Alice.[32] The land had been surrendered outside the formal framework of the manor court, but in the due presence of the hayward together with various other witnesses of the homage. The court entry then states that 'the jurors were asked if Hilary was of sound mind at the time of the surrender, and whether she made the surrender under coercion, threats or duress from John her husband.'[33] The court was reassured, and it was declared that Hilary had been 'duly examined beyond doubt in accordance with the custom of the manor from time immemorial'. It was therefore concluded that Hilary had 'freely consented to the surrender . . . without duress, coercion or flattery from her husband', and the land was thereby granted to Joan and Alice.[34] This case shows implicitly that the community recognized that the relationship between husbands and their wives was not an equal one, but that this did not mean that the husband could do with their assets as he wished without his wife's consent.

If a woman was married however, her husband was regarded as the head of the household, at least as far as the lord was concerned. It was therefore he who was held answerable to the lord for the household's holding as well as any dues, rents and customs falling on it. Female tenants were far from uncommon, but they were in a minority. In Longbridge Deverill only 2.4 per cent of

---

[31] Müller, 'Conflict, Strife and Cooperation', 316–17.

[32] The feminine surname 'Margery' is also of interest here. Perhaps John and Hilary gained their holdings through a female line?

[33] R. Lock (ed.), *The Court Rolls of Walsham le Willows 1351–1399* (Suffolk Records Society, 45, 2002) 83–4.

[34] Ibid, 84.

lay subsidy taxpayers were women, while in Badbury 15 per cent of taxpayers were female. Two of Badbury's taxpaying female tenants were rather well off, one paying 6s. 9¾ d. and another paying 5s.4d. in taxes. Women were therefore less likely to be found as tenants in their own right especially in the upper echelons of the village community. However, depending on the locality the representation could differ, and some unmarried women were clearly able to run their tenements while sustaining a decent level of income.

Women could not become local officials, such as reeves or haywards, and were therefore barred from the formal framework of much of village government. The formal tithing excluded females as all males were sworn at the age of twelve. This does not mean, however, that they were without duties and responsibilities in the village. Women participated in various forms of community policing, raising the hue and cry upon the discovery of offences committed within the village.[35] Brides also often paid for their own marriage licences, suggesting a degree at least of autonomy or spending power.[36] In this context historians have also highlighted the important role women played in the processing and retailing of food and drink, especially brewing and selling ale.[37]

In peasant communities a certain amount of cooperation was necessary, especially where open-field systems were in operation. In all communities severe divisions and strife could be detrimental to those living within them and to some degree it was in the interest of individual households and the community to attempt to cooperate, as survival depended on it.[38]

Lordship played an important role in the cohesiveness of a manorial community, which might or might not overlap with the village community. A village might be divided between two lordships, like Walsham le Willows. The manor court was merely an official, public instrument of social control run essentially in the interests of the lord, but sometimes it is possible to gain

---

[35] M. Müller, 'Social Control and the Hue and Cry in Two Fourteenth Century Villages', *Journal of Medieval History*, 31 (2005), 29–53.

[36] See for instance: J. M. Bennett, 'Medieval Peasant Marriage: An Examination of Marriage Licence Fines in Liber Gersumarum', in J. A. Raftis (ed.), *Pathways to Medieval Peasants* (Toronto, 1981), 193–246, E. Clark, 'The Decision to Marry in Thirteenth and Early Fourteenth-Century Norfolk', *Mediaeval Studies*, 49 (1987), 496–516.

[37] J. M. Bennett, 'The Village Ale-wife: Women and Brewing in Fourteenth Century England', in B. A. Hanawalt (ed.), *Women and Work in Pre-industrial Europe* (Indiana, 1986), 20–36, J. M. Bennett, *Ale, Beer, and Brewsters in England: Women's Work in a Changing World* (Oxford, 1996). See also R. H. Hilton, 'Women Traders in Medieval England', in Hilton, *Class Conflict and the Crisis of Feudalism*, 132–42.

[38] These issues have been explored in a number of studies. See for example: Dyer, *Standards of Living* esp. 22–3; Hilton, *Bond Men Made Free*, esp. 29–31.

an insight into a lord's view of the community. Manor courts at Badbury at times referred to, for example, the 'whole vill of Badbury', hence meaning those who comprised the village community, who had certain joint responsibilities, and had demands placed on them by lords. The lord therefore acknowledged the collective character of the villagers and sought to make use of this.

The manors of Monkton and Longbridge Deverill, while being separate settlements alongside the Wyle river, often attended a joint manorial court. The identification between manor, village and community may have overlapped significantly, as peasants from both communities frequently met together in the manorial courts. However, even here it was plain that while the fortunes of the two villages were closely intertwined, the manor court rolls separated Monkton and Longbridge business under clear subheadings.

Class conflict and peasant strife

From a Marxist view the village community can be seen as a crucial testing ground for class loyalties and solidarity. Demands of lordship fell both on individual tenements, but also at times on the community as a whole. Customs furthermore dictated that, excepting special agreements and circumstances, all tenants of like standing and holding size owed similar if not identical services and customs.

Shared experiences of manorial customs and obligations falling on everyone potentially unified the manorial community. Ultimately all the peasants of one community had similar cultural and economic experiences. They pursued small-scale agriculture, and they were subject to the same type of lordship. Groups of tenants had identical rents and demands for services, while all tenants might also be expected to join in the payment of tallage. In this sense poorer or richer peasant families found themselves in very similar situations as were individual households, whether they were headed either by a male or a female.

Peasant revolts have frequently been found to be organized at the village level, even when they extended themselves across wider regions. The village community, then, could act as a basis for organizing class struggle. Divisions, or stratifications were often reflected in peasant unrest, and research into the organization of peasant revolts has often shown that its leadership was composed of the village elite.[39]

---

[39] Examples might be found in the local organization of large-scale revolts, such as the rising of 1381, but also cases of perhaps less dramatic local unrest. The literature on popular revolts in the later medieval period is extensive. On these topics in particular see for instance: Hilton, *Bond Men Made Free*, esp. 214–32; Hilton and Aston (eds),

The leading villagers were undoubtedly in a difficult position: on the one side the lord and his agents could exert pressure on them to comply with their demands and on the other the community, including kin and neighbours, expected one of their own to offer them protection or favours. Manorial officials could be targets for anger and frustration, when they were seen to have sided with the oppressor.[40] These tensions could certainly intensify in the post-Black Death period of seigneurial reaction, when many lords were attempting to tighten their grip on the communities, and exert pressure on them via the officials.[41] It is therefore important to differentiate between intra-peasant conflict caused by pressure from lords, and intra-peasant conflict caused by other factors.

At Walsham le Willows no assaults on manorial officials were recorded before the first arrival of the Black Death, but three separate incidents were recorded thereafter. In 1363 John Waunzy assaulted the reeve 'beating him and handling him roughly'. We do not know what the reeve had done to annoy John so much, but John did not deny the charge when he was amerced 40d. In the same year Elias Typetot also assaulted the reeve and threatened him 'in contempt of the lord'. Elias too did not deny the charge and was amerced 2s.[42] Communities could become divided if the local officials were pitted against their neighbours, and we know of cases where seigneurial policies deliberately widened divisions.[43] At the same time we can often observe an increasing, open reluctance by both officials and other members of the community to cooperate with formal court procedures, especially after 1349.

English Rising of 1381; Dyer, 'Medieval Village Community', 416, C. Dyer, 'The Rising of 1381 in Suffolk: Its Origins and Participants', in Dyer, *Everyday Life*, 221–39; B. Cornford, (ed.), *Studies Towards a History of the Rising of 1381 in Norfolk* (Norwich, 1984); H. Eiden, *In der Knechtschaft werdet ihr verharren'; Ursachen und Verlauf des Englischen Bauernaufstandes von 1381*, Historische Forschungen, Band 32 (Trier, 1995); S. Justice, *Writing and Rebellion; England in 1381*(London, 1994); Faith, 'The Great Rumour of 1377'; Müller, 'Aims and Organisation of a Peasant Revolt', 1–20.

[40] A similar reaction perhaps to that observed in working-class communities which acted against strike breakers. In both cases the offending individual was seen to side with the enemy, which could be interpreted as betrayal: E. P. Thompson, *The Making of the English Working Class* (Harmondsworth, 1980), 562–3.

[41] For the seigneurial reaction and growing tensions between lords and peasants see for instance: Dyer, 'The Social and Economic Background to the Rural Revolt of 1381', in Dyer, *Everyday Life*, 191–219, esp.199–214.

[42] Lock (ed.), *Court Rolls of Walsham le Willows 1351–1399*, 71.

[43] R. H. Britnell, 'Feudal Reaction after the Black Death in the Palatinate of Durham', *Past and Present*, 128 (1990), 28–47.

These developments are particularly striking if we compare the evidence of different types of communities. At Brandon in the more commercialized region of Suffolk in the fourteenth century, before the arrival of the Black Death in 1349 a total of 127 cases of defaults from the manor court were recorded (excluding cases which were pardoned by the lord). This amounted to a mean of about four people per recorded year who failed to attend the manorial court which they were obliged to do. After 1349, however, 277 cases of defaults were recorded, a significantly higher figure, in spite of population decline due to the plague, leading to an annual mean average of seven cases.

In the more laid-back manor of Badbury in Wiltshire very similar developments can be observed. Here a mean of four defaults per recorded annum can be found before 1350 and a much increased mean of 10 cases per annum thereafter—recorded defaults more than doubled at this manor despite population decline. The lords of the two manors reacted differently to this growing reluctance of their unfree peasants to cooperate with their courts, which were their main tool for enforcing their rule.

In Brandon licensed withdrawals from attendance at court became very common after 1350. Up to and including 1349 sixteen licensed withdrawals, usually for a specified period of time, were recorded. After the Black Death a total of 155 such licences were recorded. Here the lord was attempting to be flexible. He offered peasants a legal way to absent themselves from court, without giving up his right to suit at court. At Badbury such licensed absences did not exist, and the abbot of Glastonbury was instead fighting an ongoing and increasingly frustrating battle to enforce suit of court. He attempted to achieve this by levying increased amercements from offenders, rising from 2d. or 3d. per head in the early fourteenth century to as much as 12d. in the later 1350s. The policy failed and from the 1360s onwards amercements plummeted down again to 2d. and even 1d. Seigneurial authority was now starting to weaken, and more defaults were now being pardoned, in total 66 per cent of all pardons for defaults after the Black Death were granted between 1370 and 1403. Two contrasting communities were experiencing very similar changing relationships with their lords. In both cases seigneurial control was slackening, and discontent with the manorial court was growing.

Local officials can also be found aiding their neighbours in concealing offences from the lord, or even participating in them. We know that manorial officials often assumed leadership in peasant revolts, but they can similarly be found participating in more mundane forms of daily conflict, of the type described by J. C. Scott as 'weapons of the weak'.[44] For example, at the manor

---

[44] For the local élite taking the lead in revolts see Dyer, 'Rising of 1381 in Suffolk', 225; J. C. Scott, *Weapons of the Weak: Everyday Forms of Peasant Resistance* (Yale University, 1985).

of East Monkton in Wiltshire John de Wyle flattened the lord's meadow with 100 sheep, and because the hayward did nothing about it, the official was amerced 6d.[45] Sometimes the wider community shielded offenders against authority. In Walsham le Willows the whole homage was sometimes presented for having hidden various offences, while on one occasion in 1333 'all the villeins' were amerced 6d. for concealing the fact that Matilda Wodebite and John Packard had failed to perform certain works.[46]

At the manor of Brandon in Suffolk the lord fought an ongoing battle with poachers which the community had a habit of concealing. Before the arrival of the Black Death twenty-three cases of poaching were presented in the manor court. After 1349 presentments rose to forty-five cases and by the 1370s conflict between the lord and his poaching tenants sharpened. In 1372 all chief pledges of Brandon were amerced 40s., because they failed to present the findings of the tithing and for concealing that Stephen son of John Gyboun and John Cavemas had destroyed the lord's warren and had taken rabbits from it.[47] In 1340 the tithing of Badbury concealed that John Tropynel had stolen barley from the lord.[48]

The warrens were also points of conflict at Walsham le Willows, but to a lesser extent than at Brandon. In Walsham peasants also poached with the help of dogs and set traps, but the warren was smaller than at Brandon. Other explanations might be that the local lords did not care so much about it, or alternatively the community was better at concealing poaching offences. Between 1303 and 1350 only seventeen hares and four rabbits were caught illicitly at the manor alongside some doves and partridges. From 1351 to 1399 the local peasantry caught even less: one doe, twelve hares and merely two rabbits.[49]

Petty forms of resistance could in places reach very high numbers. In the fourteenth century at Brandon before the Black Death 919 cases of petty offences against lordship are recorded, but a staggering 984 cases thereafter, again, in spite of population decline. Such offences included trespassing into the lord's crops, letting buildings fall into ruin, various types of labour offences ranging from performing works poorly to not turning up to works

---

[45] GADL, MS 9633, no. 7v.

[46] R. Lock (ed.), *Court Rolls of Walsham le Willows 1303–1350* (Suffolk Records Society, 41, 1998), 166.

[47] Chicago, University of Chicago Library, Sir Nicholas Bacon Collection of English Court and Manorial Documents, Manor of Brandon (hereafter UCBC) MS 291, m. 57.

[48] GADL MS 10773, fol. 18.

[49] Lock (ed.), *Court Rolls of Walsham le Willows, 1303–50*; id. (ed.), *Court Rolls of Walsham le Willows 1351–1399*.

despite being summoned. Other offences included illicitly 'rescuing' impounded animals, usually for outstanding payments to the lord, failure to pay rents, peasant flight, and petty thefts. At the manor of Badbury such cases increased from 294 before 1349 to 549 cases thereafter.[50] These peasant communities which differed in many ways can still show an increase in conflict with their individual lords in the late fourteenth century.

Cooperation and even solidarity did not, however, mean communal harmony, and there were many internal conflicts. Communities needed to regulate themselves in order to keep these divisions under control. This meant that while lordship was important, the regulation of communities went beyond the needs of lordship.

It is in its ability to regulate and control the behaviour of its members that we see the village community in action. Some conflicts might have been due to inequality among peasants, but still more research is needed to come to a firm conclusion over what roles poorer or richer members of communities played in conflict, pledging or patterns of violence. Any medieval community will have experienced among its members personal animosities, competitiveness, drunken brawls in or around its alehouses, or conflicts over boundaries, inheritance of land, or employment.

Sometimes such conflicts between peasants made it into the court records of the manor. Peasants could be very litigious, and they used the formal channels of the manorial courts to their own advantage. Beyond typical cases of debt and witholding goods, peasants sued each other over over a myriad of issues. Richer peasants can sometimes be found employing other tenants, and court records sometimes give hints of employment relationships between peasants. We note, for instance, that Agnes is 'the maidservant of Edith la Younge' in Monkton Deverill around the year 1277.[51] In the same year the hayward of Longbridge Deverill had a servant called William. A number of debt cases probably hide employment agreements, as grain, ale, wool or cash was unjustly withheld, which could have been wage payments. However, court rolls sometimes tell us about outstanding wages more directly. In Longbridge Deverill in 1277 Godfrey Parson claimed that Roger le Hayward owed him 3s. in outstanding wages from the 'time when he was the servant' of the same Roger.[52]

It would be wrong, however, to see a deep gulf between employers and employees in peasant communities. Many of those who occasionally

---

[50] The Badbury evidence excludes trespasses against the lord, as they were not always consistently recorded.

[51] GADL MS 9633, no. 6.

[52] GADL MS 9633, no. 6.

laboured for wages at some point in their own lives might employ wage labourers themselves. This is particularly common in cases where young peasants earned wages before they took land and set up their own households. In Badbury in Wiltshire in 1357 John atte Steorte was found guilty by the court of withholding wages from John Gibbes. Far from being trapped in permanent labouring jobs John Gibbes was noted in the following court records to have entered a substantial holding of one virgate of land for which he paid to the lord a very high entry fine of £10.[53] He probably needed the outstanding wages to help pay for his first instalment of the fine to the lord. In other words, wage earners could often become employers themselves, and this is not the pattern of one class exploited by another.

Hue and cry presentments in the manor court alongside entries of bloodshed and assaults certainly bear witness to violence in village communities. Men and women can be found in all of the manors raising the hue and cry against suspected or known offenders of all sorts of petty criminal behaviour of which the community disapproved. The hue and cry was a form of collective policing which aimed to call the community together in pursuit of the offender.[54] In East Monkton Alice Whither is noted as having raised the hue and cry against William le Hayward, as he had trespassed against her.[55] In Longbridge Deverill Edith the widow of Reginald Shir had a fight with Agnes de Strode and drew blood from her, which caused Agnes to raise the hue against Edith, and she was amerced 6d. for the bloodshed.[56]

The community actively attempted to contain conflict, and appears to have disapproved especially of intra-familial conflict which had turned violent, and sometimes offenders were forced to pay high amercements for having injured a close relative. In Longbridge Deverill Walter le Palmere was found to have drawn blood from his brother John le Palmere and was amerced a rather high 40d., where normal amercements for such bloodshed rarely exceeded 6d. or 12d.[57]

Conclusions

The records of manorial courts create the initial illusion that it was lordship which enforced communal order, but this is not the case. It is rather that the manorial court makes inter-peasant interactions partially visible. Profits of such community policing went to the lord, such as the amercements collected

---

[53] GADL MS 11224, no. 45; GADL MS 10634, no. 14.
[54] Müller, 'Social Control and the Hue and Cry'.
[55] GADL MS 9633, no. 5.
[56] GADL MS 9633, no. 6.
[57] GADL MS 9633, no. 5v.

from the raising of the hue and cry or the presentment of bloodshed cases. Nevertheless, the policing of the village as well as the solving of disputes between neighbours was a responsibility exercised by the community.

The peasant community harboured divisions and could witness violent confrontations. However, the peasant class was generally not split and divided; conflict, disputes, order and agreements necessarily went hand in hand. It was not only communal living, which perhaps urged peasants to keep the peace among themselves, but also the experience of lordship. Peasants generally seem to have managed to resist lordship quite effectively, and chronic divisions would have made such resistance and solidarity near to impossible. Communities might have differed in structure and their economies, but their communal experiences, both among themselves, but also vis-à-vis their lords appear to have been very similar. Communities were not only able to govern themselves and their own affairs, they also strove to contain and limit divisions among themselves, as it was in their interests to do so.

What if the Sea were Different?
Urbanization in Medieval Norway

Richard Holt

When Sir Michael Postan described medieval towns as 'non-feudal islands in the feudal seas' he was expressing the conviction that the urbanization of the middle ages was an exotic intrusion into a feudal society based on subsistence agriculture, the village and the castle.[1] Postan knew about the volume of international commerce and acknowledged its role in the local economy. In insisting, however, that the urban merchants needed to establish a legal and political detachment from the knights and villeins of the countryside, he lent support to a traditional view of urbanization, associated most with the name of Henri Pirenne, that feudal society was essentially inimical to trade and traders. Attributing the rise of Europe's towns to the interests and requirements of merchants trading in luxury goods, Pirenne had suggested that the urban community arose unintended and almost despite the surrounding society which, through its distinctive culture and activities, it would come to transform.[2]

Nobody has answered this approach to urbanization with more vigour—or indeed with more enthusiasm, one might add—than Rodney Hilton, nor to such effect: Hilton's analyses of town and country forcefully demonstrate the contrary of Postan's judgement by placing towns firmly within the context of the society that gave them birth. It was not the least of his achievements to persuade historians of all theoretical schools to approach and understand medieval urbanization as a logical and natural outgrowth of feudal society. Without that development, medieval European feudalism could not have continued to change and fulfil its potential as a social formation or mode of production. Far from being subversive of the feudal order, the medieval town was one of its distinctive expressions.

Hilton's published work on towns concentrated on France and England. What follows is intended to introduce comparative material on urbanization

---

[1] *The Medieval Economy and Society* (Harmondsworth, 1975 edn), 239.

[2] *Medieval Cities* (Princeton, 1925); *Economic and Social History of Medieval Europe* (London, 1936).

from another, very different, part of western Europe, and in the light of that material to return again to the question of the social forces acting on the growth of towns and commerce.

The character of Norwegian urbanization

A peripheral location has not excluded Norway from general European developments, as is demonstrated by the appearance of its major medieval towns in the century between 1000 and 1100. Norway's urbanization is a shadowy process. The persuasive narrative texts from the late twelfth and thirteenth centuries that construct a Norwegian past provide a basis for modern historical writing about the tenth and eleventh centuries; at the same time, however, they mask the essential lack of written sources from before about 1150. The range of contemporary sources for early towns is meagre: Trondheim with its churches and its pilgrim cult of St Olav was known to Adam of Bremen as *metropolis civitas Nortmannorum* (the metropolitan city of the Norwegians) in the 1070s[3]—a description with no secular implications—and in 1135 Orderic Vitalis could name as *civitates* (cities) Bergen and Trondheim on the west coast, and Oslo, Tønsberg, Borg and Konghelle on the eastern side of Norway. What Orderic, or his now unidentifiable source, understood in this context as a *civitas* is unclear: these were not merely ecclesiastical centres, as Orderic's source also attributed to Tønsberg a strategic role against the Danes.[4] In missing out Stavanger, an established central place and seat of a bishop from the 1120s,[5] the list would seem to be defective; Orderic's information was perhaps far from recent and his total of cities long outdated. Norway's remaining medieval towns are named in later sources, although archaeology confirms the eleventh century as the period of initial urban expansion as well as producing signs of (Danish) royal activity at Oslo in the decades before 1000.[6]

What functions did these towns have? All but one were seaports, either close to the open sea or on a major fjord; the exception, Hamar, had a good

---

[3] *Gesta Hammaburgensis ecclesiae pontificum* (Monumenta Germaniae Historica: 2nd edn, Hannover, 1876), Book IV.32, 181.

[4] M. Chibnall (ed.), *The Ecclesiastical History of Orderic Vitalis* (Oxford, 1975), vol.v, Book X, 220.

[5] K. Helle, *Stavanger fra våg til by* (Stavanger, 1975), 52–3.

[6] K. Helle and A. Nedkvitne, 'Sentrumsdannelser og byutvikling i norsk middelalder', in G. A. Blom (ed.), *Urbaniseringsprosesser i Norden, I: middelaldersteder* (Trondheim, 1977), 57–65; E. Schia, 'Urban Oslo: Evolution from a Royal Stronghold and Administrative Centre', in S. Myrvoll et al. (eds), *Archaeology and the Urban Economy: festschrift to Asbjørn E. Herteig* (Arkeologiske Skrifter 5, Bergen, 1989), 51–72.

river connection with the Oslo fjord (Fig. 1). On the basis of a scatter of evidence for commercial activity, historians have characterized them as coastal ports, which exported and imported commodities. In that respect they were successors to the coastal emporia of the early middle ages, of which one is known from Norway: the *Sciringesheale* named by the north-Norwegian Viking Ohthere in the description he gave to King Alfred (871–99).[7] This was Skiringssal, alias Kaupang (cognate with Old English *ceaping*, a marketing place), close to the mouth of the Oslo fjord, which excavation has confirmed to have been an emporium from the last decades of the eighth century until the early tenth century.[8] Whatever the reasons for Skiringssal's decline, the emergence in time of new trading places accorded with profound changes in the character and pattern of trade. Ohthere's merchandise had been prized Arctic products—furs, ivory and eiderdown—destined for consumption at the highest social levels; by 1100, new patterns of demand from consumers from a broader social background had made stockfish, dried cod from the Lofoten Islands of northern Norway, the principal export commodity. At the same time, much of the commercial focus had shifted to ports along the North Sea littoral best placed for bulk trade with England, the Low Countries and northern France.

By 1300, butter, hides, herring, and timber were major export commodities. Eighty per cent of the value of Norway's exports to England, however, was in stockfish,[9] a figure perhaps representative of Norway's total export trade. Imported commodities were manufactured goods but also, for the northern fish-producing districts in particular, corn. Town-based merchants collected and shipped these wares and distributed imported goods, although a ship-owning aristocracy also directly exported the surplus from their estates, and imported their own requirements.[10]

These, then, were very much gateway cities, their essential function being to link a regional economy to the wider economy outside. But were they more than that? Certainly they did take on other functions, reflecting the degree of social change in Norway between 1000 and 1100. Unusually for western

---

[7] J. Bately (ed.), *The Old English Orosius* (Early English Text Society, supp. ser. 6, London, 1980), 13–16.

[8] C. Blindheim, 'Kaupang in the Viks Fjord in Vestfold', in A. E. Herteig et al. (eds), *Archaeological Contributions to the Early History of Urban Communities in Norway* (Oslo, 1975), 125–73; H. G. Resi, 'Kaupang, før nye utgravninger', *Collegium Medievale*, 13 (2000), 141–64.

[9] Helle and Nedkvitne, 'Sentrumsdannelser', 96.

[10] K. Helle, *Bergen bys historie*, vol. I: 'Kongssete og kjøpstad, fra opphavet til 1536' (Bergen, 1982), 449–54

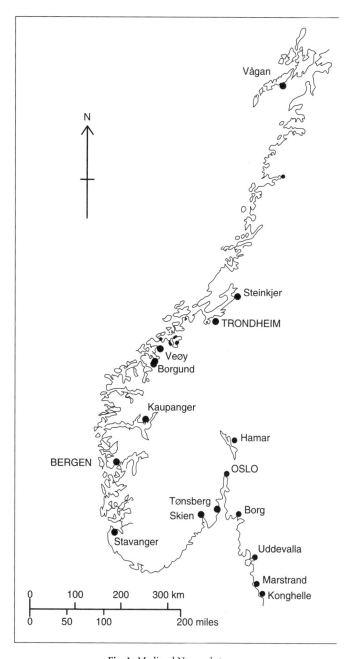

Fig. 1. Medieval Norway's towns

Europe, urbanization coincided with the triumph of Christianity over traditional religious practices. This conversion can be broadly dated to the first half of the eleventh century, so the foundation of towns and the building of major churches were thus simultaneous and presumably often linked processes. Moreover, the same period saw the successful assertion of a Norwegian national monarchy, free of the dependence on Danish kings shown by most earlier local rulers. By 1100, the major towns had begun to take to themselves the central functions of both the new state and the new Church: the character of urban society from its origins was heavily stamped by the presence both of the frequently-visiting royal court and nobility (if the narrative literature is correct) and by the clerical populations of the nation's greatest churches. The greatest urban households doubtless lived off rural rents, whilst at the same time a high proportion of imported luxury goods was destined to be consumed within the towns.

That the major towns in their early phases should have been predominantly centres of aristocratic consumption is hardly surprising, given that other early European towns followed that model.[11] What is surprising, however, is their failure to build on that and on their marketing function to achieve the transition to centres of production: that is, the failure to develop the independent role of manufacturer of both sophisticated commodities and more modest wares for a commercialized hinterland, as towns did elsewhere. To illustrate that failure we can briefly consider the evidence for Norway's three major towns.

Oslo was an important royal centre in the wealthy Viken region and became the political capital, insofar as Norway had one, during the fourteenth century. Recent historical work shows the city living partly as a trading centre and partly as a revenue-receiving centre. Medieval kings built up estates around Oslo for themselves and their followers; the urban churches also had major estates, and other townsmen owned farms. Rents were customarily paid in foodstuffs and raw materials, and it has been concluded that such revenue was easily sufficient to feed the town's projected 3000 inhabitants, leaving a comfortable surplus of commodities such as hides, furs, butter and timber for the Oslo merchants to export to England, Flanders and Germany. Oslo's resident and visiting population had other requirements besides food, of course: clothing, and a range of manufactures and luxuries, for which much of the demand was met by imported goods. The greater part of the value of imports was in woollen cloth, most of it cheap cloth rather than

[11] R. H. Hilton, *English and French Towns in Feudal Society* (Cambridge, 1992), 88–91; R. Holt, 'Society and Population 600–1300', in D. Palliser (ed.), *The Cambridge Urban History of Britain*, vol. I, 600–1540 (Cambridge, 2000), 81–2.

the better-quality sorts. Excavation evidence indicates that also many among Oslo's population wore very low-quality cloth, presumably made at home.[12] It may be that this impression of Oslo's economy will in time be modified. The evidence is thin, and its interpretation perhaps over-influenced by an expectation that town communities were consumers rather than producers, and that overseas trade was the only important urban activity. The archaeological evidence from Trondheim and Bergen, however, goes a long way towards supporting this picture.

Given the volume and importance of stockfish exports to the North Sea region from at least 1100, it is not surprising that the major ports should have grown up on Norway's west coast. Most important was Trondheim, until Bergen's rapid rise. According to the saga literature, Trondheim was founded by King Olav Tryggvason about 997, and archaeological evidence confirms settlement around that date.[13] Doubtless the intention was to establish a royal centre to rival nearby Lade, the existing cult centre and perhaps trading place belonging to the dynasty of jarls who had traditionally controlled Trøndelag and northern Norway. The rapid rise of the cult of St Olav—King Olav Haraldsson—from the mid-1030s made this in addition the focus of the new Norwegian church leading to the establishment of the Norwegian archbishopric there in 1152, and the subsequent building of the great cathedral as well as thirteen other churches and religious houses. Even so, Trondheim's early prominence may not have required any great population density or indeed any marked urban character: for example, excavation of the 3000 square-metre Library site, at the centre of medieval Trondheim, showed buildings first placed on plot frontages only around 1100, after which the number and density of buildings increased only until perhaps 1150 or more certainly 1200. One might expect Bergen's pre-eminence in the fish trade by the late twelfth century to have had an impact on Trondheim's growth. Trondheim, however, apparently stopped growing altogether, and indeed after about 1275 went into a marked decline, with a dramatic decrease in the number both of buildings and of finds of all sorts.[14] Clearly the urban economy had not developed in other directions to compensate for the loss of

---

[12] A. Nedkvitne, P. G. Norseng, *Byen under Eikaberg: fra byens oppkomst til 1536* (Oslo, 1991), 153–79, 190.

[13] A. Christophersen, 'Royal Authority and Early Urbanization in Trondheim during the Transition to the Historical Period', in Myrvoll et al.(eds), *Archaeology and the Urban Economy*, 91–135.

[14] A. Christopherson, 'Dwelling Houses, Workshops and Storehouses: Functional aspects of the development of wooden urban buildings in Trondheim from c.AD 1000 to AD 1400', *Acta Archaeologica*, 60, 1989, 101–29.

the fish trade, despite the prosperous agriculture of the Trøndelag district. Even the presence of a resident archbishop and his household, with their own quarter of the town to the south of the cathedral, seems to have done little to further Trondheim's economic development.

The archaeological evidence for craft production in Trondheim supports the proposition that it remained an undeveloped area of the city's economy. Craft activity was ubiquitous, but in all likelihood production was for household use rather than for the market. Leather production predominated before 1100, and it has been proposed that every household was producing basic leather goods for its own use. An increasing number of loom-weights has been found all over the site from the succeeding century or so—again, probably a sign of production of low-quality cloth for household use rather than for sale, given the low level of technology.[15]

Knut Helle and Arnved Nedkvitne, in their summary report on the state of research into Norwegian urbanization, were emphatic that industrial production was never a major factor in Norway's medieval urban economies, and that town craftsmen in essence worked to supply the needs of their fellow-townsmen. Shoemakers, they thought, were an exception, and in the case of Bergen some other crafts, too, probably worked to satisfy a rural demand.[16] Bergen certainly ought to have been the most industrialized of Norway's towns, economically pre-eminent as it otherwise was. It is traditionally said to have been founded by King Olav the Quiet (*Kyrre*) (1067-93), but there is as yet little archaeological evidence for significant activity before 1100. By 1200 it had become Norway's greatest emporium.[17] Yet Bergen, too, failed to develop as a manufacturing centre. Archaeological evidence comes from a range of excavations but most particularly from the major site in the heart of the town, the large quayside area destroyed by fire in the 1950s. In total, that site produced some 20,000 sherds of pottery, all imported.[18] The ceramic industry is often associated with early urban growth, but here—as indeed in other Norwegian towns—a pottery industry simply failed to develop, and wares were imported. Of the crafts we do find in Bergen, shoemaking was apparently the most important, as a recent study of both the historical and the

---

[15] S. W. Nordeide, 'Activity in an Urban Community: Functional aspects of artefact material in Trondheim from c.AD 1000 to AD 1600', *Acta Archaeologica*, 60, 1989, 130–50.

[16] Helle and Nedkvitne, 'Sentrumsdannelser', 101–2.

[17] Helle, *Bergen bys historie*, 86–90, 160–9.

[18] H. Lüdtke, 'The Bryggen Pottery, 1: Introduction and Pingsdorf Ware' (*The Bryggen Papers*, supp. ser. 4, Bergen, 1989); L. Blackmore and A. Vince, 'Medieval Pottery from South-east England found in the Bryggen Excavation 1955–68' (*The Bryggen Papers*, supp. ser. 5, Bergen, 1994).

archaeological evidence shows. However, despite Helle's and Nedkvitne's assertion, the adduced volume of work done by the Bergen shoemakers was likely to satisfy little more than the town's needs, whilst the high quality, fashionable shoes they made were certainly not intended for a mass rural market.[19]

Urban industrial production for rural markets is a classic division of labour that in the middle ages accompanied the commercialization of the local economy. Evidently, no appreciable rural market for urban manufactures existed in medieval Norway. And following on from that, the evidence all points to a general lack of commercialization of the internal Norwegian economy. One vital indicator is the volume and circulation of coinage. The close link between English commercialization and urbanization and developments in the monetary system has been traced by Richard Britnell, who has pointed out both the substantial quantity of coinage in circulation during the early period of urban growth and most spectacularly the explosion in the money supply by 1300, when an estimated thirty-six times as much cash was in circulation as there had been in the eleventh century.[20]

Norway, by contrast, did not sustain a stable coinage in the middle ages, nor any volume of coinage. Regular issues began under King Harald Sigurdsson Hardråde around 1050, with minting at Trondheim and Hamar: the quantities minted were apparently small, and the silver content quite quickly collapsed from 96 per cent to sometimes as low as 16 per cent. Peter Spufford suggested that the cause of this deterioration of the Norwegian penny was simply an inability to acquire enough silver.[21] During the long phase of political instability from the early twelfth century until well into the thirteenth, coinage virtually disappeared; the regular issues from the 1260s onwards continued to be minted in only small quantities. Finds of coins rarely come from domestic or everyday contexts but from hoards and most often from churches where they seem to have been slipped through the floorboards to reinforce prayers, which perhaps emphasizes their exotic value.

Chronic instability of both supply and value of the coinage would have discouraged its use, and indeed it is persuasively argued that neither in town nor in countryside was money the customary means of exchange. Rents,

---

[19] Jón Viðar Sigurðsson, 'Skomakerne i Vågsbotn-gård', *Bergens historiske forening*, 89 (1993), 23–54.

[20] R. Britnell, 'The Economy of British Towns 600–1300', in Palliser (ed.), *Cambridge Urban History*, 119.

[21] K. Skaare, *Coins and Coinage in Viking Age Norway: The Establishment of a National Coinage in Norway in the XI Century* (Oslo, Bergen, Tromsø, 1976); P. Spufford, *Money and its Use in Medieval Europe* (Cambridge, 1988), 83–4, 96.

taxes, and tithes were paid in kind and significantly even valued in kind—in quantities of stockfish, hides, butter and so on.[22] With at best a limited market for this commodity surplus, what was not consumed by the Church and aristocracy and their retainers had to be exported.

What is distinctive about the towns of medieval Norway, therefore, is neither their origins nor their functions as we have outlined them. It is that they never proceeded to diversify as towns did elsewhere. Whilst towns in other parts of Europe developed as markets for local produce and as providers of basic manufactured commodities and services, Norwegian towns failed to assume these roles in anything more than a rudimentary fashion. And furthermore, as the European economy continued to commercialize and diversify, new towns continued to appear until the whole countryside came within the marketing hinterland of one or more of them. Even now, the significance of this second and distinct phase of urbanization is often ignored: European economic expansion after 1200 in large measure rested on the special, and linked, roles of these new small towns—as markets for local produce, and as providers of basic manufactured commodities and services. In England, to take one well-studied example, town foundation continued through the eleventh and twelfth centuries, was at its most vigorous in the thirteenth century and came to a halt only after 1300. By then a total of some 52 larger towns and over 600 smaller towns (with fewer than 2000 inhabitants) held over 20 per cent of the country's population.[23] Yet Norway's towns, by contrast, were all in place by 1200. We see no sign there of any continuing urban expansion producing a network of local market towns. Nor do we see the emergence of the networks seen elsewhere, with the larger towns each coming to act as the focus for the small towns of its region, with a consequent evolution of a hierarchy of functions encouraging the development of sophisticated regional economies. Vågan, Veøy, Borgund, and Kaupanger acted apparently as local centres for Bergen's coastal trade,[24] but may have been little more than that, and any effect on the economies of their hinterlands is difficult to assess.

A measure of the restricted extent of urban development is how small Norway's urban population was, by contrast with other parts of Europe.

[22] K. Skaare, 'Myntøkonomi og varebytte', *Collegium Medievale*, 13 (2000), 103–16; K. Lunden, 'Money Economy in Medieval Norway', *Scandinavian Journal of History*, 24 (1998), 245–65.

[23] C. C. Dyer, 'Small Towns 1270–1540', in Palliser (ed.), *Cambridge Urban History*, 505–37; C. C. Dyer, 'How Urbanized was Medieval England?', J.-M. Duvosquel and E. Thoen (eds), *Peasants and Townsmen in Medieval Europe: Studia in honorem Adriaan Verhulst* (Gent, 1995), 169–83.

[24] Helle, *Bergen bys historie*, 117.

Against the 20 per cent and sometimes considerably higher now demonstrated to be usual elsewhere, at most only 5 per cent of Norway's medieval population lived in towns. Only Bergen's population exceeded 5000; Oslo had perhaps 3000, and there are no realistic estimates for other towns although most were clearly very small, often with populations to be reckoned in hundreds. Norway's total population is very uncertain, but on the best estimates was some 400,000 of which the urban population was no more than 20,000.[25]

Urbanization and feudal social relations

As an historical problem, Norway's failure to develop a large urban sector has implications not only for our understanding of the Norwegian economy but also of the factors promoting urban growth elsewhere. What was so different about Norway or its economy that it either did not need or could not sustain a network of towns? To begin with the obvious question: surely the reason for this failure to commercialize beyond a rudimentary level was the result simply of geographical and climatic factors? A largely mountainous and thinly-settled terrain, with often long travelling distances between settlements and scattered farms, might be thought to have hindered local market development. At the same time the long winters, when animals were kept inside and possibilities for outdoor activities were reduced, provided generous opportunities for production in the household of articles from wool, leather, wood, bone and antler. The pattern of non-commercial, domestic production of basic commodities in the Norwegian countryside remained strong until recently. But these factors are not to be exaggerated. Much of the Norwegian population lived on or close to ice-free fjords and sheltered seaways which offered advantages of transport that many elsewhere in Europe might have envied, whilst winter conditions facilitated overland transport by sledge and ski. And even in the most urbanized parts of medieval Europe the division of labour in the economy never went so far that rural production of commodities ceased altogether, and doubtless peasant households everywhere manufactured simple products for their own use. Its geography gave Norway an economy unlike those of less mountainous regions further south, but that did not necessarily hinder commercial growth and diversification.

It is more constructive to look for other forces—factors acting within and upon Norwegian society—that might have helped to retard commercialization of the local economy, and particularly in areas where geography can

---

[25] K. Helle, 'Down to 1536', in R. Danielsen et al. (eds), *Norway: A History from the Vikings to Our Own Times* (Oslo, 1995), 34–5, 39–40.

certainly be ruled out as a factor. Regions such as Trøndelag and Viken (the areas around Trondheim and Oslo) are hilly rather than mountainous, fertile districts suited to pastoral and arable agriculture and with a large and prosperous rural population. Here, especially, the absence of local market towns is most striking, where economic conditions ought to have been conducive to urbanization. But what were the conditions elsewhere in Europe that were so favourable to the development of the local market?

In insisting that medieval towns grew out of feudal social relations, it was particularly the rent relationship that Rodney Hilton perceived as instrumental in bringing about a flourishing local market, and thus urbanization. The aristocracy's demand for money rents and other dues was the essential mechanism driving their tenants to sell a substantial proportion of their produce—an involuntary surplus of foodstuffs and raw materials which the peasant household would otherwise itself have consumed.[26] That surplus was, of course, in addition to whatever proportion of the produce had to be sold or exchanged to obtain necessities. Village markets and small towns specialized in handling these surpluses, whilst the larger towns where the aristocracy spent much of their income provided the specialist markets in better-quality goods—both imported luxuries and quality, local manufactures.

Richard Britnell has stressed how essential money was, already by the time of Bloch's second feudal age, to the structure of class relationships and the exercise of authority: 'The ability to extract cash from dependants was a defining criterion of power'. In the eleventh century, money was an established, essential ingredient in the English king's relationship to his people and in the lord's relationship to his tenants, and would grow in importance through the twelfth and thirteenth centuries.[27] The transformation of the English economy followed a general European trend, associated with the substantial finds of new sources of silver from the late twelfth century;[28] yet to try to explain urbanization simply by reference to that growing commercialization and monetization of the rural economy is to fall into an easy trap. As two sides of the same coin, both need to be accounted for. The link Hilton made between urbanization and feudal class relationships emphasizes medieval urbanization as a social phenomenon arising out of the dynamics of a complexity of economic and social interaction. Towns appeared and grew not as a consequence of one particular change or another but as one aspect of

[26] R. H. Hilton. 'Towns in English Medieval Society', in R. Holt and G. Rosser (eds), *The Medieval Town 1200–1540* (London, 1990), 21.

[27] R. H. Britnell, *The Commercialisation of English Society, 1000–1500* (Cambridge, 1993), 36–47.

[28] Spufford, *Money and its Use*, 109–31, 240–63.

a period of widespread change in contemporary society. Central to the feudal revolution within the Carolingian world was a redefinition of social groups and their relationships to each other, new political structures and ideologies, the triumph of the institution of the *seigneurie* in the countryside and—not least—what Guy Bois described as a 'new dynamism' in the economy marked by the appearance of the market and an unprecedented division of labour between town and countryside.[29] In England, too, Christopher Dyer has characterized the two centuries after 880 as a 'revolutionary period', with the development of a centralized state, the emergence and proliferation of local lordship, the formation of nucleated villages and the Church's new social presence accompanying the establishment of a network of parish churches. It is too early to attribute—with confidence—cause and effect, and to establish the precise relationship of these changes to the process of urbanization, but unquestionably all were inter-connected.[30]

That process, culminating in the emergence of the small market towns, accompanied growing commercialization and specialization. Urbanization brought, inevitably, improvements in the techniques and technology of production: both a greater level of efficiency allowing lower prices but also a much better quality of manufactured goods, including products aimed at the peasant consumer as well as the aristocrat. The impressive range of advances in the technology of cloth production which had begun by the twelfth century was geared towards producing more cloth of middling quality as well as the more expensive.[31] The vast bulk of the pottery industry's production was of wares that the peasant consumer would find useful but also decorative, and even in the small market towns with their overwhelmingly peasant customers a wide range of skilled craftsmen such as locksmiths, wheelwrights and professional tailors, for example, was customarily found. And in the cloth industry that flourished also at this lowest urban level we find all the advanced trades, right up to the specialist dyeing and finishing processes.[32] Urban services, too, catered for a range of social levels: at the one end the lawyer, but at the other the numerous barber-surgeons and toothdrawers. The common obsession of historians with medieval Europe's great cities emphasizes the urban connection with the upper levels of society, yet Rodney Hilton's

---

[29] G. Bois, *The Transformation of the Year One Thousand* (Manchester, 1992), 135 and *passim*.

[30] Dyer, 'How Urbanized was Medieval England?', 178.

[31] J. H. Munro, 'Textile Technology in the Middle Ages', in J. H. Munro, *Textiles, Towns and Trade* (Aldershot, 1994), 1–27.

[32] See, for instance, E. M. Carus-Wilson, 'The First Half-century of the Borough of Stratford upon Avon', in Holt and Rosser (eds), *The Medieval Town*, 49–70.

reminder that the small local towns were flourishing communities constituting at least half of the urban population leads to a perception of urbanization as more than just a response to social situations dictated by the aristocracy, and to aristocratic patterns of demand and consumption.[33] Urbanization had developed its own momentum, based on a vigorous consumer demand for sophisticated products from all levels of society.

Comparison with the fully urbanized parts of Europe emphasizes how different the Norwegian experience was; other comparisons help explain just why it was different. The urbanizing experiences of both Ireland and Scotland, for instance, are instructive. At the Anglo-French conquest in the 1170s Ireland had five significant towns. With their easy access to the sea, the dominant function of Dublin, Cork, Limerick, Waterford and Wexford was overseas trade, a relationship which determined their limited interaction with their immediate hinterlands. A wider range of urban functions came with the foundation of inland towns by Anglo-French lords from the 1190s onwards as part of a general manorialization of their new lands. The Irish peasantry's widespread opposition to colonization, as much as the difficult terrain, reduced the effects of the feudalizing process: thus Howard Clarke explained the restricted number of towns in medieval Ireland. Even so, he could point to fifty-six places that would generally be counted as urban, with a further 250 or so second-rank local marketing places.[34] It says much about this economic network's dependence on imposed and precarious social relationships that it survived only as long as English control of the localities was certain. Increasing de-urbanization accompanied de-colonization even before the Black Death, with both Edward Bruce's Scottish invasion of 1315–18 and Irish attacks contributing to a growing weakening of English authority.[35] More accurately, the process was not the loss of urban functions entirely, but rather a regression to an older urban form in fewer centres. At the end of the middle ages, after a long period of colonial retreat, the great majority of the former market settlements had disappeared whilst some forty walled towns survived. Those that prospered were mainly seaports, and the prevailing trade pattern now was the export—by the aristocracies of both ethnic

[33] R. H. Hilton, 'The Small Town and Urbanisation: Evesham in the Middle Ages', in Hilton, *Class Conflict and the Crisis of Feudalism* (London, 1985), 187–93; 'Small Town Society in England before the Black Death', in Holt and Rosser (eds), *The Medieval Town*, 71–96.

[34] H. B. Clarke, 'Decolonization and the Dynamics of Urban Decline in Ireland, 1300–1550', in T. R. Slater (ed.), *Towns in Decline AD 100–1600* (Aldershot, 2000), 157–92.

[35] R. Frame, 'Ireland', in M. Jones (ed.), *The New Cambridge Medieval History*, vol.VI, *c.*1300–*c.*1415 (Cambridge, 2000), 375–87.

identities—of a range of primary products in return for imports of necessities and luxury items.[36]

Scotland's urban development was more restricted than England's, with perhaps no more than 10 per cent of the medieval population coming to live in towns.[37] Nevertheless, archaeology has shown extensive and varied manufacturing activity in a number of places, leading to the judgement that they were 'essential to the efficient conversion of agricultural produce into the tools of better farming and the luxuries of social status'.[38] Meanwhile, despite the general lack of written records one can perceive already in the early thirteenth century a Scottish urban cloth-making industry important enough to generate the same conflicts of interest between employers and employees as English towns were experiencing.[39] Confirming the impression of widespread commercialization in the thirteenth century, the small quantity of silver in circulation in 1200 had leapt by 1280 to perhaps £180,000, a spectacular increase and as much as a quarter of England's estimated monetary stock at that time.[40] Yet by 1400 there are signs of a steep decline in economic activity, including increasing imports of humble manufactured goods and depreciation of the coinage. 'A flight of money from remoter areas, which presumably sank back into a subsistence economy' has been suggested.[41]

Conclusion

Urbanization in both Scotland and Ireland was obviously different in detail from the Norwegian experience, but not so different in essence that we cannot find strong similarities and perhaps identify reasons for dissimilarities. In Ireland, especially, the accident of history makes very clear indeed the association between urbanization at the local level and the feudal aristocracy's efforts to reorganize agriculture and redefine their relationship with their tenants, to impose the *seigneurie* they were familiar with. That these efforts came, in the end, to nothing throws the failure of the local market towns into a

[36] Clarke, 'Urban Decline in Ireland', 178–9.

[37] E. P. Dennison and G. G. Simpson, 'Scotland', in Palliser (ed.), *Cambridge Urban History*, 731.

[38] R. M. Spearman, 'Workshops, Materials and Debris—Evidence of Early Industries', in M. Lynch et al. (eds), *The Scottish Medieval Town* (Edinburgh, 1988), 136.

[39] Holt, 'Society and Population', 90–1.

[40] I. Stewart, 'The Volume of Early Scottish Coinage', in D. M. Metcalf (ed.), *Coinage in Medieval Scotland, 1100–1600* (British Archaeological Reports 45, British Series, 1977), 65–72; Britnell, 'Economy of British Towns', 119.

[41] A. Stevenson, 'Trade with the South, 1070–1513', in Lynch, *The Scottish Medieval Town*, 189–90.

sharper light. In Scotland feudal lordship took better root, and numismatic evidence points to a flourishing commercialization of the economy in the thirteenth century, as does the evidence for extensive industrial production in towns. Even there, though, the pattern could weaken in the post-Black Death period, with a general de-commercialization and retreat from urbanization. Perhaps commercialization had not gone so deep as it had further south, and Scottish towns had always been less assured of survival: an interesting parallel with Norway is that in both countries kings—whether on their own initiative or prompted by the burgesses—granted the towns commercial monopolies in their regions. In Norway, even peddling goods around the countryside was forbidden in 1299.[42]

Norway's urbanization accompanied the very different course its social development took in the middle ages. No manorial system developed; no large-scale farming on great complexes of aristocratic landed property; no forced labour (after the disappearance of slavery); and no private jurisdiction that turned the landowner into the lord of a *seigneurie* that gave him legal rights over his tenants. Instead, the aristocracy's land was leased by tenants enjoying personal freedom. By European standards, land rents were very low: as high as one-fifth of production only in conditions of land scarcity in west Norway early in the fourteenth century—otherwise one-sixth was normal. Furthermore, a free peasantry owned one-third of the land in the early fourteenth century, against a Church holding of about 40 per cent, a royal estate of 7 per cent and only 20 per cent of the land in the hands of the lay aristocracy.[43] This was a feudal aristocracy, but a weak one, and its weakness is evident in two ways. Not only were rent levels low, but neither ecclesiastical nor lay landlords had the authority (if they had the will) to insist on an increasing proportion of their rent in cash. As a result, throughout the middle ages they continued to receive rents in kind which they could only export; they simply could not be significant purchasers of consumer goods made in Norwegian towns, even had such goods existed. Instead they were largely importers of manufactured goods, patrons of urban suppliers in Germany, England, the Netherlands and northern France—a pattern that was established early in the middle ages, and once established proved difficult to escape.[44] Medieval Norway's chief towns were, one could say, actually located outside Norway.

[42] E. Ewan, *Townlife in Fourteenth-Century Scotland* (Edinburgh, 1990), 64–5; Helle, *Norway: A History*, 47.

[43] E. Orrman, 'Rural Conditions', in K. Helle (ed.), *The Cambridge History of Scandinavia*, vol. I, *Prehistory to 1520* (Cambridge, 2003), 299, 303.

[44] The related failures to develop both a cash economy and a sophisticated urban manufacturing sector perpetuated and reinforced each other in a way that is easier to demonstrate

Towns were not islands in the feudal sea. They grew out of feudal class relations, they were a characteristic feature of feudal society, and they strengthened the feudal economy. In Norway the feudal sea really was different, and the different character of the towns was both a consequence of that, and a factor perpetuating the weakness of the aristocracy and the general weakness of the economy.

---

than to explain. The activities of overseas merchants, already before 1200 vigorously promoting imported manufactured wares in exchange for dried fish in particular (see for instance the description of Bergen at the time of the Third Crusade in M. C. Gertz (ed.), *Profectio Danorum in Hierosolynam, cap. xi* (Scriptores Minores Historiae Danicae Medii Aevi), vol. II (Copenhagen, 1970), 444–92), should be taken into account as a further factor ensuring that all of Norway's agricultural and fishing surplus was directly exported with no more than a negligible amount supporting professional manufacturing within the Norwegian towns.

Church Lords and English Urban Investment in the Later Middle Ages

Richard Goddard

Rodney Hilton's seminal article, 'Some Problems of Urban Real Property in the Middle Ages', contrasted the small-scale merchant acquisition of urban real property in the thirteenth century with the larger-scale institutional, primarily guild, property accumulations found in the fifteenth century.[1] This paper seeks to extend this analysis by looking at the acquisition of property by the church in English towns between the thirteenth and sixteenth centuries. It uses mortmain licences that included grants of property in towns in the midlands in association with other printed medieval material available for the region. It seeks to contribute to the important question of the relationship between lordship and urban development by making some observations about the investment strategies employed by church landlords, and by establishing a comprehensive chronology of church acquisition in medieval towns. Religious institutions were the most important urban landlords of the later middle ages. By the fourteenth century Westminster Abbey's urban estate is thought to have covered over 60 per cent of the area of Westminster.[2] In the early fourteenth century Londoners believed (although one must suspect some exaggeration) that a third of all city rents went to the church.[3] Rodney Hilton noted that over 60 per cent of Gloucester's fifteenth-century tenements were held by religious institutions and that, in 1486, Coventry's Holy Trinity Gild, one of the city's most powerful landlords, was receiving rents from nearly four hundred tenants.[4]

---

[1] R. H. Hilton, 'Some Problems of Urban Real Property in the Middle Ages', in C. H. Feinstein (ed.), *Socialism, Capitalism and Economic Growth* (Cambridge, 1967), 326–37.

[2] G. Rosser *Medieval Westminster* (Oxford, 1989), 46–51.

[3] C. Gross, 'Mortmain in Medieval Boroughs', *American Historical Review*, 12 (1907), 738; H. M. Chew, 'Mortmain in Medieval London' *English Historical Review*. 60 (1942), 3; S. Raban, *Mortmain Legislation and the English Church, 1279–1500* (Cambridge, 1982), 6.

[4] Hilton, 'Some Problems of Urban Real Property', 326–37.

The church and urban acquisitions

Can the acquisition by the church of urban property be considered investment, in the sense of purchase with the expectation of some future material
reward? In 1387, St. Bartholomew's Hospital in Gloucester exchanged a messuage (a plot of land containing a house and outbuildings) and 10 acres of
land in the manor of Hardwicke for a shop in Gloucester's city centre suggesting some awareness of the potential profitability of urban property.[5] The rent
per acre of urban land far exceeded that of rural land. Agricultural land in the
thirteenth century could be rented out at between 4d. and 1s. or more per
acre. Quit rents in towns—those owed to the chief overlords—were commonly 1s. for a plot roughly a quarter of an acre in area. Economic and
leasehold rents in towns were much higher with larger towns commonly
having higher rental values. Five shillings a year for a cottage and between
£2 and £3 for an imposing merchant's house were not unusual. Population
densities were also higher in towns with a constant flow of new migrants on
the lookout for places to live.[6] Thus the potential for remunerative investment certainly existed. Furthermore, land was rarely simply granted to
monastic houses. In many cases new urban property was bought for cash
in a continuing attempt to increase profits via urban rents.[7] This can be
seen with reference to Westminster Abbey's acquisition of properties in
Westminster. In 1289 the abbey purchased a house, along with a number
of other properties, in the small urban community outside their gates.[8] They
paid the donor, Stephen de Cornhill, £35 6s. 8d. for what must have been a
substantial tenement. Coventry Cathedral Priory's acquisition of Coventry
properties demonstrates how this was often achieved. One of the priory's city-
centre messuages, granted in late 1329, was a (so-called) gift from Simon and
Alice Childe to a clerk, William Passenham, here acting as an agent on the
priory's behalf.[9] He passed it on to the priory in March 1330. However, a copy
of the charter reveals that for this 'gift' William Passenham (and hence the

[5] *Calendar of Patent Rolls* (hereafter *CPR*) *1385–9*, 338.
[6] P. Schofield, *Peasant and Community in Medieval England* (Basingstoke, 2003), 30–1;
E. Miller and J. Hatcher, *Medieval England—Rural Society and Economic Change,
1086–1348* (London, 1978), 45; C. Dyer, *Standards of Living in the Later Middle Ages:
Social Change in England c.1200–1520* (Cambridge, 1989), 208; D. J. Keene, *A Survey of
Medieval Winchester*, vol. I (Oxford, 1985), 53, 64, 370–1, 395, 400–1.
[7] Rosser, *Medieval Westminster*, 48–67.
[8] B. Harvey, *Westminster Abbey and its Estates in the Middle Ages* (Oxford, 1977), 416.
[9] PRO E164/21, fol. 110.

priory) had paid Simon Childe 100s.[10] This method of acquisition was typical of many of the major religious urban investors, including Reading and Malmesbury Abbeys, and several religious houses in London, Bristol and Southampton,[11] and suggests a businesslike attitude towards investment.

One of the key components of the seigneurial economy was rent. Many of the most able urban portfolio managers, commonly Benedictine monasteries that were sited in towns, carefully administered their urban estates in order to maximize these rents. During the thirteenth and early fourteenth centuries the religious houses of Worcester Priory, Gloucester Abbey, Llanthony Priory and Coventry Priory, all similarly concerned about the value of the rent income from their urban properties, followed a policy of ridding themselves of their low-value properties and acquiring new urban tenements, or re-acquiring properties previously granted out in fee, in order to lease them at a significantly higher rent.[12] Eleanor Searle has highlighted a similar policy being followed by Battle Abbey which, during the course of the thirteenth century, bought out the messuages of their burgesses, which had previously furnished the monastery with a very low quit rent, and then re-granted them at a markedly higher economic rent.[13] Studies of towns like Westminster, Durham, and Wells have demonstrated similar policies of the monasteries and cathedrals that were landlords in these places.[14] The shift from quit rents to more remunerative leaseholds and economic rents indicates that monastic houses were conscientious and flexible portfolio managers.[15]

---

[10] E. Stokes, and L. Drucker (eds), *Warwickshire Feet of Fines*, vol. II, 1284–1345 (Dugdale Society, 11, 1939), document no. 1717. For a similar example see, Coventry Record Office (hereafter CRO), BA/B/A/8/1.

[11] D. Postles, 'Pittances and Pittancers', in M. Prestwich, R. Britnell, and R. Frame (eds), *Thirteenth Century England*, vol. 9 (Woodbridge, 2003), 178, 183–6.

[12] N. Baker and R. Holt, *Urban Growth and the Medieval Church* (Aldershot, 2004), 266–9, 279–82; R. Goddard, *Lordship and Medieval Urbanisation: Coventry, 1043–1355* (London, 2004), ch. 3.

[13] E. Searle, *Lordship and Community: Battle Abbey and its Banlieu 1066–1538* (Toronto, 1974), 144–51.

[14] Rosser, *Medieval Westminster*, 44–5, 51–4; M. Bonney, *Lordship and the Urban Community* (Cambridge, 1990), 107, 113; D. G. Shaw, *The Creation of a Community* (Oxford, 1993), 29–30. See also, Searle, *Lordship and Community;* Baker and Holt, *Urban Growth and the Medieval Church*, 268–9, 279–80.

[15] R. H. Snape, *English Monastic Finances in the Later Middle Ages* (Cambridge, 1926), 118–23.

The acquisition of urban rents, as opposed to the properties themselves, was an important component of investment by church landlords in towns.[16] All types of religious institution, except the mendicant friars, pursued urban rents. In 1279, Oseney Abbey held just one burgage (plot held by burgage tenure) in Warwick but received 4s. rent from it.[17] The Abbot of Hailes received 6s. 8d. from a third of a tenement in the Butchery in Gloucester in 1455. Worcester Cathedral Priory appears to have followed a strenuous and deliberate programme of obtaining rents from the city of Worcester. Until 1333, all acquisitions by the priory were exclusively rent-based. Only after that date, and especially between 1368 and 1393, did alienations to the house contain city messuages and land.[18] Similarly Coventry Priory gained most of its grants of rent in the final decades of the thirteenth century.[19] Winchcombe Abbey similarly invested heavily in urban rents in the early fourteenth century.[20]

Another element of portfolio management was the decision as to where to invest. This followed a simple rule of thumb. Big—or wealthy—was beautiful. The relationship between town wealth and investment is clear with reference to Table 1. Those midlands towns assessed (many probably under-assessed)[21] in the 1334 lay subsidy as having movable wealth of above £200 attracted the greatest numbers of religious investors, whilst smaller, or less wealthy, towns were considerably less popular as targets for investment, especially by monastic houses. Larger centres shown in Table 1, such as Hereford, Worcester, Northampton, Leicester, and Nottingham, demonstrate this relationship clearly. Whilst Coventry comes out top of every medieval popularity contest with by far the largest number of mortmain licences, the shire towns like Gloucester attracted significant investment. In 1455, sixteen ecclesiastical institutions held at least 338 properties of various different sizes

---

[16] For a discussion on the endowment of urban rents to monasteries, see Postles, 'Pittances and Pittancers', 178–9.

[17] W. H. Stevenson (ed.), *Rental of All the Houses in Gloucester AD 1455* (Gloucester, 1890), 17.

[18] *CPR, 1281-92*, 474; *CPR 1313-17*, 80; *CPR 1330-4*, 338; *CPR 1340-3*, 6; *CPR 1358-61*, 88; *CPR 1367-70*, 258; *CPR 1377-81*, 211; PRO, C 143 file ccclxiv/13; file cccxciii/6; file ccccxviii/29.

[19] PRO, E 164/21, fols 49-52, 85–124.

[20] *CPR 1301-08*, 141; *CPR 1317-21*, 516–17.

[21] It must be remembered that the 1334 lay subsidy allows us only a glimpse at relative, rather than absolute, urban wealth. See, S. H. Rigby, 'Late Medieval Urban Prosperity: The Evidence of the Lay Subsidies', *Economic History Review*, 39 (1986), 411–16; P. Nightingale, 'The Lay Subsidies and the Distribution of Wealth in Medieval England, 1275–1334', *Economic History Review*, 57 (2004), 29.

in Gloucester.[22] Those resident in the town, like St. Peter's Abbey and St. Oswald's Priory, and those with a primarily urban and local perspective, like the hospitals of St. Bartholomew and St. Margaret, held the most properties. Twelve other local religious houses, guilds, hospitals and houses of mendicant friars, and even the distant Eton College, all held property in the town. Those whose houses lay outside the city tended to hold fewer tenements or small parcels of land. The abbeys of Evesham (Worcestershire) and Flaxley (Gloucestershire) held small, suburban or low-value plots in Gloucester.[23] Evesham held six small properties, one of which was a toft (a plot) at the corner of Oxbode Lane 'near the town wall and latrines'.[24] By contrast St. Peter's Abbey, sited in the centre of the city and Gloucester's principal landholder, held over 200 houses at the same time.[25]

The correlation between urban wealth and investment by the church suggested by Table 1 can be seen in a comparison between Ludlow and Birmingham. Ludlow's movable wealth was assessed in 1334 at £240, thus making it a relatively wealthy small town. In 1255 when the town was surveyed by the crown, five local religious houses already held property there. Nearly all of these were clearly investments. The Hospitallers, for example, held twelve burgages in the town (more than they might need for accommodation) bringing them in 44s.[26] Between 1284 and 1392, five religious institutions, including the local hospital and guild, sought twelve mortmain licences for land there.[27] A number of these, for example the priory of Alberbury (Shropshire) and the abbey of Wigmore (Herefordshire), were outsiders. This might be compared to licences granted for land in Birmingham, assessed in 1334 at just over half the value of Ludlow, at £141. Only two local institutions, the hospital of St. Thomas the Martyr and the Holy Cross Guild, and a local parish chaplain, acquired five licences between them for land in the town.[28] Of these the guild was the most significant investor.[29]

---

[22] Stevenson, *Rental of Gloucester*, 5–113. This must be an underestimate. See Baker and Holt, *Urban Growth and the Medieval Church*, 261, 277–83.

[23] Stevenson, *Rental of Gloucester*, 111, 113.

[24] Ibid., 75.

[25] Baker and Holt, *Urban Growth and the Medieval Church*, 279.

[26] *Rotuli Hundredorum*, vol. II (Record Commission, 1818), 69.

[27] *CPR 1281-92*, 116; *CPR 1324-7*, 257; *CPR 1340-3*, 234–5; *CPR 1343-5*, 309; *CPR 1348-50*, 464; *CPR 1348-50*, 462; *CPR 1354-8*, 87, 311, 528; *CPR 1361-4*, 495; *CPR 1391-6*, 110, 115.

[28] PRO, C 143 file viii/19; file ccx/25; file cclxxxiv/19; *CPR 1350-4*, 37; *CPR 1391-6*, 137–8.

[29] W. B. Bickley and J. A. Hill (eds), *Survey of the Borough and Manor of Birmingham made in 1553* (Oxford, 1890), 36–7; R. A. Holt, *The Early History of the Town of Birmingham 1166–1600* (Dugdale Society Occasional Papers, 30, 1985).

This correlation suggests that religious institutions, in search of high rental returns, preferred investing in wealthy towns.

However, the licensing system required under the Statute of Mortmain must have shaped the investment decisions of some of the biggest players. 'General' licences became common in the early years of the fourteenth century and allowed recipients, for a fee, to acquire lands and rents to a fixed annual value rather than requiring a separate licence for each individual property.[30] Thus general licences included collections of disparate properties often collected together by clerical agents. St. Peter's Abbey, Gloucester, received such a licence to acquire £20 worth of land in 1336 and in 1405 St. Mary's Hospital, Leicester acquired a similar 'general' licence for £4.[31] These licences were both popular and convenient but for some of the major urban investors, like the abbeys of Gloucester, Winchcombe, Coventry, and Reading, a caveat was included: that they could only acquire property within their own fees. For example, Reading Abbey's only urban investment in the midlands was at Leominster, where the house already held land; Coventry Priory and Gloucester Abbey were restricted in their urban investments to the cities in which they were already landlords.[32] However, this was not commonly the case for less aggressive investors or poorer institutions. Pershore Abbey's early fourteenth-century acquisitions in Worcester were outside its own fee, as were Halesowen Abbey's new fifteenth-century properties in Lichfield.[33] Furthermore, when parochial chaplains acquired urban tenements (usually on a 'specific' rather than 'general' licence, a more suitable alternative for small-time investors) these were never required to be within their church's own patrimony.[34]

Medieval urban investment was dominated by wealthy (in terms of landed resources) monasteries that were sited within towns. Urban convents, like Worcester Priory, Gloucester Abbey, and Coventry Priory, acquired significantly more urban land over a longer period than did smaller houses and institutions such as local parish churches, chantries, friaries, and colleges, despite often being restricted to purchase within their own fees. In Coventry, 43 per cent of the mortmain licences for city land were issued to monastic houses; in Gloucester the percentage is higher at 60 per cent. The bulk of these were issued to Coventry Priory and Gloucester Abbey. But towns

---

[30] Raban, *Mortmain Legislation*, 44–58.

[31] *CPR 1334-8*, 326; *CPR 1405-8*, 109.

[32] *CPR 1338-40*, 156; *CPR 1317-21*, 516; Baker and Holt, *Urban Growth and the Medieval Church*, 282.

[33] *CPR 1301-7*, 209; *CPR 1467-77*, 16.

[34] See for example, *CPR 1340-3*, 343; *CPR 1391-6*, 151.

also spawned distinctly urban specialists. These were the, usually non-monastic, institutions that were likewise sited in towns—especially hospitals and guilds. Town hospitals, like St. Wolstan's in Worcester or St. Mary's in Leicester were significant urban specialists. They acquired the vast majority of their land close to the hospitals themselves in the towns that they served. Between 1368 and 1408 the suburban hospital of St. Mary's, Leicester, received five mortmain licences for properties, 15s. 11d. rent, and other land in Leicester and its suburbs.[35] As Rodney Hilton emphasized with specific reference to Coventry,[36] guilds acquired huge amounts of land in the towns of the later middle ages and must be considered, after the urban monasteries, principal players in the urban land market. In 1392 the Holy Cross Guild of Birmingham received a licence for eighteen messuages, several other plots, and 40s. rent in Birmingham; five years later the Holy Trinity Guild of Northampton acquired messuages, shops, and 10s. 4d. rent in Northampton.[37] Coventry's principal guild, dedicated to the Holy Trinity, acquired 153 city messuages, a mill, 94 acres of land and £22 1s. 7½d. rent in Coventry in 1392.[38] This was far larger than any previous single licence for land in Coventry, out-performing even those of the city's cathedral priory. Many of these newly acquired properties were re-leased at an economic rent.[39] The guild's revenue from urban rents was substantial. In 1486 they totalled £318 12s. 6d.[40] The wealthiest guilds were commonly found in towns. Their membership comprised local, often wealthy, business people whose assets were composed of urban tenements. Thus guilds specialized in urban investment, a portfolio that they understood well. Nottingham's Holy Trinity Guild received a licence for twenty-five city properties, some arable land and two booths in the town's Saturday market in 1460 suggesting a certain understanding of the profitability of urban commercial real estate.[41] Unlike urban hospitals, which sometimes acquired rural land in manors that lay close to the town, guilds acquired only urban tenements through mortmain.

Urban investment was also influenced by the personal input of strong individuals, usually abbots or priors, with acute business acumen. Battle Abbey's greatest participation in the land market was between 1290

---

[35] *CPR 1367-70*, 104; *CPR 1370-4*, 361; *CPR 1391-6*, 142; *CPR 1405-8*, 109, 387.

[36] Hilton, 'Some Problems of Urban Real Property', 336.

[37] *CPR 1391-6*, 137–8; *CPR 1396-9*, 162.

[38] *CPR 1452-61*, 615–17; *CPR 1391-6*, 136–7.

[39] Goddard, *Lordship and Medieval Urbanisation*, ch. 8.

[40] G. Templeman (ed.), *The Records of the Guild of the Holy Trinity, St. Mary, St. John the Baptist and St. Katherine of Coventry*, vol. II (Dugdale Society Publications, 19, 1944), 69.

[41] *CPR 1452-61*, 615–17.

and 1311, during the stewardship, and then the abbacy, of John of Whatlington.[42] Evesham Abbey's chronicle enthusiastically describes the good deeds of Abbot Henry (1256–66) and specially records his buying of property and urban rents at that time.[43] William of Brightwalton, prior of Coventry from 1248–79, was an astute and single-minded administrator keen to take advantage of the revenue-producing opportunities of urban land. He managed to acquire lordship over half of the city of Coventry (known as the Earl's Half) in perpetuity for the monastery in 1249.[44] This deal cost the monastery £300, plus £110 per annum, but by extending their fee it allowed them to invest in and develop large areas of previously unavailable urban real estate. Many of the mortmain licences granted to the house in the later middle ages were for properties in the Earl's Half of Coventry. In the priory's last mortmain licence in 1392 it purchased, amongst other properties, a messuage with a tavern and four shops in this part of the city.[45]

The decision as to whether to invest in town property or not was also partly the result of personal choice. The various orders of friars obtained a number of licences, throughout the thirteenth and fourteenth centuries, to acquire or enclose property in the towns in which they were based. In 1316 the Carmelites of Nottingham were granted a licence for a plot of land adjacent to their house (with the chapel of St. James upon it) and the lane that led to it.[46] These small mendicant acquisitions were usually for the purpose of enlarging the precincts. All of the larger midland towns contained friaries and so they were a common feature of the late medieval urban land market. Yet their mendicant ideals meant that they rarely invested in land for its intrinsic value or in the hope of a rental income over the longer term. Investment choices based on ethics or vocation can be seen again in the acquisitions made by some monastic orders. The Augustinians, for example, commonly invested in property in the towns close to their houses. For example, in 1255, Haughmond Abbey held seven properties and 12s. 6d. in rent in nearby Shrewsbury.[47] Cirencester was an Augustinian abbey that was lord of the valuable Gloucestershire town of Cirencester with its rents, market tolls, stallage, and court perquisites. In the late thirteenth century the convent of

---

[42] Searle, *Lordship and Community*, 150.
[43] D. C. Cox (ed.), *The Chronicle of Evesham Abbey* (Evesham, 1964), 47–57.
[44] PRO, E164/21, fols 77-8; Goddard, *Lordship and Medieval Urbanisation*, ch. 3.
[45] PRO, E164/21, fols. 122v.
[46] *CPR 1313-17*, 382.
[47] *Rotuli Hundredorum*, vol. II, 76

Cirencester also held rents in Gloucester, London, and Bristol.[48] By the mid-fifteenth century they continued to hold a number of tenements and other properties in Gloucester.[49] The Augustinians, as a relatively new order, had not benefited from early grants of land, like those made to many of the Benedictine houses, and thus chose to invest in the fluid urban land market. When Cirencester Abbey surrendered to the crown in 1539, 9 per cent of its income came from urban holdings.[50] Hailes Abbey, on the other hand, was a Cistercian house, an order that traditionally had spurned towns and, despite their significant estates in Gloucester and Winchcombe in the later middle ages, Cistercian sensibilities may partly explain the 0.7 per cent of Hailes's revenues that came from their urban holdings in the early sixteenth century.

Some gains of land by the church appear not to have been what one might consider true investment at all. Parochial chaplains received numerous mortmain licences throughout the period. These were commonly small alienations, usually a few messuages or rents (commonly less than £3 in value), granted by members of the local parish community. Occasionally messuages were given purposefully to a chaplain in order to furnish him with a place to live.[51] Furthermore, grants to chaplains were commonly made in exchange for prayers for the souls of the grantors and their families. Nottingham's property market was dominated by chaplains, most from the town's principal church: St. Mary's. These men gained four 'specific' licences between 1324 and 1344.[52] These were not institutional acquisitions. St. Mary's was not a collegiate church so these properties and rents did not go to the church as a corporate body. In 1326, Robert Ingram of Nottingham granted four messuages and 40s. rent from various tenements in the city to a chaplain in order for him to perform daily divine service for his and his wife's souls after their deaths.[53] However, even if chaplains lacked the resources to acquire large urban estates and had to rely on donors' generosity, these may well have been used as investments. If we assume that the Nottingham chaplain received only the grant from Ingram and that he then leased the messuages out at typical early fourteenth-century city rates of about 6s. each, then the yearly return from this grant was just over £3.[54] We know that parish

[48] Ibid.,79.

[49] Stevenson, *Rental of Gloucester*, 5, 27, 61, 71–7, 81–7, 101, 103, 107.

[50] *Valor Ecclesiasticus Temp Henry VIII*, vol. II (Record Commission, 1831), 453–6, 463–71.

[51] *CPR 1385-9*, 376.

[52] *CPR 1324-7*, 80, 249; *CPR 1340-3*, 343; *CPR 1343-5*, 317.

[53] *CPR 1324-7*, 249.

[54] For rents in Nottingham see, *Records of the Borough of Nottingham*, vol. I, 1155–1399 (Nottingham, 1882), 69, 383, 386, 409–10.

clergy in the early sixteenth century regularly pocketed yearly incomes of £10 or more.[55] Despite grants to chaplains being individually smaller than those to religious institutions, their proportional value was similar. This one grant might thus have represented a third of his yearly income. This is more than Cirencester made from the urban component of its investments (9 per cent) and about the same proportion as Coventry Priory received from its Coventry holdings (28.4 per cent).[56] Thus despite differences in scale, urban land seems to have been consistently used by nearly all members of the clergy (excepting friars) as an investment with a view to a sustained financial return.

There is however one important detail that needs to be emphasized: in reality urban landholding was only a relatively small part of most seigneurial economies. Church lords, indeed all lords, seem to have been conservative and concentrated upon the estates they understood best. For the great monasteries, these tended to be rural manors. As we have seen, their urban holdings often represented less than 10 per cent of their annual income. By comparison, at the end of the thirteenth century, the Bishop of Ely gained 40 per cent of his yearly cash revenue from demesne profits alone. Between 1288 and 1400 the crop sales of both Canterbury Cathedral Priory and Westminster Abbey represented over 51 per cent of each house's total yearly revenue.[57] This impression is reinforced by the make-up of most 'general' mortmain licences. Only a very small proportion of the lands included within each licence were, in any way, urban. Thus in 1331, Hugh de Redynges, a chaplain, collected together three messuages, 240 acres of land, 10 acres of meadow, 3 acres of pasture, 40 acres of wood and 16s. rent located in eight separate manors and granted them to Reading Abbey. Only a small part of this grant can be considered urban: the rents that came from the small Herefordshire town of Leominster.[58] Thus most monastic houses appear to have accepted anything they could lay their hands on, regardless of its location or potential profitability. However, where monasteries were lords of wealthy towns, the returns could be higher. The great royal foundation of Westminster Abbey that held land in four towns (Staines in Middlesex, Pershore in Worcestershire, Moreton-in-Marsh in Gloucestershire and Westminster itself) and these holdings in 1535 totalled 13.7 per cent of its

---

[55] P. Heath, *The English Parish Clergy on the Eve of the Reformation* (London, 1969), 173; J. C. Russell, 'The Clerical Population of Medieval England', *Traditio*, 2 (1944), 2, 179; Dyer, *Standards of Living*, 32.

[56] Calculations based upon the priory's rental of 1411, PRO, E 164/21.

[57] Miller and Hatcher, *Medieval England: Rural Society and Economic Change*, 201–3; B. M. S. Campbell, *English Seigniorial Agriculture, 1250–1450* (Cambridge, 2000), 184–5.

[58] *CPR 1330-4*, 221.

annual income.[59] As we have seen, in 1411 Coventry Priory gained just under 30 per cent of its total annual rental income from its Coventry holdings. In 1535, 21.8 per cent of the priory's total income came from its city holdings (representing 25.1 per cent of its temporal income).[60]

The chronology of investment

The church had been accumulating urban real estate for centuries before the Statute of Mortmain was introduced.[61] Towns like Ludlow and Warwick contained considerable ecclesiastical estates before 1280.[62] In 1255 Ludlow already boasted five church landlords who held twenty-four town properties and 8s. 2d. rent, and by 1279 twenty clerical lords of various different complexions held seventy-nine properties in Warwick. In the thirteenth century Battle Abbey began to focus on the acquisition of lucrative town messuages in addition to its traditional purchases of arable land. This had the effect of increasing the number of tenants paying rent to the abbey, thus increasing their yearly revenues.[63] Similarly Westminster Abbey increased its portfolio of urban land through gift and purchase in the period after 1200.[64]

The chronology of ecclesiastical acquisitions of urban land through mortmain in the later middle ages is represented in Figure 1. Two points about these data must be clarified. First, as we have seen, only rarely did 'general' mortmain licences include solely urban properties. Second, this graph only counts up the number of licences granted to religious institutions in each year, and does not reflect the amount of land, urban or otherwise, alienated in each licence. These data might be usefully compared to Sandra Raban's study of mortmain.[65] Her work examines the chronology of all mortmain licences without differentiating between urban and rural alienation. The high point for the granting of licences that include urban land in midland towns was reached in 1329. As Raban's data suggests, the steepest growth in licence

[59] This figure is an overestimate because Moreton-in-Marsh is valued only as part of Bourton-on-the-Hill. Harvey, *Westminster Abbey*, 63, 168, 334–5, 355–6, 363; Rosser, *Medieval Westminster*, 46.

[60] *Valor Ecclesiasticus*, vol. III, 49–51; A. Savine, *English Monasteries on the Eve of the Dissolution* (Oxford, 1909), 284.

[61] E. A. Kosminsky, *Studies in the Agrarian History of England in the Thirteenth Century* (Oxford, 1956), 109; R. Lennard, *Rural England, 1086–1135* (Oxford, 1959), 25; J. A. Raftis, *The Estates of Ramsey Abbey* (Toronto, 1957), 7

[62] T. John (ed.), *The Warwickshire Hundred Rolls of 1279–80* (Records of Social and Economic History, 19, 1992), 26–38; *Rotuli Hundredorum*, vol. II, 69.

[63] Searle, *Lordship and Community*, 134–51.

[64] Rosser *Medieval Westminster*, 46–51.

[65] Raban, *Mortmain Legislation*, 153–86.

acquisition for all types of land was between *c.*1300 and *c.*1340, with huge numbers of licences being granted in these years. Whilst this is apparent in the urban-licence data of Figure 1, the trend indicates a far gentler climb in licences for urban land. This suggests that urban land remained a fairly constant feature of investment by church lords that did not fluctuate wildly over time (excluding the early 1390s). These trends can be examined in more detail with reference to acquisitive behaviour of individual religious houses. In the fourteenth century, Westminster Abbey shifted their investment policies towards a more intensive exploitation of urban land.[66] Worcester Cathedral Priory and St Peter's Abbey and St Oswald's in Gloucester all appear to have gained most of their urban holdings between the late thirteenth century and the mid-fourteenth century.[67] One of the most detailed sources of information for the midland counties comes from the early fifteenth-century cartulary of Coventry Cathedral Priory which enumerates all of the house's acquisitions through mortmain in considerable detail.[68] The priory acquired land through mortmain between 1284 and 1379. However, the bulk of their urban acquisitions were licensed between 1284 and 1349. The importance of thirteenth-century urban investment can be seen in the priory's acquisitions between 1284 and 1299. In that fifteen-year period they acquired £7 10s. 2½d. in rents from within the city of Coventry alone. This represents the priory's largest rental acquisition though mortmain. The largest numbers of individual properties acquired was between 1305 and 1349, totalling ninety-three and a half individual properties all within the city of Coventry. As well as these, in the same forty-four-year period they acquired an extra £5 2s. 11d. in rent.

Whilst the chronology of investment by the church was undoubtedly affected by numerous factors, for example reduced numbers of licence grants during times of royal absence abroad or increased numbers due to changes in the law, one of the key determining factors was the economic or commercial climate. Whilst fluctuations in commercial activity can only be estimated in the broadest of terms, they do seem to have impacted upon urban investment. The period *c.*1280–1350 is recognized as a time of increasing uncertainly for most seigneurial economies.[69] As rural land became less profitable, all lords bought less of it. However, this does not seem to have been the case with urban land, despite evidence of sluggish urban economies and

[66] Harvey, *Westminster Abbey*, 168.

[67] Baker and Holt, *Urban Growth and the Medieval Church*, 268, 281.

[68] PRO, E 164/21, fols 49-52, 85–124.

[69] See C. Dyer, *Making a Living in the Middle Ages: The People of Britain, 850–1520* (London, 2002), 240–6, 293–9, 337–9.

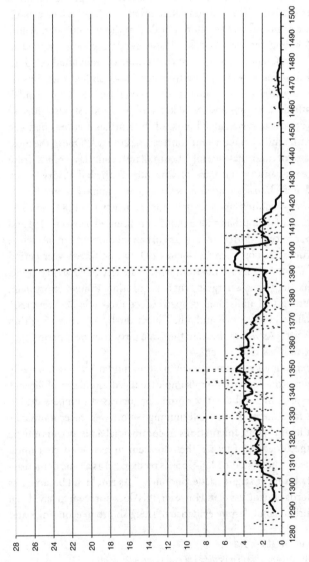

Fig. 1. Mortmain licences that include grants of urban land, 1280–1500, with 10-year moving average (N = 354). (Source: *Calendar of Patent Rolls*, 1272–1509; PRO, C 143)

falling rents between the 1320s and 1340s. Certainly the period 1315–25 with its famines and agrarian crisis, saw a levelling out of urban investment (see Figure 1), but this was followed by increased investment between 1326 and 1358 with the high point being reached in the 1330s and 1340s. This suggests that church lords, like their lay contemporaries, considered urban land a safer and more profitable bet than agricultural land during the crises of the early fourteenth century.

Raban's undifferentiated mortmain licence data suggests the period *c.*1350–*c.*1430 witnessed a dramatic and consistent fall in the number of licences granted (again excluding the early 1390s), giving almost a mirror image of the earlier period of growth. Once again this decline is observable in the urban-licence data, but as before the reduction is gentler in profile (excluding the early 1390s), and later, with the decline beginning in earnest only in the 1370s, suggesting a continuing confidence in the profitability of urban land after the Black Death. However, that conviction faltered as the century progressed. After 1350 the amount of urban real estate acquired by Coventry Priory declined considerably. Between 1350 and 1397 they acquired only twenty-five individual properties and only 2s. 9½d. in rent. A very similar urban investment profile can be observed in other monastic acquisitions. Shrewsbury Abbey's greatest period of urban acquisition was between 1340 and 1392.[70] After that they acquired no other urban land through mortmain save six Shrewsbury messuages in 1406.[71] Winchcombe Abbey's urban acquisitions in the midlands all fell between 1308 and 1401.[72] After that they received no more licences for urban land or rent. The data suggests that the church continued to acquire property in towns, albeit at a declining rate, until about 1412. Whilst trade had been disrupted in the 1350s and 60s, most authorities agree that the general level of commercial activity reached its post-plague zenith in about 1400.[73] With work available and tenements lying empty in most towns, new tenants must have been relatively easy to find. Thus landlords continued to invest in towns.

The fifteenth century, however, saw a significant drop in the number of licences for the church to acquire urban land. Furthermore, fewer properties were being granted in each licence. Thus many religious institutions simply withdrew from the urban land market for large parts of the century. In 1408, St. Mary's Hospital in Leicester acquired a licence for two messuages

[70] *CPR 1338-40*, 423–4; *CPR 1343-5*, 214; *CPR 1391-6*, 155, 141.

[71] *CPR 1405-8*, 162.

[72] *CPR 1301-8*, 141; *CPR 1317-21*, 516–17; *CPR 1391-6*, 71; *CPR 1396-9*, 139; *CPR 1399-1401*, 538.

[73] Dyer, *Making a Living in the Middle Ages*, 293–7.

and two tofts in Leicester's suburbs. In the previous century, between 1360 and 1392, St. Mary's had gained sixty-one properties and 9s. of rent in the city and its suburbs.[74] This sharp differentiation between the four-teenth and fifteenth centuries was echoed in the urban acquisitions of all religious institutions. Once again this must relate to the economic circumstances in which religious lords found themselves. In the fifteenth century lords again found their lands declining in value in the midst of a severe economic depression.[75] In most towns too rents fell in the mid-fifteenth century thus making investment less remunerative.[76] Thus we see that licences for urban land were not apparently granted between 1420 and 1452, at least for towns in the midlands. A partial recovery can just be made out between 1453 and 1472. For example, in 1467 Halesowen Abbey was granted a licence for messuages, land and rent in Lichfield and four other Staffordshire manors.[77] Most lords increased their revenues, albeit modestly, between 1470 and 1520.[78] This seems to have allowed them some freedom to invest in urban land.

However, it is also clear that other institutions, guilds in particular, con-tinued to acquire rents throughout the later fourteenth century and well into the fifteenth century. As we have seen, guilds were major beneficiaries of urban land and the most important investors in the urban property market in the post-Black Death period.[79] However, whilst it is indisputably the case that guilds were urban portfolio specialists in the later middle ages, we must be wary of the chronology of these grants. Figure 1 demonstrates that many grants to guilds occurred in 1392–3.[80] However, it must be remembered

[74] *CPR 1405-8*, 387; *CPR 1367-70*, 104; *CPR 1370-4*, 361; *CPR 1391-6*, 142. These licences include considerable grants of land, rent, and the advowsons of several churches in manors adjacent to the city.

[75] Dyer, *Making a Living in the Middle Ages*, 337; J. Hatcher, 'The Great Slump of the Fifteenth Century', in R. H Britnell and J. Hatcher (eds), *Progress and Problems in Medieval England* (Cambridge, 1996), 237–72.

[76] A. F. Butcher, 'Rent, Population and Economic Change in Late Medieval Newcastle', *Northern History*, 14 (1978), 67–77; A. F. Butcher, 'Rent and the Urban Economy: Oxford and Canterbury in the Later Middle Ages', *Southern History*, 1 (1979), 11–43; S. H. Rigby, ' "Sore decay" and "fair dwellings": Boston and Urban Decline in the Later Middle Ages', *Midland History*, 10 (1985), 55.

[77] *CPR 1467-77*, 16.

[78] Dyer, *Making a Living in the Middle Ages*, 338–9.

[79] J. Toulmin Smith (ed.), *English Gilds* (London, 1870), 231; Raban, *Mortmain Legislation*, 172–3. For Coventry, see for example, Hilton, 'Some Problems of Urban Real Property', 326–37.

[80] This is echoed in Raban's data. Raban, *Mortmain Legislation*, 155.

that the law relating to mortmain was changed in 1391.[81] The new statute widened the number of institutions that required a licence to acquire property. Church landlords were thereafter not the only perpetual corporations that required licences. This change stimulated an exceptional number of licences in the following two years, many of which were retrospective in character. Thus 61 per cent of all guild licences for urban land in the midlands were granted in 1392. It is likely, however, that many of these properties had been collected before the 1390s. In Coventry's case, all of its major guilds had been founded between the 1340s and the 1360s.[82] These guilds began amassing city properties on a huge scale at that time, long before the law required them to obtain a licence to do so. This change in the mortmain law of 1391 skews the data but also informs. The rise in the number of licences alienating urban land is significantly more pronounced than in Raban's undifferentiated mortmain figures, reinforcing the close link between guilds and the acquisition of specifically urban property.

Other fashionable institutions, such as chantries, also appear to have taken the lead in urban investment. The property market of Cirencester witnessed exactly these shifts in religious participation. Between 1305 and 1374 the abbot and convent of Cirencester Abbey were the principal ecclesiastical players in Cirencester's property market.[83] The only other early religious participant was the local hospital.[84] However, in the 1380s and 90s the market was dominated by grants to chaplains acquiring property to support their various offices at the local parish church of St. Mary and its various altars.[85] Similar patterns are observable in large towns such as Lichfield, Leicester, Hereford, and Shrewsbury and small towns like Market Harborough, Ledbury, and Winchcombe with chaplains and chantries becoming an increasingly dominant feature of the urban land market between 1350 and 1450. Furthermore, as A. Kreider suggests, the evidence of avoidance and evasion of the mortmain law by chantry donors suggests that the number of foundations is actually underestimated in the mortmain data.[86] However, shifting patterns of religious endowment or acquisition after the Black Death are somewhat illusory. Parochial chaplains gained significant numbers of donations long before

---

[81] *Statutes of the Realm*, vol. II, 79–80.

[82] CRO, BA/B/P/2/1; BA/B/P/1/2; BA/B/P/3/1; BA/B/P/4/1; BA/B/P/5/1; *Curia Regis Rolls, 1340–3*, 534; *CPR, 1343-5*, 143.

[83] PRO, C 143 file xcix/3; file cxix/12; file cxl/13; file cclxxviii/2; file cccxxviii/12; file ccclxxxv/12.

[84] PRO, C 143 file lii/11.

[85] PRO, C 143 file ccccxix/19; file cccc/19.

[86] A. Kreider, *English Chantries: The Road to Dissolution* (London, 1979), 86–90.

Table 1. Mortmain licences for the acquisition of urban property by church lords, 1280–1500 (Source: *Calendar of Patent Rolls, 1272–1509*; PRO C143)

Town name	Number of licences	1334 (£)[87]
Coventry	60	750[88]
Gloucester	45	541
Hereford	33	605
Worcester	29	300
Leicester	27	267
Northampton	26	270
Nottingham	22	371
Shrewsbury	17	800
Lichfield	15	133
Ludlow	12	240
Newark	10	390
Cirencester	10	259
Warwick	8	85
Leominster	7	45
Winchcombe	7	107
Birmingham	5	141
Stratford-upon-Avon	4	131
Ledbury	4	125
Alcester	3	94
Higham Ferrers	2	128
Market Harborough	2	64
Tamworth	2	37
Henley-in-Arden	1	42
Lechlade	1	156
Northleach	1	44
Hinckley	1	24

1350. Ninety-two per cent of Nottingham's chaplains' licences were gained before 1349, with only one more licence being sought in 1357. A similar pattern is seen in Hereford, where 50 per cent of all the grants to chaplains were licensed between 1314 and 1341, and Worcester where half of all grants to Worcester's chaplains were licensed between 1310 and 1347. Worcester's case is instructive because these early grants were licensed during the period of maximum penetration by all religious investors: Worcester Priory, the hospitals of St. Oswald and St. Wolstan, other monastic houses and nunneries, and local parochial chaplains. From 1350 onwards all grants to ecclesiastics declined in the city. For a while the chaplains bucked this trend by maintaining

[87] R. E. Glasscock (ed.), *The Lay Subsidy of 1334* (London, 1975). The figures have been rounded to the nearest pound.

[88] The figure for Coventry is widely believed to be an underestimate. See A. Dyer, 'Appendix: Ranking Lists of English Medieval Towns', in D. M. Palliser (ed.), *The Cambridge Urban History of Britain*, vol. 1 (Cambridge, 2000), 747–55.

their level of city investment and obtaining licences (50 per cent of their total) between 1353 and 1371. But after that they, along with all other church landlords, received no further donations through mortmain. Thus regardless of denomination, size, or religious function, all ecclesiastical investment ebbed and flowed with the tides of economic circumstance.

In 1967 Rodney Hilton clearly demonstrated the importance of guilds as urban landlords in the fifteenth century. This study has extended that analysis by examining the investment strategies of church landlords generally. It has revealed that town property was just one part and sometimes only a small part of the seigneurial economy. For some long-established monasteries, however, urban lordship and the higher relative value of urban land meant that their urban holdings represented a significant part of their yearly revenues. Even where the church was constrained by the licensing system (often inadvertently to its advantage), they demonstrated a preference for investment in towns where demand for property was highest—large, wealthy ones. Towns similarly spawned other urban specialists: guilds, hospitals and the parochial clergy. These, like the urban monasteries, were based in the towns in which they invested—proximity and local knowledge being the key. Urban acquisitions remained popular because their return remained fairly stable and dependable over time. The portfolio managers, whilst sometimes influenced by vocation or differing levels of business acumen, reacted to economic circumstance, increasing their urban investment in times of agrarian crisis, maintaining a reduced level of acquisition in the Indian Summer of the later fourteenth century and decreasing it when they lacked resources to do so or when rents began to fall in the fifteenth century. All church investors, even guilds and chantries, followed a similar investment profile over time.

English and French Towns in the Sixteenth Century

Penny Roberts

Comparative history, to paraphrase Rodney Hilton in the first line of his last book *English and French Towns in Feudal Society*, 'is rather a risky venture'.[1] Nevertheless, it is a valuable exercise for determining what is peculiar in a particular national context, as long as the historian is aware of the pitfalls of generalization. Hilton in this book set out to compare the relative integration of English and French urban communities into medieval economic and social structures, as well as their role in feudal society. He identified a number of trends which he posited would be consolidated in the following centuries, in particular, the dominance of officialdom in France and of a mercantile elite in England. The comparative approach will be used here not so much to establish what had changed in urban communities by 1600, but rather what perspectives a sixteenth-century viewpoint can give us on some of Hilton's conclusions. Of course, one century is far too short a period over which to expect much to have changed, and 1500 is a rather artificial divide for the essentially socio-economic developments Hilton discussed. Arguably it is 1600 rather than 1500 which marks the more significant watershed.[2] As Peter Clark and Paul Slack put it, the 'traditional, relatively closed, and semi-autonomous worlds' of early sixteenth-century towns contrast with 'the more modern, open and integrated urban society' in existence by 1700, a theme which has been continued by others.[3] At any rate, the sixteenth

---

[1] R. H. Hilton, *English and French Towns in Feudal Society: A Comparative Study* (Cambridge, 1992), xi.

[2] As highlighted in P. Benedict, 'More than Market and Manufactory: The Cities of Early Modern France', *French Historical Studies*, 20 (1997), 511–38; esp. 516, 519–20 regarding the growth in royal officials. See also M. Greengrass, *The French Reformation* (Oxford, 1987), 57, on the continuing importance of merchants in urban government in sixteenth-century France, as royal officials were often excluded from municipal posts.

[3] P. Clark and P. Slack, *English Towns in Transition, 1500–1700* (Oxford, 1976), 159. See also the contributions to P. Clark (ed.), *The Cambridge Urban History of Britain*, vol. II, *1540–1840* (Cambridge, 2000), esp. 167–450.

century is far from being a foreign country for late medievalists; certainly its urban politics and culture should be clearly recognizable.

English and French towns in the pre-modern period had much experience in common, but as Hilton recognized, their most obvious difference was size.[4] London was the only substantial urban community in England, whereas seven towns had a population in excess of 20,000 in France by 1500, a result of entrenched regionalism as well as France having a much larger overall population (estimated at some 16 million, compared with England's 2.5 million).[5] In general, England was 'lightly urbanised by European standards in 1540', with only 5 per cent of its population living in communities of over 5,000 inhabitants (rising to 8 per cent by 1600). Nevertheless, it was also distinctive for the continuing growth of its smaller towns.[6] Economically, too, England and France are traditionally held to have followed quite divergent paths. As a consequence, France suffers in comparison with England, especially with regard to their respective socio-economic developments during the early modern period. However, the usual picture of a stagnant and backward agricultural economy in France has to be offset by examples of investment and innovation, as well as an active mercantile sector which compares favourably with most other parts of Europe.[7]

Towns in Early Modern Society

Whilst recognizing 'the special features of urban existence', Rodney Hilton saw towns as very much part of feudal society, not antagonistic to it; all elements, urban and rural, formed part of a single system.[8] Definitions of 'feudal society' aside, early modernists would not demur from this view of

---

[4] Hilton, *English and French Towns*, 4.

[5] For assessments of the population of French towns at various points in the sixteenth century, see G. Saupin, *Les villes en France à l'époque moderne (XVIe–XVIIIe siècles)* (Paris, 2002), 16, where it is estimated that there were twenty towns with between 10,000 and 19,900 inhabitants in France by 1500.

[6] P. Glennie and I. Whyte, 'Towns in an Agrarian Economy, 1540–1700', and P. Griffiths, J. Landers, M. Pelling, and R. Tyson, 'Population and Disease, Estrangement and Belonging, 1540–1700', both in Clark (ed.), *The Cambridge Urban History*, 192, 196–7.

[7] For the classic position, see B. Chevalier, *Les bonnes villes de France du XIVe au XVIe siècle* (Paris, 1982), 151-71; G. Duby (ed.), *Histoire de la France urbaine*, vol. III, *La ville classique: de la Renaissance aux Révolutions* (Paris, 1981), 63–7. For a revisionist view, see P. Hoffman, *Growth in a Traditional Society: The French Countryside, 1450–1789* (Princeton, 1996).

[8] Hilton, *English and French Towns*, 154.

urban integration into the wider socio-economic and political order.[9] Yet, despite the evident continuities between the late medieval and early modern periods, there are also definite trends which begin to distinguish the period, especially after 1550: in the position of the town in relation to the countryside, and in reaction to demographic change and other factors. These should be seen, however, as consolidating existing trends, rather than in any sense innovatory. Philip Benedict identifies five characteristic developments:

1. the extension of urban control over rural landed property (through purchase by elites or reversion to them through the growing indebtedness of the peasantry)
2. the growth of rural industry, especially textiles, controlled by urban merchants tempted by cheaper labour costs (what is commonly known as the putting-out system)
3. the expansion of state and town-based administrative elites (especially men of law, but also *rentiers* who lived off rents and other investments, with time on their hands to devote to office)
4. the movement to towns of a significant fraction of the nobility (though there was already a strong tradition of noble residence in some towns, as in southern France)
5. greater crown intervention politically and financially in municipal affairs (largely the effect of centralization, the desire to control local militias and manipulate elections to office, and the growing need for taxation to fund wars).[10]

Again, these are trends that were very much under way in the sixteenth century, though far from complete by 1600, and arguably more pronounced in the following century.

There is some debate as to whether the autonomy of municipal institutions (which historians are at pains to stress were not generally descended directly from medieval communes) was being eroded or enhanced by growing central authority. Royal recognition of urban privileges was seen as the best means to maintain the loyalty that the crown lacked the force to compel, and ensured effective compliance with its will. Benedict argues that the fact that municipal

---

[9] Most recently, S. R. Epstein (ed.), *Town and Country in Europe, 1300–1800* (Cambridge, 2001); M. Prak (ed.), *Early Modern Capitalism: Economic and Social Change in Europe, 1400–1800* (London, 2001).

[10] This list is based on the opening of P. Benedict, 'French Cities from the Sixteenth Century to the Revolution: An Overview', the introductory chapter in id. (ed.), *Cities and Social Change in Early Modern France* (London, 1989), 7–8. These themes are also pursued in the essays in Clark (ed.), *The Cambridge Urban History*, 1–16, 167–450.

privileges were royal grants, meant that councillors saw their authority as a reflection of that of the king, and this tied them into an expanding patronage network increasingly controlled by the crown.[11] As will be seen later from Robert Tittler's study, this was as true of English towns as of their French counterparts in the sixteenth century.[12]

Looking further afield, aspects of social and cultural change ought to be considered too. Most obvious of these, apart from the various challenges posed by the Reformation, were the growing demands on municipalities: the responsibility for poor relief, which became more organized in response to demographic crisis from the 1520s, for educational institutions, and for hospitals, all previously the preserve of the church.[13] Likewise, the distancing of the elite from the bulk of the citizenry, as with the banning of mystery plays and *charivaris*, has been interpreted as part of the growing emphasis on law and order. Similarly, the curbing of religious festivals which once served to reinforce civic solidarity, but now provided the opportunity for violent confrontation, meant rituals were increasingly secularized, reinforcing the authority of both municipality and crown.[14]

In even a brief review of the historiography of this period, consideration must be given to the debate regarding the crisis and decay of English towns from 1450 to the mid-sixteenth century.[15] The classic examples are Palliser's York and Phythian-Adams' Coventry, but it is a variegated picture and there are problems of evidence.[16] Shortage of labour has been identified as the main

[11] On these points, see Benedict, 'French Cities', 19–20.

[12] R. Tittler, *The Reformation and the Towns in England: Politics and Political Culture, c.1540–1640* (Oxford, 1998).

[13] J.-P. Gutton, *La société et les pauvres: l'exemple de la généralité de Lyon, 1534–1789* (Paris, 1970); Chevalier, *Les bonnes villes*, 229–38; J. F. Pounds, *Poverty and Vagrancy in Tudor England* (2nd edn, London, 1986); A. Cowan, *Urban Europe, 1500–1700* (London, 1998), 157–69.

[14] Clark and Slack, *English Towns in Transition*, 149–50; Tittler, *The Reformation and the Towns*, 19–20, 336–40; Chevalier, *Les bonnes villes*, 280–5; Duby (ed.), *La ville classique*, 180–91. For a general survey of these trends, see R. Muchembled, *Popular Culture and Elite Culture in France, 1400–1750* (trans. L. Cochrane, Baton Rouge and London, 1985).

[15] See principally, P. Clark and P. Slack (eds), *Crisis and Order in English Towns, 1500–1700: Essays in Urban History* (London, 1972) and their *English Towns in Transition*; and for the counter case, A. Dyer, *Decline and Growth in English Towns, 1400–1640* (London, 1991). For a brief summary of the debate, see Dyer, *Decline and Growth*, 12–13, 52–3, and J. Barry (ed.), *The Tudor and Stuart Town: A Reader in English Urban History, 1530–1688* (London, 1990), 6–7.

[16] D. Palliser, *Tudor York* (Oxford, 1979); C. Phythian-Adams, *Desolation of a City: Coventry and the Urban Crisis of the Late Middle Ages* (Cambridge, 1979).

problem in the period 1450–1550 (compared with the continent, where population increased earlier), but the hypothesis is hard to prove. There are differences of opinion over the impact of the mid-sixteenth-century demographic increase, whether it stimulated urban growth or brought bigger problems. Clark and Slack paint a gloomy picture for larger towns, though they acknowledge that market towns prospered in response to expanding agricultural production and incomes.[17] However, others are more optimistic that growth was a positive factor. The drawbacks of the demand for poor relief, levels of violence, and taxation were manageable, and there was a reassertion of a number of regional centres in the 1520s. A slump in the cloth trade meant that textile towns were hard hit, but most, like Norwich, recovered; many went on to specialize in other areas which offset the detrimental effects of the putting-out system (contrary to the hypothesis of rural/urban antagonism) and the decline in real wages.[18]

However, from a European perspective, urban stagnation is more characteristic of the early modern period than growth; the expansion experienced in England, and also in the Netherlands, was exceptional.[19] Growth was concentrated in administrative capitals, ports (especially on the Atlantic coast), new towns and industrial cities, especially those producing luxury goods. Political protection by rulers was arguably more significant than economic factors for this increase, which may fit with the well-attested expansion of bureaucracies in the period.[20] This general overview of urban trends provides a context for the particular themes to be discussed here, in order to establish the degree of continuity or change from medieval to early modern, using Hilton's book as a baseline.

In perching on the shoulder of this particular giant, it is not possible to cover as many aspects as Hilton did even in what he himself termed 'a small book'.[21] The discussion will therefore focus on two issues which are the theme of two of the book's chapters. First to be considered will be the composition of

---

[17] Clark and Slack, *English Towns in Transition*, passim, and Dyer's analysis, *Decline and Growth*, 51–7.

[18] Dyer, *Decline and Growth*, 54–5; P. Clark (ed.), *Country Towns in Pre-industrial England* (Leicester, 1981), 11–14, provides a brief survey of the 'winners and losers' of the period.

[19] S. R. Epstein, 'The Late Medieval Crisis as an "Integration Crisis"', and J. Luiten van Zanden, 'Early Modern Economic Growth: A Survey of the European Economy, 1500–1800', both in Prak (ed.), *Early Modern Capitalism*, esp. 46, 84–5. Nevertheless, the sixteenth century is generally seen as a period of urban growth with stagnation and decline a feature of the seventeenth century, see Cowan, *Urban Europe*, 4; Duby (ed.), *La ville classique*, 44–6.

[20] Epstein (ed.), *Town and Country in Europe*, 13–16.

[21] Hilton, *English and French Towns*, xi.

urban oligarchies, since officials, especially lawyers, are characteristically believed to have taken over French municipalities by the end of the middle ages. In contrast, as already noted, Hilton stressed that mercantile elites were seen to predominate in English towns. Indeed, this is the basis for one of the standard arguments as to why England had a precocious transition to capitalism.[22] It will be necessary to establish, therefore, to what extent one can make such a sharp distinction, and what this means for the different trajectories which France and England took in the early modern period. The second issue is the incidence of conflict within urban communities, principally involving socio-economic discontent but also, characteristically in the sixteenth century, confessional tensions. Religious change is impossible to ignore in any consideration of sixteenth-century developments, and England and France provide interesting contrasting experiences of the impact of Reformation.

Urban Rulers

The social composition of the ruling elite and its relationship with feudal landowning interests were the fundamental issues for Hilton. Centralization was delayed and the feudal grip over local society lasted longer in France. The rise of the merchants came later and their power was strangled by the 'flight into officialdom' and the growth of venality (the sale and purchase of office), Chevalier's 'treason of the bourgeoisie'.[23] This trend is exemplified by the case of Montpellier, where a precocious (for France) mercantile elite had taken over by the thirteenth century.[24] By the late sixteenth century, there was a commercial downturn because of competition from nearby Marseilles and the disruption of the civil wars, but this was compensated by the growth of royal administration, because of the establishment of several financial institutions including a sovereign *cour des aides* of regional importance. Frederick Irvine has calculated that the number of offices quadrupled between 1500 and 1600, especially post 1550, and an accompanying hike in salaries led to a redistribution of wealth and property.[25] For Hilton, a comparison between London and Paris, in terms of investment in property versus trade, exemplified these contrasting trajectories already by the fifteenth

---

[22] Ibid., 104.

[23] Hilton, *English and French Towns*, 87–104 (quotations from p. 104); Chevalier, *Les bonnes villes*, 106, 129–49.

[24] Hilton, *English and French Towns*, 96–7.

[25] F. M. Irvine, 'From Renaissance City to *ancien régime* Capital: Montpellier, c.1500–c.1600', in Benedict (ed.), *Cities and Social Change*, 105–33.

century.[26] Clearly, the two capitals were exceptional in all kinds of ways, but the thesis works in general terms for some of the larger provincial centres too.

In France, such developments were dependent on the reinforcement of towns as administrative centres. There were eight with sovereign law courts, the *parlements*, which were increasing in size; for example, the Bordeaux *parlement* grew from twenty-five to sixty-two members between 1515 and 1543, and this is also true of lesser courts which acted as regional centres, as in Montpellier, Poitiers and Amiens.[27] This was often a gradual process and seemingly inversely proportional to commercial decline; as was the case for the emigration of the textile trade from Rouen and Dijon, and the pastel trade at Toulouse.[28] It was compounded after 1560 by a general increase in royal officials with legal training and the introduction of extra layers of royal jurisdiction, principally the *présidiaux* from 1552. Dijon, already the seat of a *bailliage* (the basic royal administrative unit in northern France), a *chambre des comptes* (fiscal court), and a *parlement*, gained additional chambers in the sixteenth century, with the consequence that the number of offices there doubled between 1464 and 1556.[29]

Yet caveats are also necessary; the real growth of urban royal administration was a seventeenth-century phenomenon, with the arrival of the *intendants* and their entourages, and courts often represented rival governing institutions to the municipal authorities, rather than there being any significant overlap in personnel. Officialdom was antagonistic to established feudal dignitaries too; for example, in the town of Langres there was tension between the jurisdiction of the bishop, who was also a duke and peer, and the *bailliage* established in 1561.[30] Furthermore all towns, one way or another, existed in the patronage orbit of the royal governor of a province or town or his lieutenant. The strength of municipal authorities was dependent on the size of the town, the concessions obtained from the crown, and the relative strength of the rival governing institutions already mentioned. It is also evident that the mercantile elite was still predominant in commercial centres, such as Lyons (making up 79 per cent of councillors in the mid-sixteenth century, a position of dominance which it only lost at the end of the century), and even some places where distribution had come to displace manufacture, such as

[26] Hilton, *English and French Towns*, 97–100.

[27] Benedict, 'French Cities', 26, 28, 125.

[28] Ibid., 27–8.

[29] J. R. Farr, 'Consumers, Commerce, and the Craftsmen of Dijon: The Changing Social and Economic Structure of a Provincial Capital, 1450–1750', in Benedict (ed.), *Cities and Social Change*, 140.

[30] Benedict, 'French Cities', 20.

Troyes.[31] Officialdom was clearly less prominent in the smaller towns; instead, the increasing bureaucratization of their larger neighbours often acted as a stimulus to local commercial production and trade. In contrast, the disappearance of an ecclesiastical presence on councils by the 1520s (along with a declining influence of the church over municipal activities generally) was a near universal experience, with the exception of the major ecclesiastical centre of Chartres and during the brief control of the Catholic League in some major towns in the 1580s and 1590s. In a few towns, such as Romans in Dauphiné, there was artisan and manual labourer representation on the council, but these groups were excluded from most other ruling bodies.[32] So there was a profusion of local variants, but an overall trend towards oligarchical councils and the increasing restriction of the franchise, though there could be effective resistance to the latter as Mack Holt has shown for mayoral elections in Dijon.[33]

Nevertheless, these were developments already established by the end of the middle ages, alongside a polarization of wealth.[34] The greatest privilege existed where municipal office conferred nobility, as in major towns in the south and west, such as Toulouse.[35] Here the membership of the *capitoulat* conferred real powers of patronage as well as noble status, continuing through the sixteenth century. The increasing power of the *parlement* led to tensions, but Robert Schneider argues that the court often reinforced the authority of the *capitouls* (municipal council) against rival bodies, and it was not in the *parlement*'s interests to erode their powers.[36] In Dijon, as James Farr demonstrates, the rise of officialdom was accompanied by commercial growth, and though the number of agricultural workers in the city, characteristically winegrowers, was declining, this was gradual and they still formed

---

[31] R. Gascon, *Grand commerce et vie urbaine au XVIe siècle: Lyon et ses marchands (c.1520–c.1580)* (2 vols., Paris, 1971), vol. II, 412; Duby (ed.), *La ville classique*, 161, 163; P. Roberts, *A City in Conflict: Troyes during the French Wars of Religion* (Manchester, 1996), 12, 15.

[32] Benedict, 'French Cities', 21.

[33] M. P. Holt, 'Popular Political Culture and Mayoral Elections in Sixteenth-Century Dijon', in id. (ed.), *Society and Institutions in Early Modern France* (Athens, Georgia, 1991), 98–116.

[34] On oligarchy as 'a long-established fact' by the early modern period, see C. R. Friedrichs, *Urban Politics in Early Modern Europe* (London, 2000), 19.

[35] Duby (ed.), *La ville classique*, 161.

[36] R. A. Schneider, 'Crown and Capitoulat: Municipal Government in Toulouse 1500–1789', in Benedict (ed.), *Cities and Social Change*, 195–220. However, Friedrichs, *Urban Politics*, 23, argues that 'wherever such a court existed, it served to diminish the council's authority'.

an important group. Nevertheless, the robe elite represented a massive 20 per cent of the population by 1600, as the agricultural workers had done in the mid-fifteenth century; two groups travelling in opposite directions. The percentage of artisans was declining too, though there was plenty of work in the building trades and for furniture-makers, prompted by the consumer boom stimulated by rich urban officials. Farr concludes, therefore, that the increased spending power of officeholders boosted wealth throughout Dijonnais society.[37] In contrast, Aix-en-Provence in the 1550s had a *parlement* and *cour des comptes* (fiscal court), but was also a regional marketplace involved in the wool trade, thus its single largest sector was agricultural rather than manufacture-based.[38]

So there are qualifications to be made, but Hilton's overall contrast between English and French urban society seems to hold true. It was also characteristic of French society that noble status was highly valued; the wealthy bought their way in through the purchase of land and royal letters, office-holding being only one route, and also became *rentiers*, quickly distancing themselves from their commercial origins. It is argued (by Friedrichs amongst others) that the attractions of noble status were less important in England, where wealth was the most important criterion, rather than the formation of urban dynasties.[39] The general pattern was that English urban government was open to the wealthy, who thus attained political power and social recognition. There was easy movement between the urban elite and the rural gentry, and commerce was no bar. Merchants predominated, though there was some gentrification evident too. In France, the trend was largely in the opposite direction, even where the mercantile elite was still powerful.

Reformation and Urban Conflict

Nevertheless, in certain respects these distinctions between English and French municipal experience in the sixteenth century can begin to blur on closer inspection. The Reformation took very different courses in the two countries and might be expected to have sharpened the contrasts between them, but this was not necessarily the case. In a recent book, Robert Tittler set out to incorporate religious change into English urban history as a factor

[37] Farr, 'Consumers, Commerce, and the Craftsmen', 134–73.

[38] C. Dolan, 'The Artisans of Aix-en-Provence in the Sixteenth Century: A Micro-analysis of Social Relationships', in Benedict (ed.), *Cities and Social Change*, 174–94.

[39] C. R. Friedrichs, *The Early Modern City, 1450–1750* (London and New York, 1995), 198–9; Clark and Slack, *English Towns in Transition*, 111; nevertheless, there was 'no major restructuring of the social hierarchy in English towns between the 1520s and 1660s' (114).

in influencing developments in urban politics, since, as he puts it, 'the Reformation does seem a central and formative experience in almost every individual town'.[40] This makes for some interesting comparisons with French towns, allowing us to test some of Tittler's hypotheses. In France, the Reformation was not a national state-led experience. It proved to be highly disruptive and divisive, and only took a firm grip in a few southern towns, such as Montauban and Nîmes. Tittler argues that in English towns the advent of the Reformation in the 1530s and 1540s, and its accompanying legislation, raised questions regarding the distribution of material resources (primarily as a result of the Dissolution), legal authority and political power. The Reformation's impact on political culture led to a new civic ideology; and the proliferation of royal legislation, which instituted the changes, allowed for crown intervention in urban affairs like never before. It also coincided with a time of profound economic and social change after previous stagnation, and a time of instability in which the elites sought to reinforce order. In addition, the centralization and expansion of the state lent new powers to its representatives: members of municipal councils.

For the beginning of the sixteenth century, however, Tittler proposes a contrast with the continent: that the predominant culture in England was essentially feudal demonstrating the 'shallowness of urban consciousness' there.[41] This appears to jar with Hilton's belief in France's stronger feudal grip.[42] The difference is that Hilton did not see the establishment of medieval communes as anti-feudal (nor their legacy as so decisive), and asserted that regional factors were probably more significant for their development in France. For Tittler, political autonomy was weak in all but the largest English towns; most were under the direct authority of an external and superior lay or ecclesiastical authority, and officials were not decisively differentiated from the general run of the freemanry. Ian Archer broadly supports this point, whilst acknowledging the immense variation between towns 'in the degree of political autonomy they enjoyed and in the distribution of political power within them'.[43] In the Reformation era, Tittler argues, there was a sharply accelerated transformation of urban government, society and culture, especially in larger towns, becoming more formalized and oligarchical, and

[40] Tittler, *The Reformation and the Towns*, 8.
[41] Ibid., 11.
[42] Hilton, *English and French Towns*, 129–30.
[43] I. A. Archer, 'Politics and Government, 1540–1700', in Clark (ed.), *The Cambridge Urban History*, 235–6. See also his discussion of the limitations of oligarchy, 241–6, and that 'most civic constitutions continued to blend oligarchic and participatory elements' (242).

at greater political, social, and economic distance from the governed. He acknowledges that these trends pre-dated the period, but argues that polarization became more prevalent, and the state more reliant on these urban officials. Tittler also sees the 'harmonizing effect of traditional cultural forms' or 'traditions of community' (i.e. shared values and forms of mediation) destroyed by the shift towards oligarchy and the suppression of religious rituals. So, by the early seventeenth century, urban political culture was transformed; local autonomy was overwhelmed by external intrusion, and legislative efforts to invest urban offices with royal authority changed urban politics.[44]

The major development Tittler identifies is the increasing number of 'towns corporate' through incorporation by charter, thereby establishing their powers and privileges.[45] This included forty-five boroughs between 1540 and 1558, spurred by the need to acquire the rights to the land of dissolved religious institutions, and the resources to offset socio-economic difficulties. Incorporation often conferred royal, and therefore legal, sanction on the existing institutional set-up, and was seen as a reaction to threats to local liberties and institutions rather than an act of defence by a self-interested elite. For larger towns, it consolidated oligarchy and the drive to local autonomy under the crown, excluding the lord of the manor or officials of the shire, although smaller towns often remained under the control of their lord. Many boroughs, still technically manorial, nevertheless made substantial gains in the form of self-governing powers on the basis of an established framework and a strong communal identity, as in the case of Banbury, Beverley, Bury St Edmunds, and Lichfield.[46] Not surprisingly, there was opposition from landlords to incorporation, leading to conflict at Daventry, Ipswich, and Poole.[47] But, Tittler emphasizes, other lords accepted the charter and appeared happy to continue their influence as a patron, in a redefined relationship which was mutually beneficial; or else were prepared to lend support to offset the power of a rival. Often incorporation cemented existing regional ties rather than creating new ones.

The crown's role was not necessarily seen as an unwelcome intervention either, since it shared the concerns of the urban authorities regarding law and order, rewarding them with stability. This image of mutual benefit is upheld by Archer who sees crown intervention as creating opportunities for urban

---

[44] Tittler, *The Reformation and the Towns*, 13.
[45] Though Clark and Slack, *English Towns in Transition*, 127–8, point out that this process was marked from 1440 and the Reformation simply provided 'additional impetus'.
[46] Tittler, *The Reformation and the Towns*, 153–60.
[47] Ibid., 166–7.

communities.[48] Exceptional problems of local governance during the short-term crises in the 1550s, 1590s and 1620s underlined the need to strengthen local authorities including the parish. Lichfield and Newcastle-under-Lyme made a rapid switch from broad representation via incorporation; but this process was not without challenge by rival claimants, as at Warwick and Stafford in the 1580s and 1590s, with accusations of corruption: that officials were serving their own interests, rigging elections, and oath-breaking.[49] Tittler regards this as a turning point in urban political values and outlook: co-optation increased, administration became more formalized and standardized, officers grew in stature and authority; and local government had more connection to the region and the nation and was more outward looking. But the problem for councillors remained of enforcing obedience and respect, torn between their responsibilities to the townspeople and the demands of the crown. Civic culture was designed to encourage deference and legitimize authority, but could lead to divisions and conflicts as well as cohesion.

Much of this, especially the shift towards oligarchy and the increasing intervention of the crown, is even more characteristic, as we have seen, of the urban situation in France. This familiarity is unsurprising, since many of the trends Tittler identifies were the product of wider socio-economic and political, rather than religious, change. The Reformation may have affected their direction (as a result, for instance, of the Dissolution), but otherwise its impact was not decisive. The centralizing state was a more significant factor in both France and England, manifesting itself in a proliferation of legislation, judicial reform, and pressure on urban resources. A similar debate surrounds the systematization of poor relief during the period, often seen as a protestant phenomenon, for which the church had previously been responsible, despite exact parallels in catholic countries where relief was taken over by the municipalities, as for example at Lyons and Toulouse.[50] The secularization of civic rituals, and the suppression of those seen to be disruptive, challenging authority, fits into the same pattern. Undoubtedly, though, in other ways,

---

[48] Archer, 'Politics and Government', 238–40; this argument is also made for French towns by H. J. Bernstein, *Between Crown and Community: Politics and Civic Culture in Sixteenth-Century Poitiers* (Ithaca and London, 2004), esp. 270–5.

[49] Tittler, *The Reformation and the Towns*, 192–3.

[50] Gutton, *La société et les pauvres*; N. Z. Davis, 'Poor Relief, Humanism and Heresy: The Case of Lyon', in ead., *Society and Culture in Early Modern France* (London, 1982), 17–64; B. B. Davis, 'Poverty and Poor Relief in Sixteenth-Century Toulouse', *Historical Reflections*, 17 (1991), 267–96.

'the Reformation brought with it new challenges to the unity of the urban community'.[51]

If this was true of English towns, it was much more so of their French counterparts torn apart by civil strife.[52] During the French religious wars (1562–98), the substantial Huguenot minority in many urban communities was involved in frequent clashes with catholic town-dwellers, particularly during the first decade of the conflict. The dominance of the Catholic League in many towns in the late 1580s and early 1590s put further strain on already diminishing resources and weakened defences. Furthermore, 'in the cities trade and industry was severely disrupted' by the wars, and the French economy in general was devastated.[53] The conflict not only led to bloodshed on the streets, but demonstrated the serious difficulties rebellious cities could cause for the crown. Civil strife also provided the opportunity for the feudal nobility to flex its muscle and exploit patronage networks to increase its influence over towns.[54] Thus, protestant lords extended protection to their co-religionists, and catholic leaders resisted royal pressure to accept coexistence. Not surprisingly, too, there was regular crown interference in municipal elections in an attempt to control them, but this again was a practice already established in the late middle ages.[55] The authorities increasingly felt torn between their duties to the crown and their responsibility to protect the interests of the inhabitants, divided loyalties which particularly emerged at a time of revolt.

Hilton saw no feudal antagonism in urban conflict either.[56] Despite the efforts of the authorities to maintain order and provide for the welfare of their inhabitants, conflicts were endemic if rarely violent. Most were peaceful and short-lived, although issues of political legitimacy could be more

---

[51] Cowan, *Urban Europe*, 94.

[52] On the divisive impact of the Reformation on English towns, see Archer, 'Politics and Government', 247–53, and more generally, Vanessa Harding, 'Reformation and Culture, 1540–1700', also in Clark (ed.) *The Cambridge Urban History*, 263–88.

[53] P. Benedict, *Rouen during the Wars of Religion* (Cambridge, 1981), 250; J. B. Wood, 'The Impact of the Wars of Religion: A View of France in 1581', *Sixteenth Century Journal*, 15 (1984), 131–68.

[54] There have been several urban studies on the impact of the wars; see, for example, B. B. Diefendorf, *Beneath the Cross: Catholics and Huguenots in Sixteenth-Century Paris* (Oxford, 1991); Benedict, *Rouen during the Wars*; Roberts, *A City in Conflict*; W. Kaiser, *Marseille au temps des troubles, 1559–1596* (Paris, 1992); P. Conner, *Huguenot Heartland: Montauban and Southern French Calvinism during the Wars of Religion* (London, 2002).

[55] Chevalier, *Les bonnes villes*, 104; on royal intervention in elections during the wars see Roberts, *A City in Conflict*, 16, 172.

[56] Hilton, *English and French Towns*, 127–51.

dangerous, representing not so much an attack on social inequalities as the failure of political leaders to fulfil their role as representatives of the community. As a result, the authorities were forced to take unrest seriously. William Beik concludes that, 'the latent power of the urban populace could never be lightly dismissed'.[57] However, the lack of military means to suppress large-scale disorders meant that good government was the best prevention. There were only occasional episodes which revealed that 'the normal mechanisms of social control and conflict resolution had temporarily broken down'. Thus conflict was allowed 'within a traditional framework of power relations'.[58]

Taxation was a particular focus of discontent in both countries. Hilton compared this to the conflict between peasants and lords in the countryside over rents, which, like taxes, represented the appropriation of surplus through non-economic compulsion, a burden falling on workers which the elites dodged.[59] This is a major and unsurprising continuity. Such discontent was aimed at outside agents, principally tax-collectors, but could equally turn on the authorities and the urban elite, as at Romans in 1580.[60] However, the traditional thesis that revolts during the latter decades of the French religious wars reflected the growing political tension between the crown and the Catholic League, on closer investigation appear rather to reveal traditional and localized economic concerns, as well as longstanding local political rivalries.[61] In England, urban unrest was often triggered by accusations of corruption among the ruling oligarchy. Sometimes revolts reflected factional struggles within the local elite; even an agrarian element was still present into the sixteenth century in centres such as Coventry.[62] Clashes between masters and journeymen were well established and continued throughout the early modern period, in the face of disadvantageous socio-economic trends, a decline in real wages, and the restriction of access to masterships.[63] Nervous authorities took measures to prevent the formation of illegal

---

[57] W. Beik, *Urban Protest in Seventeenth-Century France* (Cambridge, 1997).

[58] Friedrichs, *The Early Modern City*, 305, 324–5.

[59] Hilton, *English and French Towns*, 134–5, 140–1.

[60] See the classic study by E. Le Roy Ladurie, *Carnival: A People's Uprising at Romans, 1579–80* (trans. M. Feeney, New York and London, 1980).

[61] See P. Roberts, 'Urban Conflict and Royal Authority: Popular Revolts in Sixteenth-Century Troyes', *Urban History*, 34 (2007), 190–208.

[62] Hilton, *English and French Towns*, 144–5. On English urban conflicts see Clark and Slack, *English Towns in Transition*, 132–4, and Friedrichs, *The Early Modern City*, 309.

[63] See J. R. Farr, *Hands of Honor: Artisans and their World in Dijon, 1550–1650* (Ithaca and London, 1988).

fraternities and the *compagnonnages* in France which have been compared to early trade unions. Religion and patronage could and did cut across social divisions, but in general there is not much distinction to be made, either comparatively or chronologically, between late medieval and early modern protests. There was in each a well-established tradition of revolt in response to socio-economic grievances and dissatisfaction with the activities of the authorities. Differences here were in detail rather than substance, despite a lack of convergence in other respects.

Conclusions

Taking Hilton's line that towns formed an integral part of feudal society, it is necessary to consider the survival of feudal elements, broadly defined, into the sixteenth century. The argument for continuity is strong. As late medieval feudal ties and loyalties are increasingly seen to be looser, less rigid, more conditional and selfish, the more they look like those of the patronage/clientage relationships of the early modern period, as an extension of 'bastard' or 'decadent' feudalism.[64] These, too, were ties of loyalty within a mutually beneficial relationship, lasting only as long as the associated benefits. In both France and England seigneurial power still played a major role in urban communities as in society as a whole; it was a changing relationship perhaps, but part of the evolution of a system that was always mutating. The monarchies were still essentially feudal too, even in the context of increasing centralization. The crown had burgeoning influence in the towns, reinforcing loyalty and obedience, but its authority was fragile. Urban authorities were still capable of championing the interests of the citizenry and often played an ambivalent role in revolt. The main point to be made is that during both the fifteenth and sixteenth centuries, in both French and English towns, there was a consolidation of existing trends as affected by socio-economic and political change, but not yet the triumph of officialdom or capitalism in their respective urban contexts. After 1500, the less predictable impact of religious change was thrown into the mix.

It is much too hazardous for the historian to state definitively where one trend ends and another begins, even more so to posit contrasts over a one-hundred-year period. Similarities can be just as striking and informative, underlining the importance of embracing both continuity and change, exception and norm, in urban histories. If French and English towns up to 1600 look familiar enough to late medievalists, at the same time the more

[64] S. Kettering, 'Patronage in Early Modern France', *French Historical Studies*, 17 (1992), 839–62, and ead., 'Clientage during the Wars of Religion', *Sixteenth Century Journal*, 20 (1989), 221–39.

strikingly different urban landscape of the seventeenth century would have been impossible without the consolidation of trends in the sixteenth. Similarly, without Hilton's comparative study of late medieval English and French towns this present analysis would have been far more difficult. Much of Hilton's work sought continuities and discontinuities across traditional chronological, and in this case, geographical boundaries. Much less attention has been given here to small towns than he would have liked (and probably too much to religion), but it has attempted to remain true to his vision.

Serfdom and Freedom in Medieval England: A Reply to the Revisionists*

Zvi Razi

Historians of medieval England have studied serfdom extensively since the nineteenth century. However, in the 1960s M. M. Postan criticized them for paying more attention to the peasants' legal status than to their economic conditions and for overestimating the negative effects of serfdom. He claimed that the chief disabilities of servile status were balanced by the benefits of landholding and although the serfs were downgraded socially they could redeem their freedom by paying a reasonable sum of money to their lord. The fact that only a few of those who could have afforded it purchased their freedom was interpreted by him as an indication that the serfs were more interested in land acquisition than in manumission.[1] Postan's revisionist interpretation was reinforced and elaborated some twenty years later by John Hatcher in a brilliant article.[2] I will review it here in order to test the validity of the revisionist interpretation of serfdom through Hatcher's article, and also present a different view of the nature and history of this institution.

Hatcher begins his review of serfdom with demography. He argues that Kosminsky's estimate of 60 per cent unfree peasants in 1279 in the six counties for which Hundred Rolls returns survive does not represent the national picture.[3] He argues that if we take a sample of rural, urban, aristocratic, and clerical households the percentage of villeins' households does not exceed 33.[4]

---

* I am grateful to Jean Birrell for reading and commenting on my essay.

[1] M. M. Postan, 'Medieval Agrarian Society in its Prime: England', in id. (ed.), *The Cambridge Economic History of Europe*, vol I: *The Agrarian Life of the Middle Ages*, 2nd edn (Cambridge, 1966), 604–17; M. M. Postan, 'Legal Status and Economic Condition in Medieval Villages,' in id., *Essays on Medieval Agriculture and General Problems of the Medieval Economy* (Cambridge, 1966), 278–89.

[2] J. Hatcher. 'English Serfdom and Villeinage: Towards a Reassessment', *Past and Present*, 90 (1981), 4–39.

[3] E. A. Kosminsky, *Studies in the Agrarian History of England*, trans. R. Kisch (Oxford, 1956), 205–6.

[4] Hatcher, 'English Serfdom', 7.

Similarly, Edmund King has estimated that 40 per cent of peasant households were those of villeins.[5] Bruce Campbell has recently offered a more comprehensive estimate based on a national sample of 4090 manors obtained from the *Inquisitiones post mortem (IPMS)* between 1300 and 1349.[6] He calculated that during the period 1300–49, between 50 and 52 per cent of all the tenanted land was held by serfs and 48–50 per cent by freemen. Nonetheless, Campbell argues that, since the mean size of free holding was smaller than that of customary holding, the number of free tenants is likely to have equalled or even exceeded the number of servile tenants.[7] Even if Campbell's estimate is correct and the percentage of serfs was only about 50, we have to remember that the majority of the freemen in thirteenth- and fourteenth-century villages must have been related through marriage to serfs.[8] As peasants provided their relatives with land, and supported and helped each other in everyday life, hard times and old age, freemen were inevitably affected when their unfree relatives and neighbours suffered from seigneurial restrictions and exactions.[9]

Hatcher follows his demographic exercise by an examination of the status and conditions of serfs, in order to show that Robert Brenner was mistaken in claiming that serfdom was exploitative to such an extent that it caused an agrarian crisis of the late thirteenth century.[10] He argues that while unfree peasants were burdened by many obligations and restrictions, they nevertheless enjoyed security of tenure. Moreover, as the disabilities of serfdom were largely financial they were less oppressive than they appear. Labour services were often commuted, and the obligation to serve as manorial officers could be avoided by paying their landlords a fine. Similarly, for a licence fee serfs could take possession of their inheritance, marry their daughters, send their sons to be educated or to enter the church, leave the manor, alienate land, and sell animals. Even tallage, one of the hallmarks of serfdom, frequently became a fixed, often annual payment. The weight of the dues and rents was not heavy, as landlords were restrained by custom.[11] Hatcher also argues that

---

[5] E. King, *England, 1175–1425* (London, 1979), 50.

[6] B. M. S. Campbell, 'The Agrarian Problem in the Early Fourteenth Century', *Past and Present*, 188 (2005), 24–44.

[7] Ibid., 36.

[8] H. M. Cam, 'Pedigrees of Villeins and Freemen in the Thirteenth Century' in id., *Liberties and Communities in Medieval England* (London, 1963), 134–5.

[9] Z. Razi, 'The Myth of the Immutable English Family', *Past and Present*, 140 (1993), 11–15.

[10] Hatcher 'English Serfdom', 4.

[11] Ibid, 8–13.

there are many indications that by the later thirteenth century the unfree were normally paying less for their lands than they would have had to pay if their rents had been freely negotiated.[12] His claim has been recently confirmed by Junichi Kanzaka's new study of the Hundred Rolls. He showed that although customary tenants paid on average a higher rent than freeholders, they nonetheless paid significantly less than the going market rent.[13]

Hatcher and Kanzaka are probably right about the low level of rents for customary land.[14] But it is hardly likely that the serfs themselves knew it, since tenanted land was not traded commercially on most late thirteenth-century manors. At the same time they could hardly avoid seeing that they were paying much more per acre than their free neighbours and probably resented it. Therefore, when landlords attempted to increase even moderately the rents and services of their unfree tenants, they often encountered strong resistance and had to use coercive measures.[15]

Hatcher, however, plays down such conflicts. He claims that the relationships between the landlords and their unfree tenants were determined by local custom, which both sides usually honoured. Moreover, according to him, the peasants' behaviour shows that they believed that there were some advantages to serfdom; otherwise it is hard to explain why wealthy serfs were reluctant to purchase their freedom, and freemen were prepared to give up their freedom for land.[16]

It is likely that in the period under study, land-deficient freemen had no choice but to become unfree tenants in order to survive. Therefore their decision to change their legal status by itself reveals very little, if anything about their attitude to freedom. Such an attitude, however, can be inferred from the behaviour of bondmen who could afford to buy their freedom but did not. Manumissions recorded in manorial court rolls show that the

---

[12] Ibid, 17–18.

[13] J. Kanzaka, 'Villein Rents in Thirteenth-Century England: An Analysis of the Hundred Rolls of 1279–80', *Economic History Review*, 2nd ser., 55(2002), 599, 602–3, 610–12.

[14] Hatcher, 'English Serfdom', 18.

[15] R. H. Hilton, 'Peasant Movements in England before 1381', in id., *Class Conflict and the Crisis of Feudalism* (London, 1985), 122–38; R. H. Hilton, 'Freedom and Villeinage in England', in id., ed., *Peasants, Knights and Heretics: Studies in Medieval English Social History* (Cambridge, 1976), 174–91; C. Dyer, 'Memories of Freedom: Attitudes towards Serfdom in England', in M. L. Bush (ed.), *Serfdom and Slavery: Studies in Legal Bondage* (London, 1996), 277–95.

[16] Hatcher, 'English Serfdom', 24–6.

usual price for freedom was only a few shillings. In June 1281, for example, Richard de Adenebroch came to Halesowen manor court and paid 10s. to liberate John le Webbe, the abbot's bondman.[17] In the pre-plague Halesowen court rolls the names of 504 customary tenants are noted, but only fourteen of them paid for their manumission, for an average of 7s. 4d. We can see that, despite the low price charged by the abbot, only a few of Halesowen serfs bought their freedom. It seems that this was true everywhere. A comprehensive search of court rolls and other manorial documents as well as the records of the royal courts carried out by Postan reveals that a very low incidence of manumission prevailed in England in the thirteenth and in the first half of the fourteenth century.[18]

This finding is rather puzzling if we view it comparatively. In the course of the thirteenth century numerous unfree peasants in northern, central, and southern France were manumitted. In the 1240s, 1250s, and 1260s for instance, the inhabitants of some sixty villages around Paris received charters which liberated them from the main characteristics of servility. Freedom was often achieved by a combination of mass pressure and offers of money. Although the struggles against the lords were costly, the peasants succeeded, probably by borrowing, to find the large sums of money required for manumission, too. For example, the villagers of Orly near Paris gained their freedom in 1263 after a struggle of some twenty years and an enormous payment of 4000 *livres*.[19] Such large sums of money were not unusual; for example, the abbot of Saint-Pierre-le-Vif in Sens, south east of Paris, manumitted in 1257 366 of the bondmen of the monastery for 6000 *livres*, to be paid in equal parts in twelve years. William Jordan estimates that each manumitted family had to pay about 4 *livres* a year.[20]

In thirteenth-century England and France the restrictions and exactions of serfdom were quite similar, and therefore it is hard to explain why the English serfs, unlike their French counterparts, were reluctant to spend money on

[17] R. A. Wilson (ed.), *Court Rolls of the Manor of Hales*, vol. III (Worcestershire Historical Society, 1933), 103.

[18] Postan, 'Legal Status', 283–4.

[19] R. H. Hilton, *Bond Men Made Free: Medieval Peasant Movements and the English Rising of 1381* (London, 1973), 83–5; L. Genicot, *Rural Communities in the Medieval West* (Baltimore, 1990), 73–5; G. Duby, *Rural Economy and Country Life in the Medieval West* (tr. C. Postan, Columbia, SC, 1968), 242–3.

[20] W. C. Jordan, *From Servitude to Freedom: Manumission in the Senonais in the Thirteenth Century* (Philadelphia, 1986), 62–3.

manumission.[21] Postan explains the behaviour of English peasants by claiming that since land was scarce they preferred to purchase land rather than freedom.[22] This argument cannot solve our problem; in contemporary France land was short too and yet many serfs bought their freedom. It is plausible to assume that the extent of manumissions in the two countries stemmed from different policies by the landlords rather than from different attitudes to freedom by the peasants. It is likely that in England the incidence of manumission was rather low not because customary tenants were reluctant to buy their freedom, as Postan and Hatcher assume, but because their landlords were reluctant to sell it to them.

English landlords are likely to have had a manumission policy that differed from that of the French, since they ran their manors differently. It appears that forced labour had largely disappeared from the regions of thirteenth-century France which saw large-scale manumissions. These areas also witnessed the withdrawal of magnate landlords from the direct cultivation of their demesnes and the widespread use of wage labour by those who continued to farm their demesnes.[23] Unlike France, most landlords in England at that time cultivated their demesnes directly and many of them continued to use a certain amount of labour services, and therefore had a strong interest in retaining their bondmen. Their coercive powers enabled them to control the unfree tenants more effectively than the free tenants. The bondmen also filled key manorial and court offices. They had to serve, for example, as reeve, hayward, ale taster and as jurymen. Moreover, without the unfree tenants, the jurisdiction of the court, which gave the lord of the manor much power and prestige, would have been considerably diminished. Undoubtedly, English landlords must have known that the emancipation of serfs would undermine their seigneurial regime, and therefore decided to refrain from freeing them.

As landlords had kept their villeins in bondage since the beginning of the thirteenth century they were able to control them tightly and maintain a demesne economy well into the fourteenth. However, in the face of the marked demographic and economic changes in the immediate post-plague period (1350–80) which gave the peasants new opportunities to improve their conditions, the landlords stuck to their conservative policy, and increased their serfs' burdens.[24] The peasants reacted by increasing in the

---

[21] Bloch, *Signeurie francaise et manoir anglais* (Paris, 1960), 69–97; id., *Slavery and Serfdom*, 89.

[22] Postan, 'Legal Status' 284.

[23] Duby, *Rural Economy*, 260–78; Bloch, *Signeurie francaise*, 96.

[24] Hilton, *Bond Men Made Free*, 156–7.

1360s and 1370s the resistance to the seigneurial regime. Different groups called for the abolition of various, often rather local grievances, but most of them wanted to be free.[25] In the rising of 1381 the peasants became more radical and demanded that the king and his advisers should free all the serfs in England.[26]

The rising of 1381 failed as many peasants remained in bondage. Nonetheless, serfs had nearly disappeared from English villages in the early sixteenth century. This happened, as Hilton suggested, because of the massive migration of serfs during the late fourteenth and fifteenth centuries. Those who emigrated from their native villages became free when they settled on land that did not belong to their former lords or in towns. This exodus was not only the result of impersonal demographic and economic forces, but also of the serfs' determination to become free.[27] With the disappearance of serfdom from most manors in England in the course of the fifteenth century, the seigneurial system based on coercion disintegrated.

Postan and Hatcher offer a deterministic interpretation of the end of villeinage. Both of them argue that it was caused by demographic and economic changes in the later middle ages. They play down peasant resistance. Postan regards the Peasants' Revolt of 1381 as no more than a passing episode which did very little to speed up the process of serfs' emancipation, and Hatcher ignores it altogether.[28]

We have found that Postan and Hatcher underestimate the size of the servile population, claim that the peasants preferred land to personal freedom, idealize the relationship between landlords and their unfree tenants, and adopt a deterministic interpretation of the history of serfdom. Their analysis of the behaviour and attitudes of peasants and landlords alike takes into consideration only economic motives. All these cast doubts on the validity of the revisionist interpretation of serfdom.

---

[25] R. Faith, ' "The Great Rumour" of 1377 and Peasant Ideology', in R. H. Hilton and T. H. Aston (eds), *The English Rising of 1381* (Cambridge, 1984), 43–83.

[26] Hilton, *Bond Men*, 223–5.

[27] R. H. Hilton, *The Decline of Serfdom in Medieval England*, 2nd ed. (London, 1983), 55–8; Razi, 'Myth', 38–42.

[28] Hatcher, 'English Serfdom', 37–8; M. M. Postan, *The Medieval Economy and Society: An Economic History of Britain in the Middle Ages* (London, 1972), 152–4.

Popular Insurrection and the Black Death: A Comparative View*

Samuel K. Cohn, Jr

Works by Barrington Moore, Jr, Eric Hobsawm, George Rudé, and E. P. Thompson in the 1960s and early 1970s,[1] coupled with the student movements of that period, launched a new vogue for the study of revolt in comparative perspective, at least for early modern, modern, contemporary Europe and elsewhere around the globe. Curiously, this trend did not extend to medieval Europe, despite the period's large-scale revolts, especially after the Black Death. There are two exceptions, both now over thirty years old— Rodney Hilton's *Bondmen Made Free* and Michel Mollat and Philippe Wolff's *Ongles bleus*.[2] Both have become standard texts for teaching; both have stimulated further research, but this research has tended to focus on individual revolts and not on the comparative perspective. In fact, Hilton's comparative study was largely a prelude for understanding one revolt, the English Rising of 1381, and he did not draw a significant line separating the pre- and

---

* This essay derives from S. Cohn, Jr. (ed.), *Popular Protest in Late-Medieval Europe: Italy, France, and Flanders* (Manchester, 2004) and formed a preliminary study of what has now become parts of chapters 9 and 10 in *Lust for Liberty: The Politics of Social Revolt in Medieval Europe, 1200–1425 (Italy, France, and Flanders)* (Cambridge, Mass., 2006). The conclusions are based on a collection of 1112 revolts.

[1] Among those works that inspired comparative study of revolt, not just for Europe, but across Asia, North and Latin America, see B. Moore, *Social Origins of Dictatorship and Democracy* (Boston, 1966); E. Hobsbawm, *Primitive Rebels: Studies in Archaic Forms of Social Movement in the Nineteenth and Twentieth Centuries* (New York, 1966); G. Rudé, *The Crowd in History, 1730–1848* (New York, 1964); E. P. Thompson, 'The Moral Economy of the English Crowd in the Eighteenth Century', *Past & Present*, 50 (1971), 76–136. For an evaluation of the impact of the last title on global and trans-historical\ questions of pre-industrial insurrection, see A. Randall and A. Charlesworth (eds), *Moral Economy and Popular Protest* (Houndmills, 2000).

[2] R. H. Hilton, *Bondmen Made Free: Medieval Peasant Movements and the English Rising of 1381* (London, 1973); and M. Mollat and P. Wolff, *Ongles bleus, Jacques et Ciompi: les révolutions populaires en Europe aux XIVe et XVe siècles* (Paris, 1970; translated as *The Popular Revolutions of the Late Middle Ages*, tr. A. L. Lyttonsells, New York, 1973).

---

post-plague fourteenth century. By contrast, Mollat and Wolff emphasized a clustering of revolts a generation after the Black Death but failed to explain these simultaneous rebellions. This essay will re-open the question of timing and clustering of insurrections before and after the Black Death in continental Europe, north and south of the Alps.

Patterns before the Black Death

The social movements and rebellions over the hundred years prior to the Black Death show great diversity but few discernible trends. The earliest of these protests were as 'modern' as any on record in the west until the nineteenth century. By the mid-thirteenth century in northern France and Flanders, abundant evidence of working men's associations, assemblies, strikes and the destruction of tools appears in local ordinances, court cases, and chronicles,[3] and riots comprised of, organized and led by textile workers were commonplace before the Black Death.[4] Nor did such activities emerge

---

[3] Legislation against strikes in Douai in 1245: G. Espinas and H. Pirenne (eds), *Recueil des documents relatifs à l'histoire de l'industrie drapière en Flandre*, 5 vols (Brussels, 1906–), vol. II, 22; strikes and disturbances to work in Douai, 1266: ibid., 109; sentences against cloth workers on strike in Douai, 1280: ibid., II, 141–3; legislation against strikes for higher wages: F. R. P. Akehurst (ed.), *The Coutumes de Beauvaisis of Philippe de Beaumanoir* (Philadephia, 1992), 314; commoners' revolt against changes in currency and the rise of rents in Paris, 1307: J. Viard (ed.), *Les Grandes Chroniques de France*, 10 vols, *Société d'Histoire de France*, 423 (Paris, 1924), vol. VIII, 250–2, and *Chronique anonyme finissant en M.CCC.LXXXIII* in J. D. Guigniaut and N. de Wailly (eds), *Recueil des Historiens des Gaules et de la France* (Paris, 1855), XXI, 142; the breaking of tools at Saint-Omer in 1325: Espinas and Pirenne (eds), *Recueil de documents*, vol. I, 63, and 98–102; strikes at Béthune in the latter half of the fourteenth century: ibid., 313, and 328–30.

[4] See for instance the rebellion of textile workers in Ypres (Ieper) and Poperinge, 3 April 1280: Espinas and Pirenne (eds), *Recueil de documents*, III, 102–9; the revolt of textile workers in 1280, known as the Cockeruelle, Ypres, 1281: ibid., III, 686; and *Prisma van de geschiedenis van Ieper: Een bundel historische opstellen verzameld door O. Mus onder leiding van prof. J. A. van Houtte* (Ypres, 1974), especially the article by G. Doudelez, 'La révolution communale de 1280 à Ypres', 188–294; weavers' revolt in Tournai, 1281: J.-J. de Smet (ed.), *Chronica Aegidii li Muisis*, in *Corpus Chronicorum Flandriae* (Brussels, 1841), vol. II, 170; revolt of fullers, Tournai, 1307: ibid., II, 175; Revolt of Flanders, 1323–8: *Chronicon comitum Flandrensium* in J.-J. de Smet (ed.), *Corpus Chronicorum Flandriae* (Brussels, 1837), vol. I, 34–261, esp., 187, 191, and 206; Revolt of Flanders, 1323–8: *Anciennes Chroniques de Flandre*, in J. D. Guigniaut and N. de Wailly (eds), *Recueil des historiens des Gaules et de la France*, XXII (Paris, 1894), 418–19; W. TeBrake, *A Plague of Insurrection: Popular Politics and Peasant Revolt in Flanders, 1323–1328* (Philadelphia, 1993); and D. Nicholas, *Medieval Flanders* (London, 1992), 212–16.

only in major textile centres such as Douai, Tournai, Bruges and Ghent, but were also notable in provincial market towns such as Huy and Saint-Trond in the Liégeois, Béthune and Clermont-en-Beauvaisis in northern France and satellite towns and villages such as Poperinge outside Ypres, Damme outside Bruges, Termonde outside Ghent, and Nieupart.[5] Moreover, the records of northern France and Flanders show *menu peuple*, or 'those of little wealth', revolting against their city oligarchies and mayors,[6] against changes in monetary policy, rises in house rents,[7] the privileges and impositions of the French crown,[8] and above all against the imposition of new taxes.[9] Along with this remarkable array of urban revolts, early fourteenth-century Flanders witnessed the largest and most widespread peasant revolts before the German Bundschuh of the sixteenth century. But the Flemish revolts of 1297–1304 and 1323–8[10] lasted longer, won more battles, and were better integrated and coordinated with urban insurgents than any revolt seen two hundred years later in German-speaking areas.[11] Curiously, this rich vein of popular protest appears to decline with the famines of 1314–18, especially for France. Indeed, as against models drawn by historians and sociologists for supposed

---

[5] See Pirenne, *Histoire de Belgique: des origines à nos jours*, 3rd edn. (Brussels, 1922; first edition, 1900), II, 127; Doudelez, 'La révolution communale de 1280 à Ypres', and W. Prevenier, 'Conscience et perception de la condition sociale chez les gens du commun dans les anciens Pays-Bas des XIIIe et XIVe siècles', in P. Boglioni, R. Delort, et C. Gauvard (eds), *Le petit peuple dans l'Occident médiéval: terminologies, perceptions, réalités* (Paris, 2002), 175–89.

[6] Revolt in Flanders of the people of little wealth [*gens de petitte chavanche*], 1297: *Chronique des Pays-Bas, de France, etc.* in *Corpus Chronicorum Flandriae* (Brussels, 1856), vol. III, 121–2; Revolt in Bruges and Ghent against the patricians and taxes, 1301–2: H. Johnstone (ed.), *Annales Gandenses* (London, 1951), 16–18; rent strike in Paris, 1306: see above; tax revolt in Tournai, 1307: *Chronica Aegidii li Muisis*, 173–5; two clerics accused of heresy for leading a communal revolt in Carcassonne, 1306: C. Devic, J. Vaissete, et al. (eds), *Histoire générale de Languedoc*, 2nd ed., 16 vols (Toulouse 1872–1904), vol. X, cols. 645–6, n. 235.

[7] For instance the 1306 Parisian rent strike.

[8] See examples in nn. 3–5.

[9] In my database of popular insurrections, I have found twenty-five tax revolts in France and Flanders from *c.*1200 to 1348.

[10] See Pirenne, *Histoire de Belgique*, vol. II, 28–100; id., *Les Anciennes démocraties des Pays-Bas* (Paris, 1910), 181–6 and 191ff; and TeBrake, *A Plague of Insurrection*.

[11] The literature on the German Peasants' War of the sixteenth century is vast; for a good introduction, see P. Blickle, *The Revolution of 1525: The German Peasants' War from a New Perspective*, tr. T. Brady, Jr, and H. C. Midelfort (Baltimore, 1981).

'pre-industrial riots', these famines did not spark a single revolt that I know of in northern France or Flanders.[12]

Until the Black Death, no pan-European pattern in the timing of revolts can be detected. In the second half of the thirteenth and early fourteenth centuries, the revolts in central and northern Italy were different from those of Flanders; nothing akin to the Flemish strikes or revolts led and staffed by textile workers are seen in Italy, not even in places such as Florence with well-developed cloth industries and large numbers of workers without guild recognition or status as citizens. The major proponents of class struggle in the south, the *pedites* or *popolo*, pitched the interests of merchants, shopkeepers and artisans with guild recognition against landed and mercantile aristocracies including those of local bishops. In Florence, Milan, Pisa, Bologna, Genoa, Savona, Siena, Arezzo, Rome, Viterbo, Naples, Ancona, and many other smaller city-states, revolts of the *popolo* toppled aristocratic regimes and ushered new social classes into power.[13] The readiness of commoners—the *popolo minuto*—to arm themselves and defend the rule of the *popolo* shows that those beneath the status of shopkeeper played their part. However, the rebel leaders of the *popolo*, men like the wealthy Florentine major guildsman Giano della Bella, were hardly commoners;[14] they were a world apart from

[12] On such models, see for example, G. Rudé, *Paris and London in the Eighteenth Century: Studies in Popular Protest* (London, 1974), 23ff; C. Tilly, 'How Protest Modernized in France, 1845–1855', in Aydelotte, Bogue, and Fogel (eds), *The Dimension of Quantitative Research* (Princeton, 1972), 199ff; Y.-M. Bercé, *Revolt and Revolution in Early Modern Europe: An Essay on the History of Political Violence*, tr. Joseph Bergin (Manchester, 1987 [1980]), 100–2; on the famine, see W. C. Jordan, *The Great Famine: Northern Europe in the Early Fourteenth Century* (Princeton, 1996). In France, Philip the Fair set off a wave of legal protests and revolts by levying new taxes without calling the three estates. These rebellions, however, came not from the starving but from the upper reaches of the social hierarchy, and their descriptions make no mention of the famines or scarcity; see A. Artonne, 'Le mouvement de 1314 et les chartes provinciales de 1315', in *Bibliothèque de la faculté des lettres de l'Université de Paris*, 29 (1912) [entire issue].

[13] The literature on the rise of the *popolo* is immense; see E. Cristiani, *Nobiltà e popolo del comune di Pisa: dalle origini del podestariato alla Signoria del Donoratico* (Naples, 1962); C. Lansing, *The Florentine Magnates: Lineage and Faction in a Medieval Commune* (Princeton, 1991); J.-C. Maire Vigueur, 'Comuni e signorie in Umbria, Marche e Lazio', in G. Galasso (ed.), *Storia d'Italia*, vol. VII.2 (Turin, 1987), 321–606; J. Koenig, *Il popolo dell'Italia del Nord* (Bologna, 1986); P. Grillo, *Milano in età comunale (1183–1276): istituzioni, società, economia* (Spoleto, 2001), and most recently A. Zorzi, 'The Popolo', in J. Najemy (ed.), *Italy in the Age of the Renaissance* (Oxford, 2004), 145–64.

[14] See G. Villani, *Nuova Cronica*, ed. Giuseppe Porta, 3 vols (Parma, 1990–1), vol. II, 22–5 and 29–31.

self-taught Flemish rebel leaders like the weaver Peter the King, who organized thousands of textile workers and peasants to oppose patrician regimes
and the king of France.

In the first half of the fourteenth century, popular protest north and south
of the Alps continued to proceed along two different tracks. While
revolts of textile workers and other commoners began to decline in France
before the famines of 1314–18 and in Flanders after 1328, they finally arose
in the south. Butchers and blacksmiths protested the decisions of the military
elites and war policy in Siena, seriously challenging the rule of the oligarchy
of the Nine in 1318, [15] and, in coalition with notaries, judges, and younger
sons from the magnate Tolomei family, artisans and workers threatened the
rule of the Nine in 1311, 1317, 1318, 1319 and 1320.[16] Further riots erupted
in 1324 from fist-fights to martial arts competitions, again threatening the
stability of the Nine.[17] Workers formed clubs and held street parties in
Florence to the great chagrin of their social betters in 1333.[18] Florentine
workers received their own militia banners and gained new political offices
in 1342.[19] In the same year, a maverick of the Florentine elite—Andrea degli
Strozzi—ignited discontent among wool workers, rousing them to revolt.[20]
After Andrea's shamed kinsmen had caught, caged and dumped him safely
beyond the borders of the Florentine state, his son, Pagnotto, stirred wool
workers to riot again with street-corner speeches and slogans aimed at insult-
ing and provoking them.[21]

---

[15] A. Lisini and F. Iacometti (eds), *Cronaca senese attribuita ad Agnolo di Tura del Grasso
detta la cronaca maggiore* in *Cronache senesi*, Rerum Italicarum Scriptores [hereafter RIS],
vol. XV/6.1 (Bologna, 1939), 371–3.

[16] W. Bowsky, 'The Anatomy of Rebellion in Fourteenth-Century Siena: From Commune
to Signory?' in L. Martines (ed.), *Violence and Disorder in Italian Cities, 1200–1500*
(Berkeley, 1972), 229–72; *Cronaca senese attribuita ad Agnolo di Tura*, 371–3, 380, and
416–7; *Cronaca senese di autore anomino della metà del secolo XIV dall'anno 1202 al 1362*
in *Cronache senesi*, 114–15 and 128.

[17] Autore Anonimo, in *Cronache senesi*, 127–8; and *Cronaca senese attribuita ad Agnolo di
Tura*, 416–17.

[18] N. Rodolico (ed.), *Cronaca fiorentina di Marchionne di Coppo Stefani*, RIS, vol. XXX/1
(Città di Castello, 1903), 173.

[19] G. Villani, *Nuova Cronica*, vol. III, 295; and *Cronaca fiorentina di Marchionne di Coppo
Stefani*, 206.

[20] G. Villani, *Nuova Cronica*, vol. III, 350–3.

[21] Rodolico, *Il popolo minuto: note di storia fiorentina (1343–1378)* (Florence, 1899; new ed.,
1968), doc. 9, 93–4.

Historians, both those who see the *popolo minuto* as an unoriginal and conservative force (Sergio Bertelli, Raymond de Roover, Gene Brucker[22]) and those who see them as revolutionary (Niccolò Rodolico, Victor Rutenberg, Samuel Cohn, Jr, Alessandro Stella[23]) have taken this incident as quintessential of elites leading leaderless, ignorant and desperate masses by the noses. Historians of Florence have ignored, however, evidence from neighbouring Pistoia, which reveals that these workers were not leaderless but had one from their own ranks, a dyer named Corazza. After the Strozzi instigators had been arrested, the dyer proved more effective than the two Florentine knights. He organized a force of 1,300 wool workers and stormed the Florentine town hall. Instead of being smashed (as historians often assume is the result of such brazen acts),[24] the fearful priors of the city opened their palace doors and promised the insurgents whatever they wanted.[25] In the same year, the carders of Florence assembled and revolted again.[26] Two years later, a wool carder, Ciuto Brandini, organized an association of Florentine textile workers (*fraternitas*) with a strike fund (*postura seu collection*),[27] and, on the eve of the Black Death, peasants of the Florentine *contado* collected funds, passed statutes and went on their own strike.[28] Nor was Florence the only city-state to

---

[22] S. Bertelli, 'Oligarchies et gouvernment dans la ville de la Renaissance', *Social Science: Information sur les sciences sociales*, 15 (1976), 623; R. de Roover, 'Labour Conditions in Florence around 1400: Theory, Policy, and Reality', in N. Rubinstein (ed.), *Florentine Studies: Politics and Society in Renaissance Florence* (London, 1968), 277–313; Mollat and Wolff, *The Popular Revolutions*, 142–61; G. Brucker, *Florentine Politics and Society 1343–1378* (Florence, 1962); id., *The Civic World of Early Renaissance Florence* (Princeton, 1977); and id., 'The Ciompi Revolution', in *Florentine Studies*, 314–56.

[23] Rodolico, *Il popolo minuto*; id., *La democrazia fiorentina nel suo tramonto (1378–1382)* (Bologna, 1905); id., *I Ciompi: Una pagina di storia del proletariato operaio* (Florence, 1945); V. Rutenburg, *Popolo e movimenti popolari nell'Italia del '300 e '400*, Gianpiero Borghini (tr.) (Bologna, 1971; Moscow, 1958); S. Cohn, *The Laboring Classes in Renaissance Florence* (New York, 1980); A. Stella, *La révolte des Ciompi: Les hommes, les lieux, le travail* (Paris, 1993).

[24] See for instance G. Fourquin, *The Anatomy of Popular Rebellion in the Middle Ages* (Amsterdam, 1978), 25: 'revolt led only to repression and not to revolution'.

[25] S. Adrasto Barbi (ed.), *Storie Pistoresi [MCCC-MCCCXLVIII]*, RIS, vol. XI/5 (Città di Castello, 1907), 196; *Cronaca fiorentina di Marchionne di Coppo Stefani*, 215–16, also mentions a revolt involving 1,300 wool carders and others of the *gente minuta*, but this one was a good six months later (25 September 1343), and according to Stefani was smashed by the podestà and the neighbourhood militias.

[26] *Cronaca fiorentina di Marchionne di Coppo Stefani*, 215–16.

[27] Rodolico, *Il popolo minuto*, doc. 14, 102–4.

[28] Ibid., doc. n. 25, 114–5.

witness such developments in the 1340s. In 1346, textile workers in Siena came close to toppling the oligarchy of the Nine.[29]

Why did riots of workers suddenly appear in Tuscany nearly a hundred years after they had flourished in Flanders and the north of France? No one has attempted an answer; no one has even posed the question, and any answer would indeed be hard to offer at the present stage of research. My point for now, however, is that before the Black Death the development and trends of popular protest, north and south of the Alps, followed the beat of different drummers. But for the next fifty years they appear to sing more or less from the same hymn sheet, despite the fact that no evidence of any joint organisation, communication, or even knowledge of revolts links these distant insurgents across the Alps.[30]

The Black Death and its consequences

During the Black Death and its immediate aftermath, 1348–52, social movements with concrete aims of redressing economic grievances, challenging political authority or questioning social hierarchies are difficult to find either in the north or the south. In central Italy, the Black Death suddenly killed off workers' newly founded zeal to topple governments or challenge burgeoning capitalist exploitation. In Barberino Val d'Elsa, south of Florence, tempers rose at the end of the summer of 1348, leading to a bar room brawl and a minor riot of a handful of men and the barman, who happened to be a lady (and a noble one at that).[31] But the cause of the conflict pre-dated the plague, stemming from attempts to redress corrupt election results of the previous year, when a much larger riot had engulfed this walled town.[32] Two years later, city chroniclers reported a conspiracy to topple the government of the Bentivoglio in Bologna.[33] But it amounted to little, was quickly

---

[29] *Cronaca senese attribuita ad Agnolo di Tura*, p. 549; and Rodolico, *Il popolo minuto*, doc. 10, 94–7.

[30] Even among the elites, I know of no northern chroniclers to comment on any post-plague revolts south of the Alps other than the popular massacre of cardinals' retainers and other foreigners at Viterbo in 1367 and the Roman crowds' pressure to elect an Italian pope in 1378. South of the Alps, Bonaccorso Pitti, *Ricordi*, in V. Branca (ed.), *Mercanti scrittori: Ricordi nella Firenze tra Medioevo e Rinascimento*, (Milan, 1985), 383–5, is the only one to experience and to describe at length post-plague revolts north and south of the Alps.

[31] Archivio di Stato di Firenze, Atti di Podestà, n. 334, sententiae, 40r-v.

[32] Unfortunately, the sentences for this case, which would have appeared in Atti di Podestà, n. 204, do not survive; nor have I been able to find the case in the surviving inquisitions for 1347. The inquest of 1348, however, describes this revolt.

[33] A. Sorbelli, (ed.), *Cronaca A* and *Cronaca di Villola* in *Corpus Chronicorum Bononiensium*, *RIS*, vol. XVIII/1 (Città di Castello, 1910–38), vol. I, 603 and 607.

repressed, and has left no trace in the rich judicial archives of Bologna.[34] In France and Flanders revolts, even minor skirmishes, are as hard to find from the Black Death to the Jacquerie of 1358. In the immediate aftermath of the plague, a tax revolt in Rouen is an exception. Although merchants began it, workers paid the price, leaving thirty-six swinging from the gallows.[35] And in the year of the Black Death, the new count of Flanders, Louis de Male, attacked the prerogatives of the weavers, especially in Ghent, which in turn provoked riots.[36] It was not, however, until 1359 that the weavers along with other craftsmen of Ghent, Ypres, and elsewhere in western Flanders organized a successful rebellion, which challenged the domination of the count and his encroachment into their municipal liberties.[37]

To be sure, the Black Death did give rise to violence: flagellant movements and the burning of Jews swept across German-speaking areas, Spain, France and the Low Countries from September 1348 to 1351, while for Sicily, Catalans were the chosen scapegoats of 1348.[38] But this violence differed markedly from the organized protests with prior planning, numerous assemblies, and elected leaders, revolts that increased rapidly in number and developed in sophistication from the mid-1350s to the early 1380s. Rather than struggling for concrete

---

[34] The late-sixteenth-century historian P. Pellini, *Dell'Historia di Perugia* (Venice, 1664) vol. I, 909–10, mentions 'un poco di tumulto' in front of the town hall of Perugia, whose participants chant 'Long live the people', but Pellini gives no source for the incident, and I cannot find this incident in any of the published chronicles.

[35] Charles de Robillard de Beaurepaire (ed.), *Chronique normande de Pierre Cochon notaire apostolique à Rouen* (Rouen, 1870), 75–6.

[36] *Chronica Aegidii Li Muisis*, 284–8; also see Nicholas, *Medieval Flanders*, 225 and 308; and Pirenne, Histoire de Belgique, II, 135; Nicholas, *The Metamorphosis of a Medieval City: Ghent in the Age of the Arteveldes*, 1302–1390 (Leiden, 1987), 5 and 135–54.

[37] Matteo Villani, *Cronica con la continuazione di Filippo Villani*, G. Porta (ed.), 2 vols. (Parma, 1995), I, 536–7. Other areas of Europe show a similar social quiescence with few exceptions. In 1348, the smiths of Nuremberg revolted against the oligarchy to gain guild recognition, but the first wave of plague failed to reach Nuremberg; G. Strauss, *Nuremberg in the Sixteenth Century* (New York, 1966), 49. And in 1348, the cities of Aragon continued their resistance to King Pere III and were brutally repressed, but the Union of the six principal cities of Aragon and the brief success of their revolt for independence began in early 1347, well before the plague had arrived; Pere III of Catalonia (Pedro IV of Aragon), *Chronicle*, M. and J. N. Hillgarth (ed.), 2 vols (Toronto, 1980), vol. II, 439–49.

[38] The literature on the post-plague massacres of the Jews is extensive; see the following note. No one to my knowledge, however, has commented on the anti-Catalan and anti-foreign massacres that flared throughout Sicily in the plague's immediate aftermath, 1348; see A. Giuffrida (ed.), Michele da Piazza, *Chronica* (Palermo, 1980), 91–2.

goals or redressing specific political, economic or social grievances, the violence of 1348 to 1352 looked principally to forces outside society—the scapegoat and the heavens—to resolve their fears, anger, and insecurity.[39] By 1353, the number of social protests and revolts began to rise again, occurring in Rome, Poitou, Gaeta, and Viterbo. But in 1354 and 1355 their number increased more impressively, especially in Italy—Pavia, Modena, Bologna, Rimini, Rome, Siena (at least three times), Casole, Monteritondo, Massa Marittima, Montepulciano, Grosseto, Lucca, Pisa, Venice, Udine, Piedmont, L'Aquila (two revolts), Castrogiovanni (today, Enna in Sicily), Siracusa, and Catania. The most famous of the revolts of the 1350s comes, however, from the north, the Jacquerie of late May 1358, that spread through the Beauvaisis, Picardy, the Île de France, Champagne and as far east as Bar on the borders of France. Along with Étienne Marcel's Parisian insurgents, the Jacques inspired revolts in cities such as Amiens, Senlis, Caen, and Rouen.[40] A year later, fullers, weavers, and cobblers waged war against the count of Flanders, humiliated him, and took over city councils in Ypres, Bruges, and Ghent. By August 1361 the weavers had restored their power in all cities of maritime Flanders.[41]

Behind these northern revolts were certainly the realities of the Hundred Years War and the difficulties of financing increased warfare with a greatly diminished tax base because of the plagues' onslaughts. But other causes seem to have been paramount, especially for the Jacquerie, for which none of the accounts mention taxes.[42] Instead, the chroniclers point to the betrayal

[39] For examples of these immediate post-plague acts of violence, see *Breve Chronicon Flandriae*, in *Corpus Chronicorum Flandriae* (Brussels, 1856), III, 23; L. C. Bethmann (ed.), *Annales Floreffienses*, Monumenta Germaniae Historica, Scriptores, vol. XVIII (Hanover, 1859), 629; *Chronicon Aegidii Li Muisis*, vol. II, 341–8; R. Horrox, *The Black Death* (Manchester, 1994), docs 68–75; S. Simonsohn, *The Apostolic See and the Jews. Documents: 492–1404* (Toronto, 1988), nn. 373–4 and 399–400; and J. R. Marcus (ed.), *The Jew in the Medieval World: A Source Book, 315–1791*, 2nd edn. (Cincinnati, 1999), 49–55. Also, see S. Cohn, 'The Black Death and the Burning of the Jews', *Past and Present*, 195 (2007).

[40] A. Chéruel, *Histoire de Rouen pendant l'époque communale 1150–1382* (Rouen, 1843–4), vol. I, 203; and Archives Municipales de Rouen, reg. U/1 47r; D. Aiton, ' "Shame on him who allows him to live": the Jacquerie of 1358', unpublished PhD thesis, University of Glasgow (2007).

[41] See Pirenne, *Histoire de Belgique*, vol. II, 200; Nicholas, *Medieval Flanders*, 266; and M. Villani, *Cronica*, vol. II, 338–40 and 536–7.

[42] Caen was an exception, but it was an urban revolt; see the letter of remission mentioning Pierre de Montfort, transcribed in S. Luce, *Histoire de la Jacquerie d'après des documents inédits*, 2nd edn. (Paris, 1894), 291–2.

of the local nobility and their reneging on their customary protection of their peasants.[43] For the north of France, the massacres of the Jacques and the defeat of Étienne Marcel may have blunted temporarily the desire for revolt, but peasants responded to the raids of brigands and 'extraordinarily onerous taxes' with their feet, abandoning their work and heading for Paris.[44] Moreover, in several villages, which had been the battlefields of the Jacquerie, peasant resilience and self-defence continued; they organized their own resistance to the onslaughts of the English, defeating their cavalry twice at Longueil-Sainte-Marie in the Beauvaisis.[45]

Further north, taxes provoked open and successful revolts at Tournai in 1359, 1364, twice in 1365, and again in 1366, and at Valenciennes in 1364; by their examples, such revolts spread to 'all the towns of Hainault' in 1365.[46] But the south of France was the more important theatre of class struggle in the 1360s. The combination of political instability, roaming brigands, war, and new taxes weighed heavily on the mountainous areas of the Massif Central. Soldiers, peasants and townsmen formed gangs of bandits called Tuchins by their adversaries (meaning those who hid in the woods) to redress personal grievances and pursue economic advantage, but also to challenge the crown and its rising taxation in this milieu of hardship, war and half-hearted truces between the French and English.[47] This was especially true still further south

[43] See for instance J. Birdsall (tr.) and R. Newhall (ed.), *The chronicle of Jean de Venette* (New York, 1953), 76–7; and J. Lemoine (ed.), *Chronique de Richard Lescot Religieux de Saint-Denis (1328–1344) suivie de la continuation de cette chronique (1344–1364)*, Société d'Histoire de France, CCLXXVIII (Paris, 1896), 126–7.

[44] *Chronique de Guillaume de Nangis*, II, 325–8.

[45] Among the numerous chronicles that described and celebrated this heroic resistance of peasants first led by the peasant Guillaume l'Aloue and then another called the big iron man; see A. and É. Molinier (eds), *Chronique normande du XIVe siècle*, Société d'Histoire de France, CCV (Paris, 1882), 146–7; and S. Luce, 'Notice sur Gauillaume l'Aloue', *Annuaire-Bulletin de la Société d'Histoire de France* (1875), 149–56. For other cases of peasant resistance against English troops immediately after the Jacquerie; see H. Géraud (ed.), *Chronique Latine de Guillaume de Nangis de 1113 à 1300 avec les continuations de cette chronique de 1300 à 1368*, 2 vols, Société d'Histoire de France, vol. XVI (Paris, 1843), II, 304–5 and 306–7.

[46] Ibid., 349–50 and 355–6; *Chronique des Pays-Bas*, 207–9; A. Hoquet (ed.), *Croniques de Franche, d'Engleterre, de Flandres, de Lile et espécialment de Tournay* (Mons, 1938), 122–3.

[47] M. Boudet, *La Jacquerie des Tuchins, 1363–1384* (Riom, 1895). Similar bands, however, continued to pillage and organize cattle raids in the Massif Central and in other parts of Languedoc well into the fifteenth century. See. P. Charbonnier, 'Qui furent les Tuchins?' in *Violence et contestation au Moyen Age: Actes du 114ᵉ congrès national des sociétés savants*

in the regions of Toulouse, Carcassonne, and Beaucaire, where groups also called Tuchins revolted and took over villages and even the city of Nîmes.[48] Other revolts raged through southern France in the 1360s. In 1364, three hundred men of Carcassonne 'armed with various weapons and with the consent and guidance of their town councillors' made war on the royal castle of their region, setting fire to its gates and entering it. Seven insurgents were arrested. A few days later, the town council organized 2,000 men of Carcassonne to march to the prison holding the rebels, where they killed the royal officers and liberated the seven.[49] In the same year *plebes* from the market towns of Gimont and Simorre in the region of Toulouse staged their own Jacquerie, temporarily deposing aristocratic rule in the region. According to a royal letter of remission, 'like mad men', they assembled and battled against the ruling lord of the region, stormed his castle, burnt it to the ground, took his lady, three children, the servants, and movable goods to Simorre, where they burnt the servants, hanged the others from trees, and 'committed many other very great, inhumane and detestable acts of evil.' For the next thirty years the crown tried to bring these insurgents to trial and to have them pay a 25,000 franc fine. Finally, with the letter of remission, the crown admitted failure and gave up their pursuit of the insurgents.[50]

As important as the battlefields of the Hundred Years War were to instability and revolt, they were hardly the only areas of Europe to see popular rebellion during the latter half of the fourteenth century. In 1355 a combination of social forces from the richest magnate families in Siena to the *popolo minuto* successfully ended Italy's longest-standing city-state regime, that of the Nine.[51] Afterwards, the governments of Siena fell as readily as those of Italy after World War II. In five months alone in 1368–9, no fewer than six governments were toppled and replaced with new regimes.[52] In all of these permutations, artisans and workers played a significant role and secured governmental offices and privileges for themselves. Revolts in Siena

---

(Paris, 1989) (Paris, 1990), 235–47; and V. Challet, 'La Révolt des Tuchins: banditisme social ou sociabilité villageoise?' *Médiévales*, 34 (1998), 101–12.

[48] See *Histoire générale de Languedoc,* vol. X, cols. 1688–90, nn. 675–6; although the letters of remission are dated after the Duke of Berry's suppression of the Tuchins throughout Languedoc, the events they describe go back to the 1360s and 1370s.

[49] Ibid., col. 1329–31, n. 511.

[50] Ibid., 1818–20, n. 732.

[51] *Cronaca senese di Donato di Neri e di suo figlio Neri,* in *Cronache senesi,* 577–9; and G. Luchaire (ed.), *Documenti . . . del Comune di Siena dal 1354 al 1369* (Lyon, 1906), n. 12, 1–9 December 1355: Statuto 31, Riforma delle Arti, 43–46.

[52] *Cronaca senese di Donato di Neri e di suo figlio Neri,* 618–25.

culminated in 1371 with the uprising of the wool workers organized around their neighbourhood association, the club of the Caterpillar.[53] After this failure, rioting and serious threats to political stability from the lower classes in Siena died down or disappeared altogether, but unlike in Florence and most other Italian city-states, these social classes maintained a presence in Siena's government well into the fifteenth century.

Towards an explanation

Perhaps the most lasting of the conclusions drawn in Mollat and Wolff's *Ongles bleus* has been their emphasis on the sharp pan-European cluster of revolts a generation after the Black Death, in the years 1378 to 1382. Tax revolts in Languedoc, the *Harelle* in Rouen, the *Maillotins* (Hammermen) in Paris, and the 'troubles' of the Low Countries support their case. But I would argue that popular insubordination and rebellion built up from the mid-1350s to the 1370s. In fact, in Italy, after a steady rise in the number of revolts, they fell temporarily during the so-called cluster of 1378–82. The Florentine revolt of the Ciompi in 1378 was an outlier.

Because of the revolt of the Ciompi, historians have paid greater attention to popular revolt in Florence than elsewhere in Italy. Insurrections, however, were much more numerous in other regions of central Italy in the 1360s and 1370s. These included tax revolts, such as those at Bologna and Ravenna in 1357,[54] insurrections of artisans and workers in the wool industry at Lucca,[55] Perugia,[56] and Siena,[57] and various attempts by underlings (*sottoposti*) to change the political control of their city-states in Siena in 1368,[58] Lucca in 1369,[59] Cortona and Perugia in 1371 [60] and Bologna in 1377.[61] But by far the most numerous of these revolts stemmed from popular outrage over the violence, arrogance, and injustice of aristocratic behaviour and rule, whether it came from the church, a military presence, or the old local families.

[53] Ibid., 639–40.

[54] M. Villani, *Cronica*, vol. II, 94–5 and 107–8.

[55] Archivio di Stato, Lucca, Sentenze e Bandi, n. 43, np, 1370.vii.20; and S. Bongi (ed.), *Le Croniche di Giovanni Sercambi, Lucchese*, 3 vols. (Lucca, 1892), I, 204–5.

[56] *Cronaca senese di Donato di Neri e di suo figlio Neri*, 639.

[57] Ibid., 640.

[58] See n. 46.

[59] See n. 49.

[60] *Cronaca senese di Donato di Neri e di suo figlio Neri*, 639.

[61] A. Sorbelli, (ed.), *Cronaca gestorum ac factorum memorabilium civitatis Bononie a Fratre Hyeronimo de Bursellis [ab urbe condita ad a. 1497]*, RIS, vol. XXIII/2 (Città di Castello, 1911–29), 57–8.

The most important sweep of revolts occurred in the early and mid-1370s. In sheer numbers, these revolts dwarf those of Florence, as well as the supposed cluster of European-wide revolts listed by Mollat and Wolff. In one year alone, 1375, sixty cities in the Marche, Tuscany, Umbria, Emilia Romagna, and the Papal States revolted and 'freed themselves from the yoke of church rule', that is, a third more than Mollat and Wolff found for all of Europe in 1378–82.[62] A chronicle of Rimini counted even more: by 28 March 1376, 1,577 walled towns and villages (*buone castella*) from Milan to Naples had thrown off the rule of the rectors and this was not counting small or tower villages (*delle piccolo e di certe torricelle*).[63] According to Gene Brucker, this war against the papacy was 'one of the most radical revolutions in Florentine history . . . a revolution of internal politics, a critical phase of the struggle between an old order and the new'.[64] Ernesto Screpanti has gone further, seeing it as a class struggle in Central Italy 'against the old aristocratic classes and the papacy, a war against nascent capitalism and the dying medieval order'.[65] As the conservative anonymous diarist of the Machiavelli family observed for Bologna in 1376, 'the aristocrats [*grandi*] were hounded out of office and in their place merchants and artisans remained as lords'.[66]

By contrast, I know of only a handful of riots in Italy that broke out during the supposed cluster—the Florentine Ciompi; a revolt of the *popolo* in Genoa, which may not in fact have involved artisans or workers; the undefined crowd in Rome that pressured the cardinals to elect an Italian pope in April 1378; a small tax revolt against the imposition of a land tax (*aestimum*) in Parma in 1380;[67] and an insurrection of 'the people' to overthrow the ruling family in Treviso around 1380 (the chronicler is not clear about the date). In this last-named revolt, only one official was singled out and killed, a Pirinzolo, who allegedly during their last war had captured Trevigian women and forced

[62] L. Muratori, ed., *Chronicon Placentinum ab Anno CCXXII usque ad annum MCCCCII auctore Johanne de Mussis cive Placentino, Rerum Italicarum Scriptores* [hereafter, Muratori], vol. XVI (Milan, 1730), col. 521. By contrast, Mollat and Wolff, *The Popular Revolutions*, 139–41, list only 42 across Europe and some of these, such as the wars led by Philippe van Artevelde, I would not classify as popular revolts.

[63] A. F. Massèra (ed.), *Cronaca malatestiana del secolo XIV (aa. 1295–1385)*, RIS, vol. XV/2 (Bologna, 1922–4), 38.

[64] G. Brucker, *Florentine Politics and Society*, 294–5.

[65] E. Screpanti, *L'Angelo della rivoluzione: i Ciompi fiorentini all'assalto del cielo, Giugno-agosto 1378* (in press), 64.

[66] A. Gherardi (ed.), *Diario d'anonimo fiorentino dall'anno 1358 al 1389*, Documenti di storia italiano, vol. VI (Florence, 1876), 329.

[67] L. Barbieri (ed.), *Chronica abreviata, Fr. Johannis de Cornazano O.P in Chronica parmensia a sec. XI. ad exitum sec. XIV* (Parma, 1858), 397.

them 'to pull up their slips to their groins so that he could ruminate on their private parts (*ad propria remandere*)'.[68]

So how do we account for the rise of insurrections across much of Europe from the late 1350s to the 1370s and its contrast to the violence of the Black Death's immediate aftermath? Most explanations have centred on England and demography. With a sudden shrinkage in the tax base, governments were forced to raise taxes sharply to pay for more costly wars. At the same time, the dramatic demographic collapse meant that labourers were in a better bargaining position vis-à-vis their bosses, landlords, and the state. While this argument helps to explain much for post-plague revolt in England (although hardly everything, as indeed Hilton and others have shown), it settles less for Italy, where post-plague tax revolts did not rise sharply in number until the 1390s and then were located principally in the countryside. Moreover, the most famous of the revolts south of the Alps—the Tumulto dei Ciompi—turned on just the opposite demographics: Florence's wool industry declined more sharply than its population.[69] Thus a key demand of the Ciompi was the imposition of production quotas on their bosses to boost production and thereby secure employment for an industry with a surplus, not a scarcity, of workers.[70]

Further, the vast majority of revolts in post-plague Italy turned on politics; they were neither tax revolts as in the north nor disputes at the point of production as with the exceptional Ciompi. Instead, across large areas of Italy, commoners battled to end aristocratic abuse and to demand a share of governmental offices and political control. But like the tax revolts and demands to change work practices, they all were founded on a new optimism, that commoners could change their worlds, the here and now, in concrete and practical ways. The common thread linking the rush to revolt, north and south of the Alps, was a new ethos that came not with the Black Death itself but with the sharp, even if temporary, disappearance of plague followed by the steep and steady decline in rates of plague mortality

---

[68] Ser Andrea de Redusiis de Quero, Cancellario communis Tarvisii, *Chronicon tarvisinum, a. 1368–1428*, in Muratori, vol. XIX (Milan, 1731), col. 789.

[69] On the trajectory of wool production in post-Black Death Florence, see F. Franceschi, *Oltre il 'Tumulto': i lavoratori fiorentini dell'Arte della lana tra Tre e Quattrocento* (Florence, 1993), 11

[70] In August, the new Ciompi government 'passed ordinances that all the wool bosses must produce [at least] 2,000 wool cloths [*panni*] a month, whether they wanted to or not, or suffer great penalties'; *Cronaca terza d'anonimo (1378–1382)* in G. Scaramella (ed.), *Cronache e memorie sul tumulto dei Ciompi*, RIS, vol. XVIII/3 (Bologna, 1917–34), 130–1.

and morbidity from the mid-1350s to 1400.[71] Societies turned from utter despondency in the face of plague to a new self-confidence and belief in the efficacy of social action to change current affairs and even the afterlife. Such changes can be spotted in new burial practices and testamentary demands of artisans, workers, and peasants that centred on the individual and the importance and longevity of the male line.[72] Attitudes of chroniclers and doctors across much of western Europe reflect a similar change in sentiment. In the year of the plague chronicles are replete with comments condemning the medical profession, seeing doctors and their cures as only hastening the demise of their plague-patients. In the face of later plagues, their views softened; they even began to copy and recommend doctors' recipes and cures as efficacious 'shields' for fending off the disease.[73] Doctors from Portugal to Danzig also changed their minds: in 1348 and immediately thereafter they charged that the Black Death had 'dumbfounded all doctors'; Hippocrates' art was lost.[74] Prayer, repentance and recognition of church authority were the best doctors could possibly prescribe.[75] By the 1360s their opinions had changed. God hardly appears in their tracts as they boasted about their skills and the numbers of plague victims they allegedly cured. As a doctor Stefanus of Padua claimed towards the end of the century, he had 'triumphed over the plague', and with his plague tract written in the vernacular and dedicated to his fellow citizens of Padua, they too were now empowered to do the same.[76]

---

[71] On these trends, see Cohn, *The Black Death Transformed: Disease and Culture in Early Renaissance Europe* (London, 2002), 188–219.

[72] See Cohn, *The Cult of Remembrance and the Black Death: Six Renaissance Cities in Central Italy* (Baltimore, 1992); and id., 'The Place of the Dead in Flanders and Tuscany: Towards a Comparative History of the Black Death', in B. Gordon and P. Marshall (eds), *The Place of the Dead: Death and Remembrance in Late Medieval and Early Modern Europe* (Cambridge, 2000), 17–43.

[73] For these chronicles, see Cohn, *The Black Death Transformed*, 225–30.

[74] For the medical tract in rhyme of Doctor Simon de Couvain, see É. Littré (ed.) 'Opuscule relatif à la peste de 1348 composé par un contemporain', *Bibliothèque d'École des chartes*, 2 (1841), 201–43.

[75] See J. Arrizabalaga, 'Facing the Black Death: Perceptions and Reactions of University Medical Practitioners', in L. García-Ballester, R. French, J. Arrizabalaga, and A. Cunningham (eds), *Practical Medicine from Salerno to the Black Death* (Cambridge, 1994), 270–2 and 'Epistola de Maestre Jacme d. Agramont (24 April 1348)' in *Archiv für Geschichte der Medizin*, 17 (1925), 120–1.

[76] 'Ein Paduaner Pestkonsilium von Dr. Stephanus de Doctoribus', in *Archiv für Geschichte der Medizin*, 6 (1913), 356. For many more examples and a further discussion of this change in sentiment, see Cohn, *The Black Death Transformed*, 223–52.

Michel Pintoin, official chronicler of King Charles VI of France, saw the underlying cause of the revolts at the beginning of the 1380s in Paris, Rouen, and Ghent as being the same; all stemmed from a new sentiment among the *plebes*. With scorning disapprobation he lamented: 'the appetite for liberty was burning . . . the lust for new things incessant.'[77] Despite the great diversity in the forms of rebellion and differences in local economic, social, and political contexts and their immediate causes, the same, I argue, can be said of the more than five hundred revolts I have been discovering in Italian chronicles and archives from 1355 to the early 1400s. The cause of liberty became ever more pronounced in the slogans of post-plague rebels. For the hundreds of revolts against the church in 1375–6, for instance, a new flag was created that bound together insurgents across city-states. It was 'a huge banner or standard with the letters, LIBERTAS, stitched in gold'. The insurgents behind it 'proclaimed that they would come to the aid of anyone who desired liberty and wished to be rid of the tyranny and subjugation of the Church's evil pastors'.[78]

In one of Rodney Hilton's last essays, he too saw this new demand for freedom as quintessential to the spirit and ideology of the English Uprising of 1381: 'It is worth emphasising strongly that the demand for freedom was perhaps the most powerful element of inherent ideology in 1381.'[79] To be sure, earlier appeals to liberty and freedom can be spotted in popular revolts. To take one pre-plague example: with the rise of the 'second *popolo*' in Florence in 1282, the merchant chronicler Dino Compagni met fellow citizens in the church of San Pancrazio to try to persuade them of the need for change. The three Dino singled out, however, were hardly commoners; they were members of Florence's most elite merchant guild, the Calimala, and one was a member of the powerful magnate clan of the Bardi. 'They spoke of their liberty and the injuries that they had received.'[80] Quantitatively, the post-plague period shows a difference: explicit references to 'liberty' or 'freedom

---

[77] M. L. Bellaguet (ed.), *Chronique du Religieux de Saint-Denys*, Collection de Documents inédits, 6 vols. (Paris, 1839–42), vol. I, 16–23.

[78] *Annales Mediolanenses Anonymi autoris*, in Muratori, XVI, col. 659.

[79] R. H. Hilton, 'Inherent and Derived Ideology in the English Rising of 1381,' in *Campagnes médiévales: l'homme et son espace, études offertes à Robert Fossier*, Histoire ancienne et médiévale, 31 (Paris, 1995), 402. I believe that this article marks a change in Hilton's view of the ideology of late medieval popular revolts from what it had been in *Bondmen Made Free* (1973), from 'negative class consciousness' to an ideology that no matter how vague was positive.

[80] I. del Lungo (ed.), *La Cronica di Dino Compagni delle cose occorrenti ne' tempi suoi*, RIS, vol. IX/2 (Città del Castello, 1907–16), 16–18.

against tyranny' as a cause of rebellion increased four-fold in the chronicle descriptions. Previously these expressions were confined to revolts of the *popolo* and the bourgeois; it was the ideology of privilege that citizens and merchants like Dino Compagni and his elite comrades coveted. After the plague, it became the battle cry of 'the vilest sort'.[81] As Pintoin feared and as the trajectory of social protest over the later middle ages shows, the post-plague rush in the expression of this new political 'inherent ideology' was no historical constant. It had become the battle cry of artisans and peasants who challenged the social practices and political order of the elites.

[81] I have developed this point in my book, *Lust for Liberty*. In the post-plague period, liberty in the mouths of the *plebes* begins to assume a new meaning, from privileges and specific franchises toward the rights of all the native-born and equality.

Religious Dissent, Social Revolt and 'Ideology'

Steven Justice

This essay takes up a historiographical problem: the relation between the movement of religious dissent provoked by John Wyclif in the 1370s and the English peasant rising of 1381.[1] It is, strictly considered, a historiographical problem and not a historical one: since not a whit of compelling evidence has been successfully adduced in support of any direct relation, the real question is not so much whether there was one as why some of us keep looking for one. I once argued the influence of religious dissent on (or, better, the appropriation of it by) the 1381 rebels,[2] and now think that that argument, though not implausible, poses the wrong question; so the present essay involves a good deal of *retractio* and a certain amount of retraction. It is some comfort that my rashness in this matter put me in honourable company. Rodney Hilton, whose real attention was elsewhere, suggested in passing that native traditions of doctrinal dissent were part of the mix that blew up in 1381.[3] Anne Hudson made the same suggestion I did in the same year, on partly different grounds.[4] In recent years, the heresy and the rebellion keep regular company in scholarship; sometimes with simply the sense that they

---

[1] My thanks to those who offered questions and comments at the conference, especially Rosamond Faith, Zvi Razi, and János M. Bak; they have kept me thinking, and caused me even to re-treat my re-treatment of the problem.

[2] S. Justice, *Writing and Rebellion: England in 1381* (Berkeley, 1994), 73–101.

[3] R. Hilton, *Bond Men Made Free: Medieval Peasant Movements and the English Rising of 1381* (London, 1973), 213. He was speaking of a pre- or extra-Wycliffite tradition of dissent (see also p. 231); though he perhaps confused more than he clarified by calling this tradition 'Lollardy'. That choice implies a supposition probably correct, that is, that Lollardy properly so called in effect incorporated individuals and groups already, though in idiosyncratic and isolated ways, in a position of dissent; see S. Justice, 'Lollardy', in D. Wallace (ed.), *The Cambridge History of Medieval English Literature* (Cambridge, 1999), 670–1, 683–4.

[4] A. Hudson, '*Piers Plowman* and the Peasants' Revolt: A Problem Revisited', *Yearbook of Langland Studies*, 8 (1994), 96–8; see also ead., *The Premature Reformation: Wycliffite Texts and Lollard History* (Oxford, 1988), 68.

thematically belong together,[5] sometimes some substantial connection proposed or supposed between them.[6]

The most interesting case is Margaret Aston's 1994 essay querying the rising's possible connection with Wyclif's eucharistic heresy, which rejected the orthodox account of how the bread and wine at mass became the body and blood of Christ. Her conclusion is unequivocal—'No evidence exists to suggest that any of [the rebels] . . . was in any way moved by Wycliffe's arguments, or guilty of denying the worship owed to the eucharist'[7]—but her rhetoric is not. It is always risky to guess at another scholar's rejected hypotheses; but she so tirelessly catalogues sacramental resonances that one feels that she *must* have started out suspecting Wycliffite influence, and concluded by reluctantly declaring the suspicion disconfirmed. In fact, the terms in which she dismisses the case for heretical influence suggest how natural it would have seemed to her: '[The rebels'] actions may indeed have reflected radical questioning of social boundaries, *but* doubts about sacramental teaching were not on view':[8] the adversative betrays her expectation that 'questioning of social boundaries' and 'doubts about sacramental teaching' normally would be found together.

Aston's eventual conclusion is quite correct; there is no evidence linking any rebel, John Ball apart, to heresy, or linking any rebel action in 1381 to any heretical teaching, eucharistic or otherwise. (It seems at least symbolically significant that the only figure of documented Wycliffite commitments with *any* connection to events linked to the rising was a lawyer, whose connection was assessing the initial poll tax in Oxfordshire.)[9] Nor is there any language in the revolt that must have come from dissenting sources, though there

---

[5] E.g., R. F. Green, *A Crisis of Truth: Literature and Law in Ricardian England* (Philadelphia, 1999), 6.

[6] E.g., J. M. Gellrich, *Discourse and Dominion in the Fourteenth Century: Oral Contexts of Writing in Philosophy, Politics, and Poetry* (Princeton, 1995), 157, 166–8; E. Steiner, *Documentary Culture and the Making of Medieval English Literature* (Cambridge, 2003), 209–10.

[7] M. Aston, '*Corpus Christi* and *Corpus Regni*: Heresy and the Peasants' Revolt', *Past and Present*, 143 (1994), 46.

[8] Ibid; my emphasis.

[9] This is Thomas Compworth the elder, convicted of heresy concerning tithes and auricular confession in 1385; M. Jurkowski, 'Lollardy in Oxfordshire and Northamptonshire: The Two Thomas Compworths', in F. Somerset, J. Havens, and D. Pitard (eds), *Lollards and their Influence in Late Medieval England* (Cambridge, 2003), 73–95; though see W. M. Ormrod, 'The Politics of Pestilence: Government in England after the Black Death', in W. M. Ormrod and P. G. Lindley (eds), *The Black Death in England* (Stamford, 1996), 166–7.

is some that could have. Arguments for connection between the two movements have generally hinged, first, on apparently suggestive convergences of
language and concerns and, second, on assertions of historians contemporary
with the event.[10] The former we will come to shortly. The latter need to be
considered immediately, for their significance has been mischaracterized:
these assertions are not weak evidence that the rebels had Wycliffite thoughts,
but pretty strong evidence that they did not. It is generally allowed that
Walsingham's and Knighton's assertions about the rebels' Lollard sympathies
prove little, because of their evident hostility to Wyclif, and their tendentious
desire to embarrass him with responsibility for anything that might be laid at
his door.[11] But we can say more: they are so eager to produce a connection
that the tenuousness of the connections they do make is eloquent. Knighton
can say no more than that John Ball prepared the way for Wyclif, as John the
Baptist did for Christ; he almost pedantically avoids suggesting any contact or
influence between them.[12] Walsingham can scatter direct blame on the friars
for the rising, but not on Wyclif: to bring the latter into the story, he can
do no better than say that the Rising was a divine punishment for heresy,
and can assert no causal relation other than the inscrutable decorum of

[10] Hudson (n. 4 above) makes a different case for Wyclif's influence in 1381, which unfortunately confuses the question of his influence with that of his reaction. She finds that
Wyclif's comments on the revolt in *De blasfemia* are more sympathetic than they have
been thought. But that Wyclif had measured thoughts about the rebels does not prove
that they had any thoughts about him. Indeed, rather the contrary, for her argument
inadvertently discredits one piece of evidence for Wyclif's influence: by showing that
Wyclif makes no effort to distance himself from the events of June, she forces us to
conclude that Wyclif apparently saw no unlucky similarity between the rebels' actions
and his doctrines.

[11] Classically, M. Aston, 'Lollardy and Sedition', *Past and Present*, 17 (1960), 3–5; most
recently H. Eiden, '*In der Knechtschaft werdet ihr verharren . . .*': *Ursachen und Verlauf des
englischen Bauernaufstandes von 1381* (Trier, 1995), 397, who concurs with the suggestion
of R. B. Dobson, 'Remembering the Peasants' Revolt 1381–1981', in W. H. Liddell and
R. G. E. Wood (eds), *Essex and the Great Revolt of 1381* (Chelmsford, 1981), 6–7, that
their accusations either reflect or coincide with an effort by Archbishop Courtenay to do
the same. My remarks about Knighton and Walsingham apply also to W. W. Shirley (ed.),
Fasciculi zizaniorum magistri Johannis Wyclif cum tritico (Rolls Series, 5, 1858), 273–4,
but its belated testimony does not deserve separate consideration.

[12] G. H. Martin (ed.), *Knighton's Chronicle 1337–1396* (Oxford, 1995), 242. It may bear
witness to even less sense of connection between the two than even this might suggest; see
the compelling remarks on Knighton's composition in G. Martin, 'Knighton's Lollards',
in M. Aston and C. Richmond (eds), *Lollardy and the Gentry in the Later Middle Ages*
(Stroud, 1997), 33–4.

God's justice.[13] Either of these writers, it is clear, would gladly have traced the rebellion back to Oxford; it is therefore significant that neither thought he plausibly could.

This conclusion might suggest dark reflections on any attempts to trace the thinking of the rebels, and the relation of that thinking to religious sources, both of which have recently been occupations mostly of literary scholars;[14] such aspects have won less attention in the 'hard' studies that have yielded the most distinct and concrete progress in study of the revolt, by concentrating on archival material while skirting or ignoring the conceptual activities of the rebels.[15] It would be easy to conclude that less material, more intellectual elements of the uprising are irrecoverable and perhaps comparatively unreal; and while few historians would now explicitly dismiss them, 'cultural' concerns, especially conceptual ones, get rendered without much complexity or sense of pertinence, and with a sense that they are at best epiphenomenal. The persistent reluctance among historians who use

[13] Similarly, although Walsingham says (whether informedly or not is impossible to judge) that Ball taught Wyclif's doctrines, he gives no specific instances, and does not connect his allegation to the revolt itself; E. M.Thompson (ed.), *Chronicon Anglie* (Rolls Series, 74, 1875), 321. Réville alone seems to have noticed the importance of all this: 'il n'y a pas de lollards parmi eux, sans quoi le chroniqueur de Saint-Alban . . . n'eût pas manqué de leur addresser ce nouveau reproche et d'en faire le plus gros de leurs crimes'; A. Réville, *Le Soulèvement des travailleurs d'Angleterre en 1381* (Paris, 1898), 44. It is not, as I had supposed, that Réville forgot the passage in Walsingham, but that he attended more precisely than I did to what it did and did not say.

[14] For excellent examples, see the discussions mentioned in notes 4–6, and also A. Middleton, 'William Langland's "kynde name": Authorial Signature and Social Identity in Late Fourteenth-Century England', in L. Patterson (ed.), *Literary Practice and Social Change in Britain, 1380–1530* (Berkeley, 1990), 15–82; P. Strohm, *Hochon's Arrow: The Social Imagination of Fourteenth-Century Texts* (Princeton, 1992), 33–56; D. Aers, '*Vox populi* and the Literature of 1381', in D. Wallace (ed.), *The Cambridge History of Medieval English Literature* (Cambridge, 1999), 432–53; Green, *Crisis of Truth*, 198–205; A. Galloway, 'Making History Legal: *Piers Plowman* and the Rebels of Fourteenth-Century England', in K. Hewett-Smith (ed.), *William Langland's* Piers Plowman: *A Book of Essays* (New York and London, 2001), 7–39; Steiner, *Documentary Culture*, 171–7.

[15] In addition to the work of the honorand of and contributors to this volume, see for example Eiden, '*In der Knechtschaft*'; Ormrod, 'Politics of Pestilence'; E. B. Fryde, *Peasants and Landlords in Later Medieval England* (New York, 1996); A. Prescott, 'Writing about Rebellion: Using the Records of the Peasants' Revolt of 1381', *History Workshop Journal*, 45 (1998), 1–27; H. Eiden, 'Joint Action against "Bad" Lordship: The Peasants' Revolt in Essex and Norfolk', *History*, 83 (1998), 5–30; S. Federico, 'The Imaginary Society: Women in 1381', *Journal of British Studies*, 40 (2001), 159–83.

conventional record sources to credit ideas of the sort discussed here as media of historical action has re-emerged recently; it sports a more stylish look, which seems at odds with the bluff empirical sobriety of older social and economic history, but it accomplishes exactly the same thing, by insisting that to find ideas in the rising is not so much over-imaginative as coercive and in bad faith; an attempt to discover the principles and aims of the rising can be dismissed thus: 'A great event like the 1381 rising can never be subject to a single master interpretation'.[16] It is hard to imagine disagreeing with this admirable sentiment (except to wonder why only *great* events enjoy this privilege), but also hard to concede that speaking of the rebels' thoughts and purposes commits any infraction against it. For speaking of them supposes no more than that a substantial number of the rebels found their actions mutually intelligible, and inquires into nothing grander than the concrete terms of that intelligibility; and it is on these grounds that ideas may be taken as part of, not impositions on, the events. An obvious example, often discussed, is the rebels' disciplined refusal to take plunder when they destroyed the Savoy.[17] Unless we reject the accounts of that refusal altogether, and it is hard to explain why our sources or their informants would have invented it,[18] we must grant not only that some category of moral judgment was invoked, but, more importantly, that it was pertinent *enough* to *enough* of those present, as an expression of some shared self-understanding, to affect the behaviour of a crowd and therefore the shape of the event. If we do not care what the rebels thought, we risk reaffirming, with some medieval lords, that peasants had nothing but their bellies;[19] and if we do care what they thought, we need to take seriously the moral and theological vocabularies they used.

This bears directly on the historiographical question with which I began. 'If the class struggles of that time appear to bear religious earmarks, if the interests, requirements and demands of the various classes *hid themselves behind a religious screen*, it little changes the actual situation, and is to be explained by conditions of the time':[20] this is Engels, and when we think that revolt has a more natural affinity with heresy than with orthodoxy, we think

---

[16] Prescott, 'Writing about Rebellion', 18; the sentence quoted refers to Justice, *Writing and Rebellion*.

[17] Walsingham, *Chronicon Angliae*, 289; Knighton, *Chronicle*, 214–15.

[18] Justice, *Writing and Rebellion*, 91; Eiden, '*In der Knechtschaft*', 237–8.

[19] '. . . nihil extra ventrem'; the reference is to the abbot of Burton-on-Trent's maxim, preserved in G. Wrottesley, 'The Burton Chartulary', *Collections for a History of Staffordshire*, 5 (1884), 85.

[20] F. Engels, *The Peasant War in Germany*, M. J. Olgin (trans.), (London, 1926), 51; my emphasis.

as his heirs. And with such thoughts there obviously is no point investigating religion in revolt: if class relations throw off religious language as a merely superstructural expression, then understanding that language adds nothing of value to what must be fundamentally an economic account. Now this may seem the shameless construction of a straw man, since scarcely anyone would now claim that ideology works 'to assure, *in the sphere of ideas*, the social reproduction of the existing society by legitimating the prevailing relations of exploitation and the forms of expropriation of surplus',[21] that it legitimates them by enforcing particular *meanings*. Such a model takes meaning to be something implausibly determinate and manageable, and anyhow seems to imply that one could escape ideology merely by changing beliefs. But a post-Althusserian account of ideology is not finally much better. In some ways it can be more subtle and satisfying—conceptually, because it avoids some of these problems by making ideology produce subjects rather than beliefs or cognitions, and methodologically because it therefore directs our attention less to '*ideas*' than to '*practices, rituals, ideological apparatus*', to the whole life-world sustained by institutions, disciplines, and formations of all sorts.[22] This is undeniably attractive, and aligns itself with a certain 'common sense' so fully naturalized for academic discourse that it can be assumed without being argued ('If you believe, you obey').[23] But it is hard to see that anything would *not* fit the category 'ideological' on this account. An unbounded category is analytically vacuous. And in practice the category does disappear in post-Althusserian analysis: as ideology ceases to be defined by a systematic cognitive relation to economic exploitation, it either becomes absorbed into power as such, or becomes fractured into local practices and loses the systemic character that made the concept useful in the first place; that is, it approaches characteristics of Foucault and of Bourdieu, respectively.

Whatever the reason, we still have the unthinking association of revolt with heresy, a quaint habit of thought quite untouched by theoretical refinement. And I would suggest that the very notion of ideology and the discursive habits

---

[21] H. Frey, 'Religion as an Ideology of Domination', in J. M. Bak and G. Benecke (eds), *Religion and Rural Revolt: Papers Presented to the Fourth Interdisciplinary Workshop on Peasant Studies, University of British Columbia, 1982* (Manchester, 1984), 14, my emphasis; and see the state-of-nature story by which he tries to define the role of 'religion', 15–17.

[22] L. Althusser, 'Ideology and Ideological State Apparatuses (notes towards an investigation)', '*Lenin and Philosophy*' *and Other Essays* (New York, 1971), 169.

[23] '... croire, c'est obéir'. P. Veyne, *Les grecs ont-ils cru à leurs mythes? Essai sur l'imagination constituante* (Paris, 1983), 44. The passage continues: 'Le rôle politique de la religion n'est nullement une affaire de contenu idéologique'.

that go with it—in relation to such questions as these, at least—may buy nothing that historical study should want to have. Insofar as it urges upon us that some religious beliefs or practices were inherently more likely to conserve, or to disrupt, relations of production and exploitation than others, all it buys us is a deeper identification with Walsingham, Knighton, the author of the *Fasciculi zizaniorum*, and those other men of church and government whom Aston wittily describes: 'In the mind of God, and in the minds of men attuned to celestial thought, there was a link between misbelief and mayhem.'[24]

This long preamble done, let us turn to the tale, and look at three instances from the rebellion that either might be or might have been taken, by contemporaries or by historians, to indicate the presence of Wycliffite or dissenting or impious attitudes, and see how they look without that predisposition.

The first is straightforward. The various accounts of rebel demands in 1381 say little about the church; there is a desire for a general redistribution of clerical wealth that sounds like Wycliffite disendowment; I'll come back briefly to that. But there is the demand for only 'one bishop' and 'one prelate'.[25] Notice first what this demand does *not* entail. It is *not* analogous to that other demand, that there be no lordship but the king's.[26] I submit that a truly symmetrical analogy to 'no lord but the king'—where the point is the qualitatively different courts and tenants' status and rights—would be, not 'no bishop but one', but 'no bishop but God'. In keeping one bishop, the rebels would leave the episcopacy and episcopal function (also, of course, the priesthood and sacerdotal function). It in no sense rejects the principle or logic of ecclesiastical hierarchy. It would, however, eliminate many very significant and oppressive lords, and this is surely its point. The demand *separates* the episcopal office from episcopal lordship, and preserves the principle and function of church hierarchy while eliminating one of its massive incidental inconveniences. The conclusion sounds odd, to be sure; but it seems to follow from taking seriously the best evidence we have.

This instance addresses the question at a broad level of programme and principle: Did the rebels' demands regard sacramental office and lordship as aspects of a single whole? Did they evidence any desire to undo what we might think was a system of cognitive *and* material domination? On this evidence they did not. The next instance addresses the more concrete level of ritual

---

[24] Aston, '*Corpus Christi*', 46.

[25] '. . . nulle evesqe serroit en Engleterre fors une, ne nulle prelate fors une'; V. H. Galbraith (ed.), *The Anonimalle Chronicle, 1333–1381* (Manchester, 1927), 147.

[26] '. . . qe nulle seignur ne averoit seignurie fors swelment estre proporcione entre toutz gentz, fors tansoulement la seignurie la roy'; ibid.

practice and belief, and happily coincides with one of Althusser's instances of how 'regular practices . . . of the ideological apparatus' yield actions and ideas that the good subject illusorily feels he has 'in all consciousness freely chosen': '. . . he goes to Church to attend Mass, kneels, prays . . .'[27] I am thinking of the 'millstone eucharist' at St. Albans Abbey. According to Thomas Walsingham, the abbey had, long before, secured its right of multure over its tenants, and symbolized this victory by paving its parlour floor with the handmills it confiscated from them; in 1381, the rebels at St. Albans repossessed these millstones and distributed the pieces among themselves 'like bread blessed on Sundays'.[28] Two scholars have doubted that there was any eucharistic resonance in the action,[29] but that is simply baffling: the Corpus Christi date, the association with bread, the imitation not only of communion but of the fraction of the host, all make a powerful prima facie case for it. To this another has been added: the widely disseminated devotional image of Christ's passion as the milling of grain.[30] Aston thinks that Walsingham saw in this action the bad influence of heresy and thinks that he was wrong. She is obviously correct in this, but one can say more: not only is there no evidence of heresy, and no need for it in order to give a coherent account of the action, but the gesture's manifest force—associating their productive labour, the ancient rights they believed underlay and protected it, and the community to which those rights belonged with the sacredness of consecrated bread and its power to embody the community that celebrated it—depends quite precisely on those elements of orthodox eucharistic theology that Wyclif most urgently rejected.[31]

As I said earlier, Aston concludes that those contemporaries who linked revolt to sacramental heresy misconstrued the rebels' use of language and gestures with eucharistic associations. But it seems worth asking why those associations were there to be misconstrued in the first place, associations which are too consistent and richly detailed to be thought inadvertent.

---

[27] Althusser, 'Ideology', 167.

[28] Account in H. T. Riley (ed.), *Gesta abbatum monasterii Sancti Albani* (Rolls Series, 28, 1869), vol. III, 309; see the discussion in Justice, *Writing and Rebellion*, 168–9.

[29] Rosamond Faith, review of Justice, *Writing and Rebellion*, *EHR*, 113 (1998), 427; and I take this to be what Galloway suggests in his game defence of Walsingham: 'it is Walsingham, not the rebels, who provides the . . . eucharistic simile', 'Making History Legal', 37. Note, however, that Walsingham in fact provides no 'eucharistic simile'; he compares the breaking of the millstones not to the Eucharist, but to the distribution of the *pain bénit*; see Justice, *Writing and Rebellion*, 158–9 and n.

[30] Aston, '*Corpus Christi*', 27–31.

[31] J. I. Catto, 'Wyclif and the Cult of the Eucharist', *Studies in Church History*, Subsidia 4 (1985), 269–86.

However mistaken the conclusions that chroniclers drew from them, their actions show the rich use by the rebels of a still wider range of theological language. I suggest that the most plausible conclusion is the one we would more easily draw if the case in question were not a revolt, but some other and less contentious form of common action: that it drew on the language, thought, habits and imagery of the worship to which they were accustomed, in characterizing the moral and theological basis for their actions. Normative religious belief could encourage and justify rebellion as well as submission, could provide rebels as well as their lords with resources of self-explanation and self-justification; its presence in the language and thought of the revolt is not a problem, and so does not require us to contrive a Wycliffite solution.

But if this is the case, then events like the rising offer the historian an opportunity as well, which I will approach through one last episode and one last question. The episode is the capture and execution of the prior of Bury, as related in the *Electio Timworth*. Like the case just discussed, this story comes not from one of the originating areas of revolt, but from a monastic borough. The reading I offer is suppositious and speculative, and I would not claim more than plausibility for it; but it could show by what kind of mechanisms, and through what sort of practices, the local communities might have construed normative doctrines, practices, and narratives. The *Electio*, by John Gosford, abbey almoner, is not an easy source to evaluate, largely both uncorroborated and uncontradicted; the most we can confidently say is that its narrative is circumstantially detailed and generally plausible, and that is little enough. It is also generally free from obvious moralizing invention. So it is hard to know what to do with this episode in which Gosford describes how the rebels beat and mocked the prior: 'At times they genuflected before him, saying "Hail, Teacher" [*Ave Raby*]; at times they brought him a cup with nothing in it; at times they wounded him, saying "Prophesy who struck you". Thus all night long they wailed and gnashed their teeth at him, as on the night of the last supper the perfidious Jews did to Jesus'.[32] One's impulse is to dismiss this sort of stuff as mere didactic typologizing, making the prior's death a martyrdom in imitation of Christ. But there is nothing else in his account in the style of such gothic polemic. So let me suggest what I grant is only a possibility, at least to see what it might imply.

Dyer has noted the fact of Corpus Christi processions in three Suffolk parishes that produced rebels.[33] There was in fact a Corpus Christi guild in Bury itself; by the time of the 1389 guild returns (before which we can expect

[32] Thomas Arnold (ed.), *Memorials of St. Edmund's Abbey* (London, 1896), vol. III, 127.
[33] C. C. Dyer, 'The Rising of 1381 in Suffolk: Its Origins and Participants', *Proceedings of the Suffolk Institute of Archaeology and History*, 26 (1988), 274–87.

no evidence) it sponsored an *interludium*—a dramatic entertainment—for Corpus Christi.[34] It was surely not a Corpus Christi cycle of the fifteenth-century sort, though Gail Gibson has very persuasively located the N-Town cycle in Bury.[35] But we know that there were Passion plays in the south of England by the 1390s at least,[36] and some sort of cycle in York by 1376. Let me suggest that, on the supposition that this *interludium* was a Passion sequence,[37] we could imagine that if something like what Gosford described took place, it might have meant something very different to its agents than it did to him. I can only sketch this briefly. Two elements of existing Passion sequences (all of which, again, post-date the fourteenth century) are pertinent here. First, their aesthetic works from delay and intensification, drawing out the sufferings of Christ in what his captors treat as ludic diversion. Second, the accusations launched against Christ—accusations of irreverence, blasphemy and so on—apply in fact to those who accuse and torture him, the Jewish priests and guards and Roman soldiers. It is an interesting but still obvious didactic move—that those who reject goodness see their own guilt projected onto the object of their hatred—but it works with that first element to provoke the audience's desire to see the *mis*placed punishment *rightly* placed: to see the irreverent and blasphemous and treacherous torturers and judges hoist on their own petard. I have elsewhere discussed moments in which the rebels stigmatized the objects of their hatred, like Archbishop Sudbury, by dramatizing the fake claims to holiness that they claimed these prelates made. In this case, it is possible to imagine the rebels at Bury (towns-people, Gosford claims) replaying the action of a Passion sequence, but

[34] K. Young, 'An Interludium for a Gild of Corpus Christi', *Modern Language Notes*, 48 (1933), 85–6. Even Lawrence Clopper, so devastatingly sceptical about terms like *ludus* and *miraculum*, grants that *interludium* usually designates precisely dramatic perform-ance; L. M. Clopper, *Drama, Play, and Game: English Festive Culture in the Medieval and Early Modern Period* (Chicago, 2001), 132.

[35] G. M. Gibson, 'Bury St Edmunds, Lydgate, and the *N-Town cycle*', *Speculum*, 56 (1981), 56–90.

[36] The monk of Westminster records a 1393 performance by London clerics that sounds very like a cycle, and would have included a Passion sequence; L. C. Hector and B. Harvey (eds), *The Westminster Chronicle, 1381–1394* (Oxford, 1966), 476, and the *Tretise of miraclis pleyinge*, with a terminal date in the very early fifteenth century, speaks of audiences 'seing the passioun of crist and of hise seintis', C. Davidson (ed.) *A Tretise of Miraclis Pleyinge* (Kalamazoo, 1993), 39.

[37] That the *interludium* is said to be *de corpore Christi* presents no difficulty; see A. F. Johnston, 'What if No Texts Survived? External Evidence for Early English Drama', in M. G. Briscoe and J. C. Coldewey (eds), *Contexts for Early English Drama* (Bloomington, 1989), 11–12.

correcting the misprision acted therein by replaying it on those who deserve it—on the prior and Chief Justice Cavendish. If they did so—this is the point—the moral and religious basis for these gruesome and violent actions is one that could have been derived, without intervention of the slightest waver of unorthodoxy, from the vernacular but still doctrinally unobjectionable Passion plays.

One question still needs to be posed: What about disendowment? On the one hand, the proposals for redistributing ecclesiastical revenues do sound uncannily like Wyclif's programme.[38] On the other, knowing what they knew of ecclesiastical lords, one might guess that the desirability of appropriation and redistribution was a conclusion rebels might not have needed help reaching. As scholarship stands, I think that there is no way of deciding between those opposing perspectives. But one observation is in order. What most consistently drives Wyclif's arguments for disendowment is not a set of concepts (like use and dominion), but an image—a characteristically Franciscan image, familiar and by this time normative, of the destitute and suffering Christ.[39] But this image was as available to anyone even moderately instructed in the faith as it was to Wyclif, and so were the consequences that might be drawn from it. I continue to find it hard not to imagine that some word of Wycliffite disendowment had reached someone among the rebels, and have argued that there is no difficulty thinking that it might have; but if so, it could not have been, very profoundly, news.

I claimed at the beginning that exploring matters like this could help us better understand the rebellion. I want to conclude by suggesting that it could also help us to a better understanding medieval Christianity as it was encountered 'on the ground'. The last three decades or so have seen a newly vigorous scholarship on western medieval Christianity, of a character vaguely analogous to the vigorous scholarship on rural society that Hilton did so much to energize. In both the contributions are too numerous, and the achievements too rich, to be usefully represented by footnoted lists; as Hilton's name may serve as emblem for the latter, so those of André Vauchez and Caroline Bynum may do for the former. If the last generation of scholarship on medieval Christianity has shown anything clearly, it is that the doctrines, rites, practices and languages of devotion, far from freezing into an unblinking dogmatic stare, exhibited an almost alarming plasticity, that even in its most aggressively normative forms, religious belief and sentiment were conflicted, various and multivocal. The crude and tacit notion of ideology underlies the reflex association of unorthodoxy and rebellion groundlessly and

---

[38] See especially the details in Galbraith (ed.), *Anonimalle Chronicle*, 147.

[39] Justice, *Writing and Rebellion*, 83–4; Justice, 'Lollardy', 665–6.

pointlessly assumes that those who rebelled were unable to find and harness orthodoxy's provocative energies. I suggest, by contrast, that the religious elements in the thought of the rebellion are testimony to how that normative religion and ordinary worship could be construed through the experience of groups like those who rebelled; and the seeming appeal of that construction to large numbers of them shows how persuasively it must have seemed to embody what they must have seen and heard when they saw and heard their liturgies. One of Rodney Hilton's lessons was the resourcefulness of local communities; such an approach as I'm suggesting could explore how they used conceptual and imaginative, as well as material, resources available to them.

Changing Patterns of Urban Conflict in Late Medieval Castile

Pablo Sánchez León

Medieval society, in Rodney Hilton's masterly portrayal, was profoundly shaped by the antagonism between rural landlords and peasants. Although towns and cities were also 'one of its essential constitutive components', they, he insisted, should not be viewed as the loci of fundamental conflicts emerging from feudal relations.[1] Parallel to their distinctive economic structures, important differences can also be identified in the character of the social relations and conflicts in both town and country.

Lords and peasants lived in worlds apart: landlords tended to be absentees. Feudal powers interfered regularly in local life by appropriating economic surplus, which they often secured through the control of monopolies, judicial institutions and (sometimes) the appointment of local officials. But villages as such were autonomous and could not be equated with the manor: they embodied a well-established structure of self-organization, as expressed for example in the management of common rights over land and other economic resources.[2] One interesting counterweight to medieval serfdom was precisely that rural economic and political activity remained largely under peasant collective control through both informal and formal institutions of self-government.

In cities and towns things were both similar and different. In the same way that landlords ruled the countryside from a distance, merchants and the urban elite did not effectively involve themselves in craft production; they tended rather to be interested in controlling guilds. Hilton suggested important analogies between peasant communities and artisan guilds as means for collective action: both were 'institutions expressing collective identity' functioning as 'intermediate structures' between the producers and urban and

---

[1] R. H. Hilton, *English and French Towns in Feudal Society. A Comparative Study* (Cambridge, 1992), 18.

[2] Ibid., 71; see also id., *Bond Men Made Free: Medieval Peasant Movements and the English Rising of 1381* (New York, 1973), 28–32.

lordly powers.[3] But there existed also a great institutional difference between them, which may be formulated thus: apart from a means of collective cooperation and organization, peasant villages were themselves institutional units of self-government within a manor or a principality, whereas urban guilds, although in theory giving opportunities for economic and political cooperation among the artisans, were, at most, part of a wider local institutional setting. This particular character of urban popular organizations suggests that urban order was founded on a distinctive legitimacy, which bore important consequences for the shape of conflicts in towns. In this article I shall develop this argument through an overview, necessarily brief, of the changing political and social structures of the towns of Castile between the thirteenth and the sixteenth centuries. I hope to show as a result how one version of the urban politics characterized by Hilton worked out in practice.

Order in medieval towns and the distinctive urban feudalism of Castile

In the countryside lords could and often did resort to violence in order to maintain personal dependence. This is not to imply that feudal order rested only upon violence: there existed customary institutions and arrangements binding lords and peasants together morally, and often legally. That is to say, despite the inequality inherent in feudal contracts, both parties shared a minimum sense of justice as members of religious and territorial communities. Landlords tended to violate customs, though; in such cases, and given 'the political character of all essential relations' in feudal society, peasants could resist and rebel.[4] They undertook such courses of collective action because they had power to do so, which, apart from collective self-organization, included the possibility of developing interpretations of actions and other justifications based on moral standpoints. Benefiting from a common language of liberty peasants could claim their freedom, which often resulted in the incorporation of their villages into the royal demesne. Such patterns of social relations and conflicts, studied by Hilton for England, can also be found in the early medieval kingdoms of Asturias and León in the north of the Iberian peninsula.

Unlike peasants, though, artisans already enjoyed a status as freemen in towns and cities, shared by all their neighbours. Personal freedom did not of course prevent urban settlements from constituting a very unequal

---

[3] Id., *English and French Towns*, 71 and id., 'Towns in English Feudal Society', in *Class Conflict and the Crisis of Feudalism* (London, 1990), 108, respectively.

[4] Id., 'Introducton', in R. H. Hilton and T. H. Aston (eds), *The English Rising of 1381* (Cambridge, 1984), 8.

society: conflicts exploded there, for example, over the control and distribution of surplus produced by craftsmen because, much like peasants, artisans enjoyed direct access to their means of production. But in medieval towns and cities conflicts developing out of social inequalities could not allow violence to become too embedded, because urban freedom itself rested upon the maintenance of peace within the city and its jurisdiction: self-preservation, peace, unity, and urban liberties were closely associated with each other and had to be guaranteed together. A single political system was instituted for this purpose, which urged all groups, classes, and organizations reflecting social inequalities, including guilds, to adapt to it, giving up a systematic recourse to violence and claiming recognition as (partial) actors. Actually, as humanist rhetoric noted as early as the thirteenth century, the question of order in urban settlements was, precisely, how to secure and reproduce peace and unity within an acknowledged unequal society. The solutions were always found in some degree of mutual recognition and the restraint of violence.[5]

Most western European towns developed constitutions with a degree of self-government but, unlike rural customary arrangements, they were founded on a level of equality of rights (and obligations) as the basis of common justice for all neighbours. Moreover, in towns and cities the means by which all collective issues, including basic conflicts, tended to be settled was through politics, not the judicial process. This implied among other things bargaining among groups for inclusion and leverage. Compared to rural landlords, then, the urban powerful had to be much more involved in the management of local institutions. In general, they could successfully exclude large parts of the population from political participation by instituting hierarchical definitions of status and rights. In some western European cities, merchants dominated political life without major challenges thanks to their intermediate social and economic position; in others, they shared power with clerics and notaries and even with groups of local landowners, as Hilton showed when he compared English and French medieval towns. In the Iberian peninsula cities of this second kind developed in the east, in the Kingdom of Aragon.

---

[5] As stated in the *The Pastoral Eye* (*Oculus Pastoralis sive Libellus Erudiens Rectorem Populorum, c.*1220), 'those of you who live according to urban customs, share a quiet peace and a perfect relation, keeping aside all insults and evil deeds [and] offending neither superiors, nor equals or inferiors' [*quum moribus vivetis urbanis, portantes inter vos pacem tranquillam et amorem perfectum, cesantes ab injuriis et malignitatibus cunctis, non inferentes ofessam majoribus, paribus, vel minoribus ullis*]. Cf. A. Muratori (ed.), *Antiquitates Italiae medii aevii* (Milan, 1741), 97. On this anonymous piece and its relevance in the origins of humanism, see Q. Skinner, *The Foundations of Modern Political Thought. 1. The Renaissance* (Cambridge, 1978), 28–35, esp. 33–4.

Rodney Hilton also assumed that the division between town and country was the most basic structural division in the medieval economy. But this assertion, inherited from political economy, should not be read as meaning empirically that a town or city corresponded to every rural lordship; across Europe, an urban centre usually gave economic and institutional coherence to a whole territory dotted with several lordships. In Italy the pattern was partly different, due to the high degree of urban autonomy. Hilton depicted Italian urban communities as 'usurping the position of feudal landowners as exploiters of the peasants': the city became the head of territorial lordship by controlling and subordinating rural villages.[6] Urban politics also often tended to be atypical in these *comuni*: merchants did enjoy an important role in urban government, but craft guilds could exercise power as well. Indeed, in some Italian cities struggles for guild incorporation paved the way for the establishment of an inclusive political community in which all (male) neighbours enjoyed some degree of political personality as citizens.[7]

In Castile, from the river Duero down to Andalusia and also extending west along Extremadura and east to La Mancha and Murcia, towns resembled Italian city-states in their role as 'collective lordships'.[8] The pattern was pervasive: in Castile all towns or cities were the head of a lordship, and all territorial lordships had a town or city as their head. No land escaped some form of urban lordship (or *concejo*). This unique structure did not result from urban political independence, as in Italy, but rather from its opposite: royal authority exerting greater powers of coordination. Self-preservation and unity were in this case indistinguishable from the maintenance of collective freedom(s): towns captured from the Muslims or newly founded were given charters (*fueros*) by the kings. These included the prohibition of private violence and the institution of assemblies for self-government, in a society experiencing growing inequalities.[9] As a result of this granting of liberties, personal serfdom did not develop in either towns or countryside; all the same, *concejos* were given extensive jurisdictional powers over rural society.

[6] R. H. Hilton, 'Medieval Peasants: Any Lessons?', in Hilton, *Class Conflict*, 46.

[7] G. Brucker, *The Civic World of Early Renaissance Florence* (Princeton, 1977), 14–59. See also J. M. Najemi, 'Guild Republicanism in Trecento Florence: The Success and Ultimate Failure of Corporate Politics', *American Historical Review*, 84 (1979), 53–71.

[8] J. M. Mínguez, 'Feudalismo y concejos. Aproximación metodológica al análisis de las relaciones sociales en los concejos medievales castellanoleoneses', *En la España Medieval*, 3 (1982), 109–22.

[9] F. J. Martínez Llorente, *Régimen jurídico de la Extremadura castellana medieval. Las Comunidades de Villa y Tierra (siglos X–XI)* (Valladolid, 1990).

Urbanization was to become a marked character of this society from the later medieval period and onwards.[10] But its structure would greatly differ from other western European urban examples. As elsewhere, the granting of liberties included fairs and markets, and in larger cities manufactures developed. Yet merchants would never acquire the political role they enjoyed in other regions of Europe, and guilds would not become relevant political actors on their own.[11] Local government was from the fourteenth century onwards in the hands of small numbers of privileged knights, landowners (and cattle-owners), and rentiers, often retainers of the aristocracy or the royal house. Also, many peasants tended to dwell in urban centres of all sizes, from smaller towns to much bigger cities, where, together with urban producers, they were given a marginal representation in the political system.[12]

In many respects, this social and political structure resembles the features of a rural society within a formally urban mould. It partially resembled eastern European towns, but these lacked autonomy and were surrounded by vast rural jurisdictions inhabited by masses of serfs. The pattern does not seem to fit with any general account of medieval society, usually developed from other European cases. This has created difficulties for scholarly research in Spain, although the 'transition debate' has provided important sources of inspiration and analysis. As a result, significant questions arising from this peculiar example of urban feudalism have been neglected. For how, in the first place, could order be established and kept in such an urban society, in which peasants (along with other producers) lived face-to-face with resident landlords, and no significant political role was given to middlemen such as merchants? Why would rentiers and producers share a single set of urban political institutions instead of regularly resorting to violence? How were cities in Castile made into legitimate spaces for the mutual recognition of apparent class antagonists?

Answering these questions is relevant, not only for our understanding of social conflicts and change in medieval Castile and Europe, but also

---

[10] P. Sánchez León, 'Town and Country in Early Modern Castile, 1400–1650', in S. R. Epstein (ed.), *Town and Country in Europe, 1300–1800* (Cambridge, 2001), 272–91.

[11] J. M. Monsalvo Antón, 'Solidaridades de oficio y estructuras de poder en las ciudades castellanas de la Meseta durante los siglos XIII al XV', in A. Vaca (ed.) *El trabajo en la historia* (Salamanca, 1996), 39–90.

[12] Id., 'La sociedad política en los concejos castellanos de la Meseta durante la época del regimiento medieval. La distribución social del poder', in *Concejos y ciudades en la Edad Media Hispánica* (León, 1990), 359–413.

because of their theoretical implications for scholarly research and historical materialism.

Centralized taxation, tax-based urban collective organization and the limits of patronage

The relevance of the questions above becomes clear when we acknowledge that the collective lordships of Castile fell into a deep institutional crisis in the decades around 1300 as the profile of urban society became sharpened by political conflicts based on social inequalities. From the middle of the thirteenth century, groups of urban knights (*caballeros villanos*) were granted privileges of tax exemption by kings; and as a consequence of increasing social cleavages local government by general assemblies of neighbours entered a period of unsurmountable difficulties.[13] Firstly, tax exemptions were not enough to provide elite groups with sources of surplus extraction that were more substantial and stable than the ones inherited from the period of conquest and pillage. In order to overcome the threat of economic crisis, knights and other exempted groups (*hidalgos*) needed greater access to local economic resources. Furthermore, social privileges came to be based on exclusive rights, and their maintenance and exercise at the local level had to be based on the control of decision-making processes. This implied the disruption of the traditions and customs of neighbourhood self-government.

In many towns, groups of *caballeros* eventually took control of urban assemblies or even monopolized them, using a mixture of local collective action and royal consent. But popular responses resisted the attempt by the knights to become both ruling class and governor. Especially during periods of royal minorities or turmoil, brotherhoods (*hermandades*) of towns united against the abuses (*malfetrías*) of knights and magnates.[14] And from the early fourteenth century, popular upheavals exploded in major cities such as Valladolid and Segovia, demanding the perpetuation of inclusive assemblies and other communal institutions. Violence was becoming embedded in towns as well as in the country. This was not, however, the only reason why the monarchy was forced to intervene.

[13] Id., 'Transformaciones sociales y relaciones de poder en los concejos de frontera, siglos XI–XIII. Aldeanos, vecinos y caballeros ante las instituciones municipales', in R. Pastor (ed.), *Relaciones de poder, de producción y de parentesco en la Edad Media y Moderna* (Madrid, 1990), 107–70. See also P. Sánchez León, *Absolutismo y comunidad. Los orígenes sociales de la guerra de los comuneros de Castilla* (Madrid, 1998), 33–9.

[14] C. González Mínguez, 'Aproximación al estudio del "movimiento hermandino" en Castilla y León', *Medievalismo*, 1 and 2 (1992), 35–55 and 29–60.

The example of the town of Ávila reveals that, once they had acquired local power, a reasonable strategy for knights was to distribute among themselves the land pertaining to the town, a policy that headed towards the dismantling of the territorial/jurisdictional dimension of urban lordship itself.[15] But such a potential outcome openly contradicted other major trends because, from the thirteenth century, kings established towns and cities as the institutional basis for their own taxation as well. In particular, Alfonso XI (1325–50) instituted a universal tax (*alcabala*) to be collected in all the *concejos* of the kingdom. The *alcabala* was formally a payment derived from market sales, but in practice it represented a pioneering example of centralized surplus extraction.[16] Two interrelated issues thus lay behind royal intervention in its urban domain: the securing of the conditions of centralized surplus extraction, and the need to refound urban self-government on new bases, capable of reducing violence, or at least of channelling it into a new institutional setting. Both were achieved essentially by defining a set of institutions which took away self-government from local collective actors.

Alfonso's new local regime from 1348 onwards, the so-called *regimiento*, suppressed assemblies for decision-making.[17] A new political system was imposed, in which a limited number of offices to be held for life would dominate local self-government. Knights and privileged elites were given an overwhelming majority of these new offices, but it was the king who appointed them, excluding both local corporations and representative institutions. Indeed all kinds of leagues and collective organizations of local *caballeros*, including estate assemblies, were expressly banned, renewing earlier legislation on the matter. Popular assemblies were also declared illegal. The new urban government was no doubt socially biased, but its profile was narrowly oligarchic rather than just being based on a class. The vast majority of the population was effectively excluded from political participation.

The introduction of centralized taxation and the intervention in the *concejos* were not isolated acts: they were part of an overall transformation of the constitution of the kingdom which was to affect deeply the foundations of legitimacy in Castile. In 1348 a new constitutional guideline was instituted in the *Ordenamiento de Alcalá*, whereby traditional customs and *fueros* were subordinated to more recent and abstract Roman law-based

---

[15] J. I. Moreno Núñez, *Ávila y su Tierra en la Baja Edad Media (siglos XIII–XV)* (Valladolid, 1992), 73–126.

[16] The concept comes from R. Brenner, 'Agrarian Class Structure and Economic Development in Pre-industrial Europe', in T. H. Aston and C. H. E. Philpin (eds), *The Brenner Debate* (Cambridge, 1985), 55–7.

[17] The interpretation in Sánchez León, *Absolutismo*, 40–9.

reinterpretations, fostering royal authority through statutes.[18] These measures confirmed the architecture of centralized taxation, and were universally extended through the territory. The *regimiento* was reproduced in every *concejo*, from big cities to small towns, and was followed by the introduction of a royal delegate with judiciary functions, the *corregidor*. Together with the new local government, the jurisdictional power of the *concejos* over their villages was expanded and intensified: all towns and cities, independently of their size, status, or entitlement, came quickly to embody a very similar jurisdictional structure.

This fiscal revolution was to give the monarchy a huge capacity for surplus appropriation and distribution. But it also brought new problems, both within town walls and with the aristocracy of magnates. For local knights, the increasing amounts of taxation channelled towards the royal house opened up new sources of economic reproduction. As royal retainers and officials, many privileged households could get a share of the centralized revenue through several routes, including allowances (*acostamientos*) and the usufruct of taxes (*situados*). The economic structure of their patrimonies was to become more complex, combining arable land and cattle with other sources of income.[19] In all this process urban politics would still be essential, since towns were now the framework of both landowning and taxation. But the recently established *regimiento* did not turn out to be a sufficiently effective system for satisfying the redistributive needs of these privileged groups in times of structural change. Other outside influences would help to clarify this situation.

The magnates, too, had felt insecure in all this process of structural and constitutional transformation and they reacted with violence and collective action. During the civil war under Peter I (1350–68) the monarchy experimented with favours of a new kind, which were to have a successful future for keeping the loyalty of powerful allies: the granting of towns, together with their jurisdictions, to individual lineages of courtiers and magnates. The so called *mercedes enriqueñas*, named after King Henry II (Enrique de Trastamara, 1369–73) and his successors, members of a new dynasty, coincided with a transformation in aristocratic patterns of inheritance, in favour of the eldest son and also based on perpetual property rights (*mayorazgo*).[20] The upper nobility was thus economically re-established by its incorporation

[18] S. de Dios, 'Sobre la génesis y los caracteres del Estado absolutista en Castilla', *Studia histórica-historia moderna*, 3, part 3 (1985), 3–19.

[19] A. MacKay, 'The Lesser Nobility in the Kingdom of Castile', in M. Jones (ed), *Gentry and Lesser Nobility in Later Medieval Europe* (Gloucester, 1986), 159–80.

[20] B. Clavero, *Mayorazgo. Propiedad feudal en Castilla, 1369–1836* (Madrid, 1974).

into the structure of centralized surplus extraction which had originally been developed through royal institutions.

It is not difficult to predict that these measures were to put the aristocracy as a group in a position comparable with the crown, paving the way for growing competition and eventually conflict. One of its longer-run effects was to transform towns in the fifteenth century into arenas where powerful actors on the 'national' stage struggled for the control of scarce resources, both economic and political. In the towns of new aristocratic entitlement, magnates enlisted the majority of local knights and *hidalgos* as retainers; but also, in strategic royal towns and especially in the larger cities of the royal domain (*realengo*), the aristocracy started to intervene in local government by using their own retainers. The monarchy was forced to increase its own networks of retainers and allies in order to check them and keep local government under control.[21] The eventual outcome was a proliferation of different modes of 'bastard feudalism'. In the shorter run, the influence of aristocratic houses and royal clients over urban social and political life seemed to return to the pattern originally posed by the *caballeros villanos* in the twelfth century: once the majority of local rulers could balance their budgets through their relations with the higher powers of the kingdom, the *regimiento* could be considered as representing local elites as a whole.

But these policies had logical consequences for the rest of the population. The influence and reputation of royal and aristocratic houses gave the *regimiento* legitimacy to adopt policies that both filled the royal treasury and benefited magnates, courtiers, and local knights. But competition for urban control moved the monarchy to increase its own surplus extraction. Taxation soared, along with prices, from the mid-fifteenth century, becoming a burden for the non-privileged.[22] Popular mobilization, however, suffered from other long-term consequences of the establishment of centralized taxation and the *regimiento*.

The division between the taxpayers on one side, and on the other those who were both exempted from taxation and received a share of taxes as income, transformed popular protest from the late fourteenth century. The resort to collective action by the non-privileged was by now considered to be a source of violence and disorder. Guilds had been neglected for a long time as political platforms, and had been curtailed by royal authority as organizations for the regulation of production because their influence on the market threatened the monarchy, which was establishing its own financial base by taxing trade. But on the other hand taxpayers (*pecheros*) could and did successfully

[21] M. C. Gerbet, *Les noblesses espagnoles au Moyen Âge, XI–XV siècle* (Paris, 1994).

[22] M. A. Ladero, *La hacienda real castellana en el siglo XV* (La Laguna, 1973).

struggle for recognition in the new local constitution. After significant mobilization, *pecheros* were given representation in local government. It was a very limited one, though, varying from a small proportion of government officials (*regidores*) to mere presence in the meetings (*ayuntamientos*) of local officials.[23] *Pecheros* were not just limited as political actors by this marginal inclusion; they were also damaged by the structural transformations of the urban feudalism of Castile.

The label of *pecheros*, also known as the *común*, grouped together many social categories in the towns and cities of late medieval Castile. Not only producers, but also merchants and groups of landowners and notaries, were included in one single estate. It was difficult for artisans and merchants to find long-term common grounds for action; craftsmen could more easily ally with urban-based peasants, but these were on the other hand institutionally separated from those in the country for taxation and representation. A town-country cleavage weakened popular self-organization and coordination, but its greatest limitation for long-term collective action came from the overall fact that *pecheros* were a category of taxpayers and consumers, not producers. In particular, no direct relationship could be established between the category of *pecheros* and the organization of guilds, and this bore important consequences for the development and expression of class identities in the towns and cities of Castile.

Resistance against taxation, which formed the basis of urban popular demands in Castile, can be considered itself a form of class struggle, as Hilton himself argued.[24] But given their internal cleavages and the difficulties for their organization as producers, it is not surprising that in normal circumstances the non-privileged showed a rather low political profile. Merchants in particular tended to transmit popular demands in language acceptable to the powerful, and served as middlemen in coalitions of *pecheros* and *hidalgos*. This, together with the overall patronage exerted by the royal and aristocratic houses, helped to legitimize the existing local institutions: a mixture of threats and populist measures curtailed the more radical aims of the taxpayers.

In practice, royal and aristocratic houses were functioning as substitutes for traditional collective self-government. The *regimiento* was commonly supplemented by a structure of factions (*bandos*) dividing local retainers

[23] J. M. Monsalvo, 'La participación política de los pecheros en los municipios castellanos de la Baja Edad Media. Aspectos organizativos', *Studia histórica-historia medieval*, 7 (1989), 37–93.

[24] R. H. Hilton, 'Unjust Taxation and Popular Resistance', *New Left Review*, 180 (1990), 177–84.

into two opposing groups. Yet this system embedded conflicts at the local level. On one hand, factional politics were greatly dependent on the ups and downs of the relations between the crown and individual aristocrats; their conflicts at the royal court could easily end up with the exclusion of retainers of the opposing faction from local power. On the other hand, the loyalty of retainers could not be taken for granted: competition for scarce resources also developed within *bandos*. The line preventing violence was too easily crossed, with the result that, once violence became endemic, populist coalitions were doomed.

Meta-political identities and struggles for estate incorporation
The fifteenth century was a period of recurrent turmoil and civil war in the whole kingdom of Castile.[25] The continuing distribution of *mercedes*, especially when royal largesse was increased in times of disorder, further weakened the financial basis of the monarchy. The royal domain was eventually to be given a special status as the *mayorazgo* of the monarchy, thus preventing even a complete sell-off of royal jurisdictions from dismantling monarchical institutions.[26] But this did not stop the appetites of magnates for access to the remnants of centralized tax and jurisdiction. The overall constitution of Castile was maintained, but royal authority occasionally came near to collapse, deeply affecting the balance of power at the local level. The largest cities, seventeen of which were usually summoned to parliaments (*Cortes*), never passed into aristocratic possession, but their influence was in practice neutralized by one or other aristocratic faction. Given such conditions, what needs explanation is not only how did the monarchy overcome the situation, but how towns and cities with such severe social and political divisions could play a significant role, as they actually did, in restoring the authority of the crown.

To answer this question a different kind of conflict emerging in later medieval Castile needs to be taken into account, the resolution of which had the unintentional results of reuniting a complex and divided urban society, by redefining different groups as members of one single local community. The traditional community of customs and assemblies had not been supplanted by a new legitimacy just by instituting the *regimiento*. Pogroms against the Jews and, thereafter, other manifestations of social exclusion against religious minorities and against those recently converted to Christian faith (*conversos*), functioned both as a safety valve for other latent conflicts, and as a means of re-establishing the sense of identity lost to urban communities after the

---

[25] J. Valdeón, *Los conflictos sociales en Castilla en los siglos XIV y XV* (Madrid, 1975).
[26] P. Fernández Albaladejo, *Fragmentos de monarquía* (Madrid, 1992), 12–13.

destruction of inclusive self-governing assemblies.[27] Manipulation by the privileged and the church was undoubtedly part and parcel of these popular explosions of xenophobia, and the tradition of military struggle against infidels provided some of the ideological justifications for exclusionary policies. The reconfiguration of communitarian identities in terms of Christian orthodoxy, however, had other deeper, more contextual motivations. These relate to the inability of the new institutional setting of the *concejos* to provide for alternative means of reproducing unity, in urban political societies now so openly divided by privilege.

The actual connections between the 'apartheid' practices of urban authorities and the configuration of legitimacy in collective lordships still await more research. But what is already apparent is that the definition of an intolerant Catholic common identity through collective participation in pogroms and through exclusionary policies filled the vacuum left by a proper autonomous *political* community which had been prevented from developing by the establishment of the *regimiento*. The comparison with Italy is illuminating. There, by defining universal citizenship rights, politics could establish itself as an autonomous space for the mutual recognition of unequals and as a generator of social identities at least partially detached from transcendental beliefs.[28] But this was possible because popular participation in self-government contributed to a political inclusion of the majority of the population, independently of their status. In Castile, instead, once *pecheros* became an estate with a bounded position within urban society, the established juridical inequalities could not be bridged by any common identity based on inclusive citizenship. In order to assure the mutual recognition between (juridically defined) unequals—and thus secure unity, peace and order—politics had to be supplemented with meta-politics.[29]

The Catholic monarchy of the early modern Habsburg dynasty had late medieval and urban origins. The notion of ideology does not completely encompass the contents of their emerging overall Catholic identity, which went beyond religious beliefs to make a major impact on social relationships, and which pervaded the character of political and cultural institutions. This identity was the product of a complex process, involving more than

[27] A. MacKay, 'Popular Movements and Pogroms in Fifteenth-Century Castile', *Past and Present*, 113 (1972), 33–67.

[28] J. G. A. Pocock, *The Machiavellian Moment. Florentine Political Thought and the Atlantic Republican Tradition* (Princeton, 1975), 49–80.

[29] For the adaptation of humanism in Castile to an orthodox scholastic mould, see J. N. H. Lawrence, 'Humanism in the Iberian Peninsula', in A. Goodman and A. MacKay (eds), *The Impact of Humanism on Western Europe* (London and New York, 1990), 220–58.

intellectual (and propagandistic) efforts on the part of clerks and courtiers: it is otherwise hard to explain why, after converting to Christianity, thousands of Jews could be persecuted because of their ancestors' creeds, and why on the other hand in some notorious cases *conversos* helped engineer the intellectual foundations of the emerging Catholic monarchy.[30] On one side, the magnitude of social cleavages to be overcome was such that urban legitimacy seems to have had to rely not just on theology but on the creation of profoundly intolerant attitudes as a means of social inclusion. And on the other side, the fact that no heresy ever became rooted in Castilian society during the later medieval crisis, unlike in other European countries, strongly suggests that orthodox Catholic theology was in this case providing the framework of conceptual references not only for the definition of the dominant morality but also for the design of social and political institutions.

Other communitarian representations were subordinated to a Catholic language of 'people' (*pueblo*), but they were not completely erased. Discourses of legitimate self-defence, for example, were re-enacted in towns as the encroachment on urban liberties by magnates and the hounding of the commons by their retainers gathered momentum during the civil wars. Such traditions provided a crucial added legitimation for the building of coalitions between the privileged and the *común* in support of public authority.[31] Under the Catholic kings, Ferdinand and Isabella, the authority of the monarchy was restored in the whole kingdom. With the end of the disturbances, it became apparent that the overall constitution of the kingdom of Castile had developed a long-term profile which was inimical to collective organization on the part of any other social power. Unlike in England after the Wars of the Roses, parliament would not become an institution for the representation of the aristocracy. The situation inside the *concejos* was much the same.

The fifteenth-century crisis had not produced a corporate politics inside towns. Nevertheless, the older issue of the re-creation of privileged corporations, which reflected the juridical divisions of society, reappeared in a new

---

[30] One good example was Samuel Ha-Levi, the rabbi of the Jewish community (*aljama*) of Toledo, who converted to Christianity and, baptized as Pablo de Santamaría, became a bishop and one of the major apologists of royal messianic authority, followed by his son Alonso de Cartagena. See J. C. Conde, *La creación de un discurso historiográfico en el cuatrocientos castellano: 'Las siete edades del mundo' de Pablo de Santa María* (Salamanca, 1999).

[31] J. I. Gutiérrez Nieto, 'Semántica del término 'comunidad' antes de 1520: las asociaciones juramentadas de defensa', *Hispania*, 136 (1977) 319–67. See also S. Moreta Velayos, *Malhechores feudales. Violencia, antagonismos y alianzas de clases en Castilla, siglos XIII–XV* (Madrid, 1978).

230 Pablo Sánchez León

context after 1480. First the kings re-established the authority of the *regimiento* and made the *corregidores* routine royal appointments in local government. The expulsion of Jews, followed by the establishment of the Inquisition, favoured social cohesion among Christians. There was also a massive expansion of *letrados* (clerks) as legal experts, mediating in all kinds of conflicts. None of these measures could prevent *pecheros* and knights from trying to introduce representative institutions in local politics.[32] All the same, given that privilege was not challenged but rather confirmed as a legitimate expression of social inequality, the two estates of *pecheros* and knights were doomed to remain separate in their demands for self-organization and/or representation within urban institutions. Especially in the case of rentiers and knights, institutional incorporation was essential in order to assure a wider and more autonomous base for the collective redistribution of economic resources than the one offered by patron-client relations. This political strategy was also an unintentional consequence of the civil wars, when in some major cities groups of local privileged had ended up developing means of collective organization independent from patronage networks, and aiming at the inclusion of all elite lineages. In the case of the *común*, by contrast, the aim was more autonomous self-organization, freeing popular assemblies from external control by local officials, as a prerequisite for more radical agendas.

The fact that the struggles for recognition of these organizations were independent from one another shows how the towns and cities of Castile could not easily allow for the growth of an inclusive citizenship, and how, behind an overall cultural cohesion, social divisions remained and increased. Corporations were in general latent, or else kept under control by the combined power of royal authority and aristocratic *bandos*—which were nevertheless increasingly criticized for corrupting the functioning of public institutions. But the separate activities and demands of *pecheros* and *hidalgos* against an insensitive and authoritarian *regimiento* had the unintended result of setting the grounds for political cooperation between them. In a context of a crisis of legitimacy at the local level, a political association of this kind could come to the fore, and that possibility would threaten not only the king and the aristocracy, but the whole constitutional order of which the *regimiento* was a basic element.

---

[32] The interpretation is taken from P. Sánchez León, 'La constitución histórica del sujeto comunero: orden absolutista y lucha por la incorporación estamental en las ciudades de Castilla, 1350–1520', in F. Martínez Gil (ed.), *En torno a las Comunidades de Castilla* (Cuenca, 2002), 159–208.

The spectre of urban disorder: the revolt of the comuneros and its sequel

When the young Charles I (1517–51), newly arrived in Castile, was elected emperor of Germany and decided to involve the kingdom in paying his coronation expenses, he triggered a variety of different tensions.[33] In the *Cortes* of 1520, the representatives of major cities gave their consent to new taxes, but popular disturbances exploded in many *concejos*. Local officials and *bandos* found themselves on opposite sides on the matter, and a new leadership from members of the lesser nobility emerged in important cities such as Toledo, Segovia, and Valladolid. The largest and most prolonged urban revolt of western Europe in the early modern period, that of the *Comunidades*, had started. Groups of knights leading masses of artisans and other townpeople were able to defend rebellious towns against royal armies, and they gathered around Charles' mother, Juana, with the intention of repudiating the king and reforming the constitution.

At the local level, coalitions between privileged and the *común* did not revive previous experiences of paternalistic populism, but rather paved the way for attempts to establish corporative political structures: assemblies were summoned, and representatives of estates were given a voice in reformed local institutions or *juntas*.[34] In some cities, merchants acquired a prominent role, and artisans regained autonomy in their collective organizations. But no inclusive political community was born out of this constitutional crisis.

In this new context, the need for self-defence and the role of popular movements revived a rhetoric of *comunidad* that was embedded in local traditions and had slowly been appropriated by the *común*. Local *juntas* made legitimate the expression of inequalities at a political level, but the mutual recognition of groups divided by privilege was to find clear limits. It is not difficult to understand that there was a contradiction inherent in the political outcome of the revolt, that would become apparent once social and juridical antagonists attempted to found a new legitimacy. Moreover, the quest for such a goal would also reveal the boundaries of an already established political culture: not surprisingly, orthodox Catholicism was untouched by the so-called *Santa Junta*, which only questioned the role of the Inquisition. The revolt of the *Comunidades* was not a world turned upside-down. And yet it represented what, in this peculiar case of urban feudalism, could be feared as a major 'disorder': separate social groupings, recognized by law, and regarded as in a hierarchical relationship, even if not in direct opposition to each other, allied together to take direct control of

---

[33] S. Halizcer, *The Comuneros of Castile. The Forging of a Revolution* (Madison, 1981).

[34] See Sánchez León, *Absolutismo*, 212–23 and id., 'Constitución', 197–208.

urban government, in order to recover their full political personality. In order to explain such an outcome, the foundations of order and legitimacy of Castilian society need to be set out first, so as then to understand the shape that social conflicts would eventually adopt inside it. Such has been the aim of this article. One consequence of such a characterization is a theoretical one: class-based mobilization emerges as a historically-specific type of collective action, to be classified among other kinds of struggles for recognition. These struggles are also relevant for understanding social change.

The defeat of the *comuneros* in Villalar in April 1521 marked the definitive suppression of the conditions for independent collective action of both *pecheros* and *hidalgos*: the former saw the decline of their assemblies, and the latter were left with kinship and informal networks as means of organization, in a much more peaceful urban environment. Guilds would develop during the sixteenth century, but under full control of urban authorities, which were now unquestionably identified with their *pueblos*. At the moment of the conquest of America, what we would conceive of as classes were blurred in Habsburg Castile as urban collective actors, and, although caste mentality lingered, an overall Catholic identity successfully concealed social antagonisms. Only in villages, thanks to their role as autonomous institutions of self-government, could peasants reorganize and struggle for their *libertades*, breaking with their own urban lords, if paradoxically only to become themselves autonomous *villas* with their own *regimiento*—whose requirements for legitimacy they were therefore forced to satisfy.[35] An urban order, established since the fourteenth century, thus seems to have shaped these emerging rural conflicts in the long run as well.

---

[35] H. Nader, *Liberty in Absolutist Spain. The Habsburg Sale of Towns, 1516–1700* (Baltimore and London, 1990).

Peasant Politics and Class Consciousness: The Norfolk Rebellions of 1381 and 1549 Compared[1]

Jane Whittle

The county of Norfolk was heavily involved in England's two largest peasant rebellions, in 1381 and 1549. There is no question that each revolt commanded widespread popular support, and as is argued below, the rebels were drawn from a cross-section of the rural population. Whether or not these were peasant rebellions is partly a question of whether one regards the rural population of Norfolk as peasants, an issue discussed elsewhere.[2] However, they were also peasant rebellions in another sense. Other large popular revolts of this period, such as the Pilgrimage of Grace of 1536, or the Western Rebellion of 1549 involved alliances between gentlemen and the commons or ordinary rebels. They were provoked partly by discontent over religion, taxation and bad government, which united members of these two social classes.[3] By contrast, the rebellions in Norfolk in 1381 and 1549 were centrally concerned with the nature of the manorial system and terms of tenure, issues that split lords and tenants into two competing groups. Conceived in Marxist terms, as Rodney Hilton put it, these rebellions were manifestations of conflict between the two main classes in late medieval England, lords and peasants.[4]

To what degree are the two rebellions examples of peasant class consciousness, with peasants as a group uniting against lords as a group to defend and

---

[1] This chapter was researched and written during an ESRC funded research fellowship.

[2] J. Whittle, *The Development of Agrarian Capitalism: Land and Labour in Norfolk 1440–1580* (Oxford, 2000), 10–16 and 301–4.

[3] R. W Hoyle, *The Pilgrimage of Grace and the Politics of the 1530s* (Oxford, 2001); J. Youings, 'The South-western Rebellion of 1549', *Southern History*, 1 (1979), 99–122; although an argument can be made for strong anti-gentry feelings in both these rebellions, see A. Wood, *Riot, Rebellion and Popular Politics in Early Modern England* (Basingstoke, 2002), 53–4 and 57–60.

[4] R. H. Hilton, *Bond Men Made Free: Medieval Peasant Movements and the English Rising of 1381* (London, 1973), 130–4; ibid., *Class Conflict and the Crisis of Feudalism* (London, 1990), 145–7.

---

promote their own interests? Further, what do the two rebellions reveal about the nature of peasant politics? James Scott has argued that rebellions are moments when the 'hidden transcript' of oppressed people, in this case the peasantry, is made public. The ideas and capabilities held by such a group, which were always there but had no outlet, were suddenly aired openly.[5] In this sense, although rebellions are extraordinary occasions, the sentiments and capability for organization which they bring to our attention are not necessarily extraordinary. A comparison between two rebellions which occurred in the same location at different times offers an opportunity to observe the effect of changes in lord–tenant relations that had occurred in the intervening period. These changes were substantial, including the end of widespread serfdom, the abandonment of direct demesne farming, increases in tenant wealth, and a weakening of the manorial system.[6] The focus on a single county, Norfolk, provides clear limits within which these complex issues can be explored. Only certain aspects of the rebellions are discussed below: the organization of the revolts, the actions taken by the rebels, the formal demands made, and the numbers and types of rebels or participation in the revolt. Before beginning this discussion, however, it is helpful to compare the historiographies of the two rebellions.

The rebellion of 1381 is relatively well documented and has been extensively analysed. However, evidence and studies relating specifically to Norfolk are more sparse. Of the chronicles, only Walsingham describes events in Norfolk in any detail.[7] E. Powell's *The Rising in East Anglia in 1381*, with a chapter on Norfolk, was the first to supplement this basic account with the study of other types of document, while C. M. Hoare's *History of an East Anglian Soke* adds extra details.[8] Hilton undertook a useful analysis of the fragmentary 1381 poll tax returns of north-east Norfolk in *Bond Men Made Free*.[9] However, it is H. Eiden's recent article, together with an excellent pamphlet produced by Cambridge University extra-mural students, which make a detailed comparison of the events in Norfolk in 1381 with those of 1549

[5] J. C. Scott, *Domination and the Arts of Resistance: Hidden Transcripts* (New Haven, 1990).
[6] E. Miller (ed.), *The Agrarian History of England and Wales: Volume III 1348–1500* (Cambridge, 1991); B. M. S Campbell, *English Seigniorial Agriculture 1250–1450* (Cambridge, 2000); Whittle, *The Development of Agrarian Capitalism*.
[7] R. B. Dobson (ed.), *The Peasants' Revolt of 1381* (Basingstoke, 1983), 231–64.
[8] E. Powell, *The Rising in East Anglia in 1381* (Cambridge, 1896), 26–40; C. M. Hoare, *The History of an East Anglian Soke* (Bedford, 1918), 102–28.
[9] R. Hilton, *Bond Men Made Free*, 172–4.

possible.[10] Both draw on the evidence provided by indictments and manorial documents to construct detailed accounts of events in Norfolk.

The eastern rebellion of 1549 has also been relatively poorly served by historians. The authoritative account of the rebellion is provided by F. W. Russell who draws on the two near-contemporary chronicle accounts by Sotherton and Neville, as well as other local and national records.[11] S. T. Bindoff's brief pamphlet added some useful context, but subsequent books by S. K. Land, J. Cornwall and B. L. Beer have not greatly advanced our understanding of the events.[12] D. MacCulloch was the first historian in recent years to reassess the unprinted documentary evidence available on rebellion, with important results.[13] A. R. Greenwood's PhD thesis contains valuable new evidence on participation in the revolt which has never made it into print.[14] I have recently supplemented this research with a study of the surviving manorial court rolls from Norfolk dated 1548–51, to assess the social and geographical background of rebels killed in the final battle.[15] A detailed modern history of Kett's rebellion remains to be written. Kett's rebellion has often been viewed in comparative context with other Tudor rebellions, but never, in more than a cursory manner, with the great revolt of 1381. As well as comparing the events, as is attempted here, the approaches taken by historians of 1381 suggest a number of ways forward for those studying 1549. R. B. Dobson's collection of documents, Hilton's comparative analysis, the collection of thematic studies edited by Hilton and T. H. Aston,[16] and more

---

[10] H. Eiden, 'Joint Action against "bad" Lordship: The Peasants' Revolt in Essex and Norfolk', *History*, 83 (1998), 5–30, based on his PhD; B. Cornford (ed.), *The Rising of 1381 in Norfolk* (Norfolk Research Committee, Norwich, 1984).

[11] F. W. Russell, *Kett's Rebellion in Norfolk* (London, 1859).

[12] S. T. Bindoff, *Ket's Rebellion 1549* (Historical Association, London, 1949); S. K. Land, *Kett's Rebellion: The Norfolk Rising of 1549* (Ipswich, 1977); J. Cornwall, *Revolt of the Peasantry 1549* (London, 1977); B. L. Beer, *Rebellion and Riot* (Kent, Ohio, 1982). See comments in D. MacCulloch, 'Kett's Rebellion in Context', *Past and Present*, 84 (1979), 36–7; and Wood, *Riot, Rebellion and Popular Politics*, 203 n.35.

[13] MacCulloch, 'Kett's Rebellion'.

[14] A. R. Greenwood, 'A Study of the Rebel Petitions of 1549', unpublished PhD thesis, University of Manchester (1990).

[15] I studied all the Norfolk court rolls covering 1548–51 housed at the Norfolk Record Office (NRO), Cambridge University Library, the National Archive, and the British Library. The full results will be published as an article: 'Lords and Tenants in Kett's Rebellion', forthcoming.

[16] Dobson, *The Peasants' Revolt of 1381*; Hilton, *Bond Men Made Free*; R. H. Hilton and T. H. Aston (eds), *The English Rising of 1381* (Cambridge, 1984).

recently reassessments of the way certain types of documents can be interpreted by P. Strohm, S. Justice and A. Prescott, have as yet no equivalent for
1549.[17]

Organization

The organization of the two rebellions had much in common. In both 1381
and 1549 east and west Norfolk rose separately. The rebels in the west rose
first, partly under influence from Suffolk.[18] Rebellion in east Norfolk, centring on the county town and regional capital of Norwich, was later, stronger,
and more persistent. In eastern Norfolk in 1381, men were circulating around
the area north of Norwich on 14 June issuing proclamations in the name of
Geoffrey Litster. On 17 June rebels mustered outside Norwich on Mousehold
Heath and on the same day occupied Norwich.[19] Litster took control of the
castle, imprisoning a number of gentlemen there and was declared 'king of the
commons'. In the following days Litster seems to have operated an alternative
government, overseeing rebel actions and holding law sessions to settle disputes.[20] He, and other groups of rebels, remained mobile, taking actions and
holding court in various places, rather than staying in Norwich.[21] The rebellion was short lived, however, as Litster and a group of rebels were defeated
in battle in or near North Walsham by the bishop of Norwich on the 26 June,
although it took a few more days after that to quell the Norfolk rebellion
altogether.[22]

In 1549, the eastern Norfolk rebellion began in Wymondham in central
Norfolk, with Robert Kett assuming leadership there on 8 July.[23] This group
of rebels then marched to Norwich, arriving there by 10 July,[24] and setting up
camp on Mousehold Heath by 12 July. During this period, they were joined by
large numbers of men from other parts of Norfolk. Norwich was not taken

[17] P. Strohm, *Hochon's Arrow: The Social Imagination of Fourteenth-Century Texts*
(Princeton, 1992); S. Justice, *Writing and Rebellion: England in 1381* (Berkeley, 1994);
A. Prescott, 'Writing about Rebellion: Using the Records of the Peasants' Revolt of 1381',
History Workshop Journal, 45 (1998), 1–27.

[18] Eiden, 'Joint Action', 16–18; MacCulloch, 'Kett's Rebellion', 40.

[19] Powell, *Rising in East Anglia*, 27–30.

[20] Walsingham in Dobson, *Peasants Revolt*, 258; Eiden, 'Joint Action', 20.

[21] Powell, *Rising in East Anglia*, 35; Eiden, 'Joint Action', 20.

[22] Powell, *Rising in East Anglia*, 37–9; Hoare, *East Anglian Soke*, 114–9; Eiden, 'Joint
Action', 21.

[23] MacCulloch, 'Kett's Rebellion', 39; Russell, *Kett's Rebellion*, 27–9.

[24] MacCulloch implies they reached Norwich on 9 July, 'Kett's Rebellion', 39. Bindoff and
Cornwall prefer the 10 July: Bindoff, *Ket's Rebellion 1549*, 3; Cornwall, *Revolt of the
Peasantry*, 140.

straight away, although the mayor and a leading alderman were taken into the rebel camp and forced to cooperate.[25] As in 1381, Kett set up an alternative government, and the rebels seem to have abided by his rule of law. He issued warrants for rebel actions, held law courts and oversaw the imprisonment of gentlemen. Regular church services were held at the rebel camp.[26] A petition of demands was sent to the king, signed not only by Kett and the mayor of Norwich, but by chosen representatives from twenty-four of Norfolk's thirty-three hundreds.[27] The rebels twice rejected royal pardons which required them to disperse without their demands met. They took Norwich by force twice, defeated one royal army and were finally defeated themselves in a battle on 27 August, a battle during which Kett fled and hundreds of rebels were killed.[28] The rebellion had lasted for over seven weeks.

Both rebellions demonstrated a sophisticated level of organization. The raising of rebellion was coordinated, and mustering times and places were known in advance. For example, in 1381 three rebel bands moved around south and west Norfolk, taking selective actions, before meeting up in Rougham on the same day, while in 1549, the speed with which rebel camps were set up across East Anglia suggests some degree of prior planning.[29] Further details from 1549 demonstrate that some rebels at least were not desperate men drawn from the dregs of village society: North Elmham sent food and wages to their representatives at Mousehold Heath,[30] Heydon and Tunstead sent men carrying banners,[31] and from Blickling twenty-six

[25] Bindoff, *Ket's Rebellion*, 4.

[26] Beer, *Rebellion and Riot*, 93–5. These details, including a transcript of one of Kett's warrants, appear in A. Neville, *Norfolk's Furies, or a View of Kett's Camp . . .* , translated by R. Woods (London, 1615): copy from Bodleian Library, accessed via Early English Books Online, sig.C2r-C2v, C3v-C4r, D4r-D4v.

[27] The petition is printed in A. Fletcher and D. MacCulloch, *Tudor Rebellions* (Harlow, 1997), 144–6. For more details see Russell, *Kett's Rebellion*, 203–4 and Greenwood, 'Rebel Petitions', 214. The hundreds not represented were Smithdon, Freebridge Marshland, Clackclose, Grimshoe, Wayland, Shropham, Guiltcross, Diss, and Earsham, all in the south and west of Norfolk: see the map of Norfolk hundreds in P. Wade-Martins (ed.), *An Historical Atlas of Norfolk* (Norwich, 1994), 89.

[28] Bindoff, *Ket's rebellion*, 5–6; Fletcher and MacCulloch, *Tudor Rebellions*, 67–71.

[29] A. W. Reid, 'The Rising of 1381 in South West and Central Norfolk', in Cornford, *Rising in 1381 in Norfolk*, 10–33; Eiden, 'Joint Action', 18; MacCulloch, 'Kett's Rebellion', 39.

[30] Recorded in the church wardens' account, copied in Russell, *Kett's Rebellion*, 181–4.

[31] Heydon's banner was taken from the church, and had to be replaced afterwards: court with leet held the Tuesday after St Clements, November 1549, manor of Stintonhall in Salle recorded in a multi-manor court book: NRO, Towns 159 MS 1578 1D4. For Tunstead, Greenwood, 'Rebel Petitions', 305–6.

men, a large proportion of the tenants, including the majority of the manorial jury, went to the Mousehold camp.[32] In both 1381 and 1549, the rebels set up an alternative system of government, to retain order within the rebellion and also to administer what they saw as good government, offering a critique of the normal system. And on both occasions, the rebels were defeated only by military force, although there were more men under arms, and with more overt military organization, in 1549 than in 1381.

Actions

Despite these similarities however, the rebels took quite different actions in the two revolts. In 1381 the rebels' actions were direct. They burned court rolls in at least fifty-six places, and the houses of JPs, MPs, tax collectors, and John of Gaunt duke of Lancaster were systematically attacked.[33] Money was extorted from townsmen in Thetford, Norwich, and Yarmouth, as well as from various gentry households. Violence against people was limited. There were two high-profile killings: Sir Robert de Salle was killed while apparently trying to negotiate with the rebels, and Reginald de Eccles, a JP, was killed and beheaded at Heigham. It is notable that other men of similar status, such as William Clere, a JP and former sheriff, were captured and intimidated but not killed. Three Flemish men were killed in Yarmouth and at least one in Lynn, echoing the killing of Flemings in London.[34] Less dramatic, but no less significant, was the withholding of labour services, documented on the Abbey of St Benet-at-Holme's manor of Ashby and Thurne in east Norfolk.[35]

The 1549 rebellion followed a different course. In the initial stages of the revolt enclosures were thrown down near Wymondham and along the route to Norwich.[36] These actions appear almost symbolic, a way of signalling legitimacy to a government the rebels knew to have adopted a policy hostile to enclosure. Having set up camp at Mousehold, Kett issued warrants which authorized the imprisonment of gentry, the destruction of enclosures and the acquisition of food and weapons for the camp.[37] There is little evidence

---

[32] Their lord made them swear fealty anew after the revolt, resulting in a record of participation for this manor: court with leet held on Monday the day after Michaelmas 1549, Blickling court roll 1546–53: NRO, NRS 11265 26A5.

[33] Eiden, 'Joint Action', 22; Reid, 'Rising of 1381', 24.

[34] Eiden, 'Joint Action', 18–22; Hoare, *East Anglian Soke*, 110–13; Powell, *Rising in East Anglia*, 29–36. On Clere see B. Cornford, 'Events of 1381 in Flegg', in Cornford ed., *Rising of 1381 in Norfolk*, 41.

[35] Cornford, 'Events of 1381 in Flegg', 42–5.

[36] Russell, *Kett's Rebellion*, 27–31; Bindoff, *Ket's Rebellion*, 3–4.

[37] See note 26 above.

that bands of rebels went out to destroy enclosures, but they did capture and imprison gentlemen. The names of at least twenty-four gentlemen who were imprisoned can be traced. Some were certainly killed in the course of the rebellion, but it remains unclear when this took place, and it may have occurred during one of the battles.[38] There was no destruction of manorial documents, and little theft of property other than weapons and foodstuffs. It was reputed that the rebels took 20,000 sheep and 3000 cattle for their own consumption, as well as deer and poultry.[39] The orgy of men eating sheep was surely symbolic, as well as a practical means of provisioning the assembled rebels.[40] If it were not for the willingness to enter into battle, Kett's rebellion would have the profile of a mass sit-down demonstration on Mousehold Heath.

Demands

The actions taken reflect the rebels' demands and strength of feeling, but also their perception of the government's willingness to undertake reform. The 1381 rebels must have known they had little hope in asserting that their actions were legal, and all we know of their attempts at negotiation is Walsingham's account of representatives being sent to London to request freedom from serfdom and a pardon from the King: 'the commons began to grow weary. They took counsel and decided to send two of the knights, lords William de Morlee and John de Brewes, together with three members of the commons who they trusted, to the king, . . . to secure from him a charter of manumission and pardon'.[41] In 1549 the rebellion initially took a course of action that might have been understood as reasonable protest: the throwing down of a few chosen enclosures and petitioning the king. The petition which survives has twenty-nine articles, beginning with the request that 'henceforth no man shall enclose any more'.[42] Some demands are quite obscure and seem to relate to specific local disputes, but others are wideranging. Their authors wished to exclude manorial lords from farming livestock commercially, and from using and regulating common grazing land,[43] they wanted rents and copyhold fines to be set at the same levels as 1485,[44]

---

[38] Greenwood, 'Rebel Petitions', 307 and 341.

[39] Beer, *Rebellion and Riot*, 94. The figures are taken from Neville, *Norfolk's Furies*, sig.D3r.

[40] I owe this point to Andy Wood.

[41] Walsingham in Dobson, *Peasants Revolt*, 258.

[42] The impact of this demand is reduced and somewhat confused by a preceding clause asking for 'enclosed saffron grounds' to be excluded from this measure.

[43] Demands 3, 11, 13 and 29, as listed in Fletcher and MacCulloch, *Tudor Rebellions*, 144–6.

[44] Demands 5, 6, and 14, Fletcher and MacCulloch, *Tudor Rebellions*, 145.

and, in an echo of 1381, demanded that 'all bond men may be made free'.[45] They did not want an end to the manorial system, but they did seek to reduce lords' income and power. The mystery of Kett's rebellion is the contrast between its mild beginnings and relatively arcane demands, and the rebels' willingness to enter into military action and refusal to accept royal pardons and disperse. Possibly this reflects a difference in motivation between the leaders of the revolt, such as Kett, and the rank and file of the rebels.

Participation

Eiden has traced 1,214 people from Norfolk who were indicted in connection with the 1381 rebellion, or named as being involved.[46] In contrast, only 230 named rebels of 1549 have been traced.[47] Does this mean that Kett's rebellion was actually a much smaller uprising? There are no estimates of the total number of rebels in Norfolk in 1381, while estimates for the maximum number of rebels camped on Mousehold Heath in 1549 vary from a probably imaginary 20,000 to a more realistic 6,000.[48] Estimates of the number of rebels killed in the last battle of Kett's revolt also vary from 3,500 to 2,000.[49] My own attempts to trace the people who died from evidence in manorial court rolls has only identified sixty-two rebels who were killed 'at Mousehold Heath', presumably in the last battle.[50] A further six, including Robert Kett and his brother William, were hanged or outlawed soon after the rebellion.[51] Of the 128 manors with surviving court rolls for the relevant period, 28 per cent record tenants involved in the rebellion. Thus, over a quarter of manors with surviving court rolls record one or more tenants dying as a result of the rebellion. Given that not all rebels would have held land, an estimate of 1000 rebels dying in the final battle is probably realistic. So despite disparities in documentation, the two rebellions may have involved a similar proportion of the population, but the direct actions of smaller bands of 1381 rebels have left

[45] Demand 16, Fletcher and MacCulloch, *Tudor Rebellions*, 145.
[46] Eiden, 'Joint Action', 10 n.26.
[47] Greenwood traced 89 Norfolk rebels from various sources, 'Rebel Petitions', Appendix E, 378–82. Others are added from my own research.
[48] Greenwood, 'Rebel Petitions', 319. The figure of 20,000 is found in Robert Kett's indictment, printed in Russell, *Kett's Rebellion*, 221.
[49] Cornwall, *Revolt of the Peasantry 1549*, 222; Fletcher and MacCulloch, *Tudor Rebellions*, 71; Beer, *Rebellion and Riot*, 136.
[50] The date of 27 August 1549 is often also specified.
[51] The other men were John Wythe of Aylsham, Henry Bee of Burnham Overy, William Howard of Earsham, and Richard Johnson of Wymondham.

a more detailed record of involvement than the mass demonstration and battles of 1549.

Analysis of the social background of rebels from both rebellions suggests that the composition of the rebel forces reflected the social structure of the Norfolk countryside below the level of the gentry. Large numbers of craftsmen took part: of the 121 rebels identified by Greenwood from 1549, 35 per cent were craftsmen or specialists.[52] This compares to a proportion of 25.5 per cent in Norfolk's rural population in the period 1532–43, indicated by quarter sessions indictments.[53] Eiden identifies numerous craftsmen-rebels in Norfolk in 1381, while the high proportion of craftsmen in late fourteenth-century rural Norfolk is confirmed by the poll tax returns.[54] In both periods many of these men also held land. The rebels included tenants holding free and unfree land in 1381, and a variety of tenures in 1549.[55] Interestingly, however, while a number of Norfolk manors in which rebels held land in 1549 continued to enforce personal serfdom, none of the rebels identified were bondmen of blood.[56]

The 1549 rebels included smallholders, husbandmen, and larger farmers. Minimum landholding size could be established for forty-six rebels: nineteen were smallholders with 5 acres or less, nine held between 6 and 13 acres, twelve had holdings of 14 to 32 acres, while six had between 32 and 45 acres making them members of the village elite, by Norfolk standards.[57] This distribution of land is not out of line with that found more generally in mid-sixteenth-century Norfolk, again suggesting that the rebels came from a cross-section of the ordinary population, rather than predominantly from poor or wealthy sections of village society.[58] The 1549 rebels included men

---

[52] Greenwood, 'Rebel Petitions', 320 (including Suffolk rebels).

[53] Whittle, *Agrarian Capitalism*, 236.

[54] Eiden, 'Joint Action', 28; Hilton, *Bond Men Made Free*, 172–3.

[55] Eiden, 'Joint Action', 28. For 1549 the court rolls are only reliable in recording customary tenures, however a number did also mention that known rebels held free or leasehold land.

[56] These manors include Gimingham, Horningsthorpe and East Tuddenham, Sloley with Westwick, Little Framingham, and Forncett.

[57] It was relatively common in Norfolk to hold land from more than one manor. Where court rolls survive, this has been identified and taken into account in these figures, but obviously many court rolls do not survive. This, together with the poor recording of freehold and leasehold, makes these figures minimums.

[58] The land held by Norfolk rebels in 1381 awaits research. However, Dyer's study of land-holding rebels from Essex, Hertfordshire, and Suffolk suggests similar conclusions: C. Dyer, 'The Social and Economic Background to the Rural Revolt of 1381', in Hilton and Aston (eds), *English Rising of 1381*, 15.

such as John West who held 3½ acres of customary land from the Paston's manor of East Beckham, and left a widow and two year old son. John Heyward held just under 19 acres from the Townshend's manor of Stibbard. His nearest heir, William, was reputed to have died at Boulogne, presumably in the king's army, and thus the land passed to another adult son, with a third going to the widow as dower. John Purdy of Southrepps who held almost 42 acres from Gimingham manor left as coheirs his sons Thomas aged eight and Nicholas aged six. West, Heywood and Purdy all died 'at Mousehold Heath'.[59]

A handful of gentry joined the rebels in 1381: two knights and two manorial lords.[60] There were no knights among the rebels of 1549, but there were a few minor manorial lords, most notably Kett himself who owned more than one small manor in Wymondham. A shadier figure is John Wythe of Aylsham, who was specifically excluded from the parliamentary pardon of 1550, and was captured and hanged in 1551 for his part in the rebellion.[61] He held land in Aylsham, Blickling and Hevingham, and was probably the lessee of the small manor of Bolwick Hall, just outside Aylsham.[62]

Eiden notes that while events connected with the rebellion of 1381 occurred all over Norfolk, the burning of court rolls was heavily concentrated in north-east Norfolk.[63] The strong involvement of north-east Norfolk is again evident in 1549: 43 per cent of manors whose documents were examined from that region recorded events connected to the rebellion, compared to 37 per cent from south-east Norfolk, 19 per cent from north-west and only

---

[59] East Beckham Pastons court roll, NRO, WKC2/63; Stibbard is in a multimanor court book, NRO, TOWNS 159 MS 1578 1D4, William Heyward was the nearest heir but died '*apud Bulleyn ut supponit*'; Gimingham court roll, NRO, MS 5859 15C1.

[60] Eiden, 'Joint Action', 26.

[61] Beer, *Rebellion and Riot*, 204–5.

[62] Beer notes that Wythe was a prosperous copyholder in Aylsham, ibid., 205. He also held 10.5 acres in Blickling: Blickling court roll 1546–53, NRO, NRS 11265 26A5; and two acres from Hevingham, Hevingham miscellaneous roll, court held Michaelmas 1552, NRO, NRO 14487 29C1. He was the son and heir of Edmund Wythe, who was the lessee of Bolwick manor, and was accused in Hevingham court rolls of illegally enclosing land on Hevingham common where it bordered with Bolwick, in 1513. This dispute resulted in a small riot, as a result of which John Wythe appeared in Hevingham court rolls for the first time as one of the participants: see particularly Hevingham court roll 1509–47, courts held October 1513 and March 1514, NRO, NRS 13685 28D3. He occasionally dabbled in the Hevingham land market thereafter. No records survive for Bolwick manor for this period.

[63] Eiden, 'Joint Action', 17 and 22.

6 per cent from south-west Norfolk.[64] In both periods eastern Norfolk was more densely populated, while north-east Norfolk was the centre of the rural worsted weaving industry: villages and small towns involved in weaving were well represented in both revolts, although other communities were also involved.[65] Some villages such as Tunstead and Blickling were involved in both rebellions.[66]

Conclusion

Given the many similarities between the two revolts, it is perhaps surprising that no solid evidence that a popular memory of 1381 survived to 1549 has yet been found. It is possible that the demand in the rebel petition of 1549 that 'all bond men may be made free' was a deliberate reference to unfinished business from 1381, although Bindoff suggested the demand was borrowed from the German Peasants' War of 1525.[67] Personal serfdom did still exist in Norfolk in 1549, not only on the manors formerly held by the Duke of Norfolk as noted by MacCulloch, but elsewhere.[68] Certainly, servile status was less onerous, and much less widespread, than in 1381, but the peculiarity of its survival may have allowed this to become a genuine sixteenth-century grievance.

The actions and demands of the rebels demonstrate two significant changes in lord–tenant relationships and the manorial system, between 1381 and 1549. Tenants' attitudes to the manorial system, expressed by their treatment of manorial court rolls, had been transformed. Court rolls were burnt in 1381, yet by 1549 they were regarded as the records of valuable privileges. On both occasions tenants were trying to improve their terms of tenure, and on both occasions they accepted the importance of court rolls as a record of manorial custom and practice. In 1381 those customs included unfree personal status for some tenants, as well as rents and fines regarded as onerous and tiresome. During the fifteenth century, when land was relatively easily available and tenant mobility high, serfdom largely disappeared and rents and fines were lowered. Tenants in 1381 believed, sensibly, that it would be beneficial to destroy the written record and start afresh with more reasonable terms of

---

[64] Evidence from 128 series of court rolls and one rental: 40 from NE, 30 from SE, 42 from NW, and 17 from SW Norfolk.

[65] Whittle, *Agrarian Capitalism.*

[66] Eiden, 'Joint Action', 22–3; and notes 31 and 32 above.

[67] Bindoff, *Ket's Rebellion*, 12–13. A similar clause appears in the third article of 'The twelve articles' of the peasants of Swabia, see T. Scott and R. Scribner, *The German Peasants' War: A History in Documents* (Atlantic Highlands, N.J., 1991), 254.

[68] Fletcher and MacCulloch, *Tudor Rebellions*, 77–8. On the survival of serfdom see Whittle, *Agrarian Capitalism*, 37–46.

tenure. Those of 1549 could look back to a golden age, which they set, also quite sensibly, at 1485, when tenurial obligations had been lower. They knew that this golden age was recorded in the court rolls. However, this did not stop the 1549 rebels from objecting to long-lived aspects of the manorial system which they disliked, such as the remnants of personal serfdom or manorial lords' right to share the use of common land.

The second change involved lords' own farming activities and the use of resources in the agricultural economy. Norfolk's manorial lords may have abandoned arable farming on demesne land in the late fourteenth and early fifteenth century,[69] but they were still involved in livestock farming.[70] In particular, a number of Norfolk lords were engaged in large-scale sheep farming, exploiting foldcourse (sheep grazing) rights over commons and tenants' land: an enterprise that had expanded considerably in the century before the revolt.[71] This, combined with increased stocking densities on peasant farms, made the pressure on common grazing land a major issue in 1549.[72] In 1381 the issue had been the supply of labour, not land. Both the rebels' demands for the abolition of serfdom, implying a dislike of labour services and their hatred of the justices who enforced the Statute of Labourers, suggest that lords' demands for labour in demesne agriculture were causing serious tensions.[73] After the rebellion, attempts to maintain pre-plague wage levels and enforce labour services were largely abandoned, and lords switched to livestock farming as a less labour-intensive alternative. Peasant tenants seem also to have increased their emphasis on animal husbandry for similar reasons: high wages, low corn prices and relatively cheap land. Whereas

[69] Campbell, *English Seigniorial Agriculture*, 32.
[70] C. E. Moreton, *The Townshends and their World: Gentry, Law and Land in Norfolk c.1450–1551* (Oxford, 1992), 162–90; C. Oestmann, *Lordship and Community: The Lestrange Family and the Village of Hunstanton, Norfolk, in the First Half of the Sixteenth Century* (Woodbridge, 1994), 134–48; B. M. S. Campbell and M. Overton, 'A New Perspective on Medieval and Early Modern Agriculture: Six Centuries of Norfolk Farming c.1250–c.1850', *Past and Present*, 141 (1993), 78.
[71] K. J. Allison, 'The Sheep-Corn Husbandry of Norfolk in the Sixteenth and Seventeenth Centuries', *Agricultural History Review*, 5 (1957), 12–30; M. Bailey, 'Sand into Gold: The Evolution of the Foldcourse System in West Suffolk, 1200–1600', *Agricultural History Review*, 38 (1990), 40–57.
[72] Campbell and Overton, 'A New Perspective', 76–85. M. Overton and B. M. S. Campbell, 'Norfolk Livestock Farming 1250–1740: A Comparative Study of Manorial Accounts and Probate Inventories', *Journal of Historical Geography*, 18 (1992), 377–96.
[73] In Norfolk rebels destroyed or assaulted the houses of JPs at Hilgay, West Lexham, and Palgrave, and beheaded one JP in Norwich: Eiden, 'Joint Action', 18 and 20. For background on the Statute of Labourers see Hilton, *Bond Men Made Free*, 151–6.

population decline from 1348 onwards upset the equilibrium in the later fourteenth century by making labour expensive, population increase in the first half of the sixteenth century increased tensions over land use and access to land. The tensions expressed in each rebellion over terms of tenure, the manorial system and the use of land and labour in the rural economy do suggest lords and peasants saw themselves as opposing groups, with clearly defined and contradictory interests. For the period of rebellion the commons, as the peasantry described themselves, and as commentators such as Walsingham described them, were not only a class in themselves sharing economic circumstances, but a class for themselves, campaigning for their interests as a group. In both rebellions the triggers to revolt, the Poll Tax in 1381 and the anti-enclosure measures in 1549, are only partial explanations of rebel actions and demands. They led to revolts that raised a wider range of issues, revealing a 'hidden transcript' of deeper discontents with the structure of rural society and economy.

Whether the rebels felt class hatred towards the gentry and aristocracy as a group on either occasion remains unproven. Rebel attitudes in Norfolk in 1381 have to be traced from their actions, which although occasionally violent, were selective. There is no clear evidence for undifferentiated hatred of the gentry in Norfolk or elsewhere during the rebellion. Chronicle accounts claimed that rebels in Kent agreed that they 'would not give way until all the nobles and magnates of the realm had been completely destroyed',[74] while those of Essex wanted 'to kill all the lawyers, jurors and royal servants they could find'.[75] Yet a list of fifteen noblemen whom they wanted beheaded, handed to the king by the Kent rebels, suggests a rather more specific agenda,[76] while a hatred of lawyers and tax-collectors does not constitute a hatred of lords as a class. The rebels who met the king at Mile End might have demanded an end to serfdom, but, by asserting that rents should be fixed at 4d. an acre, they implicitly accepted the existence of lordship.[77] Hilton argued that these demands were 'genuinely revolutionary', and certainly they would have caused massive social upheaval if they were enforced immediately in 1381 as a consequence of the rebellion.[78] Instead these aims were achieved gradually during the fifteenth century with the widespread disappearance of serfdom and a lightening of rental payments: these changes were an

[74] Knighton in Dobson, *Peasants' Revolt*, 136; Froissart makes a similar statement, ibid, 141.

[75] *Anonimalle Chronicle*, in Dobson, *Peasants' Revolt*, 125, and repeated by the rebels in London, 160. Walsingham records a similar assertion, ibid, 133.

[76] *Anonimalle Chronicle*, in Dobson, *Peasants' Revolt*, 130.

[77] *Anonimalle Chronicle*, in Dobson, *Peasants' Revolt*, 161.

[78] Hilton, *Bond Men Made Free*, 223–4.

important social transformation, but the agrarian problems of the sixteenth century demonstrate the consequences of leaving the manorial system intact, even with improved terms of tenure. Yet, again in 1549, Kett's petition sought to redefine certain aspects of lords' rights without challenging lordship as an institution. In 1549 a number of gentlemen were captured and imprisoned by the rebels, with little indication of the selection of individuals for particular reasons. The indictment of Robert Kett claims that he shouted out, 'kill the gentlemen'.[79] A. Wood has argued from this, that 'kill the gentlemen' was the rallying cry of the rebellion.[80] Further florid descriptions of anti-gentry feeling can be found in A. Neville's description of the revolt. Yet the wording of the indictment suggests that Kett was referring only to those gentlemen that had been imprisoned on Mousehold Heath by the rebels, and in Neville's account, after the mock trial of the imprisoned gentlemen by Kett at the 'oak of reformation', it was 'the ignorant and rude multitude' who cried 'let them be hanged, let them be hanged'.[81] Oddly, there is no description of these gentlemen being killed, unlike the accounts of beheading from 1381. Some did die during the rebellion, as noted above, but how and when is unclear.

In both 1381 and 1549 the rebels proved their ability to organize and regulate their activities, and set up alternative governments, for a short time at least. By enforcing discipline and order and even mock trials, the rebels offered a critique of lords and lawyers by demonstrating that they were superfluous. By directing their anger against certain targets the rebels also demonstrated that they had a specific agenda; but whose agenda was this? Although the peasantry, the ordinary population of the countryside, united in rebellion and raised grievances which put them in direct opposition to the lordly class, it seems unlikely that they all became rebels for the same reasons. We can speculate that in both 1381 and 1549 there were at least two strands of discontent amongst the rebels, although this is easier to trace in 1549. The discontent of the peasant elite, minor manorial lords and wealthy tenants, lay in their thwarted ambitions—their direct competition with the gentry in both economic and political spheres. They led the revolt, organized the actions and framed the petitions. Yet the majority of rebels were relatively poor men, like the majority of the rural population. As they had little land or wealth, it is unlikely that they were concerned with the majority of the grievances listed in Kett's petition. They leave no specific record of their aims and discontents other than their willingness to rise in large numbers and to die in battle rather than end the rebellion in compromise. What motivated their determination

---

[79] Robert Kett's indictment in Russell, *Kett's Rebellion*, 222.

[80] Wood, *Riot, Rebellion*, 32 and 70.

[81] Neville, *Norfolk's Furies*, sig.D4r.

to die for a cause, or indeed what exactly that cause was, remains hidden behind the views of the peasant elite. The rebellion of 1549 was England's last great peasant uprising. After that date, the gulf between the village elite of wealthy farmers on the one hand, and smallholders and hired workers on the other, widened to such an extent that they no longer shared significant interests. They had ceased to belong to the same economic or political class.[82]

---

[82] Whittle, *Agrarian Capitalism*, 313.

Rodney Hilton, Marxism and the Transition from Feudalism to Capitalism*

S.R. Epstein

A founding member of the Historians' Group of the Communist Party, of the journal *Past and Present*, and a major force in a distinctive and distinguished School of History at the University of Birmingham, Rodney Hilton was among the most notable medieval historians of the latter half of the twentieth century. He was also the most influential of a small number of Marxist medievalists in Britain and Continental Europe who practised their craft before the renaissance of Marxist and left-wing history after 1968. Surprisingly, therefore, his work's historiographical and theoretical significance has not attracted much attention.[1]

Although Hilton was, first and foremost, a 'historian's historian', and made his most lasting contributions to the fields of English social, agrarian, and urban history, his engagement with Marxist historical debates cannot be lightly dismissed.[2] Hilton's Marxism, a central feature of his self-understanding as a historian, reflects both strengths and weaknesses of British Marxist historiography in its heyday, and his interpretation of a *locus classicus* of Marxist debate, the transition from feudal to capitalist modes of production, still carries considerable weight among like-minded historians.

---

* This chapter has benefited from Chris Dyer's and Chris Wickham's comments. All remaining errors of commission and omission are my responsibility alone.

[1] H. J. Kaye, *The British Marxist Historians. An Introductory Analysis* (Basingstoke, 1995), ch.3, entitled 'Rodney Hilton on Feudalism and the English Peasantry', is the shortest biographical chapter in the book (the others discuss Maurice Dobb, Christopher Hill, Eric Hobsbawm, and E. P. Thompson). See also T. J. Byres, 'Rodney Hilton (1916–2002): in memoriam', *Journal of Agrarian Change*, 6 (2006), 1–16.

[2] See E. Hobsbawm, 'The Historians' Group of the Communist Party', in M. Cornforth (ed.) *Rebels and their Causes. Essays in Honour of A. L. Morton* (London, 1978), 21–47, at 21: 'For reasons that are even now difficult to understand, the bulk of British Marxist theoretical effort was directed into historical work'. Kaye, *British Marxist Historians*, explores the charge of atheoreticism further.

This brief essay proposes to identify the salient features of Hilton's contribution to the 'transition debate'; examine his move in the early 1970s to address certain problems he identified with that debate, and his renewed concern with the question of the 'prime mover'; suggest reasons why this theoretical move was only partly successful; and, by way of conclusion, set out briefly some lines of future empirical and theoretical engagement.

Dobb's model of feudalism

The crucial theoretical influence on Hilton and most other British Communist historians formed during the 1940s and 1950s came from Maurice Dobb's *Studies in the Development of Capitalism*, first published in 1946, which proposed a model of the feudal mode of production that became the theoretical benchmark for all subsequent debates over the transition from feudalism to capitalism. Dobb followed Marx's *Capital* in explaining England's 'truly revolutionary path' to capitalism through class struggle—the 'prime mover'—and class differentiation in terms of property rights to land, and defined the historical and theoretical problems with which Hilton grappled throughout his life as a historian.[3]

Marx's theory of history rests on three pillars: a theory of class determination and class struggle; a theory of technological development; and a theory of the state, which—since the state requires a surplus to operate effectively—must include a political economy of markets.[4] However, for complex political and historiographical reasons that cannot be explored here, Dobb based his model on class struggle alone. This gave rise to two serious weaknesses in his and his followers' approach to the transition from feudalism to capitalism.

First, Dobb's model was devised in essence to explain the transition *to* capitalism, that is, to explain why the feudal mode of production was destined *to fail* in a 'general crisis' vaguely dated between the fourteenth and the seventeenth century.[5] Dobb argued that this failure was caused by systemic

---

[3] M. H. Dobb, *Studies in the Development of Capitalism* (London, 1946). For Dobb's influence on the entire Historians' Group of the Communist Party, see Hobsbawm, 'The Historians' Group', 23. R. Brenner, 'Dobb on the Transition from Feudalism to Capitalism', *Cambridge Journal of Economics*, 2 (1978), 121–40 summarizes Dobb's views in *Studies*.

[4] Chris Wickham has suggested that Marxism's fourth pillar is a 'theory of the nature of property'. But although property rights have a central explanatory function in Marx's theory of history, I'm not convinced that Marxism has yet produced a successful *theory* of how property rights emerge and get transformed. I agree however that such a 'fourth pillar' needs to be established in order to complete the Marxian intellectual project.

[5] Dobb's ambiguity regarding the chronology of the 'crisis' triggered Paul Sweezy's initial criticisms, and the subsequent debate; see below, n. 6.

disincentives to capital accumulation and innovation, including peasant over-exploitation; but he did not have a convincing explanation for why the feudal mode of production had been capable of *expanding*, territorially, economically and technologically, for more than half a millennium before the crisis. The absence of a positive theory of development—which is a central feature of the Marxist theory of history and which must, ultimately, be mediated by some kind of scarcity-based transactions—probably also expressed the 'anti-market bias' that coloured Dobb's views of socialist planned economies when he wrote the *Studies* in the 1930s and 1940s. At that time, as he later recalled, he underestimated 'the role of prices and economic incentives' in socialist economies, and his view of the feudal economy was clearly analogous.[6] That bias, and the subordination of positive incentives and markets in Dobb's scheme, were reinforced by his subsequent debate with the American Marxist economist Paul Sweezy, a debate that canonized the misleading theoretical alternative among Marxists between long-distance trade as an exogenous, independent cause of change, or 'prime mover', and petty commodity production as an endogenous source of historical evolution.[7]

The second weakness of Dobb's model was its overwhelming focus on English history. There were good reasons for this, including the paradigmatic nature of England in Marx's narrative of the transition to capitalism and the state of historical research at the time Dobb wrote. But the restriction of the transition debate to English history helped to mask the difficulties that a strictly class-based analysis faced regarding the Marxian problematic of *uneven development*. Two critical questions were never posed. First, why did the transition to capitalism occur originally in western Europe, even though parts of Asia were previously economically more advanced? And,

---

[6] M. Dobb, 'Random Biographical Notes', *Cambridge Journal of Economics*, 2 (1978), 115–20, at 120. Curiously, Karl Polanyi identified Dobb's 'extension of the scope of market laws into nonmarket economies' in *Studies* as 'drifting away from [Marxism's] fundamental insight into the historically limited nature of market organisation' and giving 'aid and comfort . . . to the enemy' (e.g. the Austrian economists Ludwig von Mises and Friedrich von Hayek). See K. Polanyi, 'Review of M. H. Dobb, *Studies in the Development of Capitalism*, New York 1947', *Journal of Economic History*, 8 (1948), 206–7. Polanyi's misidentification of the presence of price mechanisms based on scarcity with the prevalence of capitalist market institutions has plagued much neo-Marxist historiography to this day; see below, n. 41.

[7] The original debate, which appeared in the pages of *Science and Society*, was reprinted as P. M. Sweezy et al., *The Transition from Feudalism to Capitalism. A Symposium* (London, 1954). A much expanded collection of essays was published as R. H. Hilton (ed.), *The Transition from Feudalism to Capitalism* (London, 1976), with an 'Introduction' by Hilton.

second, why was the English economy between 1400 and 1700 able first to catch up with, and then to forge ahead of, previously more advanced Continental European regions? Paradoxically, Dobb's *Studies* offered a convincing demonstration that a purely class-based analysis could *not* supply a satisfactory explanation for why the European feudal mode of production was superior to its rivals, and why, despite this, it did not develop at the same rate and in the same direction. To answer comparative historical questions of this kind, it would be necessary to introduce the two pillars of Marxian analysis that were missing from Dobb's (and later Hilton's) account: a theory of technological development and a political economy of states and markets.

Class struggle and other 'prime movers'

Class struggle and self-determination through struggle were central to Hilton's Marxism, as reflected in at least two books and in the title to his collected essays.[8] His documentation of rural struggle and resistance against landlord exploitation was crucial in establishing feudalism not as a stable and static social order, but as one of contradiction, conflict and movement, and is still outstandingly important. There were two purposes in Hilton's wish to document class conflict so thoroughly. On the one hand, Hilton expressed the long-standing concern among British left-wing and non-conformist historians with the self-knowledge and self-determination of the workers, the poor and the dispossessed—with history from the bottom up.[9] This tradition of labour history and communist populism was strongly upheld by Dona Torr, an abiding influence on the Communist Historians' Group, who helped direct the members' intellectual concerns towards 'the long history of popular democracy in England, and particularly the importance of the period in which small commodity producers were losing control of the means of production'.[10] On the other hand, Hilton followed Dobb's contention that the transition from feudalism to capitalism in Britain was the outcome of the persistent struggle over rents (economic surplus) between landlords and peasants. Struggle over rent caused the self-sufficient peasantry to be ejected from the land during the later middle ages, and gave rise to growing social

---

[8] See R. H. Hilton and H. Fagan, *The English Rising of 1381* (London, 1950); Hilton, *Bond Men Made Free. Medieval Peasant Movements and the English Rising of 1381* (London, 1973); Hilton, *Class Conflict and the Crisis of Feudalism. Essays in Medieval Social History*, rev. 2nd ed. (London, 1990).

[9] See Kaye, *British Marxist Historians*, 5 and passim.

[10] See R. Johnson, 'Culture and the Historians', in J. Clarke, C. Critcher, and R. Johnson (eds), *Working-Class Culture. Studies in History and Theory* (London, 1979), 41–73, esp. 54–6.

differentiation by benefiting a section of wealthy peasants (the future rural yeomanry) which increasingly produced for the market and specialized in saleable commodities. The change generated large numbers of dependent wage earners who had to buy most of their living requirements through the market. Ultimately, class struggle gave rise to agrarian capitalism and competitive, capitalist markets of sellers and buyers: class struggle 'explained' the transition to industrial capitalism.[11]

As with Dobb, Hilton's interest in the development of the material forces of production—that is, in technological progress—was by contrast negligible. The association of technological determinism with the, then prevailing, rigid versions of Stalinist 'scientific history' would have given technological explanations a bad press from early on in his life as a committed historian.[12] 'Bourgeois' believers were if anything even less sophisticated. As the opening sentence of a famous book review suggested, 'technical determinism in historical studies has often been combined with adventurous speculations particularly attractive to those who like to have complex developments explained with simple causes'.[13]

Some twenty years later, introducing the sequel set off by Robert Brenner in 1976 to the original 'transition debate', and having noted in answer to the question, 'What caused movement in history?' that 'Marx himself, as well as many working in his intellectual domain, emphasize[d] that developments in the *forces* of production—new technology, new means by which labour is organized, the economic success of new social classes—come into conflict with the existing *relations* of production', he again dismissed this as merely a possibility, 'somewhat crudely, to give primacy to technological development'.[14]

[11] See e.g. R. H. Hilton, 'A Comment', in Hilton (ed.), *The Transition*; orig. publ. in *Science and Society*, Fall 1953. Also R. H. Hilton, 'Feudalism in Europe', *New Left Review*, 147 (1984), 84–93.

[12] *Past and Present* first appeared in 1953 with the byline 'A journal of scientific history'. This was changed a year later to the less politically charged 'A journal of historical studies', a description it still carries.

[13] 'Technical Determinism: The Stirrup and the Plough', *Past and Present*, 24 (1963), 90–100, at 90, reviewing L. White, Jr., *Medieval Technology and Social Change* (Oxford, 1962). The opening paragraph was initialled R.H.H. and P.H.S. (P. H. Sawyer), but Hilton alone signed the rest of the text. The repeated charge of 'adventurism' has strong Marxist-Leninist connotations.

[14] R. H. Hilton, 'Introduction', in T. H. Aston and C. H. E. Philpin (eds), *The Brenner Debate. Agrarian Class Structure and Economic Development in Pre-industrial Europe* (Cambridge, 1985), 1–9, at 7. As an example of Marxist techno-determinist primitivism, Hilton refers to G. A. Cohen, *Karl Marx's Theory of History. A Defence* (Oxford, 1978),

That criticism of the most materialistic variant of Marxism was consistent with Dobb's and Hilton's restrictive understanding of the opportunities for technological development under feudalism. Medieval technology, Hilton agreed with the Cambridge medievalist Michael Postan, 'was at a low level and almost static'.[15] However, he did not consider technological stagnation to be an exogenous feature of the society and economy as did Postan, but followed Marx in making technical change endogenous to the relations of production. In an essay written in 1962, published in 1965 and reprinted in 1973, on capital formation under feudalism, he concluded from a set of complex calculations that lords' investment net of capital replacement was 5 per cent. Hilton considered this to be insufficient to support thirteenth-century productivity, and inferred from this that, rather than invest, their social and political standing impelled lords to spend most income on personal display, on the maintenance of a numerous retinue, and on war. Conversely, the burden of feudal rent (including feudal exactions, ecclesiastical tithes, arbitrary royal purveyancing, and growing state taxation) and land fragmentation deprived peasants of the necessary investment in capital stock.[16]

Whereas that early essay had emphasized supply-side constraints on technological progress, Hilton increasingly identified behavioural, demand-side features as the most serious bottleneck. The following quotation, from an essay on agriculture in medieval Leicestershire, is typical of work before the 1970s that minimized the impact of medieval markets:

> Medieval agriculture . . . was much more primitive and more uniform in character than it is today. The principal reason for variety in modern times is the development of production for the market; and the search in a capitalist society for the most profitable type of

---

which argues forcefully that Marxism's only claim to being an internally consistent and distinctive theory of history that is superior to its rivals is under the guise of a weak form of technological determinism. Cohen would have been surprised at Hilton's inclusion of class formation among the forces rather than the relations of production.

[15] R. H. Hilton, 'Unjust Taxation and Popular Resistance', *New Left Review*, 180 (1990), 177–84.

[16] R. H. Hilton, 'Rent and Capital Formation in Feudal Society', in R. H. Hilton, *The English Peasantry in the Later Middle Ages. The Ford Lectures for 1973 and Related Studies* (Oxford, 1975), 174–214, at 177–96. See also B. M. S. Campbell, *English Seigniorial Agriculture, 1250–1450* (Cambridge, 2000), 17. Actually, a net rate of capital accumulation of at least 5 per cent per annum (equivalent to 100 per cent in just over 14 years) in the thirteenth and early fourteenth centuries, increasing to 10–15 per cent (100 per cent over 5–7 years) in the fifteenth century, does not seem low for a pre-industrial economy.

agricultural production has enhanced the importance of physical variations. In medieval agriculture, however, *the market did not determine the character of production. The sustenance of the farmer and his family was the main objective.* Even the urban demand was unspecialized, and hence there was comparatively little specialization in production. Everyone had to produce (on the whole) the same type of grain crop and tend the same sort of domesticated animals for meat, wool, and pulling power. Variations in the quality of land are therefore rarely referred to in medieval documents.[17]

Having early on excluded technology and markets as dynamic historical forces, and in response possibly to Postan's Ricardo-Malthusian model, Hilton came subsequently to identify the effects on class struggle of the ratio between land and population as the principal source of economic change.[18] By contrast with his analysis of technology, however, this shift in emphasis was not accompanied by a theory of endogenous demographic growth.[19]

Dobb again: from class struggle to 'petty commodity production'

Hilton's analysis of feudalism and of the feudal mode of production displays two phases separated by a theoretical watershed during the first half of the 1970s. His earlier approach had been strongly structural, centring on issues of class. Accordingly he did not engage directly with the 'late medieval crisis', although his regional 'total history' of 1967 ended just before the crisis and promised to tackle the issue at a future date.[20] Hilton took up the

---

[17] R. H. Hilton, 'Medieval Agrarian History', in W. G. Hoskins (ed.), *The Victoria History of the County of Leicester* (Oxford, 1954), vol. 2, 145–98, at 145. The statement is slightly qualified at pp. 174–5: 'While we have hitherto stressed the predominantly subsistence character of medieval Leicestershire agriculture, it nevertheless contained important sectors which were producing for the market—sectors no doubt of *qualitative* rather than of *quantitative* significance' (my emphasis).

[18] In 'Feudalism in Europe', Hilton included population among the determinant forces of production under feudalism, inasmuch as demographic collapse in the fourteenth century allowed the emergence of a yeoman class that gave rise in turn to the English agricultural revolution. He claimed on these grounds that causal primacy in social development could switch over time between class struggle and the forces of production.

[19] Such a theory was attempted for late medieval Normandy by G. Bois, *Crise du féodalisme* (Paris, 1976); Eng. trans., *The Crisis of Feudalism* (Cambridge, 1984); also Bois, 'Against the Neo-Malthusian Orthodoxy', in Aston and Philpin, *Brenner Debate*, 107–18.

[20] This stance is apparent both in his major regional study, *A Medieval Society. The West Midlands at the End of the Thirteenth Century* (London, 1967), which focused on the late

challenge in the Ford Lectures of 1973, which also signalled an albeit surreptitious change in emphasis. The lectures defined their central issue as follows: 'A question of particular importance, which some historians may think has been solved—though I do not—was whether the peasants' economy was significantly market-oriented. This is a problem of central importance for the investigation of all peasantries, medieval or not', since it affects the development of small-scale production for markets, of a competitive labour market, of internal stratification, and of capital accumulation.[21]

Hilton's statement had two subtexts, both addressed critically to Postan. These were, firstly, Postan's adoption of A. V. Chayanov's model of the 'homeostatic' peasant economy whose wealth was determined by its cyclical demographic needs, in counterpoise to V. I. Lenin's model of social differentiation among the peasantry;[22] secondly, Postan's claim—based on the assumption, which Hilton had also previously accepted, that medieval peasants preferred economic self-reliance to trade—that the late medieval economy had contracted because peasants, faced with a collapse in population and thus of demand for land, had retreated into 'non-market' subsistence. Hilton's conclusion that 'all the evidence [from the late medieval west midlands] suggests that the village economy based on the peasant households was considerably monetised' summed up both criticisms.[23]

Even so, the Ford Lectures' characterization of the late middle ages was still strikingly static. Much occurred, yet the differences between the late thirteenth and the late fifteenth centuries were unclear, and they did not add up to the epochal watershed so central to his and Dobb's chronology. Hilton's indecision may have stemmed from an inability at the time to envisage how small-scale peasant production and exchange could generate structural change, and why this change should be greater during the late middle ages than before. The answer may have arisen out of the task of re-editing and introducing a collection of essays centred on the Dobb-Sweezy 'transition debate'. The book, published in 1976, included a short paper by Maurice

---

thirteenth century but made use of far earlier material in contexts where Hilton believed there had been no significant intervening change; and in *Bond Men Made Free*, Part I: 'General Problems of Medieval European Peasant Societies'.

[21] *The English Peasantry*. The statement appears first at 37.

[22] A. V. Chayanov, *The Theory of Peasant Economy [1924–5]*, ed. D. Thorner, B. Kerblay, and R. E. F. Smith. Foreword by T. Shanin (Manchester, 1966); V. I. Lenin, *The Development of Capitalism in Russia* [1899] (Moscow, 1956); see now T. J. Byres, 'Differentiation of the Peasantry under Feudalism and the Transition to Capitalism: in Defence of Rodney Hilton', *Journal of Agrarian Change*, 6 (2006), 17–68.

[23] Hilton, *The English Peasantry*, 43–9.

Dobb, first published in 1962, which identified market incentives as the feudal prime mover.[24] Under feudalism, Dobb suggested, class struggle over the surplus output—which included the benefits of trade—had the unintended consequence of offering producers 'both the means and the motive for improving cultivation' and for engaging in petty commodity exchange, which caused class differentiation and capital accumulation within the 'economy of small producers' itself. By linking peasant-artisan class struggle and economic growth via trade, Dobb offered the key to a new Marxist explanation of the late medieval crisis, and allowed Hilton to present his Ford Lectures retrospectively as 'an attempt to discuss what made this phase of relatively unfettered small commodity production' historically so different. 'During the course of the relatively unfettered commodity production in the 15th century', Hilton now suggested,

> the necessary pre-conditions were created for later capitalist development . . . . The history of the English agrarian economy in the fourteenth and fifteenth centuries illustrates very well the consequences of successful peasant resistance to the lords' pressure for the transfer of surplus. In fact, this must be regarded as a critical turning point in the history of the 'prime mover'. The long period of the successful and multiform exploitation of peasant labour ended, at any rate in most Western European countries, between the middle and the end of the fourteenth century. Only with the successful re-imposition of forms of legally enforceable serfdom could the landowners have continued their previous success. *In the West this was politically and legally impossible. In Eastern Europe the story was different. In the West more and more of the disposable surplus was retained within the peasant economy.* When the harsh yoke of landlordism was next felt by the rural population, it was something quite different in essence, if not always in form—the beginning of the emergence and long and uneven development of a new triad, landowner—capitalist farmer—farm labourer.[25]

---

[24] M. Dobb, 'From Feudalism to Capitalism', *Marxism Today*, 6 (1962), 285–7, replying to Eric Hobsbawm, 'From Feudalism to Capitalism', *Marxism Today*, 6 (1962), 253–6, who had raised the problem of 'uneven development' discussed further below. Dobb's essay followed his shift in 1956 to a more market-based model of socialism (above, n. 6).

[25] Hilton, 'Introduction' to *The Transition Debate*, 25–6 and n. 18, 27 (my emphasis). Chris Dyer has noted *per litteram* that this interpretation of Hilton's change of stance 'presumes that he had not read Dobb's article earlier' or that working on *The Transition Debate* 'made him more aware of its significance'. Dyer recalls that Hilton 'was emphasizing the

The significance of political institutions

A more definite inclusion of trade among the determining factors of late medieval social and economic change was followed by a similar move with respect to legal and political institutions. For many years Hilton had been equally as dismissive of feudal political structure and of the feudal state as of technological progress. His regional studies tended to take political structures and institutions for granted and focused on mechanisms of rural exploitation. This was just as evident in his first study of Leicestershire estates as in his 'total history' of the west midlands a quarter of a century later, which argued that history from the bottom up could mostly dispense with national politics and central government.[26]

Although Hilton had shown an early interest in the dialectics of jurisdictional and political privileges or 'liberties', he made little effort to integrate those reflections into his mainstream research before the 1980s. The first proof of this seems to be a pamphlet on *Communism and Liberty* published in 1950 for working-class readers, which defined feudal 'liberties' as 'a very concrete expression of class privileges' that nonetheless

> in the period of feudal expansion . . . were a means by which . . . the inherent tendencies towards anarchy were controlled. But as the productive forces from which capitalism was to develop expanded, these local, cellular forms of the political, social and economic organization of the feudal nobility became a restrictive force. Local feudal liberties had to be smashed.[27]

Several years later, perhaps influenced by the more eclectic work of Perry Anderson, whose *Lineages of the Absolutist State* (1976) had introduced Weberian definitions of feudalism based on 'jurisdictional fragmentation' into the Marxist canon, Hilton came round to a more positive view of this characteristic feature of feudal society. Surveying the essential features of European feudalism in Anderson's journal, *New Left Review*, in 1984, he stated that 'fragmented (that is, localised) jurisdiction [should be] located in the *relations of production*, in the economic base of society, [rather] than in

---

market a lot by *c.*1973', by which time he would probably have been engaged in editing the volume of essays; it should be possible to verify this in the *New Left Review* archives.

[26] *A Medieval Society*, 4. An early rejection of Oxford-style 'old-fashioned politico-constitutional or narrative history' characterized the entire Historians' Group; see Hobsbawm, 'Historians' Group', 38.

[27] R. H. Hilton, *Communism and Liberty* (London, 1950), 9–10.

the superstructure', and went on to include three factors linked with decentralized power among European feudalism's five principal characteristics:[28]

1. 'The strength of the peasant communities required a local mobilization of landlord power, whether the state was strong or weak. *Decentralised power in feudalism was an essential aspect, not a weakness, of feudal society*';
2. 'Landlord power for the purpose of surplus extraction was expressed through private jurisdiction';
3. 'Feudal rent' includes payments for seigneurial monopolies (including, presumably, taxation of trade);
4. Peasant commodity production was central to feudalism and 'provided the bulk of landlord income';
5. Merchant capital and large-scale urbanization denoted 'a further development of this money element in the relations of production'.

This shift in emphasis—which defines Hilton's most original contribution to a Marxist theory of feudalism—may have also been connected with a growing interest in medieval trade and towns, foreshadowed in the Ford Lectures of 1973. In a seminal paper on small town society, also published in 1984, he emphasized the economic significance of 'certain institutional features . . . [such as] freedom of tenure and status, privileged access to the market, some administrative and even jurisdictional autonomy'.[29] His subsequent comparison between English and French towns took the argument a step further, identifying jurisdictional privilege as a key element of both the medieval urban economy and its class structure:

> Early medieval [English] urban communities, or rather the merchants which spoke for them, asked for the privileges which would give them freedom for mercantile activity. These privileges were very much the same in the French communes. In the *villes de franchise* and the *villes de consulat* as well as in the English free boroughs the urban bourgeoisie had *specific class interests in the achievement of privileges*, which not only enabled it to control its mercantile activities, but also to subordinate the artisans, to organize municipal

---

[28] Hilton, 'Feudalism in Europe' (my emphasis). Chris Dyer has suggested *per litteram* that Hilton's interest in Max Weber was stimulated already in the early 1970s by his newfound enthusiasm for urban history.

[29] R. H. Hilton, 'Small Town Society in England before the Black Death', *Past and Present*, 105 (1984), 53–78.

finance, and to use *the crucial instrument of power in feudal society, jurisdiction,* over the town's inhabitants.[30]

Remarkably, this, Hilton's last major monograph, was framed in predominantly legal and institutional terms. Despite local variations, he suggested, English and French urban privileges displayed 'considerable similarities' defined as follows:

1. burgesses had personal legal security against arbitrary feudal jurisdiction;
2. urban courts applied simplified legal processes;
3. tenure of urban real property was free;
4. burgesses were exempt from seigneurial impositions;
5. property was secured against arbitrary seizure;
6. towns had varying degrees of financial autonomy, usually granting townsmen the right to collect various dues;
7. towns had varying degrees of political and administrative autonomy.

Hilton concurrently identified several connections leading from political and institutional structure to diverging economic features in the two countries.[31] Yet, in common with other British Marxist historians of his generation, he never seriously engaged with twentieth-century Marxist theories of class and state-formation, whose main originators (Antonio Gramsci, György Lukacs and, later, Louis Althusser) were still mostly unknown in Britain before the early 1970s. To place this caveat in context, it is worth recalling that not a single member of the first three generations of the influential French '*Annales* School', including Marc Bloch, developed a significant interest in, let alone a theory of, the feudal or pre-modern state either.

The comparative method

For much of his life Hilton seems to have viewed the comparative method as a source of generalizations about a social form, feudalism, which displayed roughly similar features across the whole of Europe. His focus on class determination and class relations led him to emphasize national and international similarities in the form and manner of peasant exploitation, rather than dissimilarities and divergences in the 'intricate machinery of class domination' and in economic development.[32]

---

[30] R. H. Hilton, *English and French Towns in Feudal Society* (Cambridge, 1992), 127–8 (my emphasis).

[31] Ibid., 22–3, 45–7, 83, 91, 95–6, 100–4.

[32] P. Anderson, *Lineages of the Absolutist State* (London, 1974), 11.

Like most Marxists of his generation, Hilton did not use comparison systematically as an heuristic tool that offers the historian the closest she can hope to get to controlled, testable hypotheses. Hilton did not ignore the latter entirely, but he tended to frame comparative questions in terms of English exceptionalism rather than as a guide to causation. Thus, his early paper on feudal capital formation suggested that, since 'one of the most important ways in which the late medieval peasants contributed to capital formation was in the building up of the country's herds of cattle and flocks of sheep', 'relatively tranquil countries like [late medieval] England' might have obtained 'a vital advantage in the early stages of the economic expansion of modern times' over Continental countries more damaged by warfare.[33] Subsequently, Hilton argued that the late medieval reduction in the feudal levy was most pronounced in England, 'the weak link of European feudalism', which 'no doubt [explained] the primacy of England in capitalist development'.[34]

A lack of interest in comparative heuristics helps explain why, having spent so much effort on how to characterize the late medieval crisis as a dynamic, open-ended and general process that marked the beginning of a new epoch as much as the end of an old one, Hilton avoided the related issues of 'historically conditioned divergence' between Europe and the rest of the world, and between England and Continental Europe.[35] Maurice Dobb had identified those problems in the same paper of 1962 where he re-evaluated the role of petty commodity trade in feudal development. The major sources of 'uneven development', Dobb suggested, included the *availability of land*, which influenced the ability of poor and/or dispossessed peasants to migrate from areas of high population pressure, thereby reducing the need to find wage-employment; the *form* that feudal exactions took, which affected the strength of peasant resistance; and the *presence of markets* 'as represented by towns or inter-regional trade routes' and 'as encouraging commodity production (i.e. production for the market) *within the petty mode*', which stimulated processes of social differentiation.[36] Thus, inasmuch as class struggle over resources is mediated by political structure, and markets require political enforcement and coordination, Dobb's theory of development and underdevelopment presupposed a theory of the European feudal state and of its differences and divergences, which does not seem to have engaged Hilton's interest very much.

---

[33] Hilton, *The English Peasantry*, 202–5.
[34] Hilton, 'Feudalism in Europe'.
[35] *Hilton, English and French Towns*, 2.
[36] Dobb, 'From Feudalism to Capitalism', 286–7.

Hilton and the 'transition from feudalism to capitalism': where do we go from there?

Outside the Marxist canon, medieval social and economic historians for the past few decades have followed many of the paths first trodden by Rodney Hilton, although not always on his own terms. For historians with Marxist sympathies or with a more theoretical bent, Rodney Hilton established over four decades and nearly single-handedly a stronger empirical grounding to Dobb's theory of the transition from feudalism to capitalism, and defined many of the debate's parameters up to the present day.

For much of his life, Hilton focused disproportionately on class and property rights to land, arguing that the dispossession of economically self-sufficient peasants from the land was a necessary and a sufficient cause for the rise of a technologically dynamic, fully commoditized, capitalist mode of production. He was never greatly interested in the material forces of production (technological development), and came only late to questions related to the nature and dynamic of feudal power and the feudal state. These biases arguably weakened the import of his discovery in the 1970s of 'petty commodity production' as a source of dynamic change, and undermined his explanations for three basic phenomena, the internal dynamic (the prime mover) of the feudal economy, the transition to capitalism, and uneven development. The following notes take as their point of departure Dobb's and Hilton's work on these topics and the debates they gave rise to, to outline briefly my understanding of the current theoretical and empirical debate.[37]

A theory of the feudal mode of production and of the transition to capitalism requires a clear definition of the historical beginning and end points of the process. I would define *feudalism* as a social-economic formation featuring a prevalence of:

1. divided and competing property rights to land, capital. and labour, enforced by competing legal rights (from this follows that the military and economic competition between feudal lords gives rise to pressures for territorial political and institutional coordination, and establishes the parameters for state powers; note that serfdom is neither a necessary nor a sufficient condition for a feudal society to emerge and persist);
2. quasi-competitive markets with dispersed regulation enforced through (competing and overlapping) jurisdictional rights;

---

[37] This section follows S. R. Epstein, *Freedom and Growth. The Rise of States and Markets 1300–1750* (London, 2000), and Epstein, 'The Rise of the West', in J. Hall and R. Schroeder (eds), *An Anatomy of Power: The Social Theory of Michael Mann* (Cambridge, 2006), 233–62.

3. producer control over the means of production;
4. irregular and patchy technological innovation, which is a function of competitive market forces.

I would then define *capitalism*, by contrast, as a social-economic formation featuring a prevalence of:

1. exclusive property rights to land, capital and labour, enforced by the jurisdictional sovereignty of the state;
2. producers who earn wages and do not control the means of production;
3. competitive markets with dispersed regulation under the jurisdictional sovereignty of the state;
4. systematic technological innovation, which, as a function of competitive market forces, determines producers' (firms') chances of economic survival.

Following on from these definitions, a theory of the transition from one social-economic formation to the other must, at the least, explain the following historical questions: first, how did agricultural supply keep up with growing population and demand; second, how did exclusive property rights develop; third, how did the wage-based, non-agricultural sector expand, such that the share of population employed in agriculture fell from *c.* 90–95 per cent at the outset of feudalism (across Europe, *c.*1100) to *c.* 30 per cent as the capitalist social-economic formation was taking full shape (in England, *c.*1800); and fourth, how did technology in the energy and manufacturing sectors progress, as Marx put it, 'out of the hand-mill into the steam-mill'.

Agriculture and the feudal state.[38]

A recent, substantial body of research shows that agricultural supply in medieval and early modern—that is, feudal—Europe was far more elastic than either Marxists like Hilton or 'Ricardo-Malthusian' pessimists like Postan assumed.[39] This work has established that the major bottleneck to productivity gains in feudal agriculture was not technological, as Postan claimed, for the best technology available to thirteenth-century agriculturalists was more than adequate to supply food to a growing population; land (and possibly labour) productivity in parts of early fourteenth-century

---

[38] This section follows Epstein, *Freedom and Growth*, 40–52, with references.

[39] Little of this recent research utilizes a Marxist framework and terminology, and it also prefers the traditional periodization into medieval and early modern; in *Freedom and Growth*, I employ the term 'premodern' to highlight, along Marxian lines, the basic technological and organizational similarities between pre- and post-1500 European agriculture.

England appear to have been as high as in the mid-to late eighteenth century.[40] The most notable feature of feudal agriculture was, by contrast, the astonishing *inefficiency* with which best practice was applied. Most feudal agriculture lay very far indeed from the contemporary technological frontier. However, the relative 'distance' from the frontier differed considerably between regions with similar institutions and property rights to land. How can these differences be explained? Why did some peasants—and lords—under feudalism apply best available practice, while their neighbours apparently ignored the improved livelihoods they could achieve from technical innovation?

We saw that initially Dobb, Hilton and their followers explained these differences as a result of feudal property rights to land, and that in their eyes, only the introduction of capitalist relations of production on the land epitomized by the 'landlord–tenant–labourer' triad provided adequate incentives for systematic innovation. Their model thus predicted that lords and peasants under feudalism would behave similarly, and it excluded practically by definition the differentiating effect of market incentives. Dobb's and Hilton's 'discovery' in the 1960s and 1970s of the dynamic role of production for exchange did not significantly change this anti-market bias, because they did not associate it with a political economy and an evolutionary theory of feudal markets. This made it impossible for them to explain why market incentives, and the agricultural innovation that markets stimulate, might differ between regions, or why incentives might change over time. That is also why Hilton could not convincingly explain why English peasants became more commercialized after the Black Death, since nothing in the way markets were organized seemed (in his analysis) to have changed.

Recent agrarian studies have placed far greater emphasis on 'commercialization', and explain differences in agrarian economic performance in terms of a broad range of factors that helped to define the opportunity costs of investment (real rates of interest) and trade (transaction costs). Since real interest rates are, in the long run, a function of investment risk and investment opportunity (market size), both of which are determined by search, enforcement and transport costs, these studies suggest that the major cause of poor rates of investment and innovation arose from unusually high transaction costs under feudalism. In this view, feudal political and jurisdictional fragmentation and warfare gave rise to coordination failures and a systematic

[40] For the most recent data on land and labour productivity in fourteenth-century England, see Campbell, *English Seigniorial Agriculture*; E. Karakacili, 'English Agrarian Productivity Rates before the Black Death: A Case Study', *Journal of Economic History*, 64 (2004), 24–60.

paucity of investment in public goods, including transport and commercial arrangements, credible and predictable justice, and financial and political stability. This explanatory shift has two important implications. First, it turns agricultural supply from an *independent* variable that determined the overall rate of growth and opportunities for development of the feudal economy, as portrayed by Hilton, into a *dependent* variable that could respond elastically to changes in demand, subject to the opportunity costs of investment and trade. Second, it shifts the emphasis in explanations of agricultural productivity from property rights to land narrowly defined, to property rights over the producer surplus broadly defined. It suggests that students of the transition from feudalism to capitalism need to pay more attention to the conditions that made investment in agriculture profitable, rather than to the technical or organizational characteristics of feudal agriculture itself.

These findings can be reformulated along Marxist lines as follows. In the feudal-tributary mode of production, most rural producers owned their means of production and sold a portion of their produce on the market.[41] Therefore they responded positively to changes in supply and demand and relative prices.[42] Feudal lords (who included the ruling elites in towns with jurisdictional prerogatives over the hinterland) extracted an agricultural surplus from the peasantry through decentralized legal compulsion backed by military threat; the surplus was perceived directly as rent in cash, kind, or labour, and indirectly through taxation, levies on trade and the provision of justice. Although the relative share of income from different sources varied over time and space, the share from rights of jurisdiction (which sometimes also included compulsory labour services) was always substantial. The principal threat to feudalism thus did not come from trade; up to a point

---

[41] I follow J. Haldon, *The State and the Tributary Mode of Production* (London, 1993), in employing the term 'tributary' to emphasize that feudal incomes accrued as much through tax and tribute as through labour services and economic rent.

[42] Note that this formulation does not prejudge the composition or size of the surplus; in other words, it does not presuppose, as much Marxist and non-Marxist literature does, that a peasant household will only sell its physical surplus to subsistence. I would argue instead that the 'self-subsistent' peasant is largely a figment of nineteenth-century modernization theory, and that the choice whether to produce for personal consumption or for market exchange is the result of rational, historically contingent price-based calculus (which will include, for example, whether goods for personal consumption will actually be accessible via the market). This assumption, of course, makes no claim as to whether those prices are being formed through 'feudal' (heavily and 'competitively' taxed) or 'capitalist' markets.

feudalism thrived on trade.[43] Having said this however, feudal lords did regulate and tax markets for income. Moreover, because feudal lords as a class were less directly exposed to market pressures than peasant producers—at the end of the thirteenth century produce from the demesne sector in England, then the largest in western Europe, accounted for only about 30 per cent of the average lordly income, equivalent to under 5 per cent of GNP, much of which would have been consumed directly—they were probably less likely to take the lead in agricultural innovation.[44]

The main obstacle to agricultural growth in the feudal economy was therefore the cost of trade, which was largely defined by institutional regulation and tariffs and by political and military stability, and to a lesser extent by developments in transport technology. The lords' and towns' main purpose in stimulating trade was to maximize rent streams from their jurisdictional rights. Those rights were a basic feature of their social and political power. The introduction of jurisdictionally 'free' trade did not just lower feudal and urban revenues, but also challenged the superiority of lord over peasant and town over country. In the longer run, however, strong feudal and urban jurisdiction was incompatible with agrarian development. By the later middle ages, agricultural innovation was inversely correlated with the intensity of seigneurial rights, and rural proto-industrial growth was inversely correlated with the jurisdictional powers of towns. This suggests that feudalism had the following major 'contradiction' at its heart: the political economy of feudalism was necessary to establish markets and to coordinate economic activities during its first great phase of expansion (c.950–1250), but already by 1300 that same political economy—which combined market monopolies and the coordination failures arising from political and jurisdictional parcellization—had begun to fetter further growth. By 1300, the fundamental constraint on feudal agriculture came from feudal institutional constraints, rather than from technological inertia.

---

[43] A point made already by Dobb, *Studies*, 39–42, 70–81.

[44] B. M. S. Campbell and K. Bartley, *England on the Eve of the Black Death: An Atlas of Lay Lordship, Law and Wealth 1300–49* (Manchester, 2006), p. 76 suggests an annual mean demesne income of £22 for English lay lords in 1300–49; for an annual mean total income of c.£70, see C. Dyer, *Standards of Living in the Later Middle Ages. Social Change in England c.1200–1520* (Cambridge, 1989), ch. 2; N. J. Mayhew, 'Population, Money Supply, and the Velocity of Circulation in England, 1300–1700', *Economic History Review*, 48 (1995), 244, 249–50. For a comparison between the rate of commercialization of peasant and demesne agriculture, see R. H. Britnell, *The Commercialisation of English Society, 1000–1500*, 2nd edn. (Manchester, 1996), 121–3.

Beneath these overarching features, the political economy of feudal Europe displayed strong diversity. This explains the emergence, no later than the early twelfth century, of economically leading, or core, regions and semi- or fully peripheral ones.[45] In most of western Europe, the use of lordly powers of coercion to tax and monopolize trade, which kept the feudal economy substantially below its full agricultural potential, was counterbalanced by feudal lords' strategy of territorial expansion through localized war. Warfare was as much a part of the intrinsic mechanics of feudalism as jurisdictional exploitation. Although the main goal of feudal territorial expansion was to broaden the lord's political and economic resources, expansion also improved economic efficiency by increasing jurisdictional integration and reducing transaction costs within the new territory. Territorial 'state' formation made it possible to reduce seigneurial dues, weaken or abolish rival feudal and urban monopolies, systematize legal codes and legislation, weights and measures, help coordinate markets and reduce opportunities for pillage and warfare, and restrict rulers' opportunities to act as autocratic 'stationary bandits' against their subjects.[46]

Political centralization—the transfer of sovereignty over feudal means of coercion from subordinate lords to superior territorial authorities—transformed feudal rights of jurisdiction that sanctioned a decentralized mode of coercion, into fiscal or property rights over commercial transactions that sanctioned a centralized, state-based mode of economic coercion. Following the late medieval crisis, the evolution of decentralized feudal immunities—privileges and freedoms—into state-defined and redeemable claims to fiscal rights slowly turned the economic and legal base of the feudal class into commodities. From the fifteenth century, financial capital, rather than social status, gradually became the elites' new coin of exchange, while the state's decision whether to sell income streams to the highest bidder or to abolish them was increasingly subjected to financial and fiscal rather than political considerations. Thus, early modern 'absolutism' was not simply a form of state feudalism. By embarking on the road to centralized,

[45] For an analysis along such lines of the late medieval English economy as 'semi-peripheral', see B. M. S. Campbell, 'The Sources of Tradable Surpluses: English Agricultural Exports 1250–1349', in L. Berggren, N. Hybel, and A. Landen (eds) *Cogs, Cargoes and Commerce: Maritime Bulk Trade in Northern Europe, 1150–1400* (Toronto, 2002), 1–30.

[46] This expression, which refers to 'territorial lords [who] tax their subjects heavily and use the proceeds to serve their own interests' (rather than those of their subjects), has been popularized by M. Olson, *Power and Prosperity. Outgrowing Communist and Capitalist Dictatorships* (New York, 2000), 6–11.

monopolistic jurisdiction, early modern states also laid the institutional bases of modern capitalism and capitalist class struggle.

In sum, agricultural expansion in the feudal system was the result of two countervailing forces, one pressing for military and jurisdictional decentralization, which made trade and investment more costly, the other pushing for increased political and jurisdictional centralization, which reduced the costs of investment and trade. In the long run, centralization prevailed, leading to a slow reduction in transaction costs and stimulating commercialization and specialization. The 'prime mover' and the 'contradiction' within the feudal mode of production lay in the relations between lords, peasants, markets, and the state.

Expanding the wage-earning, non-agricultural sector.[47]

The existence during the later middle ages of regions with extensive, potentially capitalistic, property rights to land (bourgeois ownership, competitive tenancies, easy availability of rural wage labour) such as Lombardy, Sicily, the Île de France, or parts of Flanders, which nonetheless did not experience a rapid capitalist transition, proves that such property rights were necessary but not sufficient for the transition to unfold. Rather than unique property to land, the most distinctive feature of the English economy compared to its continental peers was probably the unusual elasticity of demand for surplus labour outside agriculture. In England as elsewhere, excess agricultural labour was absorbed either by towns or by proto-industrial activities in the countryside. Since rural proto-industry tended to threaten traditional urban occupations and the urban tax base, town rulers generally opposed it; therefore, successful rural proto-industries required some form of institutionalized freedom from urban prerogatives over the countryside. The extent to which such necessary 'freedoms' existed determined the elasticity of demand of the industrial and service sectors, without necessarily displacing peasants physically into towns. Conversely, the separation of a class of wage labourers from its means of production undermined feudal coercion because wage-earners could credibly threaten to migrate.

The capacity of established towns to oppose proto-industrial growth differed greatly across Europe. It was generally strongest in, however, the ancient, more Romanized and corporatized European core and weakest in the north-western periphery, and urban restrictions on proto-industrial activity were particularly ineffective in central and northern England.

---

[47] This section follows Epstein, *Freedom*, ch. 6; Epstein, 'Introduction', to Epstein (ed.), *Town and Country in Europe, 1300–1800* (Cambridge, 2001), 1–29; P. Glennie, 'Town and Country in England, 1570–1750', in Epstein (ed.), *Town and Country*, 132–55.

This institutional difference in urban 'feudal' powers provided seventeenth- and eighteenth-century England with far greater flexibility than most Continental countries in establishing 'new' proto-industrial towns based upon excess rural labour, and gave English agriculture and rural manufacture a critical competitive edge.

Technological innovation.[48]

Technological innovation in agriculture was far slower than in the rest of the economy. The reasons included the lack of botanical science that made it hard to transfer agricultural knowledge over long distances, and the unpredictability of agricultural markets discussed previously, which raised the opportunity cost of new techniques. But agricultural innovation in the sense of technical novelty (invention as opposed to diffusion) was also slow because much could still be achieved with already available techniques: in eighteenth-century France, for example, existing technology could have generated a 60 per cent higher output than was achieved in practice.[49]

As it is, without any persistent technological progress in manufacturing, mining, and the production of energy, the transition to industrial capitalism could not have occurred, and the economy of feudal Europe would have got stuck in the kind of 'high level equilibrium trap' that characterized China into the eighteenth century.[50] To understand why feudal Europe was able to catch up with and forge ahead of its 'Eurasian' peers, we need to take a closer look at the kind of technical knowledge with which pre-modern craftsmen and engineers worked. Most importantly, such knowledge was largely tacit and experience-based, which placed basic cognitive limits to how it could be expressed, processed and transmitted. Lack of codification meant that information about what was available, and the reproduction of that knowledge, depended critically on the mobility of individual experts. The essential reason why technical innovation under feudalism was so slow, therefore, was due to

---

[48] This section follows S. R. Epstein, 'Craft Guilds, Apprenticeship and Technological Change in Pre-industrial Europe', *Journal of Economic History*, 53 (1998), 684–713; Epstein, 'Property Rights to Technical Knowledge in Premodern Europe, 1300–1800', *American Economic Review*, 94 (2004), 382–7; Epstein, *Transferring Technical Knowledge and Innovating in Europe, c.1200–c.1800*, Working Papers in Economic History, LSE, November 2004.

[49] G. W. Grantham, 'Divisions of Labour: Agricultural Productivity and Occupational Specialization in Pre-industrial France', *Economic History Review*, 2nd ser., 46 (1993), 478–502.

[50] See K. Pomeranz, *The Great Divergence. China, Europe, and the Making of the Modern World Economy* (Princeton, 2000). Pomeranz's analysis of the causes of the European transition, however, is very different from mine.

the high costs of transferring experience-based, uncodified knowledge, and the weak and irregular face-to-face interactions between geographically scattered craftsmen and engineers.

From the late eleventh century, however, a distinctively 'feudal' technological system began to emerge, based on craft-based apprenticeship training, non-ascriptive membership of craft associations and, increasingly, competition for skilled workers between towns and states. These three elements defined a set of necessary and sufficient conditions for the accumulation, codification, and circulation of reliable technical knowledge. Craft-based training ensured that it met both masters' and apprentices' needs. Non-ascriptive membership meant that skilled workers could move from city to city with few restrictions or penalties, and inter-state competition for technology and high-status consumer goods meant that specialized knowledge could circulate and cross-fertilize, and that technicians could move where their skills were most required.

The costs of technical dissemination fell over time in response to growing state competition for skilled workers, and to urbanization. Urbanization—especially the development of regional and national metropolises after the late medieval crisis—offered improved opportunities for exchanging knowledge, higher average quality of labour, a greater likelihood of matching skills to demand, and stronger incentives for knowledge modelling and codification. Although it is not a priori clear whether high urbanization attracted skilled migrants, or whether migration (driven by exogenous factors like war) caused high urbanization, the evidence points to the primacy of the former, pull factors, specifically of urban commercial success. Skilled migrants enabled each new technological leader—which shifted over time from central and northern Italy (1200–1450), to the southern Rhineland and southern Netherlands (c.1450–1570), to the Dutch Republic (1570–1675) and finally to Britain after c.1675—to draw on the accumulated knowledge of its predecessors, recombine it with local experience, and develop the knowledge pool further.

Nonetheless, the secular rate on innovation was not stable. The three features shaping the provision of 'human capital' under feudalism (craft-based training, non-ascriptive membership of craft guilds, and strong inter-urban mobility) were greatly strengthened during the late medieval crisis; this gave rise to a sharp, secular increase in the rate of technical innovation and diffusion across western Europe. A second marked increase in the rate of innovation followed the 'seventeenth-century crisis', when coordination within states and competition between states increased sharply. In conclusion, the underlying, unifying factor of the two great 'feudal crises' of the Marxist canon is thus the rate of development of the productive forces.

English Towns and the Transition c. 1450–1550

Spencer Dimmock

There are few historical issues of more relevance to a critical understanding of the economic and political workings of today's societies, and their future, than 'the transition from feudalism to capitalism'. In association with its contemporary resonance, the 'transition debate' has invigorated historical theory and practice by generating a sense of structural unity to long periods of time. The debate has recognized the potential of the whole range of people's experiences and actions to determine change. State politics and everyday life are brought together and both have a claim to historical significance. In this spirit I intend in this essay to develop some new lines of inquiry on the transition in England by focusing on the interrelationships between the small town, the capitalist clothier and early enclosure.

Hilton, towns and the transition

When entering a discussion on the transition debate, Rodney Hilton always considered it necessary to spell out what he thought he was talking about and so will I. Working within a historical materialist perspective I understand feudalism and capitalism to refer to distinct societies with their own specific patterns or logic of development. There is a close relationship between the economic, political, and cultural life in each society and its predominant 'mode of production' of material goods and wealth, the latter being ultimately determinant but not mechanistically so. Each mode of production is characterized by particular social relations engaged in the process of production, and these are relations of property and social class. The feudal mode of production in the European middle ages is characterized by, on the one hand, peasants that possessed, independently of the market, their means of subsistence in the form of plots of land, and on the other, a class of lords and its state apparatus that maintained itself by the politically and legally enforced appropriation of the surplus food (in money or in kind) produced by the peasants on their plots. Although the means of surplus appropriation or feudal levy varied markedly in different regions and over time, it included labour and customary dues indicative of serfdom or villeinage, seigneurial monopolies, money and commuted labour rents and taxation.

In the developed capitalist mode of production, the peasantry no longer exist, or are certainly no longer predominant, having been separated from their means of subsistence and made dependent on the market, either as capital-owning entrepreneurs or wage-workers in both town and country-side. In this mode the direct political relationship has also disappeared and wage-workers, capital-owning entrepreneurs and commercial landlords re-late to each other as *legally* free individuals in the market place, and they are compelled to do so in order to survive. Despite the change from a direct political relationship in the transfer of the surplus to one of economic com-pulsion on the market, political coercion inevitably supports the dominant class of appropriators in ensuring the market provides an adequate supply of cheap labour.

In England where capitalist relations of production successfully emerged from the late fifteenth century, increasing labour productivity in agriculture, increases in the proportion of the non-agrarian urban and industrial sector, and modern economic growth were generated in the long run, because the new capitalist entrepreneurs were subject to competition in the market place in order to survive, and were therefore compelled to maximize profits through specialization, accumulation, innovation, and the systematic re-investment of profits in order to respond to changing demand. The landlords also depended on the market because their rents varied with the success of their capitalist tenant farmers. This competition between capitalist tenant farmers led, along with the urban and industrial sector, to the growth of the proportion of wage-workers and proletarianization, as, in economic and political terms, the weak were divorced from the land by the strong. Proletarianization was, therefore, increasingly the result, not the precondi-tion of a developing capitalist system.[1] The question is what led to the emer-gence of capitalism in the first place?

Given the role of lords and peasants as the principal feudal classes, Rodney Hilton believed that the fundamental threat to feudalism was located in the countryside; in England capitalism emerged in a rural context. For Hilton the

---

[1] For the last two paragraphs I am indebted to the clarity of the formulations in the following works: R. Brenner, 'The Low Countries in the Transition to Capitalism', in P. Hoppenbrouwers and J. Luiten van Zanden (eds), *Peasants into Farmers? The Transformation of Rural Economy and Society in the Low Countries (Middle Ages—19th Century) in Light of the Brenner Debate* (Turnhout, Belgium, 2001), 275–338; E. Meiksins Wood, *The Origin of Capitalism: A Longer View* (London, 2002); and her 'The Question of Market Dependence', *Journal of Agrarian Change*, 2 (2002), 50–87.

key to the transition was the outcome of the struggle for rent and tax between the feudal lords (including the state apparatus) and the peasantry. With the stagnation of labour productivity in agriculture, the related increase in non-productive expenditure by lords by the early fourteenth century, and the changing land–labour ratio in favour of the peasantry due to the subsequent demographic downturn, the lords faced a crisis of incomes. The seigneurial offensive designed to close the gap between lords' income and expenditure failed. By the mid-fifteenth century, peasant resistance and mobility had led to the dissolution of serfdom and further reduction of the feudal levy, ensuring more favourable terms for peasants. More of the surplus was retained by the peasantry, and this, associated with the breakdown of manorial organization and of the cohesion of rural communities, freed up peasant economies for the extension of commodity production. With landlords evicting peasant tenants by the late fifteenth century, the result was further social differentiation within the peasantry which, in Hilton's view, created 'the necessary preconditions for the capitalist entrepreneur', and capitalist development.[2]

Although recognizing the primacy of rural social relations Hilton, wishing to bring to bear all the interrelations of the system that was being transformed, became increasingly interested in the potential role of English towns. He laid down two main hypotheses in this respect: first, the survival into the early modern period of a dominant mercantile ruling elite, especially in London but also in the larger provincial towns in England, compared to the flight into the law and royal officialdom in France; and secondly, the specific nature of urbanization in England which was characterized by a relatively high density of small towns. The clear distinction between the mercantile elite of England and France must have been an advantage to the English economy in terms of distribution at least as the trade in cloth boomed again from the late fifteenth century. Hilton was impressed with the extent to which merchants had developed industrial production for export within the putting-out system in the

---

[2] This summary is based upon Hilton's contributions in R. H. Hilton (ed.), *The Transition from Feudalism to Capitalism* (London, 1976); his 'A Crisis of Feudalism', in T. H. Aston and C. H. E. Philpin (eds), *The Brenner Debate: Agrarian Class Structure and Economic Development in Pre-industrial Europe* (Cambridge, 1985), 119–137; and his 'A Study in the Pre-history of English Enclosure in the Fifteenth Century', in R. H. Hilton (ed.), *The English Peasantry in the Later Middle Ages* (Oxford, 1973), 161–73. See Wood, *Origin of Capitalism*, 34–43, for an important critique of Hilton's perspective within Marxist historiography. The dispute centres on Hilton's emphasis on the social differentiation of the peasantry and freeing up of commercial development following the dissolution of serfdom, rather than on the separation of the peasantry from the land in the enclosure movement which involved the landlords, something about which he was relatively less concerned in his published work at least.

traditional urban centres by the late fourteenth century. But, following Marx, he observed that merchant capital remained largely within the sphere of circulation and failed to transform through investment the traditional structures of agrarian and industrial production.[3] Robert Brenner's work provides strong support for this view, demonstrating that London Merchant Adventurers, who held economic and political sway in the period of emerging capitalism between 1450 and 1550 and beyond, preferred to reinforce existing trade routes through grants of coercive monopolies in a mutually supportive relationship with the English Crown, rather than seek new markets which required investment in industrial production, the latter being costly and risky. This would change with the rise of the 'New Merchants' of the early seventeenth century who emerged largely from the ranks of domestic traders and artisans and who were in direct conflict with the old monopolies. An ensuing struggle was played out in the London politics of the English Revolution.[4] Probably some of Hilton's best insights into medieval towns were achieved in the identification of an intimate relationship between towns and feudalism. He argued that the traditional urban centres were fundamentally a product of the luxury trade and aristocratic demand, the latter being dependent upon the ability of lords to maintain their income from the peasantry.[5] The dissolution of serfdom and a reduction in the feudal levy was bound therefore to have a serious knock-on effect for the old urban structure.

Hilton saw more potential for transformation at the base of the medieval economy, notably from the small towns. Following the rapid urbanization of 1100–1300 many small towns in England maintained, in some cases even increased, the size of their populations between the early fourteenth and early sixteenth centuries. By contrast, the majority of the larger towns and many village markets experienced decline, and many villages were deserted. In a seminal paper, Hilton lamented the lack of attention paid to small market towns, 'falling', as they did, 'between the two stools of research into the larger towns and peasant society'. In the context of the debate on England's supposed commercial backwardness, he argued that while England's larger towns

---

[3] Hilton, *Transition*, 22–3; R. H. Hilton, *English and French Towns in Feudal Society: A Comparative Study* (Cambridge, 1992), 84–6, and 101–4. At the Birmingham conference (2003), Halil Berktay, with the benefit of conversations with Hilton, suggested that he increasingly saw the role of merchant capital as more complex than his published views suggest.

[4] R. Brenner, *Merchants and Revolution: Commercial Change, Political Conflict and London's Overseas Traders, 1550–1653* (London, 2003). See also Brenner, 'Low Countries', 276–7.

[5] Hilton, *Transition*, 17–18; Hilton, 'Crisis', 127.

may have been much smaller than those of France, a comparison between the
west midlands, a typical English region, and Normandy in France, a region
with similar characteristics, revealed that 'the density of market foundations
in the west midlands was one and a half times to twice that of the Norman
bourgs of an urban type'. He suggested therefore that 'Given the important
subsequent role of England in the development of capitalism, this measure
of pre-capitalist commercialization may be a useful historical background to
that development'.[6]

These issues have continued to interest historians since Hilton made his
major contributions. Although he does not engage directly with the transition
debate James Galloway, in a very useful summary of up-to-date work done on
towns and commercialization in England c.1300–1570, has emphasized the
growth of London as the engine of economic change in England in the late
medieval period, both in terms of its stimulus to agrarian specialization, and
of its effect on the other towns.[7] He cites the high agricultural yields London
was able to stimulate in its hinterland even after c.1300,[8] and also its ability to
eclipse the larger provincial towns and draw the many small towns into its
orbit by the sixteenth century. He has also drawn attention to the lack of direct
political control English towns had over their hinterlands compared to those
on the continent, but argues that nevertheless the centralized political structure in England served to favour urban traders. It did so because 'the existence
of a dense network of recognized markets and fairs, a stable currency, the
standardization of weights and measures, the existence of effective procedures for the enforcement of contracts and settlement of disputes', tended
to reduce transaction costs. Galloway's overall perspective, however, in line
with an increase in influential neo-Smithian studies in recent years, appears
to view agrarian specialization and economic growth as an inevitable consequence of increases in the growth of exchange and urban demand. Hence he
talks of the 'critical mass' that towns needed to reach 'in terms of population
level and aggregation of craft-industrial production' in order 'to mould the
agricultural productive system'.[9] Robert Brenner's work provides a fundamental corrective to this view: he has demonstrated very effectively, by the
example of the heavily urbanized Low Countries in the late medieval period,

---

[6] R. H. Hilton, 'Medieval Market Towns and Simple Commodity Production', *Past and
Present*,109 (1985), 3–23.

[7] J. A. Galloway, 'Town and Country in England, 1300–1570', in S. R. Epstein (ed.), *Town
and Country in Europe, 1300–1800* (Cambridge, 2001), 106–131.

[8] High yields or increase in land productivity were achieved at this point only through an
increase in labourers due to overpopulation, resulting in reduced labour productivity.

[9] Galloway, 'Town and Country', 118.

that urban demand could not by itself bring about such an agrarian response. The impact of urban demand on agriculture in terms of specialization for capitalist production or its opposite—the fragmentation of holdings—was ultimately determined by the existing structure of 'social-property' relations and balance of class forces within a specific region.[10]

Having briefly summarized Hilton's contribution to the role of English towns in the transition, the aim of the rest of this paper is to develop Hilton's hypothesis on small towns. But rather than examine the high density of small towns in England in terms of a quantitative measure of commercialization and of non-agrarian mouths stimulating agrarian specialization, important though these issues are, I intend to pursue alternative ways in which the inhabitants and institutions of these towns may have determined the change.

The small town and the capitalist clothier

Christopher Dyer has extended Hilton's hypothesis on small town densities by comparing the regional densities of small towns *within* England (see Fig. 1).[11] Small town settlements have been identified and included in the data for the map on the basis of urban function; that is, they contained a broad range of inhabitants specializing in non-agrarian occupations, usually at least twenty different occupations being identified. This range enabled them to provide distinct services and products for their local hinterlands in exchange for cash and agricultural produce, and it therefore connected them with the wider urban hierarchy. A population above 2,000 is generally seen to mark off a town of a higher order from a small town, although quite small towns took on wider functions in some regions.[12]

What stands out from the map is a close correlation between developments in the textile industry and the density of market towns, for example, in the south-west, south-west midlands, Kent and Suffolk. This correlation is significant because while other industrial 'projects' began to take shape from the late fifteenth century, the textile industry and the export of mostly unfinished or semi-finished cloth took the lead in the emergence of capitalism at this time.

But how do we get from close networks of small towns and proto-industrialization to emerging capitalism? As market centres, small towns provided essential products and services to industrial villages, and while this may have contributed to the transition, by itself it was not a transforming function.

[10] Brenner, 'Low Countries'.

[11] C. Dyer, 'Small Towns 1270–1540', in D. M. Palliser (ed.), *The Cambridge Urban History of Britain, vol. I, 600–1540* (Cambridge, 2000), 505–40.

[12] Taken from Dyer, 'Small Towns 1270–1540', 509.

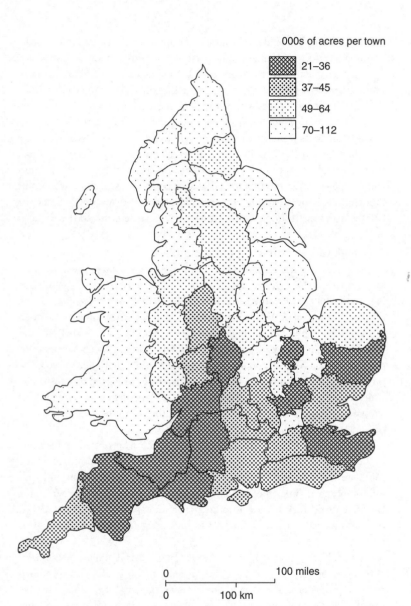

000s of acres per town

■ 21–36
▨ 37–45
▧ 49–64
☐ 70–112

0 ⊢————————⊣ 100 miles
0 ⊢————————⊣ 100 km

Fig. 1. Density of small towns in England and Wales, 1270–1540

Nor was proto-industrialization in itself an indicator of emerging capitalism. Rural industry was well established in England before the Black Death, and rural industrial expansion in north-western Europe in this period was more likely to develop as a means for the small peasantry to compensate for the fragmentation of their landholdings at a time of intense demographic pressure.[13]

As Hilton recognized, the textile industry of most of the traditional urban centres in England was relocated by the late fifteenth century in both small towns and villages. Clearly the high density of small towns in these areas facilitated this move.[14] This is an important point because the general impression is that this migration was from urban to 'rural industry'. These small towns included Dursley, Wotton-under-Edge, Minchinhampton, and Bisley in Gloucestershire; Tiverton, Cullompton, and Crediton in Devon; Malmesbury, Trowbridge, Devizes, and Bradford-on-Avon in Wiltshire; Lavenham and Hadleigh in Suffolk; Coggeshall in Essex; Cranbrook in Kent, and Newbury in Berkshire.[15] David Rollison has also emphasized the small-town nature of the textile industry by the early sixteenth century. He found that the clothiers of Gloucestershire, who were the industrial organizers, tended to be based in the small towns, while production, the spinning and weaving, mostly took place in the surrounding villages. A contemporary estimate of 1608 based on muster calculated that 55 per cent of clothiers in Gloucestershire and 36 per cent of weavers and 26 per cent of broadweavers lived in the towns.[16] This is beyond our period and we can apply these figures to the situation a hundred years earlier only very cautiously. However, using evidence from all sources between the 1480s and the 1540s, Michael Zell calculates that a third of the clothiers in the whole of the Weald of Kent lived in Cranbrook alone; and the muster of 1522 counted thirty-three clothiers in Lavenham out of a total population of only 1100.[17] Certainly the

---

[13] Brenner, 'Low Countries', 287, 300, 316.

[14] Hilton, 'Crisis', 136.

[15] D. Rollison, *The Local Origins of Modern Society: Gloucestershire 1500–1800* (London, 1992), 21–44; E. Carus-Wilson, 'The Woollen Industry before 1550', in E. Crittall (ed.), *Victoria County History of Wiltshire, vol. 4* (Oxford, 1959), 115–47; C. Dyer, *Making a Living in the Middle Ages: The People of Britain 850–1520* (New Haven and London, 2002), 308–9, 325–7; M. Zell, *Industry in the Countryside: Wealden Society in the Sixteenth Century* (Cambridge, 1994), 153–227; D. Dymond and A. Betterton, *Lavenham: 700 years of Textile Making* (Woodbridge, 1982).

[16] D. Rollison, 'Discourse and Class Struggle: The Politics of Industry in Early Modern England', *Social History*, 26 (2001), 170.

[17] Zell, *Industry*, 155; Dymond and Betterton, *Lavenham*, 12, 26.

most well-known and successful clothier families who accumulated modest fortunes in and from the second half of the fifteenth century were associated with these small towns. For example, the families of Greenway of Tiverton and Lane of Cullompton, Paycock of Coggeshall, Spring of Lavenham, Terumber alias Towker, Horton, Bailly, Langford, and Stumpe of the Wiltshire towns, Draner and Courthop of Cranbrook, Winchcombe of Newbury.[18] Rollison points out, however, that although designated in wills and other records as living in an urban parish, the larger clothiers of Gloucestershire generally lived at their mills a mile or two from the particular small town. E. M. Carus-Wilson made a similar point about the Wiltshire clothiers, although she argued that while production may have taken place in their mills just outside the towns, their business headquarters would have been in the towns. Judging by the patronage some of the wealthier clothiers lavished on these towns before 1550, and the modern survival of their substantial town houses, this must have been the case.[19]

This is as one might expect given the significance of small towns within wider commercial networks, ultimately connected with London, and also given the political institutions in small towns that would have facilitated economic organization. The growing political influence of these clothiers generated a qualitative change, as did their activities and strategies in investment, production, and marketing. They controlled all aspects of production and marketing from the production and acquisition of raw materials to the semi-finishing, and finally selling of the cloths mostly to merchants in London by the late fifteenth century for export to the rising Antwerp entrepot. They derived their wool from their own large sheep flocks, supplemented by that of local and non-local graziers. They put it out to hundreds of spinners and weavers in the local districts, and as skilled fullers and often dyers, they or their servants semi-finished the woven cloth at their own mills and premises.

All studies identify the relentless investment by clothiers of the profits from the textile industry into land and other property such as town houses. In the most detailed study to date of an expanding industrial region in England in this period, Zell reveals that in Kent *the rise of the clothiers was fundamentally based upon their ability to accumulate land*. Profits from industrial production were invested in a steady process of accumulation of property and this was rented out. But, in what was a symbiotic, interdependent process, the rents

[18] See note 15.

[19] Rollison, 'Discourse and Class Struggle', 170, and 170 n. 19; Carus-Wilson, 'Woollen Industry', 134–6; G. D. Ramsay, *The Wiltshire Woollen Industry in the Sixteenth and Seventeenth Centuries* (London, 1965), 40–3.

supported increased industrial investment. Moreover, while famous clothier families such as the Springs of Lavenham in Suffolk bought themselves into the gentry, as merchants of the large provincial towns and London were fond of doing, this does not appear to have been typical of clothiers generally. Zell selects Stephen Sharp and Alexander Dence of Cranbrook, who both died in the early 1570s and were the sons of earlier clothiers, as typical of the most successful Wealden clothier families. While they accumulated large landholdings of hundreds of acres, the income from renting was used to expand the textile business and not for ambitions within the squirearchy.[20] Three clothiers of the small towns of Bradford-on-Avon and Trowbridge in Wiltshire were identified by Leland in 1542 as having been the most successful in one of the foremost textile regions. As Carus-Wilson points out: 'each ran a clothmaking business which continued in the family for at least three generations, a business closely linked with the possession of fulling mills, and each built a modest fortune which was invested in land, houses and mills'.[21]

To add to their capitalist credentials, the clothiers in the successful clothmaking regions were market sensitive in the long term and innovative in the face of changing demand. Zell points out that the remarkable array of coloured cloth produced in the Weald of Kent by the 1560s is indicative of the response to changing market conditions, namely the general stagnation in demand for heavy broadcloths in traditional European markets, and the rise of the light and colourful New Draperies. He argues that the de-industrialization of the Weald during the seventeenth century was the result of a long-term failure of entrepreneurship in that region, holding on as it did to its exceptionally high quality but heavy broadcloths despite earlier innovation in design and colour. Cloth production in Gloucestershire in the second half of the sixteenth century successfully responded in line with the demand for lighter cloths. It did not finally collapse until the 1820s, when it was unable to compete with the growing agglomerations of small towns and industrial villages that made up the industrial complexes of modern Manchester and Birmingham.[22]

We can identify therefore by the late fifteenth century, *agency* for agrarian accumulation and specialization, industrial investment, and organization along emerging capitalist lines, all embodied in the person of the small-town clothier and his emerging yeoman class. So the significance of the survival of high densities of small towns in England into the early sixteenth

---

[20] Zell, *Industry*, 219–27.

[21] Carus-Wilson, 'Woollen Industry', 140–3. See also Ramsay, *Wiltshire Industry*, 42–5.

[22] Rollison, *Local Origins*, 29–41, 55; Zell, *Industry*, 145, 244–6.

century for the transition was not simply the comparatively large measure of commercial activity at this level. Certainly, close networks of small towns and their districts provided for an environment in which the agents of agrarian and industrial specialization had easy access to markets and labour. However, crucially, the significance lies in the extent to which a *qualitative* change in both economic and political structural terms was generated. Having said this, historians may feel that questions regarding the connection between the lords' original foundation of high densities of small towns, mostly before 1300, and their subsequent association c.1400–1600 with rural industrialization and the emergence of capitalism have not been adequately addressed in this conclusion.

The successful foundation of small towns ensured a significant increase in revenue for lords from tolls and court fines, it provided easier access to a limited range of necessary goods for the rural-based lords and peasantry, and it enabled the peasantry to exchange their surplus food for cash which lords increasingly demanded for their own expenditure. Factors determining the *densities* of the original foundation of small towns were the nature of terrain, land fertility, and particular regional economies and cultures.[23] But these early foundations were supplemented by new industrial towns after 1350 such as Stroud in Gloucestershire's industrial Stour Valley, and Pensford in Somerset, and that towns founded in one context could take on a new lease of life and develop new functions in another is to be expected.[24] This is what happened in England.

The small town, enclosure and the emergence of capitalism

A neglected aspect of the changes in the political and economic structures of English urban society in the fifteenth and early sixteenth centuries has been the enclosure movement.[25] One probable reason for this neglect is the extent to which the significance of enclosure before 1550 is played down or even denied by historians. Indeed, it has been argued in a recent study that

---

[23] Dyer, 'Small Towns', 510.

[24] Dyer, *Making a Living*, 308; C. Dyer, *An Age of Transition: Economy and Society in England in the Later Middle Ages* (Oxford, 2005), 193–4. This was published after this paper was written.

[25] By 'engrossment' and 'enclosure' I refer to the accumulation and merging of scattered or adjacent plots of land by force or otherwise for the purposes of agrarian specialization. By 'enclosure movement' I refer to the generalization and consolidation of this process in England from the middle of the fifteenth century. I distinguish this process from enclosure into small severalty which had long been a feature in regions such as Kent that were relatively free from serfdom.

significant structural changes towards agrarian capitalism in England occurred only after 1580.[26] The significance of agrarian accumulation and specialization for the rise of the small-town capitalist clothiers from the middle of
the fifteenth century has been demonstrated above. For the rest of the paper I
want to pursue further the relationship between towns and enclosure in the
period between 1450 and 1550, as it offers an explanation for the changes to
urban society as a whole by the early sixteenth century, and provides an
important dimension to accounts which tend to regard emerging agrarian
capitalism solely from a rural perspective.

Rodney Hilton's comparison of English and French towns reveals widespread landholding among townspeople in England and France of plots
within and outside the towns across the medieval period, and this has been
echoed by many other studies. It emphasizes an important aspect of the
multi-occupational character of artisan households, and the significance of
a measure of independent non-market sources of food in urban household
economies. It included access to common land as well as additional cultivated
plots. Although landholding by townspeople was not so extensive in England,
some 80 per cent of urban families' property in Hilton's French sample
included vineyards. This significance of access to land in England was brought
out in the bitter conflicts over common pasture rights in the larger English
towns between the late fourteenth and early sixteenth centuries in towns such
as Cambridge, York, Durham, Coventry and Bristol, the result of enclosure of
common pasture land in the fields around the towns by wealthy merchants
and ecclesiastical landowners based in the towns.[27] A late fifteenth-century
Coventry petition during serious troubles between the merchant oligarchy
and the artisan commoners between the 1470s and 1490s is telling. Following
the ploughing up of the city's common lands by the merchants after widespread enclosure for grazing had taken place, it stated that without the right
of pasturing their cattle and horses 'the commoners & inhabitants . . . cannot
well liff & meynteyn ther occupacions & menyall servauntes'. This was hardly
an exaggeration given the serious decline of Coventry, and the extent of the
conflict that was only finally put down in 1525 by a state military force.[28]
Rodney Hilton argued that, along with movements against taxation, enclosure disputes were more prominent in social disturbances in towns than those

[26] J. Whittle, *The Development of Agrarian Capitalism: Land and Labour in Norfolk
1440–1580* (Oxford, 2000).

[27] Hilton, *English and French*, 29, 78–83, 143–4; J. Vanes (ed.), *The Ledger of John Smythe
1538–1550*, (Bristol Record Society, 28, 1975), 23.

[28] C. Phythian-Adams, *Desolation of a City: Coventry and the Urban Crisis of the Late Middle
Ages* (Cambridge, 1979) 134, 252–7.

of specific craft grievances over merchant restrictions on their trades, and more prevalent in England because of the successful enclosure movement than in France, although it was a feature there too.[29]

The increasing restrictions by merchant governors on artisan independence and political representation, the decline in lords' incomes and luxury demand, the disruption of trade with France and the growth of London can hardly be discounted, but one can identify a central cause of urban decline in the larger provincial towns with the processes of engrossment and enclosure involving townspeople. To take the case of Coventry again, the hundred within which Coventry was situated was the most enclosed in Warwickshire, and this county was the most enclosed in the midlands.[30] The extensive turning over to pasture may have been detrimental to the grain supply to the city especially during the dearth of the 1520s when the final major conflict took place. But what was most significant was that the commoners of the town—middling artisans and traders—lost an important measure of non-market access to food with the loss of holdings, seriously affecting the balance of their household economies and having knock-on effects for craft production and the prosperity of the city as a whole. In this way the enclosure movement can be seen to have had a negative effect on the larger provincial towns in England.

I have indicated above in general terms how accumulation of land and enclosure by small town clothiers drove further investment in the textile industry. But what happened to small towns more generally? Because of the survival of substantial evidence of its urban administration and the character of landholding in its surrounding manors in the fifteenth and sixteenth centuries, the small town of Lydd on Romney Marsh in Kent may be used as an example.[31] Rentals, deeds, and wills reveal that a broad range of townspeople held land on a small scale in the first half of the fifteenth century, as Hilton found elsewhere. Dengemarsh, for which most evidence survives, was a substantial manor of approximately 950 acres including a 300-acre demesne farm extending from the town to the coast. In 1432 the assize rents were fragmented into very small plots in 'enclosed' severalty split between eighty-three holders. The rents exhibited increased fragmentation from the 1370s thereby revealing the popularity of the area at a time of demographic downturn. This was possibly due to diverse occupational opportunities and

---

[29] Hilton, *English and French*, 143–4.

[30] Phythian-Adams, *Desolation*, 57.

[31] For more detail, see S. Dimmock, 'English Small Towns and the Emergence of Capitalist Relations c.1450–1550', *Urban History*, 28 (2001), 5–25.

relatively representative governing institutions. Despite being enclosed, holdings were not consolidated but, on the contrary, were typically scattered to take advantage of diverse land-use. The eighty-three landholders in 1432 included at the very least thirty-six townsmen whom we know by their performance of offices in Lydd, and there were probably many more who do not appear in the official record. Of 468 Lydd wills examined between the 1450s and 1550s, 39 per cent of testators bequeathed land and a similar number bequeathed livestock, and this figure should be increased significantly because many testators used their wills simply to make provision for prayers and debts. These plots supported a relatively prosperous population of petty traders, craftsmen, fishermen and mariners. Some husbandmen were also present along with a few relatively large farmers who benefited from the availability of seigneurial demesne and other land within and outside Lydd parish from the late fourteenth century.

Romney Marsh became the main source of wool for the Weald of Kent textile industry. However, the traditional structures of landholding and government in the mid-fifteenth century at places such as Lydd would clearly have been a substantial obstacle to an adequate increase in supply prior to the consolidation of the industry in the second half of the fifteenth century and its take-off in the early sixteenth. In the 1460s pressure, often violent, for enclosure on Dengemarsh began, and caused middling and poorer townsmen and women to defend their holdings on Dengemarsh in the borough court from encroachment against improving manorial demesne farmers. These farmers were also townsmen of Lydd, and were backed by Battle Abbey to which the manor belonged, and its merchant sub-stewards. The highly organized resistance failed and, following an extremely violent period in the late fifteenth and early sixteenth century, the eighty-three holders had been reduced to thirty-two, holdings had been consolidated and large farms had been carved out of the old structure in addition to an enlarged demesne farm. By the 1520s social relations in the town had undergone a process of polarization, and this process was clearly congruent with the context of enclosure. This was reflected, on the one hand, by increasing numbers of people unable to pay the town tax in the 1520s as shown from annual lists of debtors in the town's chamberlains' accounts, appeals by the common council against increasing poverty, and punitive legislation against vagabondage and the imprisonment of beggars, and on the other hand by the transformation in the government of the town from a juratcy or governing council of twelve made up of a broad range of occupations with a customary 50 per cent turnover each year, to a permanent oligarchy by the 1510s increasingly made up of yeomen and minor gentry with extensive sheep flocks; this was entirely so by 1550. By the 1580s, at the latest, the members of the oligarchy of Lydd, a town with no more than a thousand inhabitants, had extended their operations well beyond the parish, and in a petition of 1583 to Chancery, two of them were said to be,

> men of wounderfull wealth, and tenauntes to diuers of the most worshipfull gentlemen of the said County of Kent of their marshe lands in Romney Marsh and theraboutes, whose ayed and frendship the said defendants so greatly expect that they thinke to coloure vp ther great faultes which are in trueth the ingrossinge vp of the greatest part of the mershe landes in those parties into there own handes and turning yt all to grasing, so that tillage for bread, keeping of melch kyne for butter and chese is not there vsed whereby the countries adioyninge are destitute of both bread butter and chese, a generall hinderaunce to the poor people theraboutes dwelling and also therby maney of the townes in the mershe there are destroyed and layed wast. . .[32]

The borough court of Lydd records that the Tudor statutes against damaging over-specialization had been ignored in this way for decades, as had traditional landmarks and common rights of way.[33]

Conclusion

To develop Rodney Hilton's hypothesis on the relationship between the relatively high density of English towns and the transition from feudalism to capitalism, and also Christopher Dyer's work on densities within England, I will make the following propositions. The survival of close networks of small towns in England through to the sixteenth century provided a crucial context for improving farmers and clothiers from the middle of the fifteenth century, enabling them to accumulate, organize, and thereby generate the transition. As markets linked to a wider urban hierarchy and increasingly within the orbit of London, they served as a practical organizational focus for the cloth industry and wool trade. As centres of administration they provided a power base that served to facilitate practical organization. For the farmers and clothiers of the small towns, to a greater or lesser extent in alliance with other groups such as merchants and landlords, the accumulation and enclosure of land on the one hand, and the consolidation of political power on the other, formed an interdependent, symbiotic process. Of course, the stimulus for these developments came from continental demand and the growth of

---

[32] PRO, C2/Eliz/B20/17.

[33] Lydd Borough Archive, Ly/JQs 1; S. Dimmock, 'Class and the Social Transformation of a Late Medieval Small Town: Lydd c.1450–1550', unpublished PhD thesis, University of Kent at Canterbury (1998), 234–54.

London, but the agricultural supply response, at once both rural and urban, was, to paraphrase Robert Brenner, conditioned by the existing property structures and balance of class forces.

The example of Lydd, and the activities of clothiers outlined above, suggests that small towns may have provided a context for early, enforced enclosure. Increasing allegations of illegal evictions of villagers and enclosure of arable land for pasture, led to the Commission of 1517. However, like the 1536 Act that followed, it was only equipped to investigate cases that took place after 1485, and yet the evidence, particularly the perceptions of high-profile contemporaries, suggests that serious damage had been done in the decades before that year. Maurice Beresford argued that this circumscribing of the Commissioners' remit was most likely the result of pressure from the landholding lobby on Chancellor Wolsey. The lords had for the previous few decades kept silent in 'dumb defiance' about the accumulations of farmers (their lessees with whom they often shared mutual interests), following the first Statute against enclosures as early as 1489 which charged them with reporting enclosures.[34] Moreover it is notable that the preamble to the 1517 Commission blamed the decay of farms and the depopulation of villages in the previous decades on urban investors and speculators who encroached on the land to enclose it for pasture.[35] Did small towns become a context for struggle between lords experiencing a crisis of income by the third quarter of the fifteenth century, and peasants migrating to areas of freer tenure and diverse occupational opportunities? And did this context facilitate the separation of the peasant elite in the form of farmers and clothiers from the rest of the peasantry as a class? If it could be demonstrated in future research that the experience of Lydd was more generalized over England, then an important feature of England's transition will have been identified.[36]

---

[34] See the discussion in M. Beresford, *The Lost Villages of England* (Gloucester, 1983), 102–33, out of fashion of late.

[35] Beresford, *Lost Villages*, 105.

[36] For evidence of evictions of peasants from manors under their control, and the invasion of common lands by clothiers of the small industrial towns, see Carus-Wilson, 'Woollen industry', 136; and Ramsey, *Wiltshire Industry*, 32, 45.

The Transition in the Low Countries: Wage Labour as an Indicator of the Rise of Capitalism in the Countryside, 1300–1700

Bas (B.J.P.) van Bavel[1]

What kind of transition?

This article deals with the transition from feudalism to capitalism. The use of these terms is no longer self-evident, perhaps because of their ideological charge. Instead, most historians now prefer to use such vague notions as 'modernization' and 'rationalization', often without being more specific. We also hear of 'the transition from the medieval to the early modern society', as if this transition involved no more than crossing a chronological boundary. This lack of specificity hampers research. Here we will use what is perhaps a subjective and very restricted but nevertheless sharp definition of the transition from feudalism to capitalism, namely the transformation of a society dominated by small, independent producers who had a strong grip on the means of production and whose produce was partly extracted by non-economic force, into a society in which there is a pronounced division between propertyless wage-earners and entrepreneurs who own the means of production, and thus have a way to appropriate the surplus.[2] This definition leads to a number of elements to be investigated in order to analyse the transition and to define its chronology. These elements are property relations, relationships involved in surplus extraction, and the rise of wage labour as personal bondage disappeared.

In order to explain structural changes in this field, historians have often looked at such factors as the rise of trade, cities and markets and the monetization of the economy. In some definitions of the transition these elements are presented as though they constitute the heart of the transition, and in others as though they were at the least the driving forces behind it. In most of

---

[1] I should like to thank Petra van Dam (VU Amsterdam), Oscar Gelderblom (Universiteit Utrecht), Jan Lucassen (IISG Amsterdam), Maarten Prak (Universiteit Utrecht), Eric Vanhaute (Universiteit Gent), Jan Luiten van Zanden (IISG Amsterdam/Universiteit Utrecht) and the participants of the conference 'Rodney Hilton's Middle Ages' for their comments on earlier drafts of this paper.

[2] This is in line with, for instance, the definition suggested by R. H. Hilton, 'Capitalism— What's in a Name', *Past and Present*, 1 (1952), 32–43.

the older studies on structural changes in the economy and society, cities were almost automatically the focus of attention, following the traditional idea that these were the new, non-feudal elements in a rural feudal sea, where developments and changes first occurred.[3] This point of view provoked criticism,[4] and resulted in an intense debate. However, recently it has become even clearer that this focus on the cities is no longer tenable. It is now clear that cities too could be an integral part of a feudal structure—for instance, with the use of privileges and force, and the exercise of non-economic power—and that they did not at all always undergo a rapid transition.[5] It seems that sometimes changes were even more rapid in the countryside. Publications on proto-industrialization, for instance, suggest that capitalist relations of production often emerged earlier in rural industries than in many cities dominated by guilds and small commodity production.[6] Some authors even maintain that the rise of agrarian capitalism was an essential prerequisite for the transition of the economy and of society as a whole.[7] These ideas are increasingly incorporated into studies published on the transition, where full attention is paid to the countryside and particularly to the interaction between town and country.

I will follow this line here, by concentrating on the rural transition. Following the definition suggested above, one of the most important elements of investigation are the production relationships, and more particularly the importance of wage labour. Although the rise of wage labour forms a crucial element in every definition of capitalism, it has not been thoroughly investigated. This applies not only to the nature and organization of wage labour, but also to its quantitative aspects. Some effort has been devoted to the development of wages, but hardly any to the assessment of the importance

[3] A tradition of historical thought advocated by such scholars as H. Pirenne, e.g. in *Medieval Cities. Their Origins and the Revival of Trade* (Princeton, 1952), esp. 193–231, and P. Sweezy.

[4] For instance by M. Dobb, *Studies in the Development of Capitalism* (London/Henley, 1978), 70–82. Cf. also the contributions by Dobb, Hilton and Sweezy in R. Hilton (ed.), *The Transition from Feudalism to Capitalism* (London, 1976).

[5] R. H. Hilton, 'Towns in English Feudal Society', *Review*, 3 (1979), 3–20; R. J. Holton, *Cities, Capitalism and Civilization* (London, 1986), esp. 64–89; and S. R. Epstein, 'Cities, Regions, and the Late Medieval Crisis: Sicily and Tuscany Compared', *Past and Present*, 130 (1991), 3–50, esp. 14–16 and 28–33.

[6] P. Kriedte, H. Medick, and J. Schlumbohm, 'Einleitung', in id. (eds), *Industrialisierung vor der Industrialisierung. Gewerbliche Warenproduktion auf dem Land in der Formationsperiode des Kapitalismus* (Göttingen, 1978), 13–35, esp. 26–33.

[7] R. Brenner, 'The Agrarian Roots of European Capitalism', *Past and Present*, 97 (1982), 16–113, esp. 18 and 110–13.

of wage labour in the pre-industrial period, least of all in the countryside. Often it is assumed that wage labour in the European countryside was not important until after 1600 or even 1700, but only a few estimates or calculations are available. With the absence of hard figures, the importance of wage labour is often equated with the degree of urbanization, considered as the best proxy for the expansion of the wage-earning population.[8] For most parts of late medieval and early modern Europe, calculations of the percentage of town dwellers will result in a low figure. If the small proportion of wage workers is often assumed to be mainly urban, the share for the countryside appears even lower.

Concrete calculations are rather scarce. The few existing estimates of the importance of wage labour in the late medieval and early modern countryside are mainly limited to England. Moreover, these estimates are based almost solely on the tax returns of 1524 and 1525, which are ambiguous in their meaning. Still, most of these calculations and the more general estimates based on censuses and other data show remarkably similar results, with the share of wage workers in the total rural population in different English regions in the sixteenth century amounting to between a quarter and a third.[9] For example, in Norfolk in around 1525, 20–35 per cent of the rural population consisted of wage labourers, a proportion which remained more or less constant during the rest of the sixteenth century.[10] In other parts of England (such as Leicestershire and Lincolnshire) in the sixteenth century, wage labour amounted to c. 20–33 per cent of the total rural population.[11] Other authors have surmised that in both the late fourteenth and the early sixteenth century about a third of the population, and sometimes even more, obtained most of their living from wage labour.[12] This is somewhat higher

[8] This equation is made, for instance, in the ingenious attempt to link coin production, wage levels, and the incidence of wage labour in the Netherlands: J. Lucassen, 'Wage Payments and Currency Circulation in the Netherlands from 1200–2000', working paper Amsterdam/Den Haag (2002).

[9] See also the general estimate for c.1600 by A. Everitt, 'Farm Labourers', in J. Thirsk (ed.), *The Agrarian History of England and Wales* part 4 (1967), 396–465, esp. 397–400.

[10] J. Whittle, *The Development of Agrarian Capitalism. Land and Labour in Norfolk, 1440–1580* (Oxford, 2000), 227–31, with some notes by the author on the reliability and interpretation of the data in the sources.

[11] J. P. Cooper, 'In Search of Agrarian Capitalism', in T. H. Aston and C. H. E. Philpin (eds), *The Brenner Debate: Agrarian Class Structure and Economic Development in Pre-industrial Europe* (Cambridge, 1985), 138–91, esp. 167–8.

[12] C. Dyer, *Standards of Living in the Later Middle Ages. Social Change in England, c.1200–1520* (Cambridge, 1989), 211–14, and R. H. Hilton, 'Some Social and Economic Evidence in Late Medieval English Tax Returns', in *Class Conflict and the Crisis of*

than the rough estimates of the share of proletarians in town and countryside in all of western Europe around 1500, that is, *c.* 25 per cent.[13]

Probably the dominance of quantitative investigations from England in this field is no coincidence, since the rural economy in England is generally thought to have been the first to undergo fundamental changes, most notably during the 'long sixteenth century'. Although recent literature reveals a more nuanced view of both the profoundness and the pace of these changes, English phenomena such as enclosure, engrossment and the rise of a rural proletariat are still the hallmarks of an early transition towards agrarian capitalism. Here, however, we will look across the North Sea to the Low Countries, where an early transition of the rural economy can also be assumed to have taken place, although it is not as well documented as the one in England. This paper will start with a general overview of our present knowledge on the rural transition in the Low Countries, with a special emphasis on the strong regional differences in the area (Fig. 1). The investigation into the rise of wage labour undertaken here will focus on two regions in the Low Countries—namely central Holland and the Guelders river area—around the middle of the sixteenth century, and the share of rural labour input provided by wage labour will be established. The results will allow us to substantiate the general overview of the transition, and to draw some comparisons with England, thus offering opportunities for understanding better both the chronology and the varied character of the rural transition.

Rural transition in the Low Countries: a general overview

All the preconditions for a rapid transition of the rural economy and society were present in the Low Countries from an early date. Forms of unfreedom and serfdom had been very weak, as in the county of Holland, or they had declined very early, with the dissolution of manorialism between the eleventh and fourteenth centuries.[14] Even in regions where manorialism had been very strong in the high middle ages, such as in the Dutch river area and the county of Namur, the manorial system declined from the eleventh century onwards

---

Feudalism. Essays in Medieval Social History (London, 1985), 253–67, esp. 261–7 (Cotswold), and id., *Bond Men Made Free. Medieval Peasant Movements and the English Rising of 1381* (London, 1977), 170–4.

[13] C. Tilly, 'Demographic Origins of the European Proletariat', in D. Levine (ed.), *Proletarianization and Family History* (Orlando,1984), 1–85, esp. 35–6. This, however, is not similar to the share of wage labour, cf. ibid., 13–17.

[14] For Flanders: E. Thoen, *Landbouwekonomie en bevolking in Vlaanderen gedurende de late middeleeuwen en het begin van de moderne tijden. Testregio: de kasselrijen van Oudenaarde en Aalst, eind 13de—eerste helft van de 16de eeuw* (Gent, 1988), 470–4.

and almost completely disappeared in the fourteenth century, except for some unimportant remnants.[15] The disappearance of elements of personal unfreedom enabled the rise of wage labour and the emergence of a labour market. Moreover, the Low Countries, and particularly their north-western parts, witnessed an early commodification of land, a development that gained momentum as early as the thirteenth and fourteenth centuries. Directly connected to this, was the early development towards exclusive and absolute property rights to land, and the rise of short-term leasing, which became the dominant form of tenancy in some regions as early as around 1300. Open, flexible, competitive, and secure land and lease markets thus emerged in the Low Countries several centuries earlier than in most other parts of the North Sea area.[16]

Furthermore, those elements which are often labelled as indicators, or even as main causes, of the rural transition were present here, namely buoyant trade, flourishing markets, a money economy, and booming cities. In the western, northern and central parts of the Low Countries all these elements were firmly established as early as the thirteenth century. From the fourteenth century onwards, the Low Countries had by far the highest percentage of the population in Europe living in towns, as well as some of the most important centres of trade, namely Bruges, Ghent, and Antwerp. But, despite the omnipresence of cities, trade, and money in almost all of the Low Countries, there were marked regional differences in the transition of the rural economy.[17]

The transition evolved very early, mainly in the fourteenth to sixteenth centuries, in the Dutch river area, coastal Flanders and coastal Frisia. Here, the transition evolved along agricultural lines. These regions saw the rise of large tenant farms, a growth in the importance of wage labour and a strong specialization and commercialization in agriculture.[18] In Holland, the transition

---

[15] L. Genicot, *L'économie rurale Namuroise au bas Moyen Age (1199–1429)*, part I (Louvain, 1943), 19–36, 75–8, 106–10, 120–1, 152–3, 299.

[16] B. J. P. van Bavel, 'The Land Market in the North Sea Area in a Comparative Perspective, 13th–18th Centuries', in S. Cavaciocchi (ed.), *Il mercato della terra secc. XIII–XVIII* (Atti delle "Settimane di Studi" e altri convegni, 35, 2003), 119–45 and 183–8.

[17] See also R. Brenner, 'The Low Countries in the Transition to Capitalism', in P. Hoppenbrouwers and J. L. van Zanden (eds), *Peasants into Farmers? The Transformation of Rural Economy and Society in the Low Countries (Middle Ages—19th Century) in Light of the Brenner Debate* (CORN Publication Series, 4. 2001), 275–338, esp. 302–25, diverging somewhat here from his earlier studies, where he compared differences between countries or even larger areas.

[18] B. J. P. van Bavel, 'Land, Lease and Agriculture. The Transition of the Rural Economy in the Dutch River Area from the Fourteenth to the Sixteenth Century', *Past and Present*, 172 (2001), 3–43.

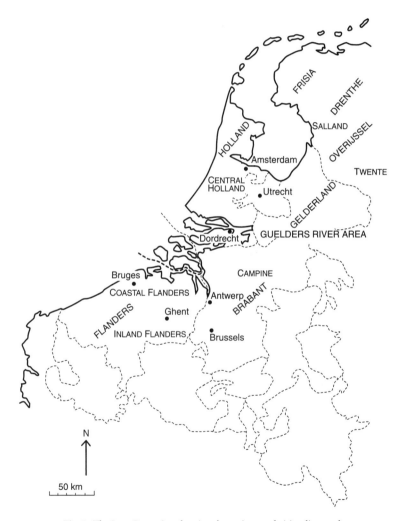

FRISIA

DRENTHE

SALLAND

HOLLAND

OVERIJSSEL

TWENTE

Amsterdam

CENTRAL
HOLLAND

Utrecht

GELDERLAND

Dordrecht

GUELDERS RIVER AREA

Bruges

CAMPINE

COASTAL FLANDERS

Antwerp

BRABANT

FLANDERS

Ghent

INLAND FLANDERS

Brussels

N

50 km

Fig. 1. The Low Countries, showing the regions and cities discussed

of the rural economy took longer and evolved in two phases. During the fourteenth century, the countryside was still mainly an agrarian peasant economy, characterized by family-sized owner-occupied holdings, but in that and the following century Holland witnessed a great expansion in proto-industrial activities, to a large extent aimed at markets in the surrounding regions or even overseas. This proto-industrial sector, and particularly the activities most typical of Holland (such as peat digging, brick production and fisheries) underwent a process by which the scale of production expanded, the means of production accumulated in fewer hands, and wage labour increased, developments which reached a peak in the sixteenth century.[19] At this point, and further evolving in the late sixteenth and the seventeenth century, agriculture started to develop along similar lines to the ones found earlier in the Dutch river area, also driven by the rise of large tenant farms, thus completing the transition to rural capitalism in the countryside of Holland.

Inland Flanders, although it was highly urbanized and also witnessed a strong rise of proto-industries, did not undergo a transition in the late medieval or the early modern period. Agriculture and industrial activities were often combined on peasants' own smallholdings, where they had their own means of production and enjoyed economic independence. Industrial activity was mainly aimed at the market—in the case of the linen sector, even at markets all over Europe—but agriculture was mainly aimed at subsistence, with a strong dominance of bread grains and, later, potatoes. It was only in the eighteenth and nineteenth centuries that a transition of the rural economy took place here.[20] In Twente and the north of Brabant, which were dominated by small cottagers, this happened even later. In the seventeenth and eighteenth centuries a process of proto-industrialization began, with a combination of putting-out and subsistence farming on small, free peasant holdings.[21] After c.1850, these rural industries were evolving towards factory capitalism, thus making these formerly peasant-dominated regions the first in the Netherlands to industrialize.[22] In Drenthe, a sandy inland region in the east of the Netherlands, the transition of the rural economy took even longer. Apart from some intensification and minor increases in the degree of

[19] See below, pp. x–x.
[20] E. Thoen, 'A "Commercial Survival Economy" in Evolution. The Flemish Countryside and the Transition to Capitalism (Middle Ages-19th Century)', in Hoppenbrouwers and van Zanden (eds), *Peasants into Farmers?*, 102–57, esp. 112–23, 137 and 147.
[21] C. Trompetter, *Agriculture, Proto-Industry and Mennonite Entrepreneurship. A History of the Textile Industries in Twente, 1600–1815* (Amsterdam, 1997), 48–54 and 64–7.
[22] J. Mokyr, *Industrialization in the Low Countries, 1795–1850* (New Haven, 1976), 99–114 (Twente) and 114–21 (Brabant).

commercialization, here the peasant structure remained largely intact.[23] On their small or medium-sized farms, and with the use of extensive common lands, the peasant families concentrated on cultivating bread grains and on some small-scale livestock farming, mainly for their own subsistence. Here, it was not until the late nineteenth century that a structural change in the economy and society took place. The same applies to the Campine, a sandy part of inland Brabant, where the last remnants of the rural subsistence economy lost their functional importance as late as the mid-twentieth century.[24]

Regional differences in the Low Countries were thus very strong, both in the chronology of the transition and in its nature. In this respect, the Low Countries must be divided into a number of regions, some twenty in total, situated close to one another yet differing sharply. Although interaction between these regions was often intense, by way of exchange of goods, products, capital, and labour, and peasant regions were linked to the capitalist regions already at an early stage, this did not even out the differences. On the contrary, the interaction at first sharpened social and economic differences between regions, and consolidated them over longer periods.

Urbanization and distance to markets did not determine this regional development, as is demonstrated by the late transition in highly urbanized inland Flanders, as opposed to the early transition in coastal Flanders and the Dutch river area. This is not to deny that markets were an essential prerequisite for the transition. Regions where an agrarian transition took place were marketing their products mainly in these highly urbanized regions, whereas Holland, for instance, was selling its proto-industrial products in exactly those regions specializing in agricultural production.[25] Through the favourable market structures, regional specialization and complementarity were increasing markedly in the Low Countries in the fifteenth and sixteenth centuries. Regions which were located further away from urban markets had fewer chances to participate in this interaction. But proximity to markets had a limited influence, as many products were easy and cheap to transport, and these could be produced for markets even hundreds of kilometres away. The presence of large cities thus did not lead automatically to the rise of

---

[23] J. L. van Zanden, 'From Peasant Economy to Modern Market-Oriented Agriculture. The Transformation of the Rural Economy of the Eastern Netherlands, 1800–1914', *Economic and Social History in the Netherlands*, 3 (1991), 37–59, esp. 38–40.

[24] E. Vanhaute, 'Processes of Peripheralization in a Core Region. The Campine Area of Antwerp in the 'Long' Nineteenth Century', *Review*, 16 (1993), 57–81, esp. 70–5.

[25] J. L. van Zanden, 'Holland en de Zuidelijke Nederlanden in de periode 1500–1570: divergerende ontwikkelingen of voortgaande integratie', in E. Aerts et al. (eds), *Studia historica oeconomica* (Leuven, 1993) 357–67.

capitalism in the countryside, nor did a region's long distance from large cities necessarily preclude a transition. The determining elements are rather found in the social and economic structures of the regions themselves. All the regions where a transition of the rural economy took place early, before c.1600, were characterized by large landownership, clear property rights, a rapid rise of short-term leasing, large tenant farms, a location where markets were accessible, and weak feudal barriers. The regions dominated by peasant landownership, on the other hand, did not experience transition until the eighteenth or nineteenth centuries, since this landownership structure reduced incentives and/or possibilities to commercialize and accumulate. Furthermore, in some cases feudal power had a continued influence there. Manorialism was rare in the Low Countries after the fourteenth century, but feudal power often took other forms, in urban settings and within market structures, for instance by way of urban privileges, monopolies and market forces.[26] In the Low Countries, this situation existed most clearly in inland Flanders, where it formed an important element in the late transition of this region despite the presence of large cities and markets. In sum, economic and institutional elements, directly linked to social structures and operative on a regional level, were setting both the pace and the chronology of the transition.

Rural wage labour in two regions

In assessing the importance of wage labour in the countryside, we have defined wage labour as contractual labour,[27] performed not independently but for an employer and rewarded by the regular payment of a wage, either in money or in kind. This leaves difficulties in demarcating the blurred boundaries of wage labour, for instance in putting-out or in cases where producers sometimes worked independently on commission, but sometimes also for wages. These varied forms of labour have been disentangled as much as possible, but some estimates or assumptions had to be made. Another aspect that needs to be mentioned is the sharply differing social and economic background of the people supplying the wage labour. At the moment, it is

---

[26] Epstein, 'Cities, Regions, and the Late Medieval Crisis', esp. 14–16 and 28–33.

[27] However, the voluntary character must be nuanced, since wage labour in the pre-industrial period was often coupled with unequal power relationships, artificially fixed low wages, all kinds of restrictions, indenture, dependence, or even unfreedom. See C. Lis and H. Soly, 'Policing the Early Modern Proletariat, 1450–1850', in Levine (ed.), *Proletarianization and Family History*, 163–228, esp. 170–2, or R. J. Steinfeld, *The Invention of Free Labor. The Employment Relation in English and American Law and Culture, 1350–1870* (Chapel Hill, 1991), esp. 3–10.

difficult or even impossible to reconstruct this on a detailed level, but we can attempt to say something about the importance of these different types of wage labour on a macro-level in different regions.

Here, we will investigate two regions for the period around the middle of the sixteenth century, namely the Guelders river area and the central part of Holland. Of the 30,000 rural inhabitants in the first region three-quarters (*c.*22,500) must have been over twelve years old and thus formed the potential labour force, whereas the countryside in central Holland had a potential labour force of 55,000.[28] Both regions have high quality sources and have been the subjects of extensive research. Also, they both witnessed a strong rural transition, but along very different lines, thus offering possibilities for a comparative analysis.

In the absence of tax records supplying data on the importance of wage labour in the countryside before the late seventeenth century, we will undertake a separate, indirect investigation for each of the four sectors in the rural economy, namely agriculture, para-agricultural work (mainly diking and digging), the crafts (including shopkeepers and other services) and proto-industries (non-agricultural, market-oriented activities in the countryside, mainly in textile production). The labour input in these sectors differed sharply between the two regions. In central Holland, labour input in proto-industries was enormous, employing 45 per cent of the rural labour force, whereas agriculture employed only 41 per cent.[29] This contrasts sharply with the situation in the Guelders river area, where agriculture was by far the most important sector (81 per cent of rural labour input), dwarfing the other sectors, namely para-agrarian work (6 per cent), proto-industries (3 per cent) and the crafts and services (10 per cent).

In the Guelders river area, of the total labour input in agriculture, probably 55–60 per cent was performed in wage labour. This high percentage is connected to the extreme proletarization, which forced countrymen to sell their labour. In the period between the mid fifteenth century and *c.*1570, lease land was increasingly accumulated by large tenant farmers,[30] resulting in a

---

[28] R. W. M. van Schaïk, *Belasting, bevolking en bezit in Gelre en Zutphen, 1350–1550* (Hilversum, 1987), 163–6 and 275–6, and J. de Vries, *The Dutch Rural Economy in the Golden Age, 1500–1700* (New Haven/London, 1978), 86–7.

[29] See the more extensive calculation in B. J. P. van Bavel, 'Rural Wage Labour in the 16th-century Low Countries. An Assessment of Nature and Importance of Wage Labour in the Countryside of Holland, Guelders and Flanders', *Continuity and Change*, 21 (2006), 37–72. Para-agrarian work engaged 6 per cent of the rural labour input in Holland, the crafts and services 8 per cent.

[30] Van Bavel, 'Land, Lease and Agriculture'.

decrease of the number of farms by between a third and a half. So, in this region proletarization was not by way of loss of landownership, but because small and medium-sized tenants lost competition in the lease market and were pushed out by large tenant farmers. At the same time, other sources of income were limited here, as the last common lands had been privatized and parcelled out during the fourteenth century, and proto-industrial activities did not develop. In this very polarized society, a large part of the population lost the possibility of working a farm independently, and had become dependent on wage labour in the agricultural sector because of the lack of other possible sources of income.

A reconstruction of the labour input on farms confirms the great importance of wage labour in this region. Agricultural labour input was strongly connected to the size of farms, since large farms often specialized in labour-extensive branches of agriculture and used capital investments to reduce labour inputs, whereas small peasant farmers often specialized in labour-intensive crops in order to use the surplus labour available in their household. Based on calculations of the labour input available for the late eighteenth and nineteenth centuries, with compensation for the rise in labour productivity in the intervening centuries, it can be estimated that farms up to 10 hectares in this region theoretically did not need any external wage labour, but the large farms with their 50 hectares on average obtained 60 per cent of their labour from wage workers.[31] On the basis of this hypothetical calculation of labour inputs, and the distribution of farm sizes in the region, at least 39 per cent of the labour input must have been supplied by wage labourers from outside the household. However, this is only a minimum, since even the smallest farms used some external labour at peak moments of the agricultural cycle. Moreover, the servants living in the household, probably making up 10–15 per cent of the population here,[32] should be added to the wage labourers. About a quarter of agricultural wage labour in this region was performed by these living-in servants, a quarter by people supplementing other means of subsistence with wages, and half by proletarian wage labourers.

Para-agrarian work, mainly digging and diking, was sometimes done by the owners of the land or by the tenants, but not as much as in other regions

---

[31] See the extensive calculation in van Bavel, 'Rural Wage Labour', where the empirical research, the calculations and the sources on which this section is largely based can be found.

[32] H. K. Roessingh, 'Beroep en bedrijf op de Veluwe in het midden van de 18ᵉ eeuw', *A. A. G. Bijdragen*, 13 (1965), 181–274, esp. 243–4 (Veluwe: 19 per cent of population over 10 years), and B. H. Slicher van Bath, *Een samenleving onder spanning. Geschiedenis van het platteland in Overijssel* (Assen, 1957), 109–15 (Overijssel: 13 per cent).

because of the dominance of large landownership and large tenant farms. By contrast, in a rural society dominated by small peasants, they fulfilled their water management obligations by working themselves. Here, most of the labour was done by hired labourers, paid out of the taxes levied for water management. Wage labourers also carried out all of the additional, irregular work on diking, such as that needed after dike bursts or construction projects. Only the regular work on the smaller dikes and the dredging of the smaller watercourses was mostly done by the smaller landowners and tenants themselves. It can be assumed that in total about two-thirds of the labour in digging and diking was performed by wage labourers.

In the crafts and services sector, most enterprises were small scale and depended on household labour. However, a fair number of craftsmen were employed in wage labour by noblemen and by religious institutions. Since no less than c.10 per cent of the population of this region was of noble or semi-noble origin (500 households) and these noblemen no longer had coerced labour or labour services at their disposal, it can be surmised that in total perhaps as many as a thousand servants and craftsmen were employed in wage labour by them. Including the small number of servants employed by independent craftsmen, this is about half of the total work force in this sector. Proto-industries were unimportant, engaging no more than 3 per cent of the total labour force.[33] Except for brick production, employing perhaps 100 workers seasonally, all non-agricultural activities here were very small scale and were performed by those possessing the means of production and working on their own account. In all, here probably a third of the total labour in proto-industry consisted of wage labour.

In Holland, the crafts sector probably accounted for relatively few wage labourers. Some craftsmen employed one or two servants, but no more, and noblemen were so few in Holland (a mere ½ per cent of the population), that hardly any craftsmen performed wage labour for noble households. However, there was one particular activity in the services sector where the importance of wage labour was increasing rapidly in the fifteenth-sixteenth centuries, that is the military. During this period, starting before 1400, there was a clear switch from feudal services and conscripted people to hired soldiers.[34] Digging and diking also took a high proportion of wage labour. An inquiry made in

---

[33] For this and the following assessment of the importance of wage labour see more extensively van Bavel, 'Proto-industrie tussen de Gelderse rivieren?'.

[34] J. A. M. Y. Bos-Rops, *Graven op zoek naar geld. De inkomsten van de graven van Holland en Zeeland, 1389–1433* (Hilversum, 1993) 46–7, 99–103, 143–6, 179–82 and 217–20.

1514,[35] shows that almost all villages contributed to the maintenance of water management works entirely in cash, which was used for paying wage labourers; the same method was used for paying for new sluices, dikes and other larger works, and also for coping with catastrophes. Only the regular work on the smaller dikes was mostly apportioned among the users of the neighbouring parcels of land. In total, around 1550, at least two-thirds of the digging and diking in central Holland was performed by wage labourers.

In the proto-industrial sector, employing no less than 45 per cent of the potential labour force in this region, most labour was originally organized within independent peasant households, but in the course of the fifteenth and sixteenth centuries there was a clear process of accumulation and proletarianization. Thus wage labour and putting-out were already becoming very important in rural industries in Holland during the late middle ages. The importance of wage labour was most pronounced in brick production, lime burning, bleaching and peat winning, and increasingly also in fishing. Urban entrepreneurs invested heavily in these sectors, which often needed very expensive capital goods, and they exploited these by way of managers and wage labourers.[36] Estimates based on extensive and detailed research into these activities suggest that in total two-thirds of the labour input in proto-industries in central Holland was supplied by wage labourers.

Agriculture had only limited importance in the Holland countryside, engaging no more than 42 per cent of the potential labour input. In the mid-sixteenth century, perhaps a good 30 per cent of labour in this sector was supplied by wage labourers: according to a calculation similar to the one undertaken for the Guelders river area the minimum share of external wage labour was 20 per cent, although 4 per cent should be added for living-in servants and some seasonal workers. This relatively low percentage, compared to the Guelders river area, was the result of the fact that the agricultural sector in Holland only was in the process of transition and still possessed traits of the peasant economy that characterized it in the middle ages, with small peasant-owned farms, worked by family labour, and an intensive agriculture going hand in hand with the fragmentation of farms. At the same time, in some parts of Holland more than in others, there were already elements of

[35] R. Fruin (ed.), *Informacie up den staet faculteit ende gelegenheyt van de steden ende dorpen van Holland ende Vrieslant* (Leiden, 1866), investigated here are 254–402.

[36] B. J. P. van Bavel, 'Early Proto-Industrialization in the Low Countries? The Importance and Nature of Market-Oriented Non-Agricultural Activities in the Countryside in Flanders and Holland', *Revue Belge de Philologie et d'Histoire*, 81.4 (2003), 181–237, esp. [xxx–xxx], and H. Brand, *Over macht en overwicht. Stedelijke elites in Leiden (1420–1510)* (Leuven/Apeldoorn, 1996), 184–7.

a new agricultural sector, with large tenant farms accumulating ever more leasehold land and increasing landlessness. In combination these elements resulted, firstly, in a high degree of landlessness, or at least near-landlessness. On the basis of the fiscal sources, available for Holland for the years around 1560, it can be calculated that 25 per cent of the households had no land at all, and that an additional 33 per cent had less than 4 hectares each.[37] Most of these countrymen who were under-supplied with land must have worked in proto-industrial activities. They probably also performed some wage labour in agriculture, though the opportunities were limited by the relative scarcity of large farms.

Conclusion

A calculation of the proportion of rural labour performed as wage labour in these two regions around the middle of the sixteenth century is summarized in Tables 1 and 2. In the central part of Holland, almost half of all rural labour was performed as wage labour, and in the Guelders river area, far more than half.

The above figures, and the strong differences in the nature of wage labour between the two regions, reflect the regional differences in the specific route of the transition. A high proportion of proletarianized labourers worked in agriculture on large farms in the Guelders river area, in contrast with a high proportion of semi-proletarianized peasants working in proto-industries in Holland. However, what the two regions had in common was that the share of wage labour was very high already around 1550, compared to other parts of Europe and even compared to England. In England according to some calculations the share of wage labourers in the total rural population in the sixteenth century amounted to between a quarter and a third. These figures cannot be compared simply, but they do suggest that the countryside in the two parts of the Low Countries investigated had a far higher share of wage labour, perhaps even as much as twice as high.

In other respects, too, there were clear differences from other parts of north-western Europe. For instance, the degree of full-time proletarianized labour must have been much larger here than elsewhere. In England, the share of rural labour performed by wage labourers could be supplied to a large extent by servants and semi-proletarianized labourers. Probably one third to one half of hired labour in early modern English agriculture was supplied

---

[37] De Vries, *Dutch Rural Economy*, 63, H. A. E. van Gelder, *Nederlandse dorpen in de 16e eeuw* (Amsterdam, 1953) 15–18, 22–4, 32–8, 78–9 and 87–9, and my own calculations on the basis of the Tiende Penningkohieren for Overschie, Twisk, Nootdorp, and Nieuwveen.

Table 1. Total labour input in the countryside in different sectors, and the wage labour and non-wage labour per sector in central Holland, mid-sixteenth century (%)

	Proportion of total labour	Wage labour	Non-wage labour
Agriculture	41	13	28
Craftsmen	8	2	6
Diking etc.	6	4	2
Proto-industry	45	29	16
Total		48	52
	100	100	

Table 2. Total labour input in the countryside in different sectors, and the wage labour and non-wage labour per sector in the Guelders river area, mid-sixteenth century (%)

	Proportion of total labour	Wage labour	Non-wage labour
Agriculture	81	47	34
Craftsmen	10	5	5
Diking etc.	6	4	2
Proto-industry	3	1	2
Total		57	43
	100	100	

by servants alone, that is to say by young adults as a part of their life cycle as peasants.[38] Much of the remaining wage labour was performed by peasants as part-time wage labour.[39] The social and economic effects of this type of wage-labour must have differed strongly from that performed by proletarian wage-labourers, both on the micro-level within the individual household and on the macro-level of the region dominated by either type of wage-labour. In the two parts of the Low Countries under discussion, perhaps as much as half of all wage labour was performed by proletarians. This applies even more to the Guelders river area than to Holland. In the latter region, a larger part of the rural population had at least a smallholding, resulting in a labour cycle which combined work on the small farm with proto-industrial work (often for wages) and wage labour on larger farms.[40] On the other hand, the number of living-in servants in Holland was probably much lower, meaning that a

[38] A. S. Kussmaul, *Servants in Husbandry in Early Modern England* (Cambridge, 1981), 3 and 11–22.

[39] Whittle, *Agrarian Capitalism*, 227–31 and 236.

[40] J. Lucassen, *Naar de kusten van de Noordzee.Trekarbeid in Europees perspektief, 1600–1900* (Gouda, 1984), 161–8.

relatively high proportion of wage labour was performed by workers from outside the household.

We can also speculate about the chronology of the rise of wage labour. In the Guelders river area the importance of wage labour must have increased sharply in the course of the fifteenth and sixteenth centuries, as the result of the emergence of large tenant farms, which both created demand for additional labour and increased the proportion of those without access to land, resulting in a growing supply of wage labourers. After the late sixteenth century, this development and the rise of wage labour halted, with a stabilization of the farm sizes and later, from the middle of the seventeenth century onwards, the rise of small independent tobacco cultivators.[41] Furthermore, no rise of factory capitalism took place here in the nineteenth century, as can be observed in many regions where an early agrarian transition took place.

In the Holland countryside, wage labour must have been unimportant in the fourteenth century. In the fifteenth century, there was an increase, but wage labour was not very substantial. Proto-industrial sectors at that time were still characterized mainly by small, independent producers who possessed their own resources, and worked for their own account. Moreover, agriculture in Holland was dominated by numerous small peasants with their own holdings. Both agricultural work and dike works were mainly carried out by way of the labour supplied by the peasant households. Only in the course of the fifteenth and sixteenth centuries was there a marked increase in wage labour, to about half of the rural labour input, mainly as a result of changes in proto-industries. This was followed in the late sixteenth and seventeenth centuries by a further strong increase, this time as a result of changes in agriculture. If the importance of wage labour in agriculture in the latter period rose here to 50–60 per cent—which can be expected in view of the similarity with the Guelders situation in the sixteenth century—this may have caused a rise in the importance of wage labour in the Holland countryside to 60–65 per cent around the middle of the seventeenth century. Thus the later transition in two phases here resulted in a higher level of wage-labour. However, after the end of the seventeenth century in the Holland countryside, too, the development of the economy and the rise of wage-labour seem to have stagnated.[42] These two cases from the Low Countries thus show that the rise of wage labour, and the transition to capitalism in general, were not

[41] P. Brusse, *Overleven door ondernemen. De agrarische geschiedenis van de Over-Betuwe, 1650–1850* (Wageningen, 1999), 45–58 and 87–92.

[42] J. L. van Zanden, *The Rise and Decline of Holland's Economy: Merchant Capitalism and the Labour Market* (Manchester, 1993), 39–40.

unilinear, ongoing developments, but could also pause or even come to a standstill altogether.

The results of the investigation into the importance of wage labour in the countryside support the more general impression that in parts of the Low Countries the transition of the rural economy was already well advanced in the sixteenth century. These regions in the Low Countries were probably the first in the world to experience a transition to capitalism. This applies particularly, though not exclusively, to those regions bordering or almost bordering the North Sea, namely coastal Flanders, Zealand, the Guelders river area, Holland, and coastal Frisia. On the other side of the sea, the coastal parts of England (East Anglia) were also among the first to experience a transition. This forces us to consider the elements held in common by the regions bordering the North Sea. In England, too, regional differences were strong, as appears from, for instance, a comparison between Norfolk and Berkshire.[43] With respect to social and economic developments, Norfolk perhaps had more in common with Holland than with the English regions located to its west. If this impression of similarity is correct, then geographical elements surely played a role in this. The eastern parts of England and the western parts of the Low Countries were located close to the sea, had access to cheap transport and often also to cheap fuel (peat). They were also located close to large urban markets. On the other hand, not all regions located close to the North Sea and/or a large urban market underwent an early transition, such as inland Flanders, while some regions further away from the North Sea and from large cities, such as the Guelders river area, did.

Other elements also played an important role in the early transition of these regions, such as freedom, the weakness of manorialism (which never existed, was only weak, or dissolved early) and secure property rights to the land. It can be surmised that power structures and social relations played an important role in this. In their turn, these regional structures show strong continuity over the centuries and appear to be rooted to a large extent in the period of occupation and reclamation of the region in question.[44] This also brings a geographical element into the picture again, not in a deterministic way, but as one of the relevant indirect factors, influencing the time and chronology of the occupation, as well as the organization of reclamation, and thus indirectly

---

[43] Cf. J. Whittle and M. Yates, ' "Pays réel" or "Pays légal"? Contrasting Patterns of Land Tenure and Social Structure in Eastern Norfolk and Western Berkshire, 1400–1600', *Agricultural History Review*, 48 (2000), 1–26.

[44] Van Bavel, 'Land, Lease and Agriculture', esp. 19–23.

the social and economic structure emerging in the region in question. Future research should attempt to make further comparisons on these points between the regions on both sides of the North Sea, in order to establish what factors underlay possible similarities in these parts of Europe where the transition took place earliest. This would help us to reveal some of the elements determining the nature and the chronology of the transition.

Conclusions

Chris Wickham

The articles in this book reflect Rodney Hilton's work remarkably well. They show us a multi-faceted set of approaches, illuminating medieval England and continental Europe from a great variety of directions, but at the core of them is a set of common assumptions and problems: that the study of the peasantry is central, that one of the most illuminating ways into understanding medieval society is through the study of conflict, that the socio-economic dynamism of the central and later middle ages had very complex roots, and that it is crucially important to tease them all out and then try to work out how they related to each other. Rodney himself, indeed, across his working life, increasingly recognized how complex the causal elements of medieval social and economic change were, while never renouncing his core principle, that 'conflict between landlords and peasants, however muted or however intense, over the appropriation of surplus product of the peasant holding, was a prime mover in the evolution of medieval society'.[1] I do not think that any of the contributors to this book would disagree with that—indeed, not many medieval social or economic historians at all would disagree with that, whether Marxist or not, although non-Marxists would put it in a different language. But it is the complexities that emerge most strongly from this volume, and its contributors have in some cases moved away from both Rodney's main interests and from his interpretations, always coming back to the Hilton œuvre in order to interact with it, but then moving on again. This is as it should be: Rodney Hilton's Middle Ages is not a closed system, but an ongoing debate.

That complexity also means, of course, that there are many ways in which a conclusion could bring these articles together. I shall do so here under three broad headings: lords and peasants; revolts; and the economic dynamism of the middle ages. These seem to me, at least, the best ways into the richness of the debate, both at Birmingham in 2003 and in this volume.

---

[1] R. H. Hilton, *Class Conflict and the Crisis of Feudalism* (London, 1985), ix.

Lords and peasants

It is a truism that the medieval world was a peasant world. 80 per cent of the population of late medieval England was rural-dwelling; the percentage was probably less in France, but only Italy and the Low Countries had a substantially lower rural population, and many parts of Europe (as Dick Holt stresses in this book) had a substantially higher one. Lords cannot be understood without the overwhelming peasant majority: how they defended their domination of that majority, as also how much money and goods they extracted from their peasant dependants, are essential elements in understanding who they were. Peasants, however, although the primary producers, and in control of their own labour power for the most part, nonetheless lived inside a world constructed by lordship, and they too cannot be approached properly unless their relationship with lords is understood. Medieval history itself turns on that permanent agonistic relationship, and most of our contributors faced it one way or another.

1. Peasant society was never uniform; it was always internally stratified. Knowledge of that stratification was important to Rodney Hilton, for at the back of his mind was always the knowledge that peasant élites, in England and elsewhere, would in the end buy up their neighbours, hire them back as wage labourers, and move in the direction of agrarian capitalism, ending the coherence of the peasantry as a class. That process was far from generalized even in a highly commercialized county such as Norfolk before the late sixteenth century, as Jane Whittle stresses; it was not a main focus of attention in this book as a result. But the way peasant élites related to their middling and smallholding neighbours, and how far internal inequalities affected the coherence of peasant communities, recurred in studies of England, Spain and France. Miriam Müller focuses on the ways communities sought to contain internal conflict between peasant strata in England; across the divergent and ever-changing social structures of fourteenth-century English villages, peasants aimed to maintain their cohesiveness in the face of seigneurial authority, despite all the potential and actual intra-village tensions, over debt, or employment, or inheritance, or inter-personal violence. Chris Dyer, focusing on a slightly earlier period, stresses among other things the dependence of lords on the collaboration of peasant leaders, who were the people who in practice ran manorial courts; as Rodney Hilton himself showed, rural élites could be obsequious to lords and bullying to their neighbours, but also leaders of the community, allied to poorer strata in their resistance to lordship. Monique Bourin, discussing thirteenth- and fourteenth-century Languedoc, similarly stresses a solidarity between village élites and at least middling peasants, as they protected their communities

from other villages and from lords (here, élites had extensive credit relations with their neighbours, but did not buy their land up on a large scale; the assertive and opportunist style of peasant leaders in England was also less in evidence). Maribel Alfonso discusses parallel divisions in central medieval León and Castile, where the poorest peasants were often excluded from a real participation in rural communities (even though, unlike often in England, they were legally free), and were often hired to do the labour services owed by their richer neighbours.

In Spain, rural élites were generally militarized, which reflects the specific history of the Christian-Muslim frontier in the peninsula; Alfonso remarks that the impact of that on élite community relations is still ill-understood. The relationship between rich peasants and their neighbours has all the same been systematically studied recently in many parts of Europe, as was seen in this book and as recurs in recent scholarship on England, France or Italy, and indeed on Spain. The choices of peasant élites, whether to ally with their poorer neighbours or whether to dominate them (either politically or economically, and either autonomously or with the help of lords) are a crucial issue for the construction of peasant solidarity, and of the institutional expressions of peasant communities, such as the *consulats* of southern France, the *comuni* of Italy, the *concejos* of Spain; they are also a crucial issue for the development of the rural economy away from feudal relations of production, as was noted earlier. But peasant inequality did not undermine a basic level of community identity in any of the societies discussed in this book; our contributors were agreed on that.

2. One reason why peasantries remained united, at least in England, was the continuing pressure of seigneurial subjection. I say 'at least in England' because it is important to bear in mind the particularity of England, among the western European societies studied in this book: until the late fourteenth century at the earliest, up to half the population of England was legally unfree. This gave lords a legal tool for coercion that they had already lost by the twelfth century in most of France, Italy or Spain. Of course, lords controlled law-courts everywhere, and peasants could seldom win at law against them; lords everywhere also had, if not a monopoly of force (peasants had weapons, and, often, a basic weapons training), at least a ready supply of military specialists whom they could use to coerce. The legal powers of lords in the French *seigneurie banale*, the Italian *signoria*, the Castilian *señorío* were great, over free and unfree alike (and even over peasant proprietors, who existed in many parts of the Continent throughout the middle ages). The extraction of peasant surplus was technically 'extra-economic' everywhere, in that it was closely related to, and legitimized by, the seigneurial control of all the levers of

political power and authority. But in England the imagery of serfdom and the resultant lordly power over the unfree suffused all lord–peasant relationships, from the late Anglo-Saxon period up to 1400, with a peak in the thirteenth and fourteenth centuries, and it is also England which is discussed from this standpoint here; so it is worth focusing on the issue from the English perspective.

There has been an ongoing debate about the degree to which peasant autonomy and protagonism were weakened by seigneurial constraints in medieval England, and the degree to which these latter were resented. Our authors here, particularly Phillipp Schofield, Chris Dyer and Zvi Razi, are sure that they were, and I am personally sure that they are right. It has been recently argued, particularly by Bruce Campbell, that thirteenth-century rents to lords were low even for unfree tenure, both if taken as a proportion of gross yields and if compared to the rents peasants could extract from sub-tenants, who arguably paid more of a 'market' rate, if such a concept yet existed.[2] Dyer here emphasizes the limitations of rent, too, and also points out that even the extra burdens brought by unfreedom—seigneurial entry-fines, merchet, arbitrary tallage—were in reality, despite the claims of lords that they were limitless, bounded by customary expectations and in practice usually predictable. Does this mean that they could be looked on as a marginal inconvenience by peasants who were prosperous enough to have a good deal of surplus after rents, services and subsistence? Razi argues that this was not the case for the surviving serfs of France, who paid a lot for freedom, and proposes that the relative absence of manumission in England was due to the reluctance of lords to grant it, given the importance of servile status in the maintenance of seigneurial control over demesne labour, and over unfree village society as a whole through the lord's manorial court. Dyer stresses that customary constraints on seigneurial dues were themselves the product of peasant resistance, and this is an important insight. Custom was, indeed, precisely one of the major terrains of lord–peasant conflict in all periods of the middle ages; both sides continually sought to shift it to their advantage, lords with the help of law-courts and main force, peasants with the help of their control of the labour process on the ground. Schofield, who has at the focus of his empirical material a case study of the Kyngs, a relatively prosperous unfree peasant family in thirteenth- and fourteenth-century Suffolk, shows that, although unfreedom did not prevent the Kyngs' prosperity, it did allow for their

---

[2] See e.g. B. Campbell, 'The Agrarian Problem in the Early Fourteenth Century', *Past and Present*, 189 (2005), 3–70.

arbitrary coercion by the local lord, the monastery of Bury St Edmunds, when that lord was desperate enough to go to the trouble to do so.

This seems to me to be the point. Lords did not have the time and inclination to police every detail of peasant lives; even brute force could only be intermittently employed (it too cost money); they relied on peasant cooperation (in running the manorial court, or in assessing and exacting rents and dues), and this both distanced lords still more from the extractive process and, doubtless, reduced the seigneurial share of the surplus further. But in the thirteenth century and many decades into the fourteenth they needed the powers they had over the unfree to maintain demesne farming, which, uniquely in western Europe, remained important in England, at least on larger estates; they needed labour services from the unfree to cultivate demesnes, or, increasingly, the money from service commutations in order to pay wage labourers. And they also needed these powers simply to be able to dominate locally, when they chose, as the Kyngs found. Lords could and did influence inheritance customs, or decide whether to facilitate or restrict the peasant land market, if their dependants were unfree; these powers were advantageous to them. Lords did not give them up easily; they were forced to, by peasant resistance in the late fourteenth century and by labour shortages in the 150 years after the Black Death. And, however low and stable, the dues paid by the unfree nonetheless marked them off from the free peasantry, and were both resented and undermined for that reason even if no other. Peasants everywhere knew the difference between rents, whose legitimacy they grudgingly accepted, and 'feudal'/seigneurial dues, which they rejected. (They also did so in France, where the latter were even lower and more stable, as the events of 1789–93 show.) Unfreedom was, famously, one of the main targets of the 1381 rebels (and even of the 1549 Norfolk rebels, at a time when it had become almost extinct, as Whittle shows), when land-lordship was not. Serfdom was only one weapon in the seigneurial armoury, but, however bounded by custom, it could tip the balance of rural control in favour of lords, so of course it was opposed.

3. Unfreedom was also important in England because of the force of the state. Wendy Davies, discussing tenth-century northern Spain, shows how in the Duero valley both kings and landowners were still relatively weak; both sides had to increase their power (in the case of landowners, at the expense of a still-strong landowning peasantry) before the devolution of seigneurial rights from kings to aristocrats and churches could begin in the later eleventh century; and those processes of increasing state and aristocratic power to a considerable extent reinforced each other. That process of mutual reinforcement occurred in England around the same time (and a little earlier) too, as

the late Anglo-Saxon state and aristocracy both slowly crystallized; a traditional historiography which sees kings and aristocrats as structurally opposed is immediately disproved by these examples, and there are others. In England, though, kings never lost their judicial centrality, and the seigneurial rights which were by 1100 a typical feature of a continental lordship were in England only held over the unfree, who were fortunately (for lords) numerous, and who, lords ensured, would become still more numerous by 1200. As time went on, indeed, the hegemony of the English state only increased, and this menaced seigneurial power in more and more areas. Hence the rearguard actions of Bury St Edmunds in the areas it still controlled (Schofield); hence also the increasing involvement of the different strata of the aristocracy in the mechanisms of the state itself, as Peter Coss effectively shows for the gentry. The gentry controlled local royal courts much as the upper peasantry controlled manorial courts: to maintain their own local dominance, and their control over their tenants and their surplus, through institutions that were supposed to restrict them. (Local aristocratic and military élites did the same with the royal institutions imposed on the cities of late medieval Spain, too, as Pablo Sánchez shows.) This book does not put a heavy emphasis on aristocracies, but Coss's work on the gentry here makes very clear how the political culture of the gentry was bound up in its relationship to the state, adversarial at times (as with some parliamentary politics) but above all collaborative. The way that the state impinged on local societies is made clearer as a result. And, as a by-product of this argument, it becomes ever clearer that it was virtually impossible for any single authority, kings or lords or communities of peasants, to control any local society entirely; power relations were harsh, but they were also strikingly diffuse. As Rodney Hilton said, feudal lords and governments, however oppressive, were no match for modern corporations and governments;[3] the network of localized collaborations was too complex. Conversely, by and large, royal and lordly hegemony in the Gramscian sense tended for the most part to be accepted as well, thanks to overlapping clienteles that stretched from the grandest court to the poorest peasant.

Revolts

But that lordly hegemony could break down. The conflictual consensus made possible by the diffusion of power, and by the agreed (even if shifting) bedrock of custom, was nonetheless built on top of a structural opposition, between producers and the people who took their products. These were

---

[3] Hilton, *Class Conflict*, 121.

traditionally landlords and seigneurial lords, of course, but, increasingly after 1200, tax-raising states took peasant surplus as well, and the hegemony of state taxation was less clearly established. Rodney Hilton dominated the study of medieval peasant and popular revolts for a long time, thanks to his empirical rigour and his enthusiastic commitment to the peasant side, and it was logical that several articles in this book should take up the topic: Steven Justice on the English Peasants' Revolt of 1381, Jane Whittle on the 1381 and 1549 revolts in Norfolk, Pablo Sánchez on urban conflicts in Castile, and Sam Cohn on fourteenth-century revolts everywhere, which he has shown to be very much more numerous, and normal, than anyone previously believed.

The organization of the 1381 rising has long been known to have been notably sophisticated, showing a resourcefulness which hostile observers had inaccurately denied.[4] Whittle's work on the Norfolk Peasants' Revolt and the Ket Rebellion makes clear that both of them show a capacity for organization, indeed for government, at least for the short timespan (ten days in 1381, six weeks in 1549) before the forces of repression could be mobilized. She also shows how peasants were fully aware of the major issues of economic conflict in each period, serfdom and taxation in 1381, enclosure and landlordly stock-raising in 1549, and used these as the focus of their demands; they were not simply opposed to power, they were acting to promote specific objectives, as a class. The breadth of the Norfolk risings reflects the importance of alliances in medieval revolts; in Norfolk they even included a handful of lords; in Flanders and Italy (Cohn) they could link very disparate social groups; in Castile (Sánchez), where effective alliances between taxpayers and disenfranchised knights were less easy, revolts were weaker as a result. All the same, peasants and artisans (either rural or urban, depending on the country) were at the core of most of these revolts; their class nature was not lessened by their links to other social groups.

Our contributors put considerable stress on the ideology of rebels. Cohn emphasizes the image of liberty, which was very prominent in post-Black Death France and Italy; he argues that, a generation after the plague, people had become more self-confident about their capacity to effect social and political change. This has an obvious parallel in the English opposition to serfdom in 1381, but on the Continent it was a banner of the legally free, not the unfree, and represented a claim to political protagonism, which was new in this period—although it had older, probably forgotten, Carolingian and pre-Carolingian roots.

---

[4] N. P. Brooks, 'The Organization and Achievements of the Peasants of Kent and Essex in 1381', now in id., *Communities and Warfare, 700–1400* (London, 2000), 266–89.

The other element of rebel ideology discussed in this context was religion. Justice elegantly dissects and doubts the common association between rebellion and heterodoxy; he shows that the rebels expressed themselves in religious language and imagery that can readily be seen as orthodox, and that mainstream Christianity, with its message of egalitarianism, could support rebellion as well as submission.[5] This is echoed by Sánchez's work on urban Spain in the more negative framework of a Catholic community of intolerance, in particular of Jews; a similarly intolerant violence just after the Black Death is seen as the opposite of organized revolt by Cohn. The protagonism that religion brings to excluded classes can often be ambiguous to our eyes, and not just in the medieval period. But we must recognize the resourcefulness of peasant protagonists in using the religious imagery that was a fundamental and inevitable part of their world-view, as indeed Justice proposes. The uncomprehending peasantry, living outside the historical time of real political events, which was being proposed for medieval Europe as late as the 1970s, is more and more being banished to the realm of myth, as a generation of scholars have followed Rodney Hilton's aim to see the world, as far as possible, through the peasantry's own eyes. We cannot do that naively, given the veils that our sources inevitably drape over the past, and given the paucity of information and lack of sympathy which our specific sources for peasant values (whether insurgent or submissive) contain. All the same, the effort after understanding pays off; we cannot fully reconstruct the meanings that a medieval peasant community gave to events, but we can see that these meanings could be coherent, thought-out, informed, to the point. These are important steps forward.

Dynamics of medieval economic change

Rodney Hilton saw class conflict between lords and peasants as the principal motor of economic change, particularly as aristocratic hegemony eroded after the Black Death. Many, even most, of our contributors might agree with that, as several of them made clear. All the same, the analyses in this book which focused most on issues of economic change, particularly in the late middle ages, stressed other factors as well, notably urbanism and the state.

1. Landowning aristocrats were inescapably linked to the peasantries they dominated; they were inescapably linked to the state which increasingly

---

[5] Justice is cautious about the word 'ideology', arguing that it has recently broken down in Foucault's and Bourdieu's styles of analysis; I would agree, while still being happy to use the word.

sought to dominate them. And they were also inescapably linked to the development of towns. Holt's illuminating article shows, through his Norwegian counter-example (backed up by the evidence of Ireland and Scotland), how if landlords were weak in their control of peasant communities, and if rents were low—if, that is to say, aristocracies (and churches, and kings) were not rich enough to be a solid source of demand—then exchange would not be strong enough to sustain urban development. I am sure he is right, and there are many parallels in early medieval Europe, where weak aristocracies were commoner than they would be later.[6] Commerce grew out of the expansion of feudal class relations, and vice versa; as Larry Epstein said, 'up to a point, feudalism thrived on trade'. So did towns, which were emphatically part of a developed feudal mode, as Rodney Hilton already argued. Indeed, lords did not only buy from towns, they founded them, and invested in them; urban rents were an integral part of landowning strategies in late medieval England, as Richard Goddard shows; and, by the sixteenth century, Spencer Dimmock makes it clear how some landowners, investing in the proto-industry of clothmaking, were themselves already clothiers, who had bought land with their profits. This tightness of relationship between towns and aristocracies was long known for Italy and Spain (Sánchez); it has sometimes been seen as a reason for the failure of southern European urbanism to move towards capitalist/industrial takeoff. But the English association between aristocratic and urban entrepreneurship was, at least in its early stages, a powerful boost to commercialization and, more broadly, economic complexity. 'Commercialization theory', with its overtones of Smithian economics, is often seen as implicitly opposed to the Marxist economic interpretations of Rodney Hilton, but, as we are reminded by Epstein and Dimmock, an understanding of the active small towns of England and of their contribution to commodity production was one of Rodney's most particular achievements. It should be emphasized that, in a late medieval context, the difference between large and small towns is a particularly important one. The density of small towns in England, where the link between small-scale artisanal production and agricultural commercialization was tight, is one of the key infrastructural features of that country, which was not matched everywhere.

Towns were also important for states, as argued by Sánchez for Castile and by Penny Roberts in a comparison between France and England that extends Rodney Hilton's work on urban difference into the sixteenth century. States could use large towns as a basis for local government, as in Castile and France, and, of course, as a major source of revenue, as the French kings did in

---

[6] See for example C. Wickham, *Framing the Early Middle Ages* (Oxford, 2005), 693–824.

the Paris region around 1200 and as states throughout Europe did in later centuries. This is itself linked to the slow development of an urban leadership largely comprised of state officials in France (unlike England), as both Hilton and Roberts underlined. At the back of Rodney Hilton's mind was the idea that this may have been one of the many elements that came together to mark a difference in English economic development in the next centuries.[7] He was very cautious about arguing this, as he knew well that medieval and early modern large towns were not the seed-bed of industrial capitalism. It is more likely, however, that it is the greater political power given to large towns in France (or Italy, or Spain) by state interest—as opposed to in England—that allowed such towns to put the brakes on rural and small-town proto-industrial competition. This argument, put in different ways by Epstein and Bas van Bavel, moves me to the last points I want to make in this conclusion, about the transition to capitalism.

2. This book covers the period up to the mid- to late sixteenth century; it therefore does not confront the major period of the 'transition debate', and it is not necessary to rehearse the enormously complex arguments about that here. As noted earlier, however, Rodney Hilton was permanently conscious of the fact of the future transition to capitalism in England, and most of his work, like the work of almost all economic historians of medieval England, had as one of its sub-themes an interest in exploring the roots of the future. This interest was picked up here in Epstein's discussions of transaction costs, technological change and the state, Dimmock's discussions of the economic context of sixteenth-century small towns in southern England, and van Bavel's discussions of wage labour and proto-industry in the Low Countries. They differ in their interpretations: with each other; with Rodney; with Robert Brenner, the most influential proponent of the argument that the local or regional balance of class forces was the key discriminator in the different paths, taken or not taken, to economic transition; and with the most active international focus of debate and recent work, the proto-industrialization school.[8] It becomes ever clearer that a future overarching theory of transition will have to engage (with as much empirical exactness as possible,

[7] R. H. Hilton, *English and French Towns in Feudal Society* (Cambridge, 1992), 104.

[8] See T. H. Aston and C. H. E. Philpin (eds), *The Brenner Debate* (Cambridge, 1985); P. Kriedte, H. Medick, and J. Schlumbohm, *Industrialization Before Industrialization* (Cambridge, 1981); S.C. Ogilvie and M. Cerman (eds), *European Proto-industrialization* (Cambridge, 1996). See also the works on this subject by several of our contributors, S. R. Epstein, *Freedom and Growth* (London, 2000); J. Whittle, *The Development of Agrarian Capitalism* (Oxford, 2000); B. J. P. van Bavel, 'Land, Lease and Agriculture', *Past and Present*, 172 (2001), 3–43.

and also comparatively) with all these elements. Here, however, with the more chronologically restricted focus of medieval Europe in mind, I will restrict myself to two observations.

First, we must recognize the importance and changing role of political structures in the economic changes of the pre-capitalist world. Epstein puts most stress on this, focusing above all on the late medieval and early modern state and its commitment to breaking down localized (aristocratic or urban, but anyway feudal) barriers to exchange and production. Looking at it from an early medieval perspective, I would put it in a slightly different way from that, while not seeking to disagree. Aristocrats, the landowning ruling class under feudalism, thanks to their wealth in rents, the solidarity of their demand, and their commitment to promoting new forms of wealth-creation in order to tax them, were *the* main early and central medieval prime movers of economic change—commercial growth, the inter-regional exchange of bulk products, and urbanism. It was only after 1300 or so that a (rural or urban) aristocratic interest in taking tolls and dues at the local or regional level meant that a fuller and more self-sustaining inter-regional economic integration was made harder—'from forms of development of the productive forces, these relations turn into their fetters', as Marx said[9]—after which only the next political level, the state, although still feudal in its basic infrastructure, could overcome that regionalism in some parts of Europe. I would still see the balance of class forces and the rise of wage labour as essential elements in the next stage of the model, much as van Bavel does, but the political and fiscal elements of the economic infrastructure cannot be set aside.

Second, however, we must avoid teleology. The economic history of medieval England (or even later) is not worth studying only because it led to capitalism, in the end, first; that was many centuries down the line, and it distorts our understanding of the lives of the real people of the middle ages to focus only on future-directed developments. Teleology lends itself to historical moralization too easily; economies are 'blocked', 'trapped', 'stagnate' because they do not obey future-directed rules. But, actually, medieval and sixteenth-century economies tended towards equilibrium, the 'high-level equilibrium' of some Chinese and Indian economic history, rather than towards transition.[10] It is well known that the great centres of thirteenth-century commercialization, Italy and Flanders, did not industrialize first; it is

---

[9] K. Marx and F. Engels, *Selected Works* (Moscow and London, 1968), 182.
[10] See R. H. Britnell, *The Commercialization of English Society, 1000–1500*, 2nd edn (Manchester, 1996), esp. 233–7, for a non-teleological account.

increasingly clear that the great centres of early modern rural proto-industry, such as south Germany, did not do so either. In England, too, proponents of a future-directed economic development in the sixteenth century based in East Anglia, Kent or Gloucestershire have to confront the fact that the core of future industrialization lay in still very commercially 'underdeveloped' regions such as Lancashire—we have to proceed regionally and microregionally in our analyses here, as van Bavel shows. And, on the macro-scale, we also have seriously to confront the increasingly compelling argument that there was nothing in the economic structures of sixteenth-century Europe (or even later, as Kenneth Pomeranz has argued most forcefully[11]) that differentiated it structurally from China and India; if this is the case, then future-directed explanatory models for our period are all empirically unfounded. This too will be the terrain of debate in the years to come. This book however holds up even if these parameters change: for it shows us the dynamism that the medieval economy, the feudal mode of production, did have. This is interesting and important to study, no matter where it led or did not lead.

Conclusion

This book gives us a good idea of the variety and excitement of current socio-economic history in the middle ages. There were absences; gender and women's history is one, even though Rodney Hilton was one of the first people to look at medieval peasant women (the issue is discussed only by Müller); the history of medieval wage labour is another (with the exception of Alfonso and van Bavel); the economic logic of the feudal mode is a third (only Epstein confronts that in any systematic way). Conversely, some elements of the medieval social landscape are now rather clearer. It is important how much the state and its political and economic structure recurs in the articles in this volume; the relationship between politics and economics has a good deal of future life in it. It is important how wide the recognition has become that commercialization was a key feature of the central and later medieval economy; this will remain a major element in future analyses, even if teleological interpretations of it die away. The articles in this book also show, more and more clearly, just how complex and regionally/microregionally diverse peasant societies in the middle ages were, and I anticipate that future work will accentuate that diversity still further; the excitement that can be generated by tracking such differences (and, I hope, comparing them) has not by any means yet vanished. And, finally, nothing in this book gives us any

---

[11] K. Pomeranz, *The Great Divergence* (Princeton, 2000).

indicator that class conflict is an outdated explanatory model for the middle ages; it just does not go away, and new insights into it can continually be presented, as many of our contributors showed us. Rodney Hilton was interested in all these issues (although he had only a muted concern for the state), and would have shared our excitement, however much he disagreed with us, loudly and forcibly, before taking us off to have a drink. It is that shared interest, shared excitement, that makes this book truly Rodney Hilton's Middle Ages.

Bibliography of Works by Rodney Hilton

Jean Birrell

Books

The Economic Development of some Leicestershire Estates in the Fourteenth and Fifteenth Centuries (Oxford, 1947)

(with H. Fagan) *The English Rising of 1381* (London, 1950).

> trans. German as *Der englische Bauernaufstand von 1381* (Berlin, 1953).

> trans. Japanese as *Igirisu nomin senso—1381 nen no nomin ikki* (Tokyo, 1961).

A Medieval Society: The West Midlands at the End of the Thirteenth Century (London, 1966), 2nd edn (Cambridge, 1983).

> trans. Italian as *Una società medievale. L'Inghilterra centro-occidentale all fine del XIII secolo* (Bologna, 1992).

The Decline of Serfdom in Medieval England (Studies in Economic History) (London and New York, 1969); 2nd edn (Studies in Economic and Social History) (London, 1983).

Bond Men Made Free: Medieval Peasant Movements and the English Rising of 1381 (London and New York, 1973), 2nd edn with Introduction by C. C. Dyer (London, 2003).

> trans. Spanish as *Siervos liberados. Los movimientos campesinos medievales y el levantamiento Inglés de 1381* (Madrid, 1978).

> trans. French as *Les mouvements paysans au moyen âge* (Paris, 1979).

> Chapter 1 reprinted in L. Kuchenbuch and B. Michales (eds), *Feudalismus—Materialen zur Theorie und Geschichte* (Frankfurt, Berlin, and Vienna, 1977), 481–522.

The English Peasantry in the Later Middle Ages: The Ford Lectures for 1973 and Related Studies (Oxford, 1975).

> Chapter 1 trans. Spanish as 'El campesinado como clase', *Estudios d'història agrària* 1 (1978), 27–37.

Class Conflict and the Crisis of Feudalism. Essays in Medieval Social History (London, 1985), 2nd edn (London, 1990).

> trans. Spanish as *Conflicto de clases y crisis del feudalismo* (Barcelona, 1988).

English and French Towns in Feudal Society. A Comparative Study (Cambridge 1992).
  trans Japanese (Tokyo, 2000).

Editions
a. Texts
(with H. A. Cronne) 'The Beauchamp Household Book (An account of a journey from London to Warwick in 1432)', *University of Birmingham Historical Journal,* 2 (1950), 208–18.
Ministers' Accounts of the Warwickshire Estates of the Duke of Clarence, 1479–80 (Dugdale Society, 21, 1952); introduction reprinted in *Class Conflict and the Crisis of Feudalism* (1985 edn).
The Stoneleigh Leger Book (Dugdale Society, 24, 1960); introduction reprinted in *Class Conflict and the Crisis of Feudalism* (1985 edn).
'Swanimote Rolls of Feckenham Forest', *Miscellany,* I (Worcestershire Historical Society, 1960), 37–52.
'Building Accounts of Elmley Castle, Worcestershire, 1345–6', *University of Birmingham Historical Journal,* 10 (1965), 78–87.

b. Books
E. A. Kosminsky, *Studies in the Agrarian History of England in the Thirteenth Century,* trans. Ruth Kisch (Oxford, 1956).
Peasants, Knights and Heretics: Studies in Medieval English Social History (Cambridge, 1976).
(with Introduction) *The Transition from Feudalism to Capitalism* (London, 1976), 2nd edn (London, 1978), 3rd edn (Delhi, 2006).
  trans. Spanish as *La transición del feudalismo al capitalismo* (Barcelona, 1977), 2nd edn (Barcelona, 1978).
  trans. German, with Postscript, as *Der Übergang vom Feudalismus zum Kapitalismus* (Frankfurt, 1984).
  trans. Turkish (1984)
(with T. H. Aston) *The English Rising of 1381* (Cambridge, 1984).

Pamphlets and Occasional Papers
Communism and Liberty (Marxism Today Series, London, 1950)
Social Structure of Rural Warwickshire in the Middle Ages (Dugdale Society Occasional Paper, no. 9, 1950); reprinted in *The English Peasantry in the Later Middle Ages.*
The Change beyond the Change. A Dream of John Ball (William Morris Society, London, 1990).
Les ciutats medievals (Barcelona, 1989).

Power and Jurisdiction in Medieval England (Our History, Pamphlet 86, Socialist History Society, 1992).

Articles

'A Thirteenth-century Poem on Disputed Villein Services', *English Historical Review*, 56 (1941), 90–7; reprinted in *Class Conflict and the Crisis of Feudalism* (1985 edn).

'Winchcombe Abbey and the Manor of Sherborne', *University of Birmingham Historical Journal*, 2 (1949), 31–52; reprinted in H. P. R. Finberg (ed.), *Gloucestershire Studies* (Leicester, 1957), 89–113; and in *Class Conflict and the Crisis of Feudalism* (1985 edn).

'Kibworth Harcourt: a Merton College Manor in the Thirteenth and Fourteenth Centuries', in W. G. Hoskins (ed.), *Studies in Leicestershire Agrarian History* (Leicester, 1949), 17–40; reprinted in *Class Conflict and the Crisis of Feudalism* (1985 edn).

'Peasant Movements in England Before 1381', *Economic History Review*, 2nd ser., 2 (1949), 117–36; reprinted in *The Middle Ages* (Institute of History of the Academy of Sciences of the U.S.S.R.) (Moscow, 1956–7), 92–111; in E. M. Carus-Wilson (ed.), *Essays in Economic History*, 3 vols (London, 1954–62), vol. II, 73–90; and in *Class Conflict and the Crisis of Feudalism*.

    trans. Japanese in *Hokensei no kiki* [*The crisis of feudalism*] (Seminar Series of Social Sciences, no. 8) (Tokyo, 1956).

'Y eût-il une crise général de la féodalité?', *Annales, Économies, Sociétés, Civilisations*, 6 (1951), 23–30; reprinted as 'Was there a General Crisis of Feudalism?', in *Class Conflict and the Crisis of Feudalism*.

    trans. Japanese in *Hokensei no Kiki* [*The crisis of feudalism*] (Seminar Series of Social Sciences, no. 8) (Tokyo, 1956).

'Capitalism—What's in a Name?', *Past and Present*, 1 (1952), 32–43; reprinted in *Transition from Feudalism to Capitalism*; and in *Class Conflict and the Crisis of Feudalism*.

'Historical Materialism', in *Essays on Socialist Realism and the British Cultural Tradition*, Arena Publication (London, n.d.), 5–14.

'A Comment', in *Science and Society*, (Fall 1953); reprinted in *The Transition from Feudalism to Capitalism: A Symposium*, Arena Publication (London, 1954), 65–72.

    trans. Turkish, in *Feodalizmden Kapitalizme Gecis* (1970).

'Life in the Medieval Manor (with a short glossary of manorial terms)', *Amateur Historian*, 1 (1953), 82–9.

'Gloucester Abbey Leases of the Late Thirteenth Century', *University of Birmingham Historical Journal*, 4 (1953), 1–17; reprinted in *The English Peasantry in the Later Middle Ages*.

'Medieval Agrarian History', in *Victoria County History of Leicestershire*, vol. II (London, 1954), 145–98.

'The Content and Sources of English Agrarian History Before 1500', *Agricultural History Review*, 3 (1955), 3–19; reprinted in *Journal of Czechoslovak Academy of Agricultural Sciences*, 29 (1956), 79–92.

'A Study in the Pre-history of English Enclosure in the Fifteenth Century', in *Studi in Onore di Armando Sapori*, 2 vols (Milan, 1957), vol. I, 674–85; reprinted in *The English Peasantry in the Later Middle Ages*.

'Dzieje Spoleczno-gospodarcze Anglii w XIV i XV w', *Przeglad Historyczny*, 48 (1957), 833–40.

'L'Angleterre économique et sociale des XIVe et XVe siècles. Théories et monographies', *Annales, Economies, Sociétés, Civilisations*, 3 (1958), 541–63.

'The Origins of Robin Hood', *Past and Present*, 14 (1958), 30–44; reprinted in *Peasants, Knights and Heretics*; and in Stephen Knight (ed.), *Robin Hood. Anthology of Scholarship and Criticism* (Cambridge, 1999), 197–210.

'Old Enclosures in the West Midlands: a Hypothesis About their Late Medieval Development', *Annales de l'Est*, mémoire no. 21 (1959), 272–83; reprinted in *Class Conflict and the Crisis of Feudalism* (1985 edn).

(review article, with P. H. Sawyer) 'Technical Determinism: the Stirrup and the Plough', *Past and Present*, 14 (1958), 30–44.

(review article) 'Medieval London', *Past and Present*, 26 (1963), 98–101.

'Freedom and Villeinage in England', *Past and Present*, 31 (1965), 3–19; reprinted in *Peasants, Knights and Heretics*.

'Rent and Capital Formation in Feudal Society', in *Second International Conference of Economic History: Aix-en-Provence* (1962), 2 vols (Paris, 1965), vol. II, 33–68; reprinted in *The English Peasantry in the Later Middle Ages*.

'Manor', 'Robin Hood' and 'Serfdom and Villeinage', in *Encyclopaedia Britannica*, 14th edn, 1967, vol. 14, 801–3; vol. 19, 394–5; vol. 20, 244–8.

(with P. A. Rahtz) 'Upton, Gloucestershire, 1959–64', *Transactions of the Bristol and Gloucestershire Archaeological Society*, 85 (1966), 70–146.

'Some Problems of Urban Real Property in the Middle Ages', in C. H. Feinstein (ed.), *Socialism, Capitalism and Economic Growth: Essays Presented to Maurice Dobb* (Cambridge, 1967), 326–37; reprinted in *Class Conflict and the Crisis of Feudalism*.

'Villages désertés et histoire économique: recherches françaises et anglaises', *Etudes Rurales*, 32 (1968), 104–9.

'A Rare Evesham Abbey Estate Document', *Vale of Evesham Research Papers*, 2 (1969), 5–10; reprinted in *Class Conflict and the Crisis of Feudalism* (1985 edn).

'Lord and Peasant in Staffordshire in the Middle Ages', *North Staffordshire Journal of Field Studies*, 10 (1970), 1–20; reprinted in *The English Peasantry in the Later Middle Ages.*

'A Crisis in England, 1376–1399', *Mediaevalia Bohemica*, 3 (1972), 149–61.

'Further Dimensions for Local Historians?', *Local Historian*, 10 (1973), 390–4.

'Some Social and Economic Evidence in Late Medieval English Tax Returns', in S. Herost (ed.), *Spoleczenstwo, gospodarka, kultura: Studies Offered to Marion Malowist* (Warsaw, 1974), 111–28; reprinted in *Class Conflict and the Crisis of Feudalism.*

'Medieval Peasants: Any Lessons?', *Journal of Peasant Studies*, 1 (1974), 207–19; reprinted in *Class Conflict and the Crisis of Feudalism.*

'Peasant Society, Peasant Movements and Feudalism in Medieval Europe', in H. A. Landsberger (ed.), *Rural Protest: Peasant Movements and Social Change* (London, 1974), 67–94

(review article) 'Warriors and Peasants', *New Left Review*, 83 (1974), 83–94.

'Soziale Programme im englishen Aufstand von 1381', in P. Blickle (ed.), *Revolte und Revolution in Europa* (*Historische Zeitschrift*, Beiheft 4) (Munich, 1975), 31–46; reprinted as 'Social Concepts in the English Rising of 1381', in *Class Conflict and the Crisis of Feudalism.*

'Feudalism and the Origins of Capitalism', *History Workshop*, 1 (1976), 9–25; reprinted in *Class Conflict and the Crisis of Feudalism* (1985 edn).

'Reasons for Inequality Among Medieval Peasants', *Journal of Peasant Studies*, 5 (1978), 271–84; reprinted in *Class Conflict and the Crisis of Feudalism.*

'Idéologie et ordre social', in *Georges Duby, L'Arc*, 72 (Aix-en-Provence, 1978), 32–7; reprinted as 'Ideology and Social Order in Late Medieval England', in *Class Conflict and the Crisis of Feudalism.*

'A Crisis of Feudalism', *Past and Present*, 80 (1978), 3–19; reprinted in T. H. Aston and C. H. E. Philpin (eds), *The Brenner Debate. Agrarian Class Structure and Economic Development in Pre-industrial Europe* (Cambridge, 1985), 119–37.

'Féodalité et seigneurie', in D. Johnson, F. Bederida and F. Crouzet (eds), *De Guillaume le Conquérant au marché commun: dix siècles d'histoire franco-brittanique* (Paris, 1979), 43–56; published in Britain with title 'Feudalism or *féodalité* and *seigneurie* in France and England', in *Britain and France: Ten Centuries* (Folkestone, 1980), 39–50; reprinted in *Class Conflict and the Crisis of Feudalism.*

'Siervos liberados', in *Siglo vienteuno de España* (Madrid, 1979).

'Towns in English Feudal Society', Review (*Journal of the Fernand Braudel Centre for the Study of Economies, Historical Systems and Civilizations*), 3 (1979), 3–20; reprinted in *Class Conflict and the Crisis of Feudalism.*

(review article) 'Individualism and the English Peasantry', *New Left Review*, 120 (1980), 109–11.

'Robin des Bois', *L'Histoire*, 21 (1980), 39–47.

'Popular Movements in England at the End of the Fourteenth Century', in *Il Tumulto dei Ciompi: un momento di storia fiorentina ed europea* (Florence, 1981), 223–40; reprinted in *Class Conflict and the Crisis of Feudalism*.

'The International Background—Some Problems of Medieval Social History', in N. Skyum-Nielson and N. Lund (eds), *Danish Medieval History. New Currents* (Copenhagen, 1981), 11–21.

'Towns and Societies—Medieval England', *Urban History Yearbook*, (1982), 7–13.

'Lords, Burgesses and Hucksters', *Past and Present*, 97 (1982), 3–15; reprinted in *Class Conflict and the Crisis of Feudalism*.

'The Small Town and Urbanisation—Evesham in the Middle ages', *Midland History*, 7 (1982), 1–8; reprinted in *Class Conflict and the Crisis of Feudalism*.

'La pagesia i l'ordre feudal', in *1.er col.loqui d'història agrària, Barcelona, 13–15 d'octubre 1976* (Valencia, 1983), 9–22.

'Feudal Society' and 'Serfdom', in T. Bottomore (ed.), *A Dictionary of Marxist Thought* (Oxford, 1983; 2nd edn, 1997), 191–6 and 494–6.

'Women Traders in Medieval England', in *Women's Studies* (special issue: H. P. Weissman (ed.), Women in the Middle Ages), (1984); reprinted in *Class Conflict and the Crisis of Feudalism*.

'Feudalism in Europe: Problems for Historical Materialists', *New Left Review*, 147 (1984), 84–93; reprinted in *Class Conflict and the Crisis of Feudalism* (1990 edn).

'Small Town Society in England Before the Black Death', *Past and Present*, 105 (1984), 53–78; reprinted in *Class Conflict and the Crisis of Feudalism* (1990 edn); and in R. Holt and G. Rosser (eds), *The Medieval Town. A Reader in English Urban History, 1200–1540* (London, 1990), 71–96.

'Introduction', in T. H. Aston and C. H. E. Philpin (eds), *The Brenner Debate. Agrarian Class Structure and Economic Development in Pre-industrial Europe* (Cambridge, 1985), 1–9.

'Pourquoi il y avait si peu de redevances a part de fruits en Angleterre médiévale', in *Les revenus de la terre, complant, champart, métayage en Europe occidentale (IXe-XVIIIe siècles)* (Flaran 7) (Auch, 1985), 107–17; reprinted as 'Why Was There so Little Champart Rent in Medieval England?', *Journal of Peasant Studies*, 17 (1990), 509–19.

'Medieval Market Towns and Simple Commodity Production', *Past and Present*, 109 (1985), 3–23.

'La société paysanne et le droit dans l'Angleterre médiévale', *Etudes Rurales*, 103–4 (1986), 13–18.

'Les tribunaux royaux', *Etudes Rurales*, 103–4 (1986), 29–38.

'Pain et cervoise dans les villes anglaises au moyen âge', in *L'Approvisionnement des villes de l'Europe occidentale au moyen âge et aux temps modernes* (Flaran 5, 1983) (Auch, 1985), 221–9.

'Les communautés villageoises en Angleterre au moyen âge', in *Les communautés villageoises en Europe occidentale du moyen âge aux temps modernes* (Flaran 4, 1982) (Auch, 1984), 117–28.

'Resistance to Taxation and to Other State Impositions in Medieval England', in J.-P. Genet and M. Le Mené (eds), *Genèse de l'état moderne, Prélèvement et redistribution. Actes du Colloque de Fontevraud 1984* (Paris, 1987), 169–77.

'Révoltes rurales et révoltes urbaines au moyen âge', in F. Gambrelle and M. Trebitsch (eds), *Révolte et société, Actes du IVe colloque d'histoire au présent*, 2 vols (Paris, 1989), vol. II, 25–33.

' "Seigneurie française et manoir anglais" Fifty Years Later', in H. Atsma and A. Burguière (eds), *Marc Bloch aujourd'hui. Histoire comparée et sciences sociales* (Paris, 1990), 173–82.

'Unjust Taxation and Popular Resistance—Marxist Theory and Practice on a Historical Problem', *New Left Review*, 180 (1990), 177–84; reprinted in *Class Conflict and the Crisis of Feudalism* (1990 edn).

'Statut et classe dans la ville médiévale', in *Histoire et société. Mélanges offerts à Georges Duby*, 4 vols (Aix-en-Provence, 1992), vol. II, 209–21.

'Le clergé rural et les mouvements paysans dans l'Angleterre médiévale', in P. Bonnassie (ed.), *Le clergé rural dans l'Europe médiévale et moderne* (Flaran 13, 1991) (Toulouse, 1995), 237–42.

'Inherent and Derived Ideology in the English Rising of 1381', in E. Mornet (ed.), *Campagnes médiévales: l'homme et son espace. Etudes offertes à Robert Fossier* (Paris, 1995), 399–405.

'Low-level Urbanization: the Seigneurial Borough of Thornbury in the Middle Ages', in Z. Razi and R. Smith (eds), *Medieval Society and the Manor Court* (Oxford, 1996), 482–517.

(with J. Cripps and J. Williamson) 'Appendix: A Survey of Medieval Manorial Court Rolls in England' in Z. Razi and R. Smith (eds), *Medieval Society and the Manor Court* (Oxford, 1996), 569–637.

'Status and Class in the Medieval Town', in T. R. Slater and G. Rosser (eds), *The Church in the Medieval Town* (Aldershot, 1998), 9–19.

'Peasant Rebellion of 1381', in P. E. Szarmach, M. T. Tavormina and J. T. Rosenthal (eds), *Medieval England. An Encyclopedia* (New York and London, 1998), 590–2.

Translation

'The Diffusion of Cultural Patterns in Feudal Society', G. Duby, *Past and Present*, 39 (1968), 3–10; reprinted in G. Duby, *The Chivalrous Society* (London, 1977).

List of Contributors

Isabel Alfonso Antón, is Investigadora Científica at the Instituto de Historia CSIC. Madrid. Her research covers medieval rural history, the Cistercians, and legal and political culture. Her publications in English include the co-edition of *Building Legitimacy. Political Discourses and Forms of Legitimation in Medieval Societies* (2004), and *The Rural History of Medieval European Societies. Trends and Perspectives* (*The Medieval Countryside*, 1). Her relationship to Rodney Hilton was based for many years on both academic and personal friendship.

Jean Birrell is Honorary Fellow, Institute for Advanced Research in the Arts and Social Sciences, University of Birmingham. She studied history at the University of Birmingham 1957–62. She has published articles mainly on the forest, hunting, and poaching in medieval England, and translated numerous works of French history. Her most recent publication is an edition of the records of the medieval Forest of Feckenham.

Having taught at Tours, Monique Bourin occupied the chair of History in the Central Middle Ages at University of Paris 1, Panthéon-Sorbonne. Now she is professor emeritus. She has devoted her research to southern French medieval society, using various approaches, in which the work of Rodney Hilton was a constant point of reference. She has coordinated the work of international research groups, one dedicated to the origins of modern personal names, the other to the study of the economy and society of the central middle ages (seigneurial exactions, serfdom, etc.).

Samuel Cohn, Jr., Professor of Medieval History, University of Glasgow, has published on the history of late medieval labouring classes, women, popular piety, the Renaissance state, social revolt, and disease. His most recent books include *The Black Death Transformed: Disease and Culture in Renaissance Europe* (2002), *Popular Protest in Late Medieval Europe* (2004), and *Lust for Liberty: The Politics of Social Revolt in Medieval Europe, 1200–1425* (2006). This last title is dedicated to the memory of R. H. Hilton.

Peter Coss holds the established chair of medieval history at Cardiff University where he is head of the School of History and Archaeology. His doctoral thesis, on the Langleys and the Langley Cartulary, was supervised by Rodney Hilton. His main area of expertise is the social history of England in the thirteenth and fourteenth centuries, with particular reference to the gentry. His most recent book is *The Origins of the English Gentry* (Cambridge, 2003).

Wendy Davies is Professor of History and Pro-Provost (European Affairs) at UCL. Recent publications include 'Sale, Price and Valuation in Galicia and Castile-León in the Tenth Century', *Early Medieval Europe*, 11 (2002), 'Looking Backwards to the Early Medieval Past: Wales and England, a Contrast in Approaches', *Welsh History Review*, 22 (2004) and 'The Celtic Kingdoms' in *The New Cambridge Medieval History*, I, *c*.500–*c*.700, ed. P. Fouracre (Cambridge, 2005). Her current research is on social and economic structures in northern Spain in the tenth century and she is writing a book for OUP on donation and its consequences, called *Giving and Dying*. She was a colleague of Rodney Hilton in the Birmingham University Medieval History department for six years in the 1970s.

Spencer Dimmock is a journeyman researcher in history. Following his doctoral research at University of Kent on the role of class and English towns in the feudalism to capitalism transition, he has undertaken research on Welsh towns at University of Wales, Swansea (see for example his 'Reassessing the Towns of Late Medieval Southern Wales', *Urban History*, 28 (2001)), and he has been involved in a team project with the *Victoria County History* and Exmoor National Park Authority researching the history of settlement on Exmoor. Although, regrettably, he did not meet them, he is convinced that Rodney Hilton and E. P. Thompson showed what was possible.

Christopher Dyer is Professor of Regional and Local History at the University of Leicester. His most recent books have been *Making a Living in the Middle Ages* (2002; paperback 2003) and *An Age of Transition?* (2005). He was taught by Rodney Hilton as an undergraduate student, and supervised by him as a postgraduate. They were colleagues at Birmingham in 1970–82.

The late S. R. Epstein wrote about medieval and early modern Italy, economic development and state formation in pre-modern Europe, and historiography; these interests are reflected in his most recent book, *Freedom and Growth. The Rise of States and Markets in Europe, 1300–1750* (London, 2000). He was Professor of Economic History at the London School of Economics and Political Science, and died at a tragically young age in 2007.

Richard Goddard is Lecturer in Medieval History at Nottingham University and is currently researching commercial and urban decline in fifteenth-century England. His most recent monograph, entitled *Lordship and Medieval Urbanisation: Coventry 1043–1355*, was published in 2004. He undertook his doctoral research at Birmingham University under the supervision of Christopher Dyer.

Richard Holt is Professor of Medieval History at the University of Tromsø, Norway. His main research interest is medieval towns, both in Norway and elsewhere in Europe; in 2004 he published (with Nigel Baker), *Urban Growth and the Medieval Church: Worcester and Gloucester*. Until 1998 he was at the University of Birmingham. Rodney Hilton was the supervisor of his doctoral thesis, a study of late medieval urban society.

Steven Justice is Associate Professor of English at the University of California, Berkeley. He is author of *Writing and Rebellion: England in 1381* (1994), and is working on a book called *Did the Middle Ages Believe in their Miracles?*

Miriam Müller was inspired by reading Rodney Hilton's *Bond Men Made Free* as a second-year student at the University of Sussex to pursue postgraduate study in medieval peasant communities, first at Cambridge, and then at Birmingham. Her research interests centre around peasant communities and forms of community policing, lord–peasant relationships, as well as wider socio-cultural aspects of hierarchical relationships, in particular the politics of food in later medieval England.

Zvi Razi is Professor of Medieval Social History in Tel Aviv University. Rodney Hilton supervised his PhD thesis at the University of Birmingham during the years 1972–5. From his post in Israel in subsequent years he visited Birmingham every summer to discuss his work and ideas with Rodney Hilton.

Penny Roberts is Senior Lecturer in History at the University of Warwick. She has written extensively on sixteenth-century French towns during the era of the religious wars, focusing on confessional conflict and coexistence, arson and popular protest. As a Birmingham graduate and postgraduate, she benefited both from Rodney's pedagogical legacy and from his invigorating company at the legendary Friday Night Seminar.

Pablo Sanchez Leon gained his PhD in history from Universidad Autonoma de Madrid in 1993. Rodney Hilton's *Bond Men Made Free* was the first book that he bought as an undergraduate, and he devoted much of his graduate studies to the 'transition debate'. He has written extensively on historical sociology, and the formation of identity. He has been a Visiting Scholar at

UCLA, and a Visiting Professor at the History Department of Sabanci University, Istanbul.

Phillipp Schofield is Professor of Medieval History in the Department of History and Welsh History at the University of Wales Aberystwyth. His research focuses upon high and late medieval English peasantry, and in particular the nature of dispute and of social structure in medieval rural communities. His recent published work includes *Peasant and Community in Late Medieval England* (Palgrave, 2003).

Bas van Bavel works at Utrecht University as the research leader of a project sponsored by the Netherlands Organization for Scientific Research, and also teaches at the Department of History and Economics. His research activities, in part inspired by Rodney Hilton's work, focus on reconstructing, analysing and explaining economic growth and social change in pre-industrial north-western Europe, emphasizing long-term transitions and regional diversity, and using comparative analysis—both in time and in space—as the main tool.

Dr Jane Whittle is Senior Lecturer in Economic and Social History at Exeter University. She specializes on rural England 1350–1650, and has found Rodney Hilton's research an inspiration throughout her career. She is author of *The Development of Agrarian Capitalism: Land and Labour in Norfolk* (Oxford, 2000), joint author of *Production and Consumption in English Households, 1600–1750* (London, 2004) and has published in various journals including *Past and Present* and *Transactions of the Royal Historical Society*.

Chris Wickham taught at the University of Birmingham between 1977 and 2005, and is now Chichele Professor of Medieval History at the University of Oxford. He is an expert on the history of Italy, 400–1250. He works on the history of Italy, 400–1250, and of early medieval Europe more generally. He was a colleague and friend of Rodney Hilton, and owes more to Rodney intellectually than to anyone else in his career.

Index

Adam of Bremen 133
Adenbroch, Richard de 185
administration 50, 69, 71, 74, 76, 77, 79,
    168, 172, 177
agricultural workers 95, 173–4, 256
agriculture 54, 244
    crisis in 183
    feudal state and 262–7
    inefficiency 262–3
    innovation in 268
    labour productivity in 271, 272
    lack of investment in 76
    livestock 244, 260
    management 69
    specialization 274, 275, 281, 290,
        293, 296
    wage labour 295–6, 298–9, 300
    wool production 283
Aix-en-Provence, France 174
Albigensian Crusades (1209-55) 113 n.
Alberbury Priory, Shropshire 152
ale, brewing and selling 124
ale tasters 186
Alfonso, Maribel 306
Alfonso VIII, king of Castile 92
Alfonso XI, king of Castile 223
Alfred, king of Wessex 134
alivrement 105–6 n.
Althusser, Louis 210, 212
amercements 80, 82, 127, 128, 130–1,
    see also fines
Amiens, France 172
Anderson, Perry 257
Angevin monarchy 38, 69
Annalistes 52, 55, 259
apprenticeships 269
Arabs, invasion of Spain 20, 22

Aragon 195 n., 219
arbitration 59, 60, 61, 230
architecture 50, 51
aristocracy 173, 174, 309, 312, 314, see also
    lordship
Arlanza, monastery of 23, 24
artisans 54, 104, 120, 138, 143, 192, 217, 256,
    268–9
    Castile 218–19, 226
    Comunidades revolt 231
    Dijon, decline in 174
    enclosure disputes 281, 282
    France, social protest 198
    insurrections of 199
    Norfolk peasant revolt 241
    wage labour 295, 297, 300
Arundel and Surrey, Richard Fitzalan, earl
    of 59
Ashby and Thurne, Norfolk 238
Aston, Margaret 205, 211, 212
Asturias 20
Augustinians 155, 156
Ávila, Castile 223

Badbury, Wiltshire 85, 119, 121, 122, 127,
    129, 130
Ball, John 206, 207
Banbury 176
banditry 36, 197–8
bans 110
barber-surgeons 143
Barberino Val d'Elsa, south of Florence 194
bastard feudalism 40, 42, 180, 225
Battle Abbey, Sussex 150, 154–5,
    158, 283
Bavel, Bas van 313, 314
bayles 105, 109–10